Overseas Shinto Shrines

Bloomsbury Shinto Studies

Series editor: Fabio Rambelli

The Shinto tradition is an essential component of Japanese religious culture. In addition to indigenous elements, it contains aspects mediated from Buddhism, Daoism, Confucianism and, in more recent times, Western religious culture as well – plus, various forms of hybridization among all of these different traditions. Despite its cultural and historical importance, Shinto studies have failed to attract wide attention also because of the lingering effects of uses of aspects of Shinto for the ultranationalistic propaganda of Japan during the Second World War. The Series makes available to a broad audience a number of important texts that help to dispel the widespread misconception that Shinto is intrinsically related to Japanese nationalism, and at the same time promote further research and understanding of what is still an underdeveloped field.

The God Susanoo and Korea in Japan's Cultural Memory
David Weiss
Mountain Mandalas: Shugendo in Kyushu
Allan G. Grapard
The Origin of Modern Shinto in Japan: The Vanquished Gods of Izumo
Yijiang Zhong
Religion, Power and the Rise of Shinto in Early Modern Japan
Edited by Stefan Köck, Brigitte Pickl-Kolaczia and Bernhard Scheid
The Sea and the Sacred in Japan
Edited by Fabio Rambelli
Shinto, Nature and Ideology in Contemporary Japan
Aike P. Rots
A Social History of the Ise Shrines
Mark Teeuwen and John Breen

Overseas Shinto Shrines

Religion, Secularity and the Japanese Empire

Karli Shimizu

BLOOMSBURY ACADEMIC
LONDON • NEW YORK • OXFORD • NEW DELHI • SYDNEY

BLOOMSBURY ACADEMIC
Bloomsbury Publishing Plc
50 Bedford Square, London, WC1B 3DP, UK
1385 Broadway, New York, NY 10018, USA
29 Earlsfort Terrace, Dublin 2, Ireland

BLOOMSBURY, BLOOMSBURY ACADEMIC and the Diana logo are
trademarks of Bloomsbury Publishing Plc

First published in Great Britain 2023
This edition published 2024

Copyright © Karli Shimizu, 2023

Karli Shimizu has asserted her right under the Copyright, Designs and
Patents Act, 1988, to be identified as Author of this work.

For legal purposes the Acknowledgements on pp. ix–x constitute an
extension of this copyright page.

Series design by Dani Leigh
Cover image: 'Taiwan Shrine, Taihoku', Postcard published by
Taihoku Niitakadō, 1930s (Undated) (Author's collection)

All rights reserved. No part of this publication may be reproduced
or transmitted in any form or by any means, electronic or mechanical,
including photocopying, recording, or any information storage or retrieval
system, without prior permission in writing from the publishers.

Bloomsbury Publishing Plc does not have any control over, or responsibility for,
any third-party websites referred to or in this book. All internet addresses given
in this book were correct at the time of going to press. The author and publisher
regret any inconvenience caused if addresses have changed or sites have ceased
to exist, but can accept no responsibility for any such changes.

A catalogue record for this book is available from the British Library.

Library of Congress Control Number: 2022936790

ISBN: HB: 978-1-3502-3498-7
        PB: 978-1-3502-3499-4
        ePDF: 978-1-3502-3500-7
        eBook: 978-1-3502-3501-4

Series: Bloomsbury Shinto Studies

Typeset by Integra Software Services Pvt. Ltd.

To find out more about our authors and books visit www.bloomsbury.com
and sign up for our newsletters.

To
Yukitaka Raistlin Kaikaliʻia Shimizu
Onore ga tame ni suru wa kunshi no gaku nari.

Contents

List of figures	viii
Acknowledgements	ix
Notes on text/translation	xi

1	Introduction: Religion, secularism and Japan	1
2	The birthplace of Japan: Kashihara Jingū and the Home Islands	29
3	The northern capital: Hokkaido and Karafuto in the near periphery	57
4	A model colony: Taiwan at the far periphery	89
5	Of the same lineage: Korea as annexed territory	125
6	A multiethnic empire: Manchuria and Asia outside of Japan	153
7	A distant land: Hawai'i on the East–West border	179
8	Conclusion	213

Notes	229
Character glossary	249
References	264
Index	276

Figures

2.1	Kashihara Jingū today	30
2.2	School slate	35
2.3	Postcard of Fukada Pond at Kashihara Jingū (1940)	36
2.4	Postcard of Jinmu's Tumulus (1940)	41
3.1	Hokkaidō Jingū today	60
3.2	Hokkaidō Gokoku Jinja today	71
3.3	Furano Jinja today	80
3.4	A postcard of Kamikawa Jinja	84
4.1	A postcard of Greater Imperial Shrine Taiwan Jinja	95
4.2	Koxinga	107
4.3	Kenkō Jinja	115
5.1	The stone stairs of Chōsen Jingū's main approach (c. 1930s)	135
5.2	Calendar of October, Showa 18 (Imperial Year 2603, Western Year 1943)	136
5.3	'Warrior Dolls'	149
6.1	A postcard of Kenkoku Chūreibyō (1940s)	159
6.2	Kenkoku Shinbyō (1940)	163
6.3	A postcard of Shinkyō Jinja	172
7.1	Commemorating Hilo Daijingū's fortieth anniversary (1939)	191
7.2	Hawaii Kotohira Jinsha today	200
7.3	Hawaii Izumo Taisha (1923)	204

Acknowledgements

How could I fully express the debt of gratitude I owe to all those who have helped and supported me in the writing of this book? Even so, I want to give my deepest thanks to the many friends and colleagues whose advice and friendship have made this work possible. First and foremost, the advice and expertise of Dr Philip Seaton of Tokyo University of Foreign Studies, Dr Jeffry Gayman of Hokkaido University and Dr Eiko Tsuchida of Hokkaido University have been inestimably valuable throughout this project. I truly hope that this book does justice to their high standards.

This book has also hugely benefitted from the suggestions and insights of colleagues at both my home institute of Hokkaido University and those I have met through conferences and symposiums. Especially, the stimulating conversations and thoughtful feedback of Dr Mira Sonntag of Rikkyo University, Dr Aleksandra Jaworowicz-Zimny of Nicolaus Copernicus University, Dr Georgy Buntilov of Hokkaido University, Dr Ellen Van Goethem of Kyushu University, Dr Edward Boyle of Kyushu University and Dr Steven Ivings of Kyoto University have all directly or indirectly improved this work.

I would also like to acknowledge the helpful assistance given to me by many Shinto shrines over the course of this research. In particular, I must thank Rev. Naohiro Hotta formerly of Hilo Daijingū, Rev. Masa Takizawa and Mrs. Irene Takizawa of Hawaii Kotohira Jinsha, and Bishop Daiya Amano and Rev. Jun Miyasaka of Izumo Taishakyo Mission of Hawaii. I also want to thank Rev. Keisuke Yamada of Kashihara Jingū and Rev. Mitsuhiko Nishikawa of Furano Jinja, as well as the priests and experts at Hokkaidō Jingū and the Hokkaidō Jinja-chō.

Chapters 2 and 7 contain portions of previously published journal articles. Reprinted with permission are parts of 'Shintō Shrines and Secularism in Modern Japan, 1890–1945: A Case Study on Kashihara Jingū' in the *Journal of Japanese Religion* 6:2 (2017); and 'Religion and Secularism in Overseas Shinto Shrines: A Case Study on Hilo Daijingū, 1898–1941' in the *Japanese Journal of Religious Studies* 46:1 (2019). I thank Brill and the Nanzan Institute of Religion and Culture, respectively, for this permission as well as their editors and anonymous readers for their enlightening comments.

My heartfelt appreciation goes to everyone at Bloomsbury Academic. This book could not have been written without their thoughtful suggestions and kind support. Especially, Series Editor Dr Fabio Rambelli provided invaluable encouragement and feedback, while Publisher Lalle Pursglove and Assistant Editor Lily McMahon's clear advice and immeasurable patience are what brought this book to fruition. Furthermore, the feedback from the anonymous reviewers arranged through Bloomsbury on both the proposal and manuscript was extremely helpful and has certainly made it a better work. Of course, any errors remaining in the book are mine alone.

My gratitude also belongs to all my students who supported me during the research and writing of this book. Their questions and energy motivated me throughout Hokkaido's long winters, and they endured with remarkable grace the lengthy impromptu lectures on the finer details of overseas Shinto shrines to which I subjected them.

Finally, this work would not have been possible without the encouragement and support of my family: my mother Randi Gammell-Bjornton, who always emphasized the importance of education for her daughters; my father Scott Lawson, who passed down his interest in religions to me; and my beloved husband Yōichi Shimizu, who endured countless days of neglect during the writing of this book. I also want to thank my brilliant brother Makai Lawson and his wonderful family Ame, Constantine and Julius for putting up with my lengthy stays at their house while writing. I hope I can impose on you again! My other brother Derek Paulus and my sister Stacie Laux also have my gratitude for always expanding my worldview and being all-around awesome siblings. Further thanks go to Arvid Bjornton for countless Hawaiian breakfasts and ferrying me around the island. My schooldays *onshi* Mr Scott Jeffrey, too, has been an unwavering source of encouragement throughout this project. This book, however, is dedicated to my newborn son, Yukitaka Raistlin Kaikaliʻia. I hope you will grow up to love learning as much as I do.

Notes on text/translation

- East Asian names are written family name first followed by given name. Mixed names, such as those with an English first name and Japanese last name, are written in the Western style: given name first followed by family name. When a personage has a well-known English name, that has been used. The Revised Hepburn system is used to romanize Japanese, Pinyin is used for Chinese and McCune–Reischauer is used for Korean.
- The Japanese reading of place names has been prioritized, although relevant Chinese and Korean readings have been added for well-known place names. The use of the Japanese reading prevents obscuring the connections between place and shrines that are obvious when written in Chinese characters. Furthermore, the Japanese reading is sometimes more reflective of the original local term than the current Mandarin reading. For example, the place name pronounced Kagī in Taiwanese Hokkien is pronounced Kagi in Japanese, but Chiayi (Jiāyì) in Mandarin. Shinto sites often had multiple names throughout their history, but in principle, the 1945 name of the site is used.
- Foreign words are italicized, except in the case of common words used in English, such as Tokyo, Shinto and kami. The Japanese names of organizations are not italicized, but diacritics are retained.
- The term History is capitalized when used as a specific noun to refer to the historical idea of a single progressive linear History. Likewise, the term True/Truth is capitalized when referring to the historical idea of a single True religion or secular Truth in comparison to incomplete or mistaken 'lesser' religions.
- Following precedent found in Hawaiian studies, attributive locational nouns are used to designate geographic references. For example, a Hawai'i Japanese or a Taiwan Shintoist is one that resides in Hawai'i or Taiwan, respectively, not someone who is ethnically or racially Hawaiian or Taiwanese.

1

Introduction:
Religion, secularism and Japan

What is 'religion'? While most people can give examples of religion, few can give a definition that is broad enough to include all the typically accepted world religions, yet narrow enough to exclude non-religious concepts like communism or sports fandoms. The definition of religion in the *English Oxford Dictionary* reflects this. It relies upon a theocentric idea of 'god/s' as being definitive of religion, while the subsidiary definitions add faith ('belief in the doctrines of a religion') and worship ('adoration of a deity') as aspects of religion. Conversely, the dictionary's second definition allows religion to refer broadly to anything 'followed with great devotion'.[1] But this sort of theocentric definition falls apart when applied to such accepted world religions as Buddhism, which does not worship a 'controlling power', much less a personal God. The same is largely true for Taoism and Confucianism, so much that the latter is often not considered a religion at all.

Dictionary definitions tend to reflect the popular usage of words, and scholars have devised more academic definitions of religion. Scholarly definitions in the nineteenth and early twentieth centuries assumed the relationship with a Christian-like God as definitive, but as scholars attempted to be universally inclusive, definitions tended to move towards what Josephson has called a hierocentric conception of religion. This obscured the Eurocentricity of the definition more than resolved it. This sort of definition assumes an innate divide ('an irreducible dimension of human experience') between the sacred/ transcendent and the secular/immanent. It positions personal experience and a set of doctrines (beliefs) as definitive of religion (Josephson 2012, 9). Yet this definition aligns poorly not only with the so-called Japanese religions (Josephson 2012, 10) but also with pre-modern conceptions of 'religion' in the West (Asad 1993, 29).

Anthropological definitions of religion which try to universalize theocentric Christian ideas by replacing 'God' with the 'transcendent' still hinge on a group of Protestant Christianity-based elements such as salvation, a Church, belief in a doctrine and personal experience. In other words, 'the word "religion" is a fundamentally Eurocentric term that always functions, no matter how well disguised, to describe a perceived similarity to European Christianity' (Josephson 2012, 9).[2] Despite its lack of historicity and universality, today the modern concept of religion does exist. It has had a deep influence on societies as they have encountered it, and the term can be useful in pre-modern/non-Western contexts, if it is used in a manner Nongbri describes as 'redescriptive' (Nongbri 2013, 21). Although it can be useful, or even necessary, for explaining modern society and phenomena, we must remain aware of its historical origins and meanings. In nineteenth-century Japan, the modern concept of religion influenced the newly created Japanese concept of *shūkyō* ('religion'). But it is a mistake to assume that 'religion' is universal – historically or geographically.[3] To understand the position of Shinto shrines in modern Japan, they must be released from the ill-fitting category of 'religion' and looked at in the context of secularism as a whole.

The invention of religion

How was the modern concept of religion was born from its European Christian past? The term 'religion' or, rather, its Latin antecedent *religio* extends back to ancient times. However, its modern meaning has little in common with its original meaning as something similar to 'scruples' (Josephson 2012, 17). The medieval separation between 'religion' and the 'secular' was not the modern divide between a religious sphere of private belief and a public sphere of universal fact; rather it drew a difference between lay people and those in monastic orders (Nongbri 2013, 21). Nongbri traces the rise of the modern concept of religion – religion as a private sphere of personal belief – to the breakdown of the heresiological framework in the seventeenth century (Nongbri 2013, 57, 125). The heresiological framework, which interprets different beliefs as perversions of Truth, was also how Europeans interpreted Buddhism when encountering Japan for the first time in the sixteenth century (Josephson 2012, 45).

The religious conflict of the Reformation in Europe led to a privatization of the concept of religion, while belief in the right religion – rather than the act of belonging to the Church – became key to salvation. Furthermore, the rise of the 'nation-state gave rise to religious pluralism as a means of subduing citizens' (Nongbri 2013, 91–7). In other words, as states were unable to stamp out heresies, they converted former heresies into 'religions' or later religious sects. Europeans began to search for the common denominators that united all these religions, which led to the idea of Deism. Nongbri sees Locke's 'Letter Concerning Toleration' written in the 1680s as a turning point in the development of the modern concept of religion. In this Letter, religion had begun to take on most of its modern characteristics: 'a group of individuals who freely choose to associate with each other and adhere to a particular set of writings for the purpose of salvation, and who ideally operate in ways that do not interfere or overlap with the concerns of the state' (Nongbri 2013, 103).

The concept of religion did not develop in Europe unaffected by the rest of the world. By the nineteenth century, a fourfold categorization of religions had developed. On the one hand religion had come to refer to private, doctrinal beliefs. But True religion was distinguished from lesser religions in a hierarchy that located Christianity at the top as the only True religion, followed by Islam, Judaism and, finally, paganism. In this scheme, all but the True religion of Christianity was seen as mistaken idolatry, which Masuzawa terms 'Un-Christianity' (Masuzawa 2005, 51). However, increasing contact with the non-West, especially the West's discovery, or invention, of Buddhism, led to a flattening of the concept into world religions.

The West's encounter with Buddhist and Hindu thought led it to reorganize the pre-modern traditions of India into 'world religions'. Hinduism became a Judaism-like 'ethnic religion', founded by the genius of a nation, while Buddhism was its Protestant-like reformed version, with Siddartha Gautama as its Jesus-like founder. Contemporary practices of Indians were discounted as corruptions of 'True Buddhism', and it was only the West that was able to locate 'True Buddhism' in ancient texts like the Vedas. Encounters like this, as well as the growing idea of atheism, led to 'the destabilization, the collapse, and the reconstitution of the classificatory logic' (Masuzawa 2005, 307) of religion in the late nineteenth to early twentieth century.

The hierarchical, fourfold concept of world religions, after a period of confusion, developed into a flattened list of up to twelve world religions: Christianity, Islam, Judaism, Sikhism, Zoroastrianism, Buddhism, Jainism, Hinduism, Shintoism, Confucianism, Taoism and 'Primitivism'[4] (Masuzawa 2005, 44). The flattening of the category of religions was not a single linear process. Especially during the late nineteenth century, when the idea of religion was being introduced to and adapted by Japan, both the hierarchical and the flattened idea of religion were coexistent in the West (Fluhman 2012, 27). To a certain degree, a hierarchy remained, with 'world religions' (those with founders and a developed doctrine) such as Buddhism and Christianity as the most True, 'national (ethnic) religions' (with scriptures and doctrine, but without a founder and a tendency towards reliance on rite) as less evolved versions of religion, and primitive religions (those which lack a founder, scriptures or even much doctrine, but rely on rites) as little better than superstitions. This distinction was important for Japan, because the 'Shinto' upon which Japan as a new nation-state based its legitimacy had far more in common with the Western concept of primitive religions than that of world religions.

The concept of religion was often thrust upon nations by the West in the context of imperialism. Despite the power imbalance, the nations subjected to the concept rarely adopted the concept without modification. Instead, they adapted it, sometimes to better fit the local situation and other times to actively resist imperialism.[5] In turn, these adaptions of religion influenced the concept as a whole (Josephson 2012, 5). In the case of Japan, the concept of religion came tied to the struggle of avoiding the colonial disasters neighbours like China and Hawai'i had suffered, and to Japan's quest for recognition as a civilized nation-state by the West. The new Meiji government of Japan made an early effort to formulate what has been seen as a sort of Shinto-influenced state religion with the Great Promulgation Campaign. In the early 1870s, around the start of the Campaign, diplomatic concerns pushed the Meiji government to consider a state religion with religious toleration as politically expedient.

But the translation of the Western concept of religion into the Japanese language and context was in flux throughout this period, becoming embedded in Japanese society only in the early twentieth century (Isomae 2012, 241–2). The failures of the Great Promulgation Campaign played a role in defining what 'religion' itself meant. As the Campaign was shut down, its focus on a 'national doctrine' was abandoned. Religion (*shūkyō*) came to mean a personal belief that should be kept separate from the state, even while the public ritual of shrines was separated from doctrinal teachings, thus allowing the Meiji Constitution of 1890 to guarantee freedom of belief while protecting the legitimacy of the imperial institution from contestation (Maxey 2014, 242). The modern concept of religion, as part of the political system of secularism, was put into the service of the state.

The political system of secularism 'presupposes new concepts of "religion", "ethics", and "politics", and new imperatives associated with them' (Asad 2003, 1–2). When discussing religion in the context of secularism, rather than being a countable noun enumerating different 'world religions', it becomes a generic mass noun designating a discrete sphere which is often positioned as opposed to the sphere of the secular. Josephson argues that this binary is actually a trinary, with the opposite of the secular being 'superstition' and with religion serving as a sphere mediating between them. This can be seen in Meiji period Japan where superstitions (*meishin*) were targeted for elimination by the government. Meanwhile religion as a category protected recognized religions from persecution while limiting their influence by relegating them to a private sphere that was not allowed in schools or politics. The secular, on the other hand, was considered universal to all imperial subjects and formed an ideological basis for the state (Josephson 2012).

Although the Japanese government had to consider international opinion and popular sentiment, it acted as the final arbitrator for deciding how the many kami-related pre-modern traditions would be divided into the secular, superstitious or religious spheres. The popularity of new religions, which often relied on 'superstitious' practices like faith-healing, demonstrates how the government used religion to moderate practices it perceived as superstitious. After continued state repression failed to squash these practices' popularity, the government legally recognized many Sect Shinto groups as religion, as long as they modified themselves to become more moderate. This trinary of secularism is also relevant to countries in the West. Similarly in the United States, a secular sphere was built historically upon the idea of a divine Creator, while the conflicting doctrines of the various Christian and Jewish sects were relegated to the sphere of religion. Despite this, parts of the doctrine of some sects, such as the polygamy of the Latter Day Saints, were seen as beyond the pale and persecuted as superstition, as will be discussed below. And like many of the Sect Shinto groups in Japan, the Latter Day Saints were able to gain legal recognition by giving up those parts of their doctrine that were impermissible to the state.

Religion developed in a specific temporal and geographic context, and it developed in the context of international relations, the nation-state and secularism. The term **secularism**, then, can be defined as the 'political doctrine' (Asad 2003, 16) included within the project of modernization that recategorizes the world into **secular** (*mushūkyō*), **superstitious** (*meishin*) and **religious** (*shūkyō*) spheres (Josephson 2012, 260-1). The term **secularity** indicates the consensus of reality promoted within a political system of secularism.

American secularism, Japanese secularism

A secularity posits itself as universal, as containing facts which are true for all people. This is similar to how the hierarchical conception of religion placed Christianity at the top as the only True religion: the only religion that contained the whole Truth.⁶ Despite a secularity's legal position as universally True, more recent scholarship has recognized that multiple, sometimes conflicting secularities exist (Burchardt et al. 2015). Even within the West, various states have had differing concepts. While the United States embraced a Judaeo-Christian concept of a single monotheistic Creator (Providence) as a universally accepted fact, France with its history of conflict with the Catholic Church adopted a much stricter idea of a secularity known as Laïcité.

Before looking at Japan, it may be helpful to first consider what sort of assumptions a Western secularism – a concept of secularity English speakers are likely to be intimately familiar with – does and does not take as real. The United States is particularly relevant as an example, because it was the first to introduce the concept of religion into Japan during the mid-1800s when it pushed for freedom of religion in Japanese treaties. The United States was also the main Western country overlapping the Pacific area Japan eventually came to see as within its domain. One of the key elements of the US foundation is the separation of Church and State. Many of the European settlers who came to the American continent had been motivated by religious persecution; thus, the ability to freely practice their own beliefs or to build their own 'city on the hill' was dear to the early colonists' hearts.

When the thirteen colonies united together to declare independence from Britain, the new American governments drew legitimacy from God or Providence, the existence of which was considered a universal fact among diverse Christian sects, and to a lesser extent the Jewish population, residing in the United States. However, these sects had diverse ideas about the exact nature of God and his relationship to humankind.⁷ The separation of Church and State as established in the First Amendment of the Constitution in 1791 prohibited the federal government from promoting any one religious sect over another.⁸ It did not prohibit individual states from establishing a state religion,⁹ and it did not disallow the invocation of God by the federal government. In other words, at the time of the US legal establishment of secularism, the existence of a Creator, the bestowal of individual souls and other Christianity-derived concepts fell within the common consensus and formed a cornerstone of the secularity upon which the new government's legitimacy was built.

These mainstream Protestant ideas dominated the definition of religion in nineteenth-century America, while acts like homosexuality and polygamy were considered by this majority as barbaric superstitions, and thus subject to legal and social persecution. However, as the American population expanded and diversified, changes in the common consensus and the concept of religion also developed. The example of the Church of Latter Day Saints (LDS), or Mormonism, demonstrates how the categories of religion and superstition were negotiated in nineteenth-century America.

When Joseph Smith, the founder of the Church of the Latter Day Saints, first began gathering followers, he was seen as a fraud who deluded ignorant people into giving him money and women. To explain away the many instances of otherwise rational and upstanding men following Smith, some followers, while considered sane in every other area of life, were diagnosed as insane only in matters of religion (monomania) (Fluhman 2012, 49). Smith was often compared to the Prophet Muhammed, who was seen in the eyes of Christians of that time as also having invented 'visions' from God and a new book to supplant the Bible, in order to deceive the ignorant (Fluhman 2012, 35). Thus in the mid-nineteenth century, Mormonism was seen by mainstream Americans as a corruption (heresy) of the True religion, which was mainstream Protestantism. Being taken in by this 'fraud' was pathologized as a mental illness.

As Smith's following grew, they formed communities, which gave them significant voting power. Fears over this voting power led states to drive the Mormons out, often with violence. This sat badly with the idea of 'religious toleration'. But it was rationalized, for example in Illinois, by insisting the state was only persecuting 'political' Mormonism, that is, actions such as gathering together in a city, while 'religious Mormonism', that is, doctrinal tenets like believing Christ came to America, was still tolerated (Fluhman 2012, 91).

After the lynching of Smith, the Latter Day Saints fled to Salt Lake Valley (modern Utah) in 1847, but they faced persecution again when the United States annexed the area in 1850. At this point an important change in the discourse occurred. Previously Mormonism had been considered a state-specific problem, but annexation and discussion over eventual statehood for Utah made Mormonism a federal problem. In particular, the practice of polygamy became a key issue seen as beyond the pale of civilization. The US government enacted a series of Acts aimed at stamping out polygamy. The justification often used for this was that polygamy was oppressive to women. However, LDS women who spoke out in defence of the practice were often treated as ignorant and thus dismissed (Fluhman 2012, 117), while women who spoke against polygamy were given due attention. The LDS church attempted to defend the practice by arguing it was based upon the theology of the Church of the Latter Day Saints and was thus a 'religious practice'. Correspondingly, as a religious practice, it should be protected under the ideal of freedom of religion. However, the court case *Reynolds v. United States* (1878) ruled that while religious doctrine was protected, actions guided from religious doctrine, that is religion-related praxis, were not (Fluhman 2012, 104). This court case established a significant legal precedent defining only doctrine, and not praxis, as religion eligible for protection under the ideal of religious freedom.

Utah was able to become an American state, that is, gain full legal rights, only after the Church of the Latter Day Saints renounced the practice of polygamy. After decades of legal pressure, the Church renounced the practice in 1890 and Utah was admitted into the union of states in 1896. This shift from persecution to grudging acceptance reflects the changes the concept of religion was undergoing more broadly. In the early 1800s, Americans largely saw Protestant Christianity as the only True religion and other 'religions' as being corrupted versions of it. The LDS Church was criticized from this point of view. However, as the concept of religion both broadened and flattened in the late 1800s to include Buddhism and other systems, Mormonism was allowed entry into the ranks of 'religion', providing it divested itself of unaccepted praxes and limited itself to religious doctrine. The American federal state arbitrated through legal acts and court cases what could be allowed as religion and what could not be allowed as harmful delusion. This example of the legal acceptance of Mormonism as 'religion' demonstrates how the modern concepts of religion and superstition were constructed in the United States, and how the state was a major arbitrator of the categories of secularism. It provides a basis for comparison against similar processes which occurred in Japan and other non-Western nations.

The late nineteenth to early twentieth centuries were a period of confusion leading to the flattening of the concept of religion. While the Latter Day Saints were refused admittance to the 1893 World's Parliament of Religions despite their active petitioning, Seager (2009) sees the Parliament as a major turning point for the American concept of religion. The Parliament was opened with the aims of uniting the ten 'great religions' of the world against irreligion and of indicating 'the impregnable foundations of theism' (Seager 2009, xxvii). In this international and ecumenical undertaking, the American organizers hoped to firmly establish a universal common consensus. However, as the reference to theism indicates, 'its universalistic agenda turned out to be particularistic' (Seager 2009, xxxix). The unarticulated ambition of the Parliament was to fit all other religions into the framework of Christianity. Buddha, Brahma and kami all become equivalents of God. This proved the 'fact' of theism, which was being increasingly called into question by the growing acceptance of atheism. The Parliament failed in its aim, however. The division between the Protestant denominations and the eloquence of the Eastern delegates 'generated universalistic religious discourses rooted in the traditions of the East' (Seager 2009, 113).[10] In short, the United States was founded upon what Seager calls the 'Colombian Myth' of patriotism, classical philosophy and Christianity. But as the concept of religion continued to flatten in the early twentieth century, the American secular sphere broadened to allow for more Eastern ideas into the common consensus, even while keeping its basic framework derived from Christianity. Far from being confined to a private sphere, ideas such as God-given ('natural') rights formed the basis of the state's legitimacy, becoming part of the secular sphere and what Bellah (1991) referred to as 'civil religion'.[11]

Whether a separation between 'religion' and 'the secular' can be found in premodern Japan is contested,[12] but it is clear that the modern concept of religion was first encountered in the context of unequal treaties with Western nations. Isomae (2012) has identified four stages through which the concept of religion came to be translated by the neologism *shūkyō* – originally a Buddhist term referring to a sectarian teaching – and embedded within Japanese society. This process lasted most of the Meiji period; thus, the confusion around the term 'religion' in the West during this period was mirrored in Japan. The secular sphere was defined as the opposite of *shūkyō*: *mushūkyō*, literally 'not-religion'. During this process, the Great Promulgation Campaign of the 1870s and 1880s constituted a major effort by the Japanese government to indoctrinate a 'state teaching' into the populace. While in some ways this can be seen as an attempt to create a 'state religion', this interpretation relies upon the idea of 'teaching' as being definitive of religion, something that was not yet firmly established in Japan when the Campaign was in progress. However, the government's efforts were influenced by the hierarchical model of religion, which saw True religion as truth. Shinto had difficulty fulfilling the requirements of a True religion (based as they were on Protestant Christianity) and was more likely to be considered mere superstition by Westernizers than as a civilized religion. As the West leaned towards a flattened concept of religion that demoted True religion to just one of many contestable religions, Japan followed this trend, adopting a secularism based on religious freedom, rather than religious toleration, with the Meiji constitution.

The enactment of the constitution and the discourse around the failed 1900 Religion Bill established a 'religious settlement' (Maxey 2014) that positioned Shinto shrines within the non-contestable secular sphere. At the same time, they limited Buddhism, Christianity and Sect Shinto to the permissible, but contestable, sphere of religion. The discourse around the 1900 Religion Bill also developed a generic vocabulary of religion, and it became an important way religion was separated from Shinto shrines. Terms like *kyōkai* (church), *kyōshi* (cleric/instructor) and *kyōha* (denomination), which evoke the image of doctrine through the character *kyō* (teaching), were designated religious things.[13] Meanwhile Shinto shrines utilized a separate set of terms such as *jinja* (shrine), *shinkan* (ritualist) and *shakaku* (rank), which evoked different concepts. These differences in vocabulary also conveyed information about the defining characteristics of their bearers. *Kyō* in religious categories suggests doctrine as defining, while terms like *kan* and *gū* associate those Shrine Shinto terms with the government and imperial court. Thus the end of the Meiji period saw a division of old customs into the new categories of the secular, religion and superstition. *Shūkyō* lacked the image of True religion which still lingered around its English equivalent 'religion', but instead strongly possessed connotations of denominational doctrine. Furthermore, the secular sphere as conceived in Japan differed from the theism-based secularity of the United States.

Although legal concepts had to align at least partially with popular conceptions, the Japanese government was the major arbitrator of the secular and religious spheres. Japan adopted the framework of secularism, a modern Western construct, but not without modification. While the Colombian myth underpinning American secularity was supported by classical philosophy and Christian morality (Seager 2009, 4), Japan founded its secularity upon a Confucian-Shinto morality in addition to a scientific modernity adopted from the West, in what Josephson calls the Shinto-scientific secular (Josephson 2012, 19).[14]

Since secularities claim to be universal, significant problems arise when they conflict. Japan dealt with this in two ways. One was to advocate that Japanese secularity was only universal to the Japanese sphere. The other was to utilize a reverse-Orientalist claim, embracing the image of the mystical east while adopting Western technology. Since Japan had swiftly modernized its technology to catch up to the West, ideologues argued that Japan had mastered the physical side as much or better than the Occident, while still possessing the superior Oriental understanding of the mystical side. This supposed mastery of both physical and mystical let them argue that Japan's understanding of universal Truth was more complete than that of the West.

In this way, the Japanese government formulated its secularity in antagonism to the West. The term 'antagonism' emphasizes how the relationship was 'more complex than direct opposition' and had elements of 'borrowing and adaption' (Buntilov 2016, 6). The government did not reject the Western idea of time as linear and progressive.[15] It quickly adopted the Western calendar, including the seven-day week with Sunday as a day of rest, and abandoned its tradition of using the cyclic sexagenary system of time and dividing months into three ten-day weeks. Yet at the same time, the Japanese government took the (theoretically) scientifically calculated date of the first Japanese emperor's enthronement in 660 BC,[16] rather than the birth of Christ, as the start of linear time. Thus the Japanese government did not directly oppose Western secularity, but adopted and then subverted it to make Japan's claim to Truth trump that of the West.

Three important elements of secularity are conceptions of space, time and ethics. These elements are some of the basic building blocks upon which people's perception of reality rests. Space and time might seem like concrete things that can be defined physically through science, but cultural aspects affect the perception of geography and time in significant ways. For example, the American understanding that seven continents (Europe, Asia, North and South America, Australia, Africa and Antarctica) make up the land masses of world may seem like an objective fact of geography,[17] but that framework was completed only in the 1950s. In the late eighteenth century, the world was generally conceived as consisting of four continents. In the late eighteenth to early nineteenth centuries, the 'fact' of four continents became linked to new racial sciences connecting a different race to each continent. The genealogy of this 'myth of continents' can be traced back to medieval T and O maps. These maps, which had precedent in ancient Greek divisions, divided the world into three parts as settled by the three sons of Noah with the holy city of Jerusalem at the centre. America, as the 'new world', was added as the fourth division of the world (Lewis and Wigen 1997, 29–33).

The Eurocentricity of Western metageography[18] was not lost on Japanese elites. Power relationships made this metageography difficult to reject entirely, but early Meiji period textbooks dealt with this incongruence by separating geographical continents (*tairiku*) from political-cultural continents (*taishū*) (Monbushō 1874, 3).[19] While world maps placing the Prime Meridian (and thus England) at the centre of the world were not uncommon in Japan, maps dividing the globe into Eastern and Western hemispheres, thus placing Asia at the centre of the East, were also common. Furthermore, the trend of placing Japan and Oceania at the centre of world maps grew in popularity in the Showa period and is now standard on Japanese world maps today. Japan sustained the divide between Europe and Asia, but refocused this Europe-centred geography on Japan and the East.

The Japanese government did the same with time and ethics. It abandoned its Chinese-based system of measuring time, and by extension history, and adopted a Western model. The Western model was more scientific than the Chinese lunar model, which fit well with the government's claim to technological mastery. But the model it adopted was not a pure adoption. Rather, it deliberately antagonized the Western version by counting the Japanese start of linear time as being older than the start of the Christian era. While the Meiji government-based national morality upon Confucian ideals such as harmonious relationships, it was couched within the framework of Shinto mythology which positioned these moral ideals as indigenous to Japan. In particular, the ideals of loyalty to the emperor and the emperor's benevolence were prominent. Japan did not reject many Western moral values, but went to great lengths to instil a Victorian morality into the populace through campaigns against 'superstitions' and uncivilized customs, such as prohibiting co-sex bathing and fox-expelling rituals, and encouraging meat-eating. By expelling 'uncivilized' customs, the Japanese government hoped to gain equal treatment by the West. Yet the method by which 'Japanese people were being won over to the civilization called for by Fukuzawa [was] not through appeals to British social mores but by being taught about Shinto' (Josephson 2012, 153). In other words, this morality was reconstructed to be based on Confucian-Shinto ideas rather than Classical-Christian ideas. In summary, Japanese secularity was adapted from Western secularity and modified in order to position it as not only more suitable for the East but also as possibly superior to Western secularity.

Communicating a Japanese secularity

This modern Japanese secularity had to be communicated to and instilled into Japanese subjects: Home Islanders and colonial subjects alike.[20] This meant that even the Home Islands had to undergo what Caprio has called internal colonization (Caprio 2009, 9). As the empire expanded, this task of colonization was extended into new territories such as Hokkaido, Taiwan and Korea. School education, physical geography, holidays and war dead commemoration were all methods the government had at its command to aid it in this task. Japan developed a modern system of education which taught a national curriculum. Schools encouraged a single 'national language', based on a middle-class Tokyo dialect. They also instilled a broader sense of the international community and Japan's place in it. Morality (*shūshin*) was an important part of this school curriculum. Morality textbooks collected a range of stories inspired by great Japanese and Western personages that demonstrated values such as bravery, patriotism and loyalty. However, the most succinct example of the morality promoted by the government is the Imperial Rescript on Education. Both this Imperial Rescript and the morality textbooks drew on a Confucian foundation of ethics, along with the modern values of the 'international community', while being framed within the Shinto-based imperial myths.

The Japanese secularity was also communicated through metageography. Metageographies 'constitute ideological structures' (Lewis and Wigen 1997, xi), and this is true not only on the global level but also on the lower taxonomic levels of regions, prefectures and cities. Thus Japan's modernization included new ideas about city planning and transportation networks. New cities and train lines were constructed to reinforce a geographic idea of concentric centres and peripheries. New cities like Sapporo were constructed upon a grid aligned with the cardinal directions, which indicated a modern rationality while evoking the layout of the classical Japanese capitals. Railways, a key symbol of modernity, were constructed to connect the Japanese centre to the periphery. Shrines were included in this. Trains allowed the city's denizens easy access to the public space of the shrine, often located at the periphery of a major city. Furthermore, train stations became the centre of the towns, with government offices, schools and department stores often located directly in front. The daily life of Japanese subjects became ordered around new centres and connected by train and other modern transportation to larger centres. Especially in the overseas territories, 'public spaces became targeted points of intervention aimed at transforming non-elite inhabitants from disobedient objects of rule into self-regulating, if not self-governing, subjects of power' (Henry 2014, 4). In addition, as discussed above, maps often relocated Japan into the centre of the world, and positioned the Greater East Asian sphere as imagined by Japan concentrically around it.

A way the Japanese state helped instil a new sense of time was by adopting a new calendar. This calendar embraced scientific modernity in its astronomical accuracy. But it also embraced the mythic Shinto history in that it located the start of History at the year of the first human Emperor's enthronement rite. The linear time of this imperial calendar (*kōki*) was evoked in school textbooks and became the focus of massive celebrations in 1940. The government adopted a cyclic method of measuring eras that is still used today, the regnal year. In contrast to the pre-modern period when the regnal year was often changed based on calamities and other events, the regnal year from the Meiji period onwards was tied to the reign of each emperor, posthumously combining the emperor and the era. Within the yearly cycle of time, the government established a set of national holidays. These holidays were largely based on Shinto court ritual, combining the modern solar calendar with holidays based on Shinto rite. In the Showa period, holidays increasingly became the focus of attention and the government utilized a form of 'rule by time'. Rule by time is a term used by Hara (2011) in discussing the synchronized practice of bowing towards the centre (*yōhai*).[21] Thus the calendar and the celebrations connected to it became an important method by which a changed sense of time and space was instilled within Japanese subjects.

The war dead played an important part in the construction of the modern nation-state. Japan's victory in the Russo-Japanese war marked a turning point in its development, and war memorials and commemorative events celebrated that victory on a wide scale. One of the requirements of a modern nation-state is to instil a strong enough sense of patriotism in its subjects that they are willing to give their lives for the nation in exchange for posthumous honour and assurance of care for their families. Since this honour was a requirement for the state, it had to be incontestable, that is, located in the secular sphere. After some experimentation, Japan established a system of cenotaphs (*shōkon-sha*), later converted into *gokoku* shrines, that was able to manage the ever-increasing war dead produced by Japan's continuing expansion into Asia. These war memorials were organized in a concentric fashion, so that local memories of the dead were distinctive but still 'subsumed within the broader context of national and global memories of the conflict' (Seaton 2016a, 9).

Shinto shrines, meanwhile, were used in conjunction with schools, geography, holidays and war memorials to help instil this new Japanese secularity into the populace. Schools planned field trips and community service events at shrines, while shrines featured in school morality textbooks. Train lines were often specifically constructed to allow city residents easy access to shrines, while shrines served as public spaces equipped with museums, sport arenas and gardens. Shrines became an integral part of modern Japanese city planning. National holidays coincided with the national system of shrine festivals, so the shrine was a site where holidays were publicly celebrated, with sport or music events often being held after solemn shrine rites. Finally, the system for commemorating the war dead led to the creation of a new type of shrine, specifically for venerating those who had died for the emperor. While the political system of secularism developed in a Western context, and modern Western countries developed their own varying secular spheres based on Christian and Classical morality, Japan adopted the same system of secularism, but adapted it by utilizing Shinto and Confucian morality even while retaining many aspects of Western civilization and morality. Japan was not the only non-Western nation-state to do this,[22] but it serves an important example of how a non-Western state adapted secularism during its project of modernization.

Japanese colonialism and the expanding Japanese sphere

The Japanese government, even while holding that Japan had a fuller understanding of truth than the West due to Japan's mystical 'oriental' nature, dealt with the problem of contrasting ideas of secularity by practically limiting Japanese secularity to the Japanese sphere. The Japanese sphere in this sense is not limited to the areas directly controlled by Japan. It delineates the expanding sphere of influence to which the Japanese government ideologically laid claim. At the start of the Meiji period when Japan was in a weak military position, the Meiji government worked quickly to secure its northern and southern borders by incorporating Hokkaido (Ezochi) and Okinawa (Ryūkyū) into the state. While both these places had a history of strong Japanese influence,[23] this can be argued to be the start of modern Japanese colonialism (Mason 2012; Seaton 2016a, 26). Hokkaido was immediately claimed by the Meiji government, since the fear of Russia claiming the sparsely populated island was great and Ainu living in Hokkaido had no recognized state or modern military to prevent Russia or Japan from doing so. Okinawa was a recognized kingdom, but was annexed by Japan in 1872, her kings being demoted to mere nobility. Although Okinawa was subject to many of the same colonial measures as Hokkaido, it was considered developed enough to not require a new shrine like Hokkaido and other overseas areas did.[24] During this early period, Japan's main concern was in protecting its narrow interests, as can be seen by its negative response to the request of King Kalākaua of Hawaiʻi in 1881 for a protectorate-style relationship with Japan to counter American influence in the Pacific.

The Japanese government worked hard to prove that Japan was a civilized country in the eyes of the West and thus deserving of equal treatment. Slogans like 'rich nation, strong military' captured the government's ambition to enrich the nation and build up the military enough to be considered a 'great power' on the international stage. The government first looked to expand Japan's sphere of influence to include Korea, which brought about a conflict of interest with Qing China, who historically claimed suzerainty over Korea. This led to the first Sino-Japanese War (1894–5), where Japan surprised the international community by winning a decisive victory. As a part of the war spoils, the Qing passed Taiwan over to Japan. Taiwan differed from Hokkaido and Okinawa in that it lacked a long history of close interaction with Japan. Furthermore, Taiwan was also the first territory Japan gained through the common method of imperialism through war. As Japan's first territory internationally recognized as a formal colony, Japan was determined to turn Taiwan into a model colony and took pride in the West lauding Japan's colonial efforts in Taiwan.[25]

Conflict over Korea next led to the Russo-Japanese War in 1904–5. Again Japan surprised Western nations by winning against Russia. In particular, Japan's victory over Russia demonstrated Japan's ability to compete militarily with a Western power. Japan began to be seen as a possible threat by the West. Japan's victory established Korea as a protectorate of Japan, leading to Korea's annexation in 1910. Furthermore, during the First World War, Japan allied with Entente powers (Britain, France and Russia) against Germany, which allowed it to expand its influence in China by taking over German colonies in Asia and the Pacific. Japan became the only non-Western great power in the League of Nations formed after the First World War, and was granted the South Seas Mandate. This gave Japan control over Germany's former colonies in the Pacific, giving the task of civilizing Micronesia to Japan as a 'sacred trust' (Peattie 1992, 82).

The rejection by the United States and Britain of the Racial Equality Clause proposed by Japan to the League of Nations was also significant in driving Japan away from the idea of Western-based 'universal' values. It pushed Japan away from a style of colonialism that saw the assimilation of colonial people as not possible, and towards a style that aimed to assimilate colonial people into full subjects. This attitude towards colonialism also influenced the establishment of shrines overseas. Major overseas shrines in the earlier days of Japanese colonialism enshrined the Three Pioneer Kami (Kaitaku Sanjin) and allowed for adaption to local circumstances. This has been referred to as a 'pioneer theology' (*kaitaku no shingaku*) (Suga 2014, 141). However, beginning in the early to mid-1900s, a shift in attitudes towards seeing Shinto as universal or as a True religion was reflected in a trend towards enshrining Amaterasu Ōmikami rather than the Three Pioneer Kami in overseas shrines. This shift led to what might be called a universalized theology, in contrast to the earlier pioneer theology.[26]

Pan-Asianism, or the idea of united Asian values in contrast to the West, developed as an anti-colonial discourse that aimed to unite Asia in the face of Western imperialism. Thinkers like Okakura Kakuzō, well known in the West for his treatises on Tea and the value of oriental art, drew upon the pre-modern metageography of the Three Countries united by Buddhism. While this theory traditionally placed India (Tenjiku) as the original enlightened country, the mediaeval Shintoist Yoshida Kanetomo used the theory of Japan as the Land of the Kami to argue that it was Japan, not India, that was the 'primal nation' (Hardacre 2017, 216). In the Meiji period, this idea combined with Japan's rapid adoption of Western technology and military, leading many Japanese pan-Asianists to see Japan as the obvious leader to unite Asia and bring their Asian 'brethren' into civilized society. Civilization in this case meant a Japanese civilization, based on, but not the same as, Western civilization. While many Japanese pan-Asianists thinkers sincerely, if chauvinistically, hoped to unite all of Asia into one equal brotherhood, this ideology was also used by the military to rationalize colonialism and the construction of puppet states in Asia. Shintoists often defined the wartime slogan 'the world under one roof' (*hakkō ichiu*) as meaning 'universal brotherhood', but it also implied it was only under the Japanese emperor's benevolent care that such a brotherhood could be achieved.

In the late 1930s, the idea of the Greater East Asia Co-prosperity Sphere became popular, and at its greatest extent included the Provisional Government of Free India, the Kingdoms of Cambodia, Laos and Thailand to the East and the Japan's South Seas Mandate over Micronesia to the West. In the 1940s the Japanese government had even broader plans for the Co-prosperity Sphere to include Hawai'i, southern India, Australia, New Zealand and possibly the coastal areas of the Americas where significant communities of Japanese had already migrated. As Japan imagined its sphere of influence expanding, efforts began to incorporate the inner colonies such as Taiwan and Korea more fully as Japanese through the process of imperialization (*kōminka*). This included efforts to erase outward differences such as non-Japanese names and to require of colonial subjects the same duties required of citizens in the Home Islands such as military service.

In summary, Japan adopted a worldview that adapted the Western idea of East versus West. Within the East, or Asia, Japan utilized a concentric idea which saw the Japanese sphere of influence as increasingly expanding to include all of the Asia-Pacific. The ideological goal was to civilize, that is Japanize, the entire area, but until that end point was reached, the region could be arranged into a hierarchy of territories more or less 'Japanese'. Under this definition, being Japanese was defined by praxes, such as speaking Japanese at home or venerating at shrines. However, this ideological view allowed Japan to claim to be working towards racial equality while still justifying systemic discrimination against non-Home Islanders.

The progressive evolution of civilization

The late-nineteenth-century popularity of evolution theory also influenced Japanese conceptions of space and time. This theory was applied not only to biological processes as argued by Charles Darwin, but also to religion, language and, more generally, culture. Under the fourfold hierarchical concept of religion, European superiority was located in Christianity as the only True religion. This was confirmed by the idea of progressive evolution: the newest form of Christianity – Protestantism – was the most advanced, while other older religions like Catholicism or Judaism were less so (Fluhman 2012, 132). As religion flattened, the secular worldview came to be increasingly advocated as the most advanced and even Protestant Christianity was demoted to an imperfect precedence. Using progressive evolutionary theory, the world could be neatly ordered into an arrangement which positioned Europe as superior at first by merit of its Christianity, and later by merit of its 'rational secularism' (Masuzawa 2005).

As Fluhman has observed, 'science itself was deeply implicated in colonist ideologies' (Fluhman 2012, 131) and the neo-Lamarckian ideas of social evolution and progressive History have often underpinned the rationale for colonialism and slavery. In the nineteenth and twentieth centuries, the West divided the world into three categories. Civilized nations were those of the West, while most of the darker-skinned peoples of the rest of the world – lacking writing, complicated technology and monotheism – were considered barbarians. Non-whites who possessed literacy were given the mediating status of semi-civilized. This tripartite scheme was aligned with the division of race and continents and backed up with 'scientific' and religious justification (Lewis and Wigen 1997, 23–4). The inferiority of black-skinned Africans could be explained both by their racial decent from Noah's youngest son, Ham (who committed the unforgivable crime of seeing his father naked), and by the arid climate of Africa which had supposedly stunted the African 'race'. In a similar manner, Europe's superiority could be had by its merit of being 'Christian' (descended from Noah's eldest son) and, when this lost currency, by arguments that Europe's temperate climate fostered intellectual and technological superiority. Civilized habits, religion and technology could be adopted by non-white nations and were, but this rarely convinced Western nations to treat these nations as equals. Hawai'i was one example of this colonial discrimination: when its Christian monarchy was overthrown by American businessmen the Western world looked the other way. 'Semi-civilized' nations such as India and Japan were very much aware of this example.

In comparison, the traditional metageography in Japan also divided the world into three sections, but was an adaption of two ideas from continental Asia. One idea was the Buddhist-based Three Countries model of the world used by Pan-Asianists. In this, India, as the birthplace of the Buddha, was the centre of the world and Japan lay on the very periphery, to where Buddhism had only been brought after it had been accepted in China and Korea. Alongside this, another metageography theory that influenced Japan was the Chinese *kai* theory, which positioned China as the centre of civilization surrounded by barbarian states. Japan, on the periphery of China, was again positioned as a barbaric place merely adopting the civilized habits of China. These theories were combined with the idea of Japan as the Land of the Kami (*shinkoku*), which had prominence in the development of Kokugaku thought. Kokugaku thinkers attempted to invert the traditional position of India or China as the centre of the civilization and Japan in the barbaric periphery. Instead, people in Japan had innately lived in harmony with the kami in Japan, and it was not until Japan was 'corrupted' by foreign creeds that strife arose. Other lands, on the other hand, were quickly corrupted from the start, and thus needed to develop high-sounding creeds like Buddhism and Confucianism in order to prevent the people from falling into strife. Despite this inversion of civilization's source country, the basic view of the 'three countries' of India, China and Japan remained.

In the Meiji period, Japanese intellectuals quickly consumed the latest Western research, including that on the hierarchy of races and nations, and applied it to their own past. Japan adapted the Christian-based metageography of the West in that it accepted a distinction between Europe and Asia. Along with this, Japan adopted the idea of race. Thus ideologues drew upon pre-modern ideas about Japan as the Land of the Kami to support its position as the 'natural' leader, but only of Asia and Asians. This idea of the Land of the Kami deserves a closer look. Although Japan accepted the idea of social evolution as scientific and the resulting categorization of societies on a spectrum from barbaric to civilized,[27] it based the state's legitimacy on 'the hallowed past of the Age Divine',[28] an age when people and kami lived in perfect harmony, in other words, an idealized past. So while other nations lacked this past, Japan as the Land of the Kami had maintained its connection to the 'Age Divine', especially through the ancient rites of Shinto shrines.

Social evolution in this view was cyclical: Japan's social progression was not moving towards an unknown future Utopia, but rather towards a return to a higher version of the timeless idealized past: what might be called an idealized modernity.[29] While the centre of the nation might be the most civilized, the peripheries often preserved elements of that idealized past. Thus the modernity of the centre and the antiquity of the periphery were both vital to the progress towards recovering that idealized past. Shintoists[30] often depicted geographic travel into the periphery as a trip into the temporal periphery (Christy 1997, 158). This aligned with the ideas of the Hirata Kokugaku school of thought that were popular before and around the time of the Meiji Restoration. The administration of the Japanese empire was arranged in a concentric model. Tokyo as the capital was in the centre, but each prefecture also had its centre, while within each prefecture or territory, each county had its own centre and so on. Shrines reflected this concentric administration structure and played a significant role in connecting the centre and the periphery together.

The reinvention of 'Shinto'

The origin of Shinto as a system has been much contested. The older view is that 'Shinto' is an indigenous religion extending back to age immemorial.[31] This view has been criticized by scholars who argue that Shinto was an entirely modern invention of the Meiji period (Kuroda 1981) or that a system called 'Shinto' can only be traced back as far as the innovations of Yoshida Kanetomo (1435–1511) (Breen and Teeuwen 2010, 222). Hardacre, however, notes the lack of continuity between Kanetomo's Shinto and what is called Shinto today, and argues that the 'Ritsuryō system represents the institutional origin of Shinto, based on the concept of *jingi*, the instantiation through Kami Law (*jingiryō*) of an annual calendar of state ritual, and the establishment of the Council of Divinities (Jingikan) to administer the rites' (Hardacre 2017, 18). Despite claims of indigeneity, shrine rites and folk customs across the Sinosphere shared many traits (Inoue 2003, 7). This similarity, especially between shrines and Chinese mausoleums (*byō*), would become important to Shinto during Japan's colonial project. Regardless of where the origin of Shinto as a system is placed, it is clear that the cluster of customs and networks that are considered 'Shinto' today were diverse and often without strong relation to each other. The process of 'Shintoization' (Breen and Teeuwen 2010, 221) – when discrepant or 'foreign' elements are subsumed into the framework of Shinto – occurred not just in the Home Islands but also at shrines overseas.

The role shrines and other social institutions would have in supporting the Meiji state was not clearly determined at the start of the Meiji Restoration. While shrines were declared sites for the ritual of the state in 1871, this was not the establishment of Shinto as a state religion, nor was it a declaration of shrines as secular. At this early point, the modern idea of religion was not yet embedded within Japan, and the term ritual (*sōshi*) included *sō/shū*, a character that implies sectarianism in the later neologism of *shūkyō* (Josephson 2012, 7). The Great Promulgation Campaign, which began in 1870, was an early attempt to harness the power of 'religion', or at least doctrine, for the state. While the movement was largely considered a failure by 1875, it was formally ended only in 1884 when the national instructor (*kyōdōshoku*) system of the Campaign was abolished. But the Great Promulgation Campaign was an important experiment by the Japanese government in formulating the relationship between the state, religion and shrines. This can be seen by the many rapid changes the government offices which governed shrines underwent during the period. With the Meiji Restoration in 1868, the Jingikan was renewed as a major government department after years of being divided between the Yoshida and Shirakawa houses. Yet in 1871 it was abolished to be replaced by the Jingishō, a degradation of rank. The same year, the modern shrine ranking system was established while Buddhist rites were ceased at the imperial court. The next year, the Jingishō was merged into the Kyōbushō, which had been established the year before to manage the Great Promulgation Campaign. In 1873, the Great Teaching Institute (Taikyōin) was established as a part of the Campaign only to be disbanded after a mere two years, in 1875. In 1877, the Kyōbushō, which had managed the Campaign's doctrine alongside managing shrines and temples, was abolished. Efforts to wean shrines off state support began with the Shrine Preservation Fund in 1880. In 1882, the government prohibited shrine priests from being national instructors, clearly drawing a line between the praxis of shrines and the state doctrine of the Campaign. Finally, the Campaign was officially ended in 1884 (Hardacre 2017, 355-402). This rapid series of often conflicting changes concerning shrines, as well as temples, demonstrates the lack of predetermined vision on the relationship of shrines to the state. The modern idea of religion and the secular were also fluid and undetermined during this period. Thus while the 1870s in Japan were characterized by a government effort to form and propagate a state doctrine, it is anachronistic to see Great Promulgation Campaign as the government's attempt to establish Shinto as a 'state religion'.

In the 1880s, the growth of the Freedom and People's Rights Movement led the government to consider the creation of a constitutional monarchy with democratic representation through the Diet. This led to the promulgation of the Meiji Constitution, which established the Japanese state as secular with a limited guarantee of freedom of religious belief.[32] During the same period, discourse over the establishment of the failed 1900 Religion Bill formulated a vocabulary that separated shrines from generic religion (Maxey 2014, 220) and the academic study of religion in Japan developed with the first chair of Religious Studies being established as Tokyo Imperial University in 1905 (Isomae 2012, 201). The failure of the Campaign led to Shinto becoming incorporated into the common consensus; that is, it led to the successful secularization of Shinto. With the legal and popular establishment of the political system of secularism, shrines were located into the secular sphere, and Buddhism was formed into a Japanese religion (Josephson 2012, 258).

The modern shrine ranking system

In the late Edo period, shrines were organized loosely through a system of licences and sartorial standards by the Shirakawa and Yoshida families. But this changed with the Meiji Restoration. The government declared shrines as sites for conducting the ritual of the state (*kokka no sōshi*) and organized them into the modern shrine ranking system. Despite the hopes of many Shinto ritualists, the Meiji state was unable to financially support all shrines. After a series of trials, all but the most important shrines were required to rely upon their local communities for a majority of their financial support, although these shrines still received small offerings from the state or local government according to their rank (Hardacre 2017, 397–9).

The shrine ranking system organized shrines into two main categories: imperial and national shrines (*kankoku heisha*) and the various shrines (*shosha*). Each of these categories was further organized into ranks. Imperial and national shrines were divided into greater, intermediate, lesser and 'special' ranks, while the various shrines were ranked according to their geographic domain from prefectural shrines to the lowest category of unranked shrines. This ranking scheme united shrines into a single system that extended beyond governmental ministries. While most shrines were under the charge of the Home Ministry, overseas shrines were put under the charge of their respective colonial governments. Likewise, Yasukuni Jinja and the new *gokoku* shrines created in 1939 formed an exception, being partially under the domain of the Ministry of War. The ranking system also united shrines without regard for sectarian boundaries or lineage, such as shrines venerating[33] the same kami. This was in contrast to Sect Shinto, which was divided along sectarian lines.

The modern shrine ranking system united all Shinto shrines across the empire, but it also defined their positions in relation to each other both vertically and horizontally. Vertically, the relatively unregulated unranked shrines were at the bottom. Each village theoretically had a dedicated village shrine, which was the protector (*chinju*) kami of the village. Above village shrines were district shrines, which functioned as a protector of the district. Above these were the prefectural shrines, which protected a major section of the prefecture. Thus each prefecture was clearly ranked in a geographically concentric manner. Furthermore, shrine

Introduction: Religion, Secularism and Japan 23

mergers dictated by the government in the 1870s aimed to align shrines with administrative divisions, reducing the number of shrines in each area so that each village or district was ideally allocated only one shrine of the appropriate rank. This ideal was based off the idea of 'territorial hierarchy' from Hirata Kokugaku (Thal 2005, 116). A major motivation for the shrine mergers in the Home Islands was economic concerns. But similar attempts in the colonies were more concerned with realigning the 'imagined community' (Anderson 1991) of colonial residents with the metageography put forth by the Meiji government.

Ranked above the various shrines were the national and imperial shrines. Imperial shrines, which received offerings from the imperial court, included the twenty-two official shrines designated in the early Heian period, and focused on shrines with connections to the imperial house. National shrines, which received offerings from the state, included many of the shrines designated as 'first shrines' (*ichinomiya*) under the Shogunate. Furthermore, the category of 'special imperial shrines' included shrines such as Minatogawa Jinja and Yasukuni Jinja, which were dedicated to those who gave their life for the emperor. While some national and imperial shrines fit into the geographically concentric structure seen in the ranking of the various shrines, this was not always true. Many of these shrines attracted reverence from across the empire. The shrine ranking system united all Shinto shrines into a single system organized geographically concentric, where reverence was funnelled from the periphery to the centre.

Secularizing shrines, religionizing temples

Shrines in the early twentieth century were largely seen and treated as secular institutions. In the political system of secularism, the secular sphere designates those things that are considered public and universal to all citizens, and thus can form the basis of laws and be taught in public education. Shrines were not *innately* secular: the secular and religion are both constructs.[34] But after the end of the Great Promulgation Campaign, shrines were increasingly located in the newly formed secular sphere. This meant emphasizing shrines as historical sites, rather than mythological sites, as public facilities rather than private ones, and as an essential part of modernity, while treating antique shrine customs not as barbaric, but as relics from the idealized past.

First, History is a linear construction of the past, but the construction of History goes beyond the uncovering or explaining of facts and inevitably includes the interpretation of those facts. Newly constructed shrines in the Home Islands were built on sites perceived to be the scientifically validated physical sites of historical events, and the kami enshrined were, or at least depicted as, historical personages. This sometimes happened with overseas shrines, although geography or practical concerns often took precedence over historical connection when deciding the location of a new shrine. Older shrines also repositioned their kami as historical personages, rather than mystic divinities, and began to emphasize the concrete history of the shrine's site, rather than its miraculous powers. Thal provides an example of this in her case study on Kotohiragū, which in the Meiji period re-identified its miraculous kami Konpira Daimyōjin, as the 'historical' kami Ōmononushi no Kami and Emperor Sūtoku. It also downplayed the site's mysterious powers in favour of emphasizing Emperor Sūtoku's supposed retirement there (Thal 2005, 142, 246). Furthermore, shrines became sites not just for commemorating History, but also for learning about it, with museums and other public facilities being built on shrine grounds and school children visiting shrines on field trips.

Second, shrines were treated as public facilities. Public facilities such as sports tracks and pleasure gardens were also built at shrines. Public transportation such as railroads were constructed specifically to allow the public easy access to shrines, just as access was provided to other government facilities such as the city hall. The open construction of shrine grounds, the entrance marked by the open *torii* gate, and the expansive forest-like garden, meant shrines were accessible to all members of the public at any time day or night, in contrast to most Buddhist temples, which were protected at night by massive gate doors and in principle reserved only for members of that temple's sect.

Third, shrines were positioned as a natural part of modernity that evoked an idealized past. As previously explained, Japanese modernity was conceived as circular: it was a race forward towards an idealized past. Rather than shrines seeing themselves as museums committed to lifeless re-enactments of an outdated past, they portrayed themselves as living efforts to revive the idealized past when humanity supposedly lived in perfect harmony with the kami. This past, furthermore, was a futuristic one, where the ancients had access to modern technology and understood not just how to utilize such technology, but also the workings of the kami behind it. Thus Josephson (2012) describes this Japanese secularity as 'Shinto-scientific'. Rather than the amalgam of technology and Shinto being a paradox, it was posited as the natural coming together of two parts of a whole.

In the late nineteenth century, Japan settled on a secular state with shrines located in the public, praxis-focused sphere of the secular. In this way, Meiji

Shinto was a new construct. But the Meiji ideologues brought about 'the birth on one hand of "Shinto", and the birth on the other of a new entity called Buddhism' (Breen 2009, 248). As shrines were pushed into the secular sphere, Buddhist temples – along with Christian and later Sect Shinto churches (*kyōkai*) – were relocated into the private sphere.[35] But as the secular (*mushūkyou*) was defined in opposition to religion (*shūkyō*), Buddhist temples were 'religionized' in the same process in which shrines were 'secularized'. To refer back to the development of a generic vocabulary of religion, many terms in the grammar of religion were constructed from or utilized traditionally Buddhist terms, including the term *shūkyō* itself (Krämer 2013).

The Shinshū sect of Buddhism was an influential political actor during the Meiji period. It had developed a doctrine against venerating the kami, and, since it lacked the degree of dependence many other Buddhist temples had on amalgamation with shrines, fared better after the Meiji government required shrines and temples to separate (Breen 2009, 249). The Shinshū sect was originally an enthusiastic supporter of the Great Promulgation Campaign, but became disillusioned by the strong Shinto focus and internal bickering that occurred among the Shinto ideologues. The withdrawal of the Shinshū sect in 1875 signalled the eventual failure of the Campaign. Shimaji Mokurai, a Shinshū priest, played a significant role in constructing the concept of religion in Japan. Shimaji, who had studied in Europe and was familiar with the Western idea of religion, argued that religions such as Buddhism and Christianity focused on the transcendent and gave moral guidance and solace to souls after death. As a religion, Buddhism was freed from the burden imposed by the Great Promulgation Campaign of promoting the national doctrine. Shinto, on the other hand, was not a religion, for if it were, it would be of the most primitive sort, which was unthinkable (Krämer 2013; Nitta 2009). Thus the argument for shrines as secular and Buddhism as a religion was used by Shinshū Buddhists to protect themselves from unwanted government interference.

Ama (2011), in his book on the modernization and globalization of Shinshū Buddhism, discusses how Shinshū Buddhism in Hawai'i was not only 'Americanized' but also 'Japanized'. At first glance, it seems counterintuitive to suggest that Japanese Buddhism could Japanize as a process equivalent to Americanization. But this Japanization might also be described as religionization: Shinshū Buddhism in Hawai'i adopted many changes to align itself with the practices of Shinshū Buddhism in Japan, which was undergoing its own transformation into a modern religious institution. This included reforms like flattening the structure of the sect and creating a Buddhist wedding ceremony. But one of the changes that is most relevant to the discussion of religion and the secular was the reinterpretation of the 'two truths' teaching of Mahayana Buddhism.

The two truths teaching divided truth into the absolute Truth of Buddha's laws and the relative truth of mundane society. Shinshū Buddhists of the Edo period stressed the importance of enduring the laws of realm in daily life, while looking towards the Buddha for salvation in the afterlife (Ama 2011, 21). In the Meiji period, Shimaji reinterpreted this 'two truths' teaching to mean a divide between mundane truths, which included Shinto rituals honouring the imperial ancestors, and the spiritual Truth that Buddhism taught. Shinshū Buddhists began enshrining *taima* talismans from the shrine Ise Jingū in their temples and conducting imperial rites, despite Shinshū's historical prohibition against venerating kami. This was so much so that Ōmi (2017) argues that pre-war Buddhism can be considered 'State Shinto'.

Japanese subjects living under American rule operated under two different versions of secularism: American and Japanese. Japanese Buddhist institutions in Hawai'i both Americanized and Japanized (religionized) in order to better fit within the category of religion in both Japanese and American secularism. Hawai'i Shinto shrines, on the other hand, found themselves categorized as secular in Japan, but religious in Hawai'i. Shrine communities managed this conflicting categorization through a process of translation. In the same process of translating Japanese terminology into English, shrines were translated out of the Japanese secular sphere and into the American religious sphere. This translation involved the re-categorization of shrine practices considered secular in Japan as religious in America, rather than the adoption of elements modelled on American religious practices such as the hymn-writing and theological innovations seen in some Buddhist temples. Thus shrines could become religious in the English-language context of American secularism, while remaining mainly secular within a Japanese secularity.

Overview of the work

The establishment of secularism and the ideology of imperialism provides the backdrop against which modern Shinto shrines were developed. The modern concepts of religion and the secular are not self-evident categories, but are rooted in a specific genealogy that can be traced back to early modern Europe and the development of the nation-state. As such, it is necessary to look at

Shinto shrines within the broader context of the political system of secularism in order to understand the development and position of Shinto shrines within Japan as a modern nation-state. Doing this allows us to examine shrines' role in promoting the state's attempt at embedding a new, modern consensus of reality – a Japanese secularity.

Just as 'religion' and *shūkyō* do not point to exactly the same thing, Japanese and American secularities also differ from one another. The Japanese government and shrines adapted ideas about secularity from the West to fit their specific circumstances, often utilizing ideas like progressive History, the East-West divide and the modern concept idea of religion, even while replacing their Eurocentricity with a focus on Japan. Meanwhile Japanese subjects overseas were forced to navigate between the pressures of differing secularities. The transformation of Japan into a modern secular state included both the secularization of Shinto shrines and the religionization of Buddhist temples and Sect Shinto groups. The chapters in this book explore how Shinto shrines were both secularized and religionized, as well as how this process affected their position within society.

The argument that shrines were considered secular sites should not be mistaken for an argument that Shrine Shinto or 'State Shinto' was not part of Japan's imperialism and colonialism. Establishing a Japanese secularism committed violence against local customs in the Home Islands but even more so in the colonies. In Taiwan and Korea, many Chinese and indigenous customs were suppressed as barbaric or superstitious, while the secularization of shrines also stripped Home Islanders of pre-modern traditions of such as funeral customs, faith healing and divination practices by delegitimizing them as shrine practices. Furthermore, shrines often directly supported Japanese militarism during this period. This includes not only the veneration of war dead at *gokoku* shrines but also the ideological justification shrines provided for the continuing expansion of the Japanese sphere. Indeed, shrines demonstrate that secularism can be just as oppressive as a state religion.

This book begins its journey in the Home Islands at the centre of Japanese empire and travels across the seas to the distant reaches of Japan's perceived sphere of influence. Before setting sail overseas, the book, in Chapter 2, examines how modern Shinto shrines were established and then operated as secular sites within the Japanese Home Islands. Chapter 3 moves north to Meiji Japan's earliest colonial space, Hokkaido, to examine how changing ideas about religion and the secular led to the development of a 'pioneer theology' adopted by both large and smaller shrines. It also examines how the war dead were gradually Shintoized in the first half of the twentieth century. Chapter 4 moves south to Japan's first formal colony, Taiwan. There, four different shrines are examined to trace the shift in shrines from aiming to create good imperial subjects which still had room for selected Taiwanese customs, to creating assimilated Japanese subjects.

Chapter 5 then travels to Korea to unpick the changes that led to a new 'universalized theology' that adopted a hierarchical view of religion, even while the Japanese government continued to insist on a secular view of Shinto. This encouraged the inclusion of selected Korean customs into Shinto, but also caused conflicts around the freedom of religion. Looking at Manchukuo in Chapter 6 demonstrates the gaps between the government, army and settler population's ideas about shrines and Shinto. While the Manchukuo and Japanese governments imagined a multiethnic Shinto secularity that might serve as the basis of the state, Home Islander settlers clung to an ethnic conception of shrines which preserved them as exclusively Japanese sites. Chapter 7 at last takes us to Hawai'i, where five different shrines are examined to see how shrines conceived as secular adapted to existing under an American secularism that located shrines in the religious sphere. The final chapter draws out the shifts that affected modern overseas Shinto shrines and how their pre-war relationship with the constructed categories of religion and secular has affected their destruction or their continued existence post-war.

2

The birthplace of Japan: Kashihara Jingū and the Home Islands

11 February 660 BC.[1] *Framed by the verdant slopes of Mt. Unebi, Emperor Jinmu sat at Kashihara Palace, surveying the wide expanse of his newly established Capital. Below him arrayed were his loyal retainers, many of whom had made the long, difficult trek eastward from Himuka to at last settle here at the centre of the Land of the Rising Sun. Foremost among them was Amenotomi no Mikoto, chief ritualist, and Amenotaneko no Mikoto, prime minister. At the gates stood the imperial guard, washed clean of blood and dirt. Their bronze helmets shone in the sunlight, reflecting golden rays like the wings of the Golden Kite had reflected the morning sun to blind the enemy at the Battle of Tomi. Jinmu looked up towards the sun. While bandits still roamed in distant lands, here at the centre the citizens of Yamato could at last lay their heads down in safety and peace. All this was due to the benevolence to his ancestress, Amaterasu Ōmikami, who had given this land's great treasure – the people – into Jinmu's care. From today, he vowed, a new age of peace and security would begin, and the work of Heaven would one day expand to all the eight corners of the world. Emperor and subject alike bowed in reverence as voices rose in chorus: 'May this reign be unshakeable for a thousand, yea, for eight thousand generations, Here and now the cornerstone of the Great Japanese Empire is laid' (Uta 1921, 101).*[2]

Kashihara, above lauded as the site of the foundation of the Japanese empire, is today a little-known city in Nara Prefecture, whose main attractions include mountain hiking and some early Asuka period ruins. But during the early 1940s, Kashihara was famed across the empire as the birthplace of Japan. Kashihara Jingū is the shrine founded upon the site designated as the location of the enthronement rite of Emperor Jinmu, the legendary founding Emperor of Japan. Thus the site serves as a prominent example of a modern Home Islands shrine which establishes a comparative basis for looking at overseas shrines. Through

Kashihara Jingū, this chapter examines the relationship of modern Shinto shrines to the newly embedded concepts of the secular and religion, and finds that Kashihara Jingū was largely conceived and treated as a public, historical and modern site, despite early connections to semi-private reverence organizations. Kashihara Jingū also had a role in affirming the new Japanese secularity promoted by the Japanese government. Since Kashihara Jingū was founded at the site seen as the birthplace of Japan in 1890 just as the modern concept of secularism was becoming embedded in Japan, it serves as a particularly useful example for examining how a changed sense of time and space was communicated to Japanese subjects. Although unique as the 'birthplace of Japan', Kashihara Jingū shares similarities with other shrines in the Japanese Home Islands.[3]

A brief history of Kashihara Jingū

Kashihara Jingū (Figure 2.1) venerates the traditional first human emperor of Japan, Jinmu (Kamu-yamato-ihare-hiko-hohodemi no Sumera Mikoto) and his empress consort (Hime-tatara-isuzu-hime no Mikoto).[4] The shrine was

Figure 2.1 Kashihara Jingū today. (Author's photograph.)

established in 1890, but the movement leading to its foundation extends back to the Edo period (1603–1868), when Kokugaku scholars and other nativists took a growing interest in the physical location of imperial tombs (Itō 2002, 67). The Tokugawa Shogunate, in order to boost its legitimacy in the face of growing criticism that it was disrespectful to the emperor, designated a site near Mt. Unebi in Kashihara, Nara, as the historical tumulus of Emperor Jinmu in 1863. When the Meiji government came to power, it affirmed the Shogunate's designation as accurate, and local interest in the site grew. In 1887, the first petition for a monument at the archaeological site of Jinmu's palace, in addition to the tumulus, was submitted to the Osaka government by Nishiuchi Narisato, a local imperial tomb guardsman and the man who became Kashihara Jingū's first chief ritualist. A year later the same petition was submitted to the Minister of Home Affairs, which led to official permission being granted in March 1889 (Takagi 1997, 270).

While the movement to establish a monument at the site of Jinmu's palace began mainly as a local effort, the imperial household began to take an active interest. The Meiji government decided to grant the new Kashihara shrine the rank of greater imperial shrine, the highest rank in the modern shrine ranking system established in 1871. Significantly, the imperial house donated the Kashikodokoro and Shinkaden buildings from the Kyoto Imperial Palace to be recycled as the shrine's main buildings. These two buildings were part of the Three Imperial Palace Sanctuaries (*kyūchū sanden*), which formed the heart of the restored Council of Divinities (Jingikan).[5] The imperial residence had shifted from Kyoto to Tokyo in 1869 and thus the Council of Divinities had also been moved to the Tokyo Imperial Palace. The support the national government granted Kashihara Jingū is significant because, at this time, it was moving away from supporting shrines after the perceived failure of the Great Promulgation Campaign. Major shrines were granted a lump sum preservation payment[6] to help them become self-sufficient, and the newly established Kashihara Jingū received a sum of 10,000 yen (Uta 1940, 249). Kashihara Jingū had its enshrinement rite (*chinza*) on 2 April 1890, just in time to celebrate the national holiday of Emperor Jinmu's Anniversary (Jinmu Tennō-sai) as a major festival. Its annual festival (*reisai*) was established as 11 February, to align with the previously established national holiday of Foundation Day.

From 1911 to 1926, the shrine underwent its first major expansion (Uta 1981b, 216). A new train line was constructed to improve access and the shrine grounds were almost doubled in size from 6.7 hectares to 12.1 hectares

(Kashihara Jingū-chō 1989). Another significant addition to the shrine was the formation of the 13.2-hectare Unebi Park. Kashihara Jingū, like Jinmu's tumulus, was established on an archaeological site recognized by the state. While the sites were nearby each other, they were separated by a stretch of land where villagers resided. Local groups had long advocated for the shrine and tumulus to be connected by establishing a public park between them. After the chief ritualist of Kashihara Jingū added his petition for the park, the national government agreed to purchase the land. The villages within the new park's area were relocated, and Unebi Park was formed. To help fund these improvements, Kashihara Jingū Kōsha was established in 1912. Donations collected by this association and other private donations, in addition to public funding from the imperial house and government, made the shrine's expansion possible (Takagi 2006, 59).

Kashihara Jingū reached its height of popularity in 1940, the year the empire celebrated the 2600th anniversary of Jinmu's enthronement. In preparation for this anniversary, the shrine again underwent major improvements. The train line was moved to bring a station, named Kashihara Jingū Entrance, directly in front of the shrine's main approach. The shrine's outer garden also underwent considerable landscaping.[7] Funding from the national and local government, in addition to private financial and labour donations, aided the planting of over 20,000 trees. The construction of a new enlarged shrine building, athletic facilities, a dormitory and a museum were also funded (Kashihara Jingū-chō 1989). In 1940, a record number of visitors came to Kashihara Jingū, with 1.25 million visitors recorded during the first three days of the year. The shrine's annual festival that year attracted 700,000 visitors (Ruoff 2010, 99). Tied up as it was in the pride of empire, the shrine's enormous popularity disappeared at the end of the war. Today the forested shrine grounds still impress the visitor with their majesty, but the shrine lacks the national appeal shrines like the Ise Jingū and Meiji Jingū still maintain.

An historical, public, modern site

Shinto shrines like Kashihara Jingū were one of the most visible institutions promoting a Japanese secularity. But before looking at this connection, a broader look at their relationship with the political system of secularism is necessary. Kashihara Jingū was conceived and treated as a secular site – that is, as a historical, public and modern site – in imperial Japan, even while efforts were made to separate it from the category of religion.

Kashihara Jingū as historical

The secular sphere is characterized by its perceived factual nature. Kashihara Jingū from its foundation was treated as a site of historical events that existed as a part of, rather than outside, physical space and time. Interest in Emperor Jinmu as the first emperor of Japan began increasing with the popularity of Kokugaku thought in the Edo period. This and the desire to bolster its own political legitimacy led the Shogunate to enquire into the historical location of Jinmu's tumulus and then in 1863 to grant official recognition to the current site (Itō 2002, 69). While political considerations, in addition to textual, oral and archaeological evidence, determined this recognition, the Meiji government confirmed the tumulus's legitimacy after it came to power.

Calls for public veneration at the tumulus began in the late 1870s, but it was the 1888 petition to the Minister of Home Affairs by Nishiuchi Narisato that led the government to hold enquiries and investigations into the location of Jinmu's palace (Takagi 1997, 270), which was the site of his enthronement rite and thus marked the (mythic) start, or the birthplace, of the Japanese empire. As is discussed below, the semi-private nature of Jinmu's tumulus as the grave belonging to the imperial house also encouraged the creation of a site separate from the tumulus itself. Early documents petitioning for the recognition of the Kashihara palace site did not call specifically for a shrine, but called for preserving it as a historical site and erecting a monument there (Uta 1981a, 3, 20). Thus the site that became Kashihara Jingū was not conceived specifically as a Shinto site at first, but as a monument to a national historical site. This ambiguity between shrines and generic monuments was not exclusive to Kashihara Jingū.[8] It became a complaint among some Shinto ritualists that shrines were denigrated by the national government's treatment of them as 'mere' monuments.

After the 1888 petition, the government identified the site to the south-east of Mt. Unebi as matching the description of the Kashihara palace described in the classics. While the project originated as a local initiative, the imperial and national government took interest and plans grew into something more than a mere monument. By April 1889, specific discussions about a shrine were being held and the official foundation of the shrine as the greater imperial shrine Kashihara Jingū occurred on 2 April 1890 (Uta 1981a, 47). This was the same year the Meiji Constitution, which established Japan as a secular state, was enacted, and the same period when the modern concept of religion was becoming embedded in Japan. Even while the effort to establish a state doctrine under the Great Promulgation Campaign was being scrapped as a failure and state funding for shrines was being phased out, a shrine – Kashihara Jingū – was still seen as the superlative way to commemorate a historical site considered central to Japanese History.

While modern scholars who dismiss Jinmu's existence as a complete fiction might find the idea of searching for evidence of his palace ridiculous, Jinmu's existence during this period was largely accepted as a fact in both Japan and the West.[9] In addition to the surveys done before the shrine's foundation, the government continued to value the site's factuality. The Ministry of Education undertook a project from 1937 to 1940 in preparation for the empire's 2600th anniversary, where a committee of professors from Japan's top universities investigated the historical legitimacy of thirty-six 'sacred historical sites' related to Jinmu based on written documentation and fieldwork. Kashihara was one of only two sites given unqualified recognition by the committee (Ruoff 2010, 40–1), affirming Kashihara Jingū as a site of factual History.

Kashihara Jingū's abbreviated histories also emphasize the surveys and research that went into legitimating the site and note the many historical sites located on or near the shrine grounds (Uta 1981a, 178). The shrine was an active distributor of educational materials directed towards a more popular audience. Uta Shigemaru, the fifth chief ritualist of the shrine, authored multiple books in the 1920s that detailed the history of Jinmu and the Kashihara site as the first capital of Japan.[10] These books drew on academic works (Uta 1981b, 499) and included historical maps, illustrations based on archaeological evidence, lineage charts and study questions asking readers to recall exact names and dates relating to the history discussed in the book. The second expansion of the shrine also saw a historical museum built within the shrine's outer gardens, making Kashihara Jingū not only a historical site, but also a site to learn about History. Originally a National History Museum sponsored by the 2600th Anniversary Celebration Bureau was planned, but due to bureaucratic issues, the Yamato National History Museum was constructed instead using private donations (Ruoff 2010, 42).

The depiction of Kashihara Jingū as a historical site was not limited to shrine-initiated works, but was common across broader society. School children learned about Jinmu's Kashihara palace from their school textbooks. For example, a morality textbook published for fifth-grade students in 1928 wrote matter-of-factly that over 2,580 years had passed since Jinmu had his enthronement rite and included a lithographic illustration of Jinmu performing his 'great filial' rite (*taikō*)[11] on nearby Mt. Tomi. School supplies featured illustrations of Jinmu reminiscent of popular prints,[12] often alongside other historical role

The Birthplace of Japan   35

Figure 2.2 School slate: The front features Ninomiya Sontoku, while the back features Emperor Jinmu and the golden kite. (Author's collection.)

models like Ninomiya Sontoku (Figure 2.2). Particularly in the late 1930s, the government, along with the commercial sphere such as travel companies and department stores, encouraged the growth of Jinmu in the popular imagination with exhibits, art, promotions and publicity stunts based on the legend of Jinmu, often with his enthronement at Kashihara palace featuring at the climax (Ruoff 2010, 77, 95).[13] In this way, national and local governments, as well as civilian works, treated Kashihara Jingū as a historical site similar to other secular sites of Japanese national History in both official and popular contexts.

Kashihara Jingū as public

Kashihara Jingū also served as a public facility. The decision to build a shrine separate from Jinmu's tumulus was influenced by the semi-private nature of the latter site. Civilian groups had suggested plans as early as 1882 for building a shrine at the tumulus, but the identification and maintenance of tumuli were part of an effort to provide the imperial house with a history to match that of Western imperial houses. Thus the tumulus became a private asset of the imperial house (Takagi 2006, 180). The establishment of Kashihara Jingū at Mt. Unebi rather than at the tumulus led to a division of ritual, with the shrine focused on rites for the public and the tumulus site focused on the imperial house's private rites. A similar division would be later seen between Meiji Jingū in Tokyo and Emperor Meiji's tumulus in Momoyama (Yamaguchi 2005, 200). As a public site, convenient and modern access specifically to the shrine itself was necessary. Thus the shrine's first improvement project extended the railway in 1893 to Unebi Station. As the popularity of the shrine grew, the rail system further expanded to open up two more stations near the shrine: Kashihara Jingū Entrance in 1923 and Yamato Ikejiri in 1929. During the improvements for the 2600th anniversary, the old Kashihara Jingū Entrance station was moved to its current location and Yamato Ikejiri Station was renamed Kashihara Jingū West Entrance.

The shrine improvement projects also beautified the shrine grounds, turning it into a forested park and lakeside to be enjoyed by the public (Figure 2.3). The stated purpose included the idea of returning the land to the forested purity of Jinmu's era. However, the construction of a serene forested outer garden around a shrine was a modern characteristic, influenced by new ideas about the importance of public parks to civilized nations. The term 'outer garden' (*gaien*) itself originally referred to the outer precincts of a palace, and the practice of constructing the pure forests was pioneered at the Ise Jingū and Meiji Jingū before

Figure 2.3 Postcard of Fukada Pond at Kashihara Jingū (1940). (Author's collection.)

Kashihara Jingū (Yamaguchi 2005, 82-4). Volunteer labour and the donation of money and trees from Japanese subjects across the empire to construct the outer garden connected not only residents of the local Kashihara area, but all imperial subjects to the shrine, thus making it inclusive of all Japanese subjects: 'a shrine by the people, for the people' (Yamaguchi 2005, 201). Diverse media, including illustrations of the shrine sold at department stores, and radio and television broadcasts about the shrine ceremonies, fostered this empire-wide emotional connection by allowing those unable to travel to the shrine to still experience it. Activities at the shrine were not limited to the passive enjoyment of nature. The Kashihara Arena in the outer gardens included the Yamato Kokushikan museum, a conference hall, dormitory, library, athletic facilities and an outdoor theatre. Kashihara Jingū also became a popular destination for school field trips for local children as well as students from the colonies (Ruoff 2010, 99). Thus Kashihara Jingū provided many other public services in addition to its main function of performing ritual.

Kashihara Jingū as Modern

The secular sphere was also conceived as modern, as opposed to those primitive or outdated superstitions believed by 'uncivilized' peoples.[14] As peoples were organized by their degree of civilization, correspondingly civilized peoples were seen as modern or the most progressive, while less civilized peoples were conceived as being stunted or stagnant, trapped in an ancient time period. The concept of religion was tied into the idea of this 'progressive History'. If Shinto rites were to form the incontestable basis of the nation, it was vital that Shinto shrines positioned themselves as modern, in addition to (or rather, as a part of) being a site restoring the idealized past. Thus an idealized modernity – as represented by technology and internationalism linked with ancient customs – was incorporated as an integral part of Kashihara Jingū.

First, Kashihara Jingū was linked to encounters with modern technology. Constructing railways to provide public access to the shrine has already been mentioned above. But trains in particular were a key symbol of modernity. Many visitors took advantage of this new transportation, with an average of 367,000 passengers a year debarking from the Sanpai Insen line at Unebi station near Kashihara Jingū between 1915 and 1918 (Uta 1981a, 745). Radio, photography and film also brought the shrine into the everyday life of imperial subjects. The deep beat of the taiko drum over the radio during rites at Kashihara Jingū left a deep impression on school children in Korea (Ruoff 2010, 31), while photographs displayed visitors in sharp morning coats mingling with shrine priests in classical Japanese garb. Colourized photography and printing captured the brilliant dress of the Kashihara Jingū's shrine maidens (Uta 1981b, front matter), and the masses could watch the emperor's entourage in sleek automobiles pay their respects at the shrine on news reels (Nippon Nyūsu Eiga-sha 1940). For many Japanese subjects, experiencing Kashihara Jingū in person or from afar was inseparable from modern technology.

Second, Kashihara Jingū was associated with the international and the new. An example is found in a pamphlet published by the shrine called *The First Capital* (*Hajime no Miyako*). Published in 1922 and distributed by public offices such as police stations (Uta 1981b, 70), the pamphlet begins with a brief history of the Kashihara palace in antiquity. But the majority of it consists of a Socratic dialogue between various persons. The dialogues depict Kashihara Jingū as representative of the new international Japan. In one dialogue, a 'government official' expresses his resolve to 'pioneer a new example' of visiting Kashihara Jingū in addition to Ise Jingū. In another dialogue, a husband and wife discussing where to bring their newborn child for its first shrine visit ritual decide on Kashihara Jingū because Japan is now 'ranked among the world's three strongest nations' and modern Japanese citizens must make their children into 'international people' (Uta 1981b, 33–6). The shrine also concerned itself with international affairs. Kashihara Jingū performed rites for international events,[15] and in 1899 made efforts to accommodate foreign visitors by translating its signs into English (Uta 1981a, 351). In this way, Kashihara Jingū distanced itself from the image of an antiquated religious cult, and instead acted as a symbol of the international and new.

While Kashihara Jingū positioned itself as modern, its connection to the Japanese past was essential.[16] This was not a past of primitive barbarism, but like the Garden of Eden, an idealized period when Man and Nature lived in harmony. Yet unlike the Garden of Eden, the Japanese past was within this world and could be restored, which allowed the government 'to disguise change as a return to normalcy' (Kasulis 2004, 168). Another shrine pamphlet, *The First Emperor* (*Hajime no Tennō*), written by chief ritualist Uta Shigemaru and utilizing modern research and academic methods, demonstrates this. The pamphlet consists of an account of Jinmu's eastward expedition to Kashihara. The simple illustrations in the small book depict clothing and tools like swords, boats and dishes in the manner that was presumed to be used during that period. The text portrays the age of Jinmu as already possessing the equivalent to cutting-edge technology, implying that modern technology was indigenous to Japan, but had merely been lost in the following years due to corrupting influence from foreign nations. In the text Jinmu laments the loss of Japan's purity and states that his motivation for establishing his capital at Kashihara is to restore it:

> at that time [of Ninigi no Mikoto], the country was still undeveloped and people's hearts were pure ... but [now] in the faraway countries over there, there are bad people who conduct themselves selfishly. Thus the good people cannot lay their heads down safely to sleep. It is very pitiful.... If I recall, the man who had previously visited that country was my relative Nigihayahi no Mikoto. Since this is so, I want to hurry and go to establish a capital there.
>
> (Uta 1981b, 799-800)

This passage is followed by factual questions such as 'Who was the man who had previously ridden an airship to the Yamato basin?' and accompanied by an illustration of the airship which looks remarkably like a dirigible balloon. The joining of an idealized past and modernity was not limited to literature. In 1940, a *naorai* meal, attended by 1,900 people, was held after the ritual announcing the completion of improvements to the shrine. While this meal celebrated an improvement project impossible to complete without modern technologies, it was served on commemorative dishes copied from Sue pottery, the 'ceremonial pottery of our ancient ancestors' (Uta 1981b, 706-17). The shrine advocated itself as an institution both modern and able to restore a 'modernity' from the past that was Truer than the superficial modernity of the West. Thus until the end of the war, Kashihara Jingū acted and was seen as a historical site, public and modern in character, similar and superior to other secular institutions like public parks and museums.

Kashihara Jingū and religion

While Kashihara Jingū was treated as factual, public and modern – all characteristics definitive of the secular sphere – its central purpose of performing ritual was connected to 'gods' (kami), an aspect popularly associated with the religious sphere. But the question of whether shrines are *innately* religious or secular is nonsensical, and not the concern here. The more relevant question is about which sphere shrines were located in within the political system of secularism. Thus to understand Kashihara Jingū's relationship with the sphere of religion, it is helpful to see how it related to its predecessor and neighbouring site, Emperor Jinmu's tumulus. While located nearby the shrine and eventually connected to it by Unebi Park, the shrine and tumulus were not combined into a single entity, but remained governed by separate parts of the government. Shrines were governed by an entity under the Ministry of Home Affairs[17] while the tumuli as property of the imperial house were managed by the Ministry of the Imperial Household (Uta 1981b, 32). This separation was not a given, but neither was it surprising. The presence of cemeteries at shrines was experimented with during the early Meiji period,[18] but the practice remained a rare exception.

As discussed previously, interest in Jinmu's and other imperial tumuli began in the Edo period, and Meiji government's recognition of the site was an affirmation of the Shogunate's previous designation. In the mid-Meiji period, local movements began calling for a shrine for venerating Jinmu to be built at the tumulus. In 1882, Shinkai Umemaro of nearby Imai Town formed the Unebi Kyōkai and in 1889, the national instructor Okuno Jinshichi helped form the Unebi Kashihara Kyōkai Hon'in. Both organizations drew up unsuccessful plans to build shrine buildings near Jinmu's tumulus. Yet, as the term *kyōkai* ('church') in their names implies, these societies differed in intention from Kashihara Jingū. Drawing influence from the semi-religious Great Promulgation Campaign, they promoted a doctrinal-based reverence for Jinmu focused on his tumulus. These groups continued activities separately alongside Kashihara Jingū until 1903, but the relationship was less than cordial: Nishiuchi, finding a problem with Okuno's radical personality and disinclination to differentiate between private and public, succeeded in having Tokyo revoke Unebi Kashihara Kyōkai's permission in 1903 (Takagi 2006, 25–7). The tumulus as a physical tomb was inseparable from the other world (*meikai*), and the *kyōkai* focused on it were, like the Great Promulgation Campaign, too doctrinal to be useful in a secular state.

Furthermore, the tumulus (Figure 2.4) was not entirely a public site (Takagi 2006, 189). As the tomb of an imperial ancestor, it was managed as property of the imperial house. The emperor was 'head of the Empire'[19] which meant that his ancestors were relevant to all Japanese subjects,[20] so rites held there were of public interest, with newspapers and newsreels reporting on them. But the general public was not free to participate in these rites, in contrast to the rites held at shrines.[21] The shrine pamphlet *The First Capital* explicates the difference between the shrine as a public site and sites such as tumuli and the Imperial Palace Sanctuaries which are reserved for the imperial house. While lamenting that the relationship between *jingū* shrines and tumuli has yet to be clearly determined by law, the pamphlet explains that unity between the imperial house and the people is essential to the Japanese national character. *Jingū* shrines, based on the example of the Ise Jingū, are places where emperor and subject pay reverence together in the case of public matters. Kashihara Jingū in particular,

The Unebi-Goryo　　　　　　　　　　　　　　　陵゠北 東 山 傍 畝 皇 天 武 神

Figure 2.4 Postcard of Jinmu's Tumulus (1940): Access to the site by the public is blocked off by a wooden gate fitted within the *torii*. (Author's collection.)

since it venerates Jinmu and his empress as imperial ancestors as part of the ritual of the state, is a spiritual palace where the imperial house and the people are united as one in their veneration (Uta 1981b, 30–3). Thus the shrine saw itself as a public site for the performance of state ritual, outside of the grammar of religion, through which the emperor and the populace were united as one, in contrast to Jinmu's tumulus or the Imperial Palace Sanctuaries.

'True' religion

Kashihara Jingū as a public site was positioned within the secular sphere under the system of secularism in Japan, but what was its connection to the older, but still in use, hierarchical concept of religion as True Religion? In the early part of the twentieth century, Kashihara Jingū embraced the designation of shrines as secular and downplayed elements that hinted at 'religion', True or not. Jinmu, for example, was referred to as the 'Imperial Ancestor Emperor Jinmu' rather than a title that hinted at a transcendent status.[22] Furthermore, Kashihara Jingū rejected close association with possibly religious organizations. The Unebi Kyōkai organization discussed previously focused its veneration on the same kami[23] as the Great Promulgation Campaign, in addition to Emperor Jinmu, making it similar in character to legally religious sects like Shintō Taikyō. Some shrines such as Izumo Taisha and Kotohiragū formed close relationships with their (semi-)religious counterpart organizations.[24] But Kashihara Jingū formed its own unrelated fundraising organization rather than co-opt a connection with the Unebi Kyōkai or Unebi Kashihara Kyōkai Hon'in.

Despite this, the importance of distancing shrines from 'religion' lessened as the power imbalance with Western countries decreased as Japan grew in military might and national confidence in the 1930s. Furthermore, as Japanese expansion began to be increasingly rationalized through the use of pan-Asianist ideology based on Jinmu's quest for 'universal brotherhood' (*hakkō ichiu* lit. eight cords one roof), some ideologues positioned Shinto as the True religion of Asia,[25] in parallel to how Christianity was the True religion of the West. While Kashihara Jingū continued to see itself as a secular institution, it also became a sacred site beyond a mere monument in the wartime ideology.[26] Similar to how human rights are treated as one of the highest incontestable ideals in liberal secularism, Kashihara Jingū was imbued with an inviolable sacred nature of Truth.

Promoting a Japanese secularity

The term 'secularity' can be defined as the consensus of reality promoted within a political system of secularism. In Japan's case, this included changed senses of space, time and ethics formed in antagonism with the Western secularities. Shrines played a significant role in anchoring and communicating this new Japanese secularity. The modern shrine ranking system organized all shrines into a spatial model connected both vertically and horizontally, and the merging of shrines from 1905 to 1910 as a part of the government's Local Improvement Movement worked to make shrines more closely reflect administrative units (Hardacre 2017, 416–18). Kashihara Jingū, as a greater imperial shrine ranked at the top of this system, was a particularly visible institution that communicated these new concepts to the populace especially as the birthplace of Japanese History.

Space

Kashihara Jingū was one of several major 'centres' of Japan. The various shrines (*shosha*) of the shrine ranking system were organized according to the geographic area they watched over, but imperial shrines were positioned as relevant on an empire-wide scale. The location of Kashihara Jingū was decided based on classical evidence and tradition, but the choice of Kashihara in Nara prefecture over Miyazaki prefecture – the other possible candidate for being the birthplace of Japan – placed it within relatively close reach to Tokyo by train. Particularly from the viewpoint of overseas subjects, Kashihara Jingū was quite near the geographic centre of Japan. Thus Kashihara Jingū's geographic location affirmed its status as a centre in the larger concentric metageography that the Japanese government was constructing through methods like the categorization of inner and outer territories and the shrine ranking system.

The formal shrine ranking system was not the only way shrines were connected to each other. The recycling of materials from one shrine by another lesser-ranked shrine was a relatively frequent practice. At Kashihara Jingū, the Kashikodokoro and Shinkaden buildings of the Imperial Palace Sanctuaries were recycled as Kashihara Jingū's main buildings, which provided an important link from a higher centre to a lesser one. Being a Japanese centre did not mean Kashihara Jingū neglected its local territory,[27] and those closest to the shrine were the most likely to donate their labour and resources. But its major festivals emphasized the state rituals all shrines were required to celebrate, such as the national holidays, and it performed, modern nationwide *kagura* dances like Urayasu-no-mai, which written in 1940 to accompany a poem by Emperor Showa.

Among greater imperial shrines, Kashihara Jingū was given special attention due to its major festivals coinciding with two national holidays: Foundation Day (Kigen-setsu) and Emperor Jinmu's Anniversary. Shrines across the nation were required to celebrate the national holidays, but the practice of *yōhai* ('veneration[28] from afar') towards Kashihara Jingū on these holidays emphasized the physical position of the shrine as a centre. *Yōhai* on a small scale originated from practical reasons, allowing people or ritualists to venerate an object at a distance. Many times, a particular spot was designated as a *yōhai* site, which could be temporary or permanent, elaborate as a full shrine building or merely a crude marker of wood or stone. The line between an unranked shrine and a *yōhai* site was vague, and some *yōhai* sites developed into shrines.[29] However, *yōhai* began to be used as a national practice only in 1937, when the government began intensifying efforts to homogenize the empire under the policy of imperialization (Hara 2011, 415). After 1937, Kashihara Jingū, along with Meiji Jingū, Yasukuni Jinja and the Imperial Palace, became a centre upon which the focus of the entire Japanese sphere, emperor and subjects alike, were united.

Kashihara Jingū, beyond being *a* centre of Japan, was also positioned as *the* original centre of Japan, the birthplace of the empire (*kōkoku*) where

Japanese History began. The Meiji government traced its legitimacy back to the Yamato court legendarily founded by Jinmu with his enthronement rite at Kashihara – thus a 'restoration' brought the change of government in 1868. Kashihara Jingū was constructed to commemorate, or in contemporary terminology 'to preserve' the site the Meiji government recognized as that enthronement rite's historical location. Yet the Kashihara site was not the only possible choice for the birthplace of Japan. The legend of Jinmu's eastward expedition begins in Miyazaki Prefecture in Kyushu and ends with him settling at Kashihara. In the late 1930s, Miyazaki Prefecture on the merit of this legend unsuccessfully campaigned to be recognized as Japan's birthplace.[30] But it was Kashihara which retained the official designation. Thus while historical events occurred before Jinmu's enthronement rite, the History of Japan did not begin until he underwent it.

As the conception of the Japanese sphere expanded, so did the area of the world to which Japanese History became relevant. Although the legend of Jinmu originally had little to no connection to the peripheries of the Japanese sphere, nor to the more distant parts of the Home Islands, Kashihara Jingū became their birthplace as they were incorporated into that Japanese sphere. In this capacity, the invocation of the foundation of the empire focused the attention of the entire nation on Kashihara Jingū. As the legend of Jinmu was increasingly utilized by Japan in expansionist propaganda, the shrine was also pointed to by the slogan *hakkō ichiu* ('eight cords one roof'). The phrase was derived by the Nichiren Buddhist scholar Tanaka Chigaku from Jinmu's words at the point of his departure from Hyūga (Miyazaki Prefecture) on his eastward expedition to Kashihara. It cast Jinmu as the first pioneer, travelling to a distant location to bring order and peace to benighted peoples. This pioneer consciousness was widespread across the Japanese sphere, and inspired Japanese migrants from Hokkaido to Hawai'i. Jinmu as a pioneer particularly served as an example for Japanese living overseas, allowing them to take pride in their location outside of the Home Islands. The importance of Kashihara Jingū can be seen during the Congress of Overseas Brethren, held in 1940 and sponsored by the Ministries of Foreign Affairs and of Colonial Affairs. The Congress took Jinmu's golden kite as part of its symbol and included *yōhai* focused towards Kashihara Jingū (Ruoff 2010, 154–7, 171).

The new metageography imagined by the Meiji government and developed through to the end of the war largely adopted the European division of the world into East and West. Yet within that Eastern hemisphere, the Japanese

Home Islands became seen as the centre of the world and the start of History. Within this order, the entire Japanese sphere was connected through a series of concentric relationships both vertical and horizontal as laid out by the modern shrine ranking system. Kashihara Jingū as a greater imperial shrine was not only one of the top-level centres of Japan in this network, but it was also the geographic centre of all Japanese History, especially for Japanese subjects living at the periphery of the Japanese sphere. Yet history involves not only space, but also *time*, which is the next subject.

Time

Kashihara Jingū as the site of Emperor Jinmu's enthronement rite also marked the temporal start of Japanese History. Calculated from the Japanese classics to have occurred in 660 BC, that year marked the start of Japanese linear time using the new imperial calendar. Similar to how the year Christ is traditionally said to have been born marks the start of the Western calendar and thus events previous to Christ are counted backwards, events that occurred before that date were calculated negatively. Far from being a reversion to an outdated calendar, the adoption of linear time using the imperial calendar supported the government's move from the lunisolar calendar based on Chinese models to the modern solar calendar.

Connecting the start of Japanese linear time to the foundation of Japan by Jinmu and placing that start before the start of the Western calendar allowed the government to position the solar calendar not as a Western imposition but something predating the West. It intimately connected the calendar to the original pure Japan of an idealized antiquity, making it more relevant to the average Japanese subject than an arcane explanation based on foreign science. Having the imperial calendar predate the Western calendar also allowed the government to claim superiority to the West as the oldest nation of the world, despite the West's technological advancement.

Kashihara Jingū directly exhorted the value of the new solar calendar. The shrine-published pamphlet *The First Capital*, previously mentioned, suggests a conversation between two 'country folk' where the first laments that despite the new calendar being in use for fifty years, people cannot seem to let go of the old calendar. He then wonders how this situation might be resolved. His fellow replies by suggesting they transfer their lunar new year traditions to the nearby national holiday of Foundation Day (11 February) as the first step to improving their lifestyle (Uta 1981b, 33-4). This also illustrates how the praxis of celebrating the new holidays was more important than the internal reasoning attached to the celebration (Josephson 2012, 139; Thal 2005, 285).

Ruoff (2010) has amply demonstrated the increasing prominence of the imperial calendar in Japanese society as the anniversary year of 2600 (1940 AD) approached. Popular works chronicled Japan's '2600 years of History', international scholars gave lecture series on the topic and department stores across the empire held exhibitions about the Jinmu story (Ruoff 2010, 73-6). Residing at the centre of these celebrations of Japanese History was Kashihara Jingū. The major renovations and expansions the shrine underwent in anticipation of the anniversary and the millions of visitors the shrine received have already been described, but Kashihara Jingū's influence was not limited to those who could physically visit the shrine. Newsreels (Nippon Nyūsu Eigasha 1940) and radio (Ruoff 2010, 31) brought the ritual of Kashihara Jingū to Japanese subjects throughout the empire.

In addition to the linear time of the imperial calendar, Kashihara Jingū also affirmed the yearly cycle of time established by the Meiji government. In 1873, the Meiji government, along with the solar calendar, created a new set of national holidays considered appropriate for a modern nation-state. While some of the holidays overlapped pre-modern celebrations, the new holidays mostly lacked ideological connection to the holiday practices of the Tokugawa government. The new year was shifted a month back to the solar new year and was celebrated with the lengthy national holiday of Genshi-sai. Foundation Day on 11 February celebrated Jinmu's enthronement rite at Kashihara, 3 April saw the anniversary of Jinmu's passing memorialized and the autumn was marked by the Shinto harvest rites of Niiname-sai and Kanname-sai. Kashihara Jingū, as discussed above, honoured the above holidays with rites and in the case of the two holidays directly connected to Jinmu not only celebrated them but also became the focal point for celebrations held across the empire.

Here, it might be enlightening to make a brief foray into terminology. The term 'national holiday' (*shukusai-jitsu*) refers to two types of holidays: celebratory days (*shuku-jitsu*) and festival days (*sai-jitsu*). By 1927, the four celebratory days were esteemed as the Four Great Seasons (*shidaisetsu*) while the rest of the holidays remained festival days. The difference between these two types of holidays seems to have been importance rather than quality. For example, the beloved Emperor Meiji's birthday was designated a celebratory day while the short-reigning Emperor Taisho's birthday remained a festival day. Furthermore, while the government eventually recognized only seven national festival days, shrines celebrated a large number of local festival days, from their annual festival (*reisai*) to their regular monthly festival (*tsukinami-sai*). Subjects were encouraged to mirror this festival day schedule in their homes with things such as placing additional foods before their home shrine. This overlap of terminology reinforced the idea that local shrine festivals were of the same secular nature as national festivals.

Many large shrines in the modern era stood at the top of a vertical lineage. Ise Jingū, while receiving reverence from all Japanese subjects through the distribution of Jingū *taima*, was connected to those shrines bearing the appellation *daijingū*. Similarly, Kotohiragū served as the parent shrine for shrines across the empire called Kotohira Jinja. Izumo Taisha, which venerates Ōkuninushi no Mikoto and is lauded as second only to the Ise Jingū, utilized a religious organization, setting up Izumo Taisha-kyō churches. While there were shrines across Japan which venerated Jinmu Tennō, Kashihara Jingū lacked this sort of vertical-concentric network of branch shrines. Yet, like Meiji Jingū's treatment on the holiday of Meiji-setsu, Kashihara received veneration from all other shrines on Emperor Jinmu's Anniversary. Thus with the major festivals of Kashihara Jingū aligned with, or the focus of, national holidays, its rites served as a significant way the yearly cycle of time was communicated to subjects of the nation.

Finally, the practice of *yōhai* towards Kashihara Jingū played a part in instilling a sense of daily time in imperial subjects. Japan had traditionally measured time using the temporal hour, meaning the length of an hour differed as the length of daytime increased or decreased during the year. With the change to the solar calendar in 1873, Western-style equinoctial hours began to be used. This new method of timekeeping, consistent across the empire regardless of when the sun rose or set locally, was more convenient for establishing precise railway, and later radio, schedules. Local governments informed their cities of noon and sometimes the end of the day with a bell, whistle or other siren. However, mass timed *yōhai*[31] only began in 1937 when the imperialization efforts led to the establishment of a single empire-wide time zone. Thus in addition to instilling a physical sense of direction, *yōhai* rites were also precisely timed to the very minute. Japanese subjects, whether at home, at work or on a street car, for a single precise minute, turned their bodies towards the centre of focus – Kashihara Jingū, or another centre – to bow. Diaries from the Home Islands and the colonies record how many subjects felt deeply united in time with the rest of the distant Japanese sphere, but even for those who felt ambivalent about the practice, 'their consciousness was spellbound by time itself' (Hara 2011, 437).[32]

Ethics

Kashihara Jingū, as the birthplace of Japanese space and time, was an especially important anchor for the new Japanese secularity. However, shrines played a part in another aspect of the secular sphere: ethics, or a national morality. In the West, religion (that is, Christianity) was often seen essential for sustaining morality.[33] Western nation-states also constructed a secular national morality, often derived from the values upon which the state was ideologically founded. This secular morality did not exclude God, but often assumed a deistic basis, sometimes described as 'natural morality'. The Japanese government was determined to win the respect of Western states and distinguish itself from barbarous peoples by instilling a new set 'civilized' values, from punctuality to modest dress, in the populace. Yet in this project, the customs of the West were not merely copied, but adapted to help bring the previously disparate identities of Japanese subjects under a unifying national morality.

The single document that most succinctly encapsulated the basic ethics of the Japanese state was the Imperial Rescript on Education, promulgated on 30 October 1890, the same year the Meiji Constitution was enacted. It became a regular fixture of public school life: it was read out loud on school holidays, memorized by the students, and its veneration came to serve as a test of patriotic loyalty. The ethics invoked in the Rescript were mainly Confucian, but like the Meiji Constitution, the Rescript was framed with the invocation of imperial ancestors and the founding of the nation (Maxey 2014, 157). So here again the legend of Jinmu provided the framework in which national morality rested. While Kashihara Jingū was a major physical anchor in relation to the increasingly invoked legend of Jinmu, it had little direct connection to the Rescript. In other words, shrines like Kashihara Jingū played a supporting role to a broader national morality that incorporated shrines, but this morality cannot be said to have been founded on them. This indirect connection of national morality to shrines is illustrated by how Kashihara Jingū appears in school textbooks. Jinmu appears in morality textbooks, but as a historical figure whose enthronement marks the start of Japanese History.

The Jinmu legend also played an important role in legitimizing leisure activities as patriotically moral during wartime. Even during the so-called dark valley of Japanese history in the late 1930s and early 1940s, Japanese subjects continued to consume media, buy commercial goods and engage in leisure travel (Ruoff 2010, 18).[34] Kashihara Jingū was one of the main focuses of this activity, especially around the 2600th anniversary. The shrine served as the final stop on tours of the Sacred Jinmu Sites, and it became a common destination for patriotic road trips by both residents of the Home Islands and visiting groups from overseas.[35] Reminiscent of how the invocation of the empire's foundation framed the text of the Imperial Rescript on Education and the rite of the Constitution's promulgation, leisure travel too was framed as taking part in a sacred nationalism.

Kashihara Jingū underwent major improvements twice after its foundation, with the second expansion largely using volunteer labour brigades. Based upon the youth brigades that helped construct Meiji Jingū in the 1920s, youth groups, factory workers, neighbourhood associations and many other groups came to the shrine to donate their labour. At the shrine, volunteers not only laboured at things like tree-planting, but followed a punctual schedule which included ritual, songs, lectures and the following of social etiquette (Ruoff 2010, 65). Thus Kashihara Jingū became a site for 'hands-on citizenship training', where national morality could be enacted in an ideal closer to what might be done in everyday life (Ruoff 2010, 5). The Kashihara Arena (Kashihara Dōjō) really was a *dōjō*, not just for sports and martial arts, but for practising how to be properly Japanese, as imagined by the national morality.[36]

Besides becoming a site for practising Japanese morality, Kashihara Jingū also directly encouraged modern morality in shrine pamphlets. One example is *The First Capital* (1922), one of the shrine-published pamphlet discussed previously. It begins with a history of Jinmu's life told by chief ritualist Uta that emphasizes Jinmu's virtuous legacy (Uta 1981a, 29). Jinmu followed the 'True Path' – glossed as the path of 'Great Filial Piety' – and the 'Correct Path'. This is explained as governance (*matsurigoto*) united with ritual (*matsurigoto*), which are glossed as having love for the people and respect for the kami, respectively (Uta 1981a, 28). Kami are defined, not as powerful transcendent beings, but as 'the spirits of our ancestors and of those who made great achievements for the sake of the nation and the world' (Uta 1981a, 28). The pamphlet affirms the duties of the emperor and his subjects, and in language similar to the Imperial Rescript on Education, invokes their obligation to protect this ancestral moral legacy.

This pamphlet's history drew a clear equivalence between the modern Japanese government and that which was established by Jinmu at Kashihara. Thus this was not musty history with little relevance to modern readers, but rather history that served as a model for restoring an idealized past in modern times. The Socratic dialogue following the history, divided into ten questions and answers, speaks more directly to readers. While the purpose of the pamphlet clearly includes promoting the shrine, it does so by arguing that contributing to

Kashihara Jingū will develop the person into a modern, international person and contribute to public good.[37] Question One, for example, explains how Kashihara Jingū is a place for public ritual where the emperor and the people are united as one, in contrast to the Kōreiden of the Imperial Palace Sanctuaries, which can be accessed only by the imperial house. Thus visiting Kashihara Jingū even individually contributes to the greater unity of the empire.

Questions Three and Four, meanwhile, explain the importance of using the modern, more accurate imperial calendar, instead of the outdated lunisolar calendar, which encouraged subjects to adopt the government's modernization reforms. Question Seven emphasizes how donations to the shrine help Kashihara Jingū contribute to public welfare projects and Question Ten emphasizes how modern Japanese citizens must think like members of an international community. In short, Kashihara Jingū positioned Jinmu Tennō and his court as a role model for modern Japan and promoted the virtues of a modern Japanese secularity such as community spirit, modern timekeeping and an international mindset. Shrines like Kashihara Jingū cannot be credited with creating a full 'Shinto morality', but they, along with other social institutions like schools and the military, contributed by facilitating the enactment of a national morality and directly encouraged these moral virtues by promoting their enshrined kami.

Imperial ritual

In pre-war Japan, the imperial house and its ritual formed the keystone of Japanese secularity. From the beginning of the Meiji period, Shinto ritual was incorporated as an ideological basis that the new government formed around and drew its legitimacy from the emperor. The rites performed by and surrounding the imperial house were part of the incontestable secularity upon which the new nation-state was built (Maxey 2014, 22). The ritual of Kashihara Jingū reflected this imperial ritual and was seen as connecting subjects to the imperial house as one body. The manner in which the ritual of Kashihara Jingū reflected imperial ritual can be seen by looking at the types of festivals celebrated, shrine architecture and the status of those participating in the rites.

The major festivals of Kashihara Jingū, like those of all state shrines, largely aligned with the previously established national holidays[38] of the nation (Hardacre 1989, 101–2; Thal 2005, 157). Majority of the pre-war national holidays in Japan were established in 1873 with the enactment of the holiday ordinance. These new holidays mostly focused upon the imperial house and were celebrated in the imperial palace with solemn rites. The two most important festivals of

Kashihara Jingū, Foundation Day (Kigensetsu, 11 February) and Emperor Jinmu's Anniversary (Jinmu Tennō-sai, 3 April), overlapped the previously established national holidays.

The architecture of Kashihara Jingū also emphasized the site's history as an imperial palace, rather than a site confined to conducting religious rituals. Actual buildings from the Kyoto Imperial Palace were handed down to be utilized by Kashihara Jingū as the main building (the seat of the kami) and the oratory. Popular illustrations and books depicting the dwellings of the ancient emperors as resembling shrine architecture further strengthened this impression. Pamphlets published by the shrine typically described or depicted not only Jinmu's original Kashihara Palace, but also other ancient palaces as having the raised floors and prominent crossbeams (*chigi*) now distinctive of shrine architecture (Uta 1981a, 802). Likewise, the surrounding forest of the shrine was referred to as the *shin'en* or *gaien*. Gaien originally refers to the outer garden of the imperial residence. But it also came to be used for the outer forest surrounding large shrines dedicated to imperial ancestors (*jingū*) (Yamaguchi 2005, 84). Thus Kashihara Jingū was explained as a sort of palace (*miya*) surrounded by a palace garden (*gaien*).

The type of visitors the shrine received also connected Kashihara Jingū to the imperial house. Emperor Meiji lauded Kashihara Jingū in his poetry, and the shrine had *kagura* dances (Ōgi-no-mai and Sakaki-no-mai) composed to his and the empress' poems. Members of the imperial house, including the emperor, frequently paid official visits to Kashihara Jingū. The shrine directly stated in pamphlets how the visits of the emperor or his representative to Kashihara Jingū on public occasions unite the ruler and people (Uta 1981b, 33). These shrine visits generally included not only a financial donation to the shrine, but active physical participation in the form of clapping and offering an evergreen branch, and then recording the visit with the visitors' official title (Uta 1981a, 862; 1981b, 943). They were often publicized in news reports, making visible to the public the connection between Kashihara Jingū and the imperial house. Thus Kashihara Jingū and the imperial rites whence Japanese secularity drew its legitimacy were aligned and visibly linked together.

Kashihara Jingū in the periphery

Imperial shrines such as Kashihara Jingū were positioned as relevant to all Japanese subjects. Due to this, these shrines had influence on even the distant reaches of the empire. Subsequent chapters discuss the role of shrines outside of the Home Islands, but let us examine here how Kashihara Jingū, as a shrine located geographically and ideologically in the centre, helped promote a Japanese secularity in the peripheries of the Japanese sphere.

Most shrines in Meiji Japan, despite their various possible historical origins, were limited to their individual protector domains: the geographic area over which the shrine watched. Higher-ranked shrines watched over larger areas that generally included lower-ranked shrines watching over correspondingly smaller geographic areas. While Kashihara Jingū was connected to its local community, its domain was limited less by space and more by an imagined community, similar to what is called a *sūkei* (veneration) shrine today. This ranked organization of shrines was linked to government offerings and loosely followed the government's administrative organization of the territory. Visits to Kashihara Jingū by members of the imperial house, government officials and overseas dignitaries attracted the attention of national news, and the shrine directly encouraged government officials to consider visiting Kashihara Jingū as a regular part of their duty as a government official (Uta 1981b, 34–5). As the visitor statistics to Kashihara Jingū in 1940 show, a large portion of ordinary Japanese subjects visited the shrine. This included not just pilgrims from within the Home Islands, but thousands from Korea, Taiwan, Karafuto and Manchuria.[39] In addition, the shrine was featured in film and radio broadcasts, and also appeared in commercial goods, including picture scrolls, children's books and dioramas. This broad network of media and consumerism allowed Japanese subjects who were unable to visit the shrine in person to experience the site and sound of Kashihara.

Commercial media may have been a way for Japanese in the peripheries to experience Kashihara Jingū, but *yōhai* was a way for them to actively participate in that experience. Despite Kashihara Jingū's lack of branch shrines, the celebration of Foundation Day and Emperor Jinmu's Anniversary was required of shrines. Citizens could visit their local shrines to participate directly in this ritual, or perhaps take comfort vicariously through the understanding that their locality's protector shrine was connected to the birthplace of Japan. Kashihara Jingū was also just one (if possibly the most important) of the many historical/sacred sites or monuments related to Jinmu. Considered from this angle, monuments, historical sites or shrines related to Jinmu in one's own locale connected the local town to a larger network of Jinmu-related sites in what Ruoff called a 'national topography' (Ruoff 2010, 86).[40] Kashihara Jingū, especially in this case, was just one of the many sites which supported the ideology surrounding Jinmu that helped formed a basis for a Japanese secularity.

When a modern Shinto shrine was constructed, Japanese subjects had the opportunity to leave their physical mark upon the shrine grounds through volunteer labour. This occurred at shrines both large and small overseas, but the effort at Kashihara Jingū, like the efforts at Meiji Jingū and Miyazaki Jingū, particularly stands out due to the national scale on which it occurred. During the second expansion of the shrine from June 1938 to November 1939, about 1.2 million volunteers organized into volunteer labour brigades helped construct the outer garden of the shrine. While the nearest prefectures sent the most volunteers,[41] over four and a half thousand volunteers came from Korea, over a thousand each from Taiwan and Manchuria, as well as double digits from Germany, China and the South Pacific (Uta 1981b, 523). Their work included the planting of 76,000 trees with the aim of restoring the area to its ancient appearance (Kashihara Jingū-chō 1989). Thousands of these trees were donations, including from overseas areas such as Taiwan and Manchuria (Uta 1982, 687). In the form of trees, living parts of the periphery were incorporated into Kashihara Jingū.[42] Thus Kashihara Jingū, by allowing not only local residents but all Japanese subjects a connection to the shrine, helped promote a Japanese secularity as being relevant to Japanese subjects in both the Home Islands and overseas.

Conclusion

Kashihara Jingū demonstrates how modern Shinto shrines were conceived and treated as secular institutions. Although some of the antecedents to the Kashihara shrine had embraced the semi-religious doctrine of the Great Promulgation Campaign, the government and public saw Kashihara Jingū as a historical site of factual History and treated it as a public institution much like a public park or museum. Modern Shinto shrines also had a significant role in communicating the changed sense of reality required for a modern Japanese secularity. Seen as the birthplace of History, Kashihara Jingū especially served as a centre towards which the entire Japanese sphere paid reverence, affirming a new metageography with the Japanese Home Islands at the centre. It also affirmed a new sense of modern time, becoming the fount from which linear time on the imperial calendar began and celebrating the new cycle of time based around the national holidays. Finally, the shrine served as a training ground for Japanese subjects where they could practice a national morality.

Kashihara Jingū was unique in its position as the birthplace of History in the Japanese secularity, but the conception of Shinto shrines as secular and their role in communicating the changed sense of reality required by a new secularity seems to have been common at shrines across the Home Islands. While it is impossible to comprehensively overview the many shrines of the Home Islands here, Kashihara Jingū has similarities with other modern or modernized shrines. Shrine grounds at most major shrines were treated as public sites during this period and the construction of public museums, gardens and monuments at them was not uncommon. Kashihara Jingū was also not alone among major shrines in the construction of a vast garden, with Ise Jingū, Meiji Jingū, Heian Jingū and Miyazaki Jingū all landscaping their shrine grounds to evoke majestic tree groves reminiscent of ancient days.[43] Furthermore, while some shrines embraced the semi-religious project of the Great Promulgation Campaign, they moved away from it after 1890 when the Meiji Constitution established Japan as a secular state.[44] Thus Kashihara Jingū was typical among Shinto shrines in its location in the secular sphere.

Other shrines in the Home Islands also played a role in communicating and affirming a changed sense of space, time and ethics similar to Kashihara Jingū. Like Kashihara Jingū, other major shrines that became centres by receiving *yōhai* include Ise Jingū, Yasukuni Jinja, Meiji Jingū, as well as the imperial palace which contained the Three Imperial Palace Sanctuaries. Furthermore, the shrine ranking system included all shrines within Japanese governed territory and located each shrine and its community vertically and horizontally as a small, but integral, part of the Japanese empire. Shrine lineages – the connection between lesser shrines and parent shrines who venerate the same kami – supplemented this spatial orientation.[45] All shrines celebrated national holidays, affirming the new sense of cyclical time adopted by the Japanese government. Ise Jingū published the Jingū calendar, which counted time both linearly from Jinmu's enthronement rite, and cyclically through the regnal year and annual cycle of holidays. Finally, all shrines to some extent served as sites for the practice of a Japanese morality. Large or small, participation in modern shrine ritual bound subject and emperor together and attendance at major shrine festivals became standard for government and village elites. The village shrine's rank became connected to the status of the village as a whole and, as examined in the next chapter, communities often vied with each other for the higher shrine rank. The Japanese secularity promoted by the Japanese government was not invented by, nor entirely based on, shrines. But Shinto shrines in the Home Islands played an important role in communicating and affirming the secularity that the Japanese government constructed as a part of the project of modernization.

Now we leave Kashihara at the centre of Japan and make our way north nearly 1,500 kilometres to Sapporo, the snowy capital of the island of Hokkaido. There we shall see how the Japanese secularity embraced by many shrines in the Home Islands also served as the founding ideal for shrines large and small in the near periphery. In addition, Hokkaido's position as a frontier land guarding against the threat of Russia provides an ideal opportunity to look at a new and unusual type of Shinto shrine – shrines venerating the war dead – and how they served to sustain a secularity supportive of the modern nation-state.

3

The northern capital: Hokkaido and Karafuto in the near periphery

Autumn 1869. Shima Yoshitake made his way by ship and by horse from Tokyo to the northern periphery of Japan. His destination was the Ishikari plain, the yet-wild land that was to become the northern capital for which he had so long advocated: Sapporo. On this journey through mud and snow, Shima carried a precious burden, entrusted to him in the hallowed halls of the revived Jingikan. Within it was the sacred mirror of the Three Pioneer Kami. This kami, to be enshrined at the imperial shrine of Sapporo and at countless smaller shrines across the island, was to become the foundation and protector of not only Sapporo but also the entire island of Hokkaido. Although a small and hastily constructed government office first served as residence for the kami, Shima had located a beautiful site worthy of the 'new Great Shrine of Hokkaidō' (Hokkaidō Jingū-shi Hensan Iinkai 1991, 31). Standing among the snowy pines in November, Shima praised the site in delicate Chinese verse, 'Surrounded on three sides by mountains and opening up on another, clear streams run across double hills. Ah! this place between mountain and brook was surely created for the shrine' (Hokkaidō Jingū-shi Hensan Iinkai 1991, 31).[1]

The history of human habitation in Hokkaido (Ezo) extends back into Palaeolithic times. As early as the seventh century, there was an exchange of goods, cultures and persons between the Ainu residents of Hokkaido and Yamato Japanese in northern Honshu (Segawa 2015, 52–3). The Ainu peoples also developed trade links with Chinese and Russian groups across the Asian continent (Walker 2001). In 1590, the Shogun Hideyoshi gave the Kakizaki (Matsumae) clan from northern Honshū land on the southern tip of Hokkaido as a fief, which led to increasing interaction between the Ainu in Hokkaido and Japanese in Honshu. The Matsumae presence also meant the establishment of a number of Buddhist temples, Shinto shrines and other sites for the veneration of the kami and buddhas in southern Hokkaido. Despite this, the History of Hokkaido is popularly conceived as only starting in 1869, when Ezo was renamed Hokkaido, Sapporo was established as the capital, and the island formally became imperial land (*kōdo*). The romanticized story of Hokkaido's foundation as described above evoked the same pioneer ideals found in the legend of Emperor Jinmu. Shima Yoshitake seemed to be echoing Emperor Jinmu's legendary journey from Kyushu into not-yet civilized lands to establish a new Capital. Just as the History of Japan did not begin until Jinmu's enthronement rite at Kashihara, the History of Hokkaido did not begin until it was incorporated into the empire (*kōkoku*).

After winning the Battle of Hakodate in 1869, the Meiji government took control of Hokkaido and formed the Colonization[2] Commission (Kaitaku-shi). This organization was charged with turning Hokkaido into productive land for the empire. Under Shima, who was a rehabilitated Shogunate loyalist appointed as Hokkaido's Development Magistrate, the Colonization Commission set about establishing the city of Sapporo to serve as the headquarters for the development of the entire island. The city was laid out on a grid pattern of wide streets aligned with the four cardinal directions, evoking both a modern scientific rationality and hearkening back to the grid pattern that had once characterized the classical capitals of Japan like Heian-kyō and Fujiwara-kyō.[3] Sōsei-gawa River roughly divided the city East from West and a long public park, Ōdōri Kōen, separated the public service buildings in the North from the private enterprises in the South, and served as a firebreak. Sapporo, as the capital of Hokkaido, was not only imagined as the northern capital of Japan, but it also served as a model modern Japanese city, rationally planned to demonstrate 'that modern and western were not coterminous and that the new was in fact the old' (Blaxell 2009, 6).

Shima's 'new great shrine of Hokkaidō', Sapporo Jinja, became the new territory's most prominent shrine. One of the earliest actions the Meiji government undertook for developing Hokkaido was the enshrinement of the Three Pioneer Kami (Kaitaku Sanjin), along with the establishment of Sapporo. This kami, specially chosen to aid the planned colonization efforts in Hokkaido, was entrusted to Shima Yoshitake and Higashikuze Michitome. In 1869, they physically carried the sacred mirror of this kami up to the planned location of Sapporo, and settled it temporarily in the hastily constructed government office. In 1871, the kami was transferred to the shrine's current location upon a small mountain to the west of Sapporo city, overlooking Ōdōri Park. This shrine was not only significant to Hokkaido as its general protector (*sōchinju*), but it also became the pioneer model upon which other colonial Shinto shrines were based (Suga 2014, 134).

Hokkaidō Gokoku Jinja, another major shrine in Hokkaido, demonstrates the relationship between war memorials and Shinto shrines. An early pressing concern for the Meiji government was the incorporation and defence of Hokkaido against the danger of invasion from Russia (Mason 2012, 114). One policy put in place by the Meiji government to combat this fear was to recruit farmer-soldier migrants to settle the land. Often drawn from displaced samurai who had been loyal to the Shogunate, they were lauded as pioneers, given land to cultivate, and were expected to be ready to fight in the event of a Russian invasion. In 1888, a more formal defence of Hokkaido was arranged with the establishment of the Seventh Division of the Japanese Imperial Army. Although mainly charged with the defence of Hokkaido and Arctic warfare, this division was assigned to combat under the Kwantung Army[4] and in the Pacific from the late 1930s. Hokkaidō Gokoku Jinja originated as a war memorial in connection to the Seventh Division.

Home Islander migrants to Hokkaido also set up local shrines, such as Furano Jinja. While there were premodern shrines especially in the south of Hokkaido which underwent a process of modernization,[5] the majority of shrines in Hokkaido today were established by migrants after the Meiji Restoration in 1868. Furano Jinja as one of these small settler shrines demonstrates how the secular functions of Shrine Shinto extended to even small shrines with relatively little interference from the central government. Although Karafuto (Sakhalin) was a separate prefecture and incorporated into Japan at a later date, it was often grouped with Hokkaido in matters concerning shrines. It was colonized on the same model as Hokkaido, which included the enshrinement of the Three Pioneer Kami at Karafuto Jinja and the construction of Karafuto Gokoku Jinja to look after its war dead.

Sapporo Jinja: Pioneering new imperial lands

The Three Pioneer Kami of Sapporo Jinja first arrived in Hokkaido carried by Count Higashikuze Michitomi, who had been appointed chairman of the Colonization Commission. At Hakodate, Shima took charge of the kami's 'spirit proxy' (*mitamashiro*), arriving in Sapporo in December 1869 (Enomoto 2011, 108). The kami was temporarily enshrined in the Sapporo government's office until the next year, when it was transferred to a newly built, but still temporary, shrine on the banks of the Sōsei-gawa River. A formal shrine system had not yet been solidified by the Meiji government at this point and thus Sapporo Jinja became known as Hokkaido's first shrine (*ichinomiya*), using a popular premodern shrine ranking system. Shima, with the help of long-time Hokkaido resident Sōyama Seitarō, decided upon a hill west of Sapporo as the permanent location for Sapporo Jinja. Shima was dismissed from his post as magistrate on 19 January 1870, but his successor, Iwamura Michitoshi, kept the location as the permanent site for Sapporo Jinja, renaming the area Maruyama.[6] While financial constraints meant only a temporary shrine building could be constructed there, Sapporo Jinja was given the rank of lesser national shrine (*kokuhei shōsha*) when the shrine ranking system was enacted in 1871.

The gradual increase in rank of Sapporo Jinja reflected Hokkaido's increasing importance and population. In 1872, the shrine was raised to a lesser imperial shrine, a significant change removing the shrine from the jurisdiction of the prefectural government to that of the national government. In 1889, Ise Jingū was rebuilt and Sapporo Jinja's temporary shrine building was replaced with the former shrine building of Ise Jingū's outer shrine. In 1893, Sapporo Jinja was raised to an intermediate imperial shrine, and finally in 1899 it was raised to the highest shrine rank, greater imperial shrine (Figure 3.1).

Figure 3.1 Hokkaidō Jingū today: Sapporo Jinja was renamed Hokkaidō Jingū in 1964 after Emperor Meiji was enshrined. The current shrine building dates from 1978. (Author's photograph.)

A Modern Public Site

Shinto shrines like Kashihara Jingū were largely treated as secular institutions and played a role in confirming a new Japanese secularity promoted by the Japanese government. This function, however, was not limited to the Home Islands, but was a key element in the process of turning new territory like Hokkaido into a part of Japan, into imperial land. Like Kashihara Jingū, Sapporo Jinja was also conceived as a modern, public site, and it worked to affirm new conceptions of time, space and ethics. Perhaps the most apparent indicator of Sapporo Jinja's public conception was its top-down foundation as a public institution by the Meiji government. The first years after the Meiji Restoration were deeply influenced by the ideal of *saisei itchi*, in which political affairs and Shinto ritual were considered of the same importance. This was reflected in the priorities of the Colonization Commission: The spirit proxy, a mirror, of the Three Pioneer Kami, was given to the Hokkaido government, which first temporarily enshrined the kami at the main Sapporo government office. While a chief ritualist was appointed to Sapporo Jinja after its establishment, the civil government continued to be intimately involved in the shrine's affairs.

The Three Pioneer Kami enshrined at Sapporo Jinja – Ōkunitama no Kami, Ōnamuchi no Kami and Sukunahikona no Kami combined into one seat (*za*) – are also of a public character. The latter two kami are most famously enshrined at Izumo Taisha shrine, but appear in the Japanese classics where they are involved with developing the land and creating medicine. Ōnamuchi no Kami is often identified with Ōkuninushi no Kami, who governs the other world. However, Ōnamuchi of the Three Pioneer Kami retained none of Ōkuninushi's association with a transcendent concept of life after death. Ōkunitama no Kami, on the other hand, is a term for the kami of a land, and thus indicated the kami of the land of Hokkaido itself (Hokkaidō Jingū-shi Hensan Iinkai 1991, 19–20). Thus the Three Pioneer Kami were conceived as focused on the immanent matter of physically developing Hokkaido into imperial land. Established before the modern concept of religion was embedded in Japan, Sapporo Jinja participated in a variety of activities, including the semi-religious Great Promulgation Campaign in the 1870s. However, by the 1890s when the Meiji Constitution positioned Japan as a secular state and the modern idea of religion was becoming embedded in Japan, Sapporo Jinja, as a greater imperial shrine, was positioned on the secular side of the religion/secular divide.

Sapporo Jinja, like Kashihara Jingū, continued to be treated as a public facility. The ritualists serving at Sapporo Jinja often had previous experience in, or went on to become, government officials in departments unrelated to shrines.[7] Furthermore, Count Kuroda Kiyotaka, who succeeded Count Higashikuze as chairman of the Colonization Commission,[8] established Sapporo Jinja's annual festival (*reisai*) on 12 June as a public holiday in Hokkaido from 1873 (Noto 1994, 66). Public access to the shrine was also a concern for the Sapporo government. The shrine's relatively distant location at Maruyama made it difficult for the public to visit, especially during the snowy winters. To resolve this, a *yōhai* site, where veneration towards Sapporo Jinja is performed from afar, was constructed by 1878 in the city centre. Tramlines were also laid to give public access to first the *yōhai* site and then the shrine itself. In 1918, the Hokkaido Semi-Centennial Exhibition (Kaidō 50-Nen Kinen Hokkaidō Hakuran-kai) was held to celebrate the fiftieth anniversary of Hokkaido. Preparations for this event included constructing an electric tram system providing access from the city centre to the Exposition grounds in Nakajima Park. While the tram line to Nakajima Park failed to be completed in time for the Exposition, the government continued to expand the tram railway to connect public buildings such as schools, public parks, government buildings, hospitals and Sapporo Agricultural College (later Hokkaido University). The First Avenue line was connected to Sapporo Jinja's *yōhai* site in 1920, and by 1924 had been extended out to Sapporo Jinja and Maruyama Park.[9]

The public character of the shrine was also seen in the volunteer work contributed by Hokkaido residents. The grand festivities of the annual shrine festival were possible due to the volunteer work of the surrounding districts, which contributed dedicatory events and built elaborate floats for the parade. One of the most visible volunteer works was the planting of 150 cherry blossom trees in memory of Shima Yoshitake by Fukutama Senkichi, a long-time resident of Hokkaido.[10] In particular, access to the shrine at Maruyama by tram led to its popularity as a public site for leisure, with woodcuts and paintings showcasing the shrine as a famous place for cherry blossoms (Hokkaidō Jingū 1989, 15–17). Many of these cherry trees were of the local Ezo-zakura variety whose colouring and blossoming pattern differs from varieties popular in the Home Islands like Somei-yoshino. This allowed residents to participate in the stereotypically Japanese activity of cherry blossom viewing, yet with a distinct Hokkaido flavour.[11] The construction of a sports arena in the outer garden in 1934 further promoted the site as a place for public leisure.

A difference between Kashihara Jingū and Sapporo Jinja was the latter's lack of History, that is, the lack of a perceived past with a connection to the Japanese nation-state. Unlike Kashihara Jingū, Maruyama and the whole of Hokkaido were imagined as virgin land in the Japanese narrative (Mason 2012, 59). Despite this, historical practices brought from the centre were utilized at the shrine. The first permanent shrine building was the recycled building of the Ise Jingū's outer shrine, built in the ancient *shinmei* style, while the rites conducted at the shrine followed revived practices of the ancient Ritsuryō state (Hardacre 2017, 107–8, 362). But it was the act of Sapporo Jinja's establishment that brought Maruyama, and thus Hokkaido, into the flow of Japanese progressive History. Because of this, Sapporo Jinja actively commemorated the History of Hokkaido that had begun in 1869.

For example, in 1938 a subsidiary shrine of Sapporo Jinja, Kaitaku Jinja, was established within the shrine garden. It enshrined thirty-seven historical personages connected to Hokkaido, including Shima, Higashikuze and Kuroda discussed above. Its annual festival was set on 15 August, the day the island was renamed Hokkaido. Also, a campaign to enshrine Emperor Meiji in a second seat beside the somewhat abstract Three Pioneer Kami began in 1933, due to the active interest that the emperor had taken in Hokkaido's development (Miyamoto 2014, 58). Furthermore, inspired by Heian Jingū, Sapporo Jinja added a marching band dressed as imperial loyalists from the Meiji Restoration to its festival in 1926 (Noto 1994, 78; Shirano 1994b, 106). Historical figures such as the mediaeval warlord Katō Kiyomasa and Emperor Jinmu also began to be featured in festival floats from 1912 (Shirano 1994a, 98). Thus Sapporo Jinja, while not founded on a specific historical site, incorporated both ancient and modern Japanese History into its activities, and placed Sapporo within the 'national topography' (Ruoff 2010, 86) of Japan.

Sapporo Jinja not only commemorated modern History, but it also utilized modern technology. Hokkaido, imagined as virgin land, presented a blank slate upon which a Japanese modernity could be constructed. The government brought in Western experts, built grand Western-style buildings of wood or stone, and promoted Western agriculture like wheat and milk. Sapporo Jinja was part of this by including elements of Western modernity within its activities. The shrine's history was commemorated with woodcuts utilizing Western artistic perspective, which gave way to photography. Festivals included the Heian-style court dress of the ritualists alongside the bowler hats and morning coats of dignitaries, and utilized Western horse-drawn carriages and later automobiles.[12] At festivals some *torii* gates were decked entirely in green garlands following the Western trend of triumphal arches (Hokkaidō Jingū 1989, 34). Photography captured the splendour of the shrine's ancient ritual against the backdrop of the grand redbrick building of the Government Office, commemorating this seamless combination of ancient and modern (Noto 1994, 74). Thus Sapporo Jinja, like shrines in the Home Islands, was a secular institution integral to Japanese modernity.

Incorporating Hokkaido into Japanese space and time

Sapporo Jinja was one of the many modern public institutions, such as the civil government, the military and schools, that helped embed a Japanese secularity in Hokkaido. As demonstrated by Emperor Meiji's visit to Hokkaido in 1876 and again in 1881, incorporating the space of Hokkaido into the empire was an important priority for the government. While Emperor Meiji did not visit Sapporo Jinja in person, likely due to logistical reasons, Emperor Taisho visited as Crown Prince in 1911, while Emperor Showa venerated at the shrine both as Crown Prince Regent in 1922 and then as emperor in 1936.[13] Sapporo Jinja, as Hokkaido's only greater imperial shrine, placed Hokkaido within the network of the modern shrine ranking system in the same category as elite Home Island shrines. But more significantly, it was the first of a pattern of giving each newly incorporated imperial territory a single greater imperial shrine to act as the general protector of the region. Furthermore, the inclusion of Sapporo Jinja's main festival on the Jingū calendar – the new national calendar issued by the Jingū Shichō – further located Hokkaido as not only a regional space within Japan but also as a part of national yearly cycle of time.

Sapporo Jinja was also a key element of Sapporo as a modern Japanese city. Sapporo was carefully planned out by the Colonization Commission as modern 'northern capital'. Sapporo Jinja was located above the main city, overlooking it from Maruyama. The shrine's main approach ran along the northern block of Ōdōri Park, the dividing line between the city's northern and southern halves, with Sapporo Jinja's first *torii* gate[14] at North 1 West 25. In 1920, the main approach was lengthened, bringing its beginning near the red-brick Hokkaido Government Office (constructed in 1888) at West 6. Sapporo Jinja's back approach ran along the southern block of Ōdōri Park, sandwiching the centre of the city. The shrine's annual procession, which followed the main approach until passing under the first *torii* gate and then toured the city stopping at important sites such as the Government Office (North 2 West 6) and its own *yōhai* site (South 2 East 3), reminded residents of Sapporo Jinja's spatial relationship with the city.[15] This relationship between the protector shrine and the rest of the city became a template which other modern Japanese cities in the periphery followed.

New senses of space, time and ethics in residents

Sapporo Jinja's festival was incorporated into the annual cycle of time on the modern Jingū calendar. But the shrine also helped instil the modern solar calendar into Hokkaido residents. In 1872, before Japan's adoption of the solar calendar, the government established Sapporo Jinja's annual festival to be the 15th day of the sixth month (*6-gatsu 15-nichi*), a full moon on the lunisolar calendar. However, a 1872 ordinance[16] shifted Japan to the solar calendar. Thus from 1874, Sapporo Jinja celebrated its festival on 15 June (*6-gatsu 15-nichi*) on the new solar calendar (Noto 1994, 68; Shirano 1994b, 107).[17] As this festival was a prefectural holiday, this directly affected Hokkaido residents, reminding them that 15th of June – still the sixth month – no longer corresponded to the moon, but to the modern imperial calendar. Sapporo Jinja also raised awareness of the linear imperial calendar through festivals venerating Emperor Jinmu. It annually celebrated the national holidays of Foundation Day and Emperor Jinmu's Anniversary, and in 1940 took part in the 2600th anniversary celebrations, including performing the new Urayasu-no-mai *kagura* dance. Already by 1913 Emperor Jinmu had gained enough popularity among Sapporo residents to be featured in effigy on one of the procession's floats (Shirano 1994b, 106). The procession further lionized the regnal eras of cyclic time by commemorating the Meiji Restoration with the Ishin Kin'ō-tai marching brass band, discussed previously.

Sapporo Jinja, like shrines in the Home Islands, became a site for moral 'hands-on citizenship training' (Ruoff 2010, 5). While Sapporo Jinja had no organized mass effort of volunteer labour as occurred at Kashihara Jingū or Hokkaidō Gokoku Jinja (discussed later), there were many opportunities for residents to practice 'Japanese' activities at the shrine. The shrine became a popular leisure site for engaging in typical Japanese activities like cherry blossom viewing, and formal groups such as the Japanese poetry club Kōfūkai were meeting at the shrine from as early as 1907. Like at Kashihara Jingū, organized patriotic groups began gathering regularly at the shrine after the outbreak of the Sino-Japanese war in 1937. Women's, students' and public servants' groups gathered regularly to pray for the raising up of Asia and military success. This encouraged Sapporo residents to see themselves as part of a broader Japanese sphere.[18] Furthermore, a self-cultivation group was also started at the shrine, directly encouraging the formation of a Japanese morality (Hokkaidō Jingū-shi Hensan Iinkai 1991, 362).

The shrine also played a part in children's education. After the shrine's school entrance ritual, the children received morality textbooks which included a history of Sapporo Jinja. The shrine was also featured, alongside topics ranging from fishing and snowflakes to Toyotomi Hideyoshi and Emperor Jinmu, in the Hokkaido Elementary Reader, a set of readers published specifically for Hokkaido by the national government. After a brief history of the shrine, the Reader's passage points to the illustration, modelling students who, on the instruction of their teacher, are marching up the shrine's approach. The passage notes that these are not just any students, but students from Sapporo, presumably just like the students reading the passage (Monbushō 1897, Vol. 5 Lesson 11).

Perhaps the most visible chance for Hokkaido residents to participate in shrine events was the annual festival. Farmers contributed their produce to the shrine as offerings, while artistic groups contributed dedicatory performances. The city of Sapporo was divided up into districts, increasing in number as the population grew, each of which was charged with a portion of the palanquin procession. This included building elaborate floats topped with trees and/or the effigies of popular kami such as Susanoo, Sarutahiko and Katō Kiyomasa. Other volunteers carried the palanquin, marched in the brass band and carried the brocade banners evoking the splendour of the imperial house. A woodcut from 1897 shows a joyful procession with figures in Heian-style, modern Japanese and Western dress, while Taisho period photographs show district members in Heian-style dress posed seriously in front of the shrine (Hokkaidō Jingū 1989, 13, 35). The Ainu, as Japanese subjects, were not left out of this celebration, with Ainu sometimes contributing dedicatory performances or leading the palanquin procession (Hokkaidō Jingū 1989, 12; Noto 1994, 68). This foreshadows the trend of subsuming local elements into the larger national ritual performed at shrines.

Sapporo Jinja and the Ainu

Although Ainu were specifically included in earlier festivals at Sapporo Jinja, it is worth taking a moment to consider why they were not more prominently included. In Taiwan, there was limited, but visible, incorporation of Taiwanese customs at shrines. But this does not appear to have occurred much in Hokkaido. One reason is because of demographics. In relation to settlers from the Home Islands, Taiwan Islanders made up a significantly larger percentage of the population of Taiwan than the Ainu did in Hokkaido. Also, the Taiwan Islanders and Taiwan's Takasago tribes were recognized as distinct ethnic groups, not yet fully Japanese.[19] Ainu, although still subject to severe discrimination as 'former aborigines', were officially assimilated Japanese subjects to be treated like other residents in Hokkaido. Sapporo Jinja did not see the need nor have the spare resources to focus on a group that was already officially (if not treated so in practice) fully Japanese.

Furthermore, Taiwanese customs with their origin in classical Chinese culture were considered more civilized than Ainu customs, which were treated as quaint customs of a barbaric culture soon to die out (Siddle 1996). This was particularly important for shrines due to the similarities shared by some Ainu customs and shrines rites. Shinto shares vocabulary with the same origin as some Ainu words, not the least of which was 'kami' ('kamui' in the Ainu language). They also shared customs. For example, both Shinto and Ainu ritual practices use a similar looking tool that shares the term *nusa*, and they both include purification rituals that involve passing multiple times through grass rings (Jp. *chinowa*) (Segawa 2015, 218, 209-11, 225-8). Shinto shrines were careful to present themselves as modern institutions, since they were in danger of being classified as little better than superstitious relics themselves under the Western conception of religion. There was the possibility that subsuming Ainu customs into shrine practices would damage Sapporo Jinja's reputation as a civilized site of ritual. It seems likely the above reasons are why Sapporo Jinja rarely associated itself with Ainu customs. That said, Shinto rites were used to instil a patriotic identity at some Ainu schools. For example, in 1916, a school in Fushiko, Obihiro, constructed a Shinto site dedicated to Emperor Meiji on the grounds and had its students perform *yōhai* towards the imperial palace (Sasaki 2013, 218-19). It is unclear whether this was typical for Ainu schools and the use of *yōhai* became common at all schools regardless of location by at least the late 1930s.

Sapporo Jinja and religion

Sapporo Jinja, like Kashihara Jingū, acted as a secular institution and helped instil a new Japanese secularity in Hokkaido residents. But as it was founded before the concept of secularism was embedded in Japan, it provides an opportunity to examine how a modern shrine adapted to the shifting ideas around religion and state in the early Meiji period, particularly the Great Promulgation Campaign and shrines' relationship with the recent dead through funerals. The Great Promulgation Campaign in the 1870s was the Meiji state's main effort to create a national doctrine.

To promote this doctrine, the Great Teaching Institute was formed in Tokyo in 1873, and each prefecture was directed to establish a single Intermediate Teaching Institute to train and coordinate 'national instructors'.

Hokkaido was an exception to this rule in that the government gave permission for establishing two Intermediate Teaching Institutes. The first, located in the open port of Hakodate at the Shinshū Buddhist temple Ganjōji, focused on combatting the encroachment of Christianity. Hakodate had earlier contact with Westerners and Christianity than other places in Hokkaido, since it was designated in 1854 as the first Japanese port opened to foreign trade. The second Intermediate Teaching Institute was focused on propagating the Great Teachings among Hokkaido residents rather than combatting Christianity. The settler residents of Hokkaido were a diverse lot and included many groups that were considered less than exemplar citizens and in need of citizenship education. This second Intermediate Teaching Institute was to be set up in Sapporo at the Shinshū Buddhist Kansatsu-sho. Despite additional support from Sapporo Jinja's ritualists, a lack of funds and suitable location prevented the Sapporo Intermediate Teaching Institute from being realized (Hokkaidō Jingū-shi Hensan Iinkai 1995, 127–46).

In 1875, Shinshū Buddhism pulled its support from the Great Promulgation Campaign and the Great Teaching Institute was dissolved. The Shinto faction of the Campaign was reorganized into the Shinto Secretariat (Shintō Jimukyoku), which likewise established branches in the various prefectures, including Hokkaido (Hardacre 2017, 632). In Sapporo, the Shinto Secretariat shared space and ritualists with Sapporo Jinja, although ritual and finances were kept separate. Thus Sapporo residents seem to have sometimes confused them as a single institution (Hokkaidō Jingū-shi Hensan Iinkai 1995, 149–50). The struggle to finance shrines and the breakup of the Campaign also led to the creation of various Shintō sects (*kyō*). One such group was Jingū-kyō, which was formed as the doctrinal and fundraising branch of the Ise Jingū in 1872. Jingū-kyō established Divine Wind Associations (Jinpū Kōsha) across Japan (Hardacre 2017, 380). As the Jingū *taima* was at first distributed through these Associations, entire villages in Hokkaido, such as Shimoteine-mura, often joined (Hokkaidō Jingū-shi Hensan Iinkai 1995, 154–5). In 1899, however, Jingū-kyō would abandon the doctrinal format and reorganize itself into the secular Jingū Hōsaikai.

These three organizations – Sapporo Jinja, Shinto Secretariat and Jingū-kyō – were officially separate organizations. In the late 1870s there was not yet an established divide between secular and religious spheres in Japan. However, a divide between ritual sites (Sapporo Jinja) and doctrinal organizations (Jingū-kyō) was beginning to form, even if organizations like the Shinto Secretariat retained their ambiguous relationships to both. These organizations shared the same personnel and spaces, at least in Hokkaido, and thus appeared as a part of the same system to many citizens. For example, in 1878, the chief ritualist of Sapporo Jinja was Ōnuki Maura. He had previous experience as a Shinto ritualist at Nikkō Tōshōgū shrine, but he was also a national instructor in the Great Promulgation Campaign. He also had already helped establish Divine Wind Associations in Hokkaido. Ōnuki petitioned and then in August received permission from the Minister of Home Affairs to construct a *yōhai* site for Sapporo Jinja, which would also serve as the headquarters of the Shinto Secretariat in Sapporo. In September, he was appointed head of the Sapporo Shinto Secretariat. The same month, Ōnuki was appointed a first-degree assistant instructor of Jingū-kyō, and in 1879 enshrined a 'divided spirit' of the Ise kami at the Sapporo Jinja *yōhai* site (Hokkaidō Jingū-shi Hensan Iinkai 1995, 151–2). Thus by 1879, the kami of Sapporo Jinja, the Shinto Secretariat and Jingū-kyō were all being venerated by Ōnuki from the *yōhai* site of Sapporo Jinja. While Ōnuki saw his position and rituals as distinctly separate, this was not readily apparent to residents in Hokkaido.

Sapporo Jinja began with a close relationship to state doctrinal efforts, but as the national government's policy changed, it slowly separated them from the shrine, even if this was not clearly indicated to the average citizen. In 1882, the Shinto Secretariat became the Classics Institute, a secular institution for training ritualists, and in 1899, Jingū-kyō transformed into the Jingū Hōsaikai, a secular organization for distributing the Jingū *taima*. Thus by 1900 Sapporo Jinja's lingering connections to religious-style doctrine were cut. In addition to doctrine, Sapporo Jinja's relationship with the other world also underwent a reversal in early Meiji. In 1871, a site for Shinto-style funerals was located near Akeno Cemetery in Sapporo (Hokkaidō Jingū-shi Hensan Iinkai 1995, 165). In 1873, the national government promoted Shinto-style funerals, so Sapporo Jinja started conducting funerals for those who desired them. While this policy lasted less than two years, funerals became an important source of revenue for the public, but chronically underfunded, shrines. Reservations about the polluting association of funerals at shrines were managed by Shinto ritualists though the method of conducting funerals as national instructors, rather than as Shinto ritualists (Hardacre 2017, 379). In 1877, Wakabayashi Yoshimichi, a ritualist of Sapporo Jinja, began formally conducting Shinto-style funerals at the Akeno site.

However, on 24 January 1882, the Ministry of Home Affairs prohibited shrine ritualists at imperial and national shrines, including Sapporo Jinja, from serving as national instructors and conducting funerals.[20] Thus Wakabayashi was forced to give up his position as ritualist, and instead associated himself with the religious Shinto sect, Shintō Honkyoku, as a Shinto instructor. Shinto-style funerals continued to be popular in Hokkaido, and private donations allowed for the construction of a more permanent funeral hall. In 1885, Wakabayashi petitioned the Minister of Home Affairs for permission to formally establish the funeral hall as the shrine Shinonome Jinja. The request for a secular shrine (*jinja*) was denied, but the Ministry gave permission for a religious Shinto hall (*shiu, sorei-sha*) (Hokkaidō Jingū-shi Hensan Iinkai 1995, 165–8). Thus Shinonome Shi was officially founded. This demonstrates again how the central government's control of vocabulary drew a line between secular shrines (*jinja*) and ritualists (*shinshoku*) on the one hand, and religious institutions (*shi*) and instructors (*kyōshi*) on the other. The conversion of Shinonome Shi into Sapporo Sorei Jinja after the Second World War indicates the institution's supporters were never fully convinced of a clear separation between shrines and Shinonome Shi. But similar to the separation between Jinmu's tumulus and Kashihara Jingū in the Home Islands, the central government's definition of shrines as this-worldly and non-doctrinal was reflected in the near periphery of Japan.

Sapporo Jinja demonstrates how major Shinto shrines came to be treated as secular sites, not only in the Home Islands, but also in the near periphery. Like Kashihara Jingū, Sapporo Jinja had a significant role in communicating the new Japanese secularity to the often less-than-exemplary imperial subjects residing in Hokkaido. Sapporo Jinja also had an essential role in transforming Hokkaido, new imperial land, into an integral part of the empire. It did this by positioning Hokkaido within modern Japanese space through its rank as a greater imperial shrine, and through its geographic and ideological position as the general protector shrine of the colonial capital of Sapporo. It positioned Hokkaido within Japanese time, through practices like its annual festival and *yōhai* rites both towards Sapporo Jinja itself and from Sapporo Jinja towards the imperial palace and Kashihara. The location of Sapporo Jinja in the secular sphere was a process that occurred over several decades as the Japanese government adopted and refined a system of secularism. While the Meiji government required a separation between Shinto shrines (*jinja*) and Shinto facilities for the recent dead (*sorei-sha*), a clear distinction between secular shrines and religious Shinto sites was not always fully embraced by Hokkaido residents.

However, there was one Shinto facility dedicated to a special kind of recent dead that was allowed shrine status: Yasukuni Jinja, established in 1879. Takenaka (2015) has already given an excellent account of Yasukuni Jinja's unusual development into a shrine. Yasukuni Jinja remained unique as a shrine until 1939, when the Ministry of Home Affairs ordered that war memorials (*shōkon-sha*) be converted into a new category of shrines called *gokoku* shrines.[21] The next section examines the path Hokkaidō Gokoku Jinja took from being a private military commemorative site to becoming the leading public shrine dedicated to the war dead in Hokkaido. This process also demonstrates how the site worked to incorporate the near periphery into imperial land and how the relationship between shrines, secularism and the war dead changed.

Hokkaidō Gokoku Jinja: A shrine for the war dead

Hokkaidō Gokoku Jinja (Figure 3.2) was not the only *gokoku* shrine in Hokkaido. The 1939 directive to convert *shōkon-sha* into shrines organized this new type of shrine into two ranks – designated and non-designated – with each

Figure 3.2 Hokkaidō Gokoku Jinja today. (Author's photograph.)

prefecture in principle to have only a single designated shrine.²² Hokkaido was unusual in that it had a total of three designated *gokoku* shrines, the most of all prefectures.²³ Rather than the Sapporo Gokoku Jinja located in central Sapporo, or the Hakodate Gokoku Jinja with its longer history, it was Hokkaidō Gokoku Jinja located in Asahikawa city that served the entire island as a regional version of Yasukuni Jinja.

Hokkaidō Gokoku Jinja traces its beginnings back to the Seventh Division of the Imperial Japanese Army. A key priority when settling Hokkaido was building a significant military presence, and in 1888, the Seventh Division of the Japanese Imperial Army was formed to protect Japan's northern border. While first based in Sapporo, in 1902 the division headquarters were moved further north to Kamikawa district, where the 'garrison town' of Asahikawa grew up around it (Seaton 2016b, 165). Hokkaidō Gokoku Jinja traces its start to the *shōkon* rite performed by Lt. Gen. Ōsako Naotoshi, commander of the Seventh Division, shortly after this move. *Shōkon* rites were an innovative method for commemorating the war dead that developed from a mix of Buddhist, Shinto and Confucian traditions at the end of the Edo period (Takenaka 2015, 29–36).²⁴ The rites started by Ōsako evolved into the Seventh Division Shōkon Ritual Site, and in 1907, they were transferred to a new location located on army land next to the parade ground, but rented from the city. At this point, the site was popularly conceived as a *yōhai* site, and it held its annual rite on 5 and 6 May, the date of Yasukuni Jinja's main festival (Shimemura 1981, 565).

In 1910, Lt. Gen. Uehara Yūsaku, Commander of the Seventh Division, and Kawashima Atsushi, Director-General of the Hokkaido government, petitioned for and received permission to construct a *shōkon-sha* as a permanent site (Shimemura 1981, 567). This facility, called the Dai-Nana Shidan Kan Shōkon-sha (Seventh Division Administrated Shōkon-sha), shifted the annual *shōkon* rite to June, a month after Yasukuni Jinja's rite and the role of lead officiant was passed alternatively between the mayor of Asahikawa and the commander of the Seventh Division. In 1916, as the site was being used jointly by the city and military, the site was renamed the Hokkaidō Shōkon-jō. This name change indicated both the site's relevance to all residents of Hokkaidō and clarified its status as a site to where the spirits of the war dead were not permanently in residence.²⁵

The site increased in significance and popularity, but remained the Hokkaidō Shōkon-jō for nineteen years. In 1935, the Ministry of Home Affairs granted the petition of the Seventh Division commander Lt. Gen. Sugihara Miyotarō, Hokkaido government's Director-General Sagami Shin'ichi, Asahikawa mayor

Watanabe Kan'ichi and sixty-six others to convert the site into a *shōkon-sha*, understood as a site where the venerated war dead remained in permanent residence (Shimemura 1981, 590). This change was also significant in that it was the first time Shinto ritualists were allowed involvement with the site, even while the site remained largely under military-civil control.[26] In 1939, the Ministry of Home Affairs ordered that all *shōkon-sha* be converted into *gokoku* shrines, and the site became the Hokkaidō Gokoku Jinja.

Despite becoming a shrine, the site was distinguished from regular shrines in several ways. *Gokoku* shrines were not given into the complete control of the Shrine Bureau in the Ministry of Home Affairs. Like at Yasukuni Jinja, the military and civil government shared administration of the shrine. This was reflected in the ritual of Hokkaidō Gokoku Jinja. Fujieda Nagahira, the sixteenth-generation Shinto ritualist of Ubagami Daijingū[27] in southern Hokkaido, was assigned to the shrine as its chief ritualist. However, the head of the Seventh Division and the mayor of Asahikawa continued to be charged with the annual rite.

Furthermore, the difference between *gokoku* shrines and regular shrines was also indicated by their limited inclusion in the shrine ranking system. Rather than shrine ranks, the new *gokoku* shrines were divided into designated and undesignated shrines. While designated shrines were equated to the same rank as prefectural shrines and non-designated shrines were equated with the rank of village shrine, they remained in a category separate from regular shrines (Inoue 2019). This was somewhat similar to the special category of imperial shrines (*bekkaku kanpeisha*) created to hold nationally relevant shrines dedicated to kami who had died in service of the emperor, which included Yasukuni Jinja. Both these categories were separated from regular shrines, but not clearly ranked above or below regular shrines of a similar status.

Space, time and ethics at Hokkaidō Gokoku Jinja

While for most of its pre-war history Hokkaidō Gokoku Jinja was unconnected to shrines or Shinto ritualists, it did share many similarities with them. Early on its military community saw it as a *yōhai* site towards Yasukuni Jinja, its architecture and ritual were based upon that of Yasukuni Jinja, and Major Kajiura Ginjirō, the adjutant general who enthusiastically directed the site's expansion in the 1930s,[28] based his plans for the shrine on the idea of a northern version of Yasukuni Jinja (Shimemura 1981, 586).

As an institution venerating the war dead only from Hokkaido, the site located Hokkaido within the more expansive topography of imperial lands. While the government began standardizing war dead memorials as early as 1874 (Takenaka 2015, 45), Hokkaidō Gokoku Jinja's connection to shrines was formally made only in 1935 when the government began transitioning *shōkon-sha* into Shinto shrines. This connection was solidified in 1939 when the *gokoku* shrine ranking system formally linked former *shōkon-sha* into an empire-wide network. Like how the modern shrine ranking system linked Sapporo Jinja vertically under the Ise Jingū and horizontally to other prefectures' leading shrines, the *gokoku* shrine network placed Hokkaidō Gokoku Jinja under Yasukuni Jinja and linked it with the designated *gokoku* shrines of other prefectures.

The 1934 petition for raising the site to a *shōkon-sha* also demonstrates how physical geography was an important element in determining which sites would be marked on the national topography. It cites Asahikawa's location in the centre of Hokkaido, along with its history and connection to the Seventh Division, as reasons it should be raised in status (Shimemura 1981, 591). *Yōhai* was also an important physical practice that reinforced the spatial position of Hokkaido as represented by Hokkaidō Gokoku Jinja in a Japanese metageography. The site was not only seen as a *yōhai* site, but like Sapporo Jinja, it later became the focus of *yōhai* for Hokkaido residents. In 1937, Japan entered the Second Sino-Japanese War and *yōhai* began to be practiced on an empire-wide scale (Hara 2011, 415). For example, the Hokkaido government directed all Hokkaido residents to perform *yōhai* and offer a minute of prayer on 5 June during Hokkaidō Gokoku Jinja's 1945 major festival (Shimemura 1981, 633). We also see during this same festival how the smaller communities surrounding Asahikawa contributed the aid of their own shrine's ritualists to Hokkaidō Gokoku Jinja. Thus ritualists in the periphery, who represented their shrine and thus community, were gathered to the centre of Hokkaido at Hokkaidō Gokoku Jinja.[29]

Hokkaidō Gokoku Jinja also raised awareness of modern time. The shrine had its origins in an effort to 'educate wordlessly' recruits who were accustomed to an agricultural calendar into the strictly regimented life of a modern soldier (Shimemura 1981, 560). Records show that in 1933 the major festivals being celebrated at the shrine included its own festival in June, Yasukuni Jinja's annual and irregular festivals in October and April, and the Army and Navy Memorial Days in March and May (Shimemura 1981, 584). So even before becoming a shrine, the site reinforced the yearly cycle of Japanese time. The regular festivals of the site were also organized according to a strict hourly schedule. Like at Yasukuni Jinja, civilian participants – the newly bereaved – were required to be seated two hours before their rite began, and the rite was conducted according to a predefined timetable.

Perhaps the most precise example of promoting national time in connection to the site was on 24 May 1935, when the registry of the Hokkaido war dead was delivered from Yasukuni Jinja to Hokkaidō Gokoku Jinja as its 'spirit proxy' (Shimemura 1981, 595). Resembling how Higashikuze and Shima carried the spirit proxy of Sapporo Jinja from Tokyo to Sapporo, Murasakita Naotane, the chief ritualist of Kamikawa Jinja which was the highest-ranked shrine in the Asahikawa area, personally carried the registry from Yasukuni Jinja to Asahikawa. Kajiura, who so enthusiastically supported the site's development that he was nicknamed the 'Shrine Adjutant' (Shimemura 1981, 578), met Murasakita at Hakodate, and they transported the registry by rail in a specially designated train carriage. The Hokkaido government directed officials, residents and community groups to see off the registry, which departed from Hakodate at 6:00 in the morning, and then to welcome it into Asahikawa. The registry arrived at precisely 4:38 in the afternoon, and the Seventh Division lined the entire route from the station to the shrine, standing at attention (Shimemura 1981, 595). This precise timing is an example of how shrines reinforced modern time as measured by the minute.

Linear time was also marked by the site in 1940 with the celebration of the 2600th anniversary of Jinmu's enthronement rite. Shrines across the Japanese sphere planned major renovations and events to celebrate (Ruoff 2010, 61–7), and Hokkaidō Gokoku Jinja was no exception. The shrine began a major renovation project in celebration of the anniversary. The 2600th anniversary also overlapped with the 50th anniversary of Asahikawa's establishment in 1890. As Hokkaidō Gokoku Jinja had only formally become a shrine the previous year, these renovations began in 1940, with the first stage completed in 1945 (Shimemura 1981, 608, 622).[30] While the anniversary celebrations might also be seen as excuses to enlarge the shrine along with its elevation in rank, the projects affirmed the importance of those anniversaries. Just as Kashihara Jingū was more concerned with the act of celebrating 11 February (Foundation Day) than the reasons for it, the praxis of celebrating the year, rather than the significance individual citizens attached to it, was what made them into good imperial subjects. Thus the site, first as a *shōkon-sha* and then as a shrine, instilled an awareness of modern Japanese time and space among its supporters.

Hokkaidō Gokoku Jinja also worked to build a geographically rooted difference between Hokkaido and the standard version of Japan as represented by the centre. The site worked to assimilate Hokkaido residents into a new national secularity, while providing a space to create a narrower local identity particular to Hokkaido, but subordinated to the larger conception of being Japanese. While the *shōkon* site was originally founded to aid new recruits in learning to be modern military men, it became a site representing the contribution of Hokkaido residents to Japan. Hokkaido residents were able to die for the nation/emperor, giving proof that Hokkaido, despite its geographic and cultural differences from the Home Islands, was fully a legitimate part of the empire.

Similar to how Shima envisioned Sapporo as the 'northern capital' of Japan (Blaxell 2009, 6), organizers of Hokkaidō Gokoku Jinja often saw it as a northern version of Yasukuni Jinja.[31] The site imitated Yasukuni Jinja in many elements: architecture, rites, enshrined spirits, museum and garden. Yet these elements were given a northern character. The site used the same architecture as Yasukuni Jinja, but the towering wooden *torii* gate was constructed from massive one meter in diameter trees donated by Higashi Asahikawa village (Shimemura 1981, 579). The rites followed Yasukuni's precedent, but were shifted by a month when the weather was slightly warmer. The site venerated the war dead enshrined at Yasukuni, but only those from the North. The museum was modelled on Yasukuni Jinja's museum, Yūshūkan, but called the Hokuchin Military Museum (Shimemura 1981, 587), using a term (*hokuchin*) emphasizing the settling of the spirits in the 'north'.[32] Like Yasukuni Jinja, the site displayed military weapons in its garden, but they were 240 mm howitzers from Hakodate in southern Hokkaido (Shimemura 1981, 578).[33]

Hokkaidō Gokoku Jinja's garden in particular emphasized the site as reflecting the north. During the 1933 renovations, the site's grounds were drained and landscaped to create two lakes over which the main approach passed. While donations from Hokkaido residents made these renovations possible, the members of the Seventh Division were used for much of the manual labour. The lakes they dug were shaped into the same form as Karafuto and Hokkaido (Shimemura 1981, 574). The seaside city of Rumoi donated a lantern made of local stone, which was placed at the same spot on the lake as Rumoi is located in Hokkaido (Shimemura 1981, 580). Thus the entire 'north' was literally carved into the garden of the site.

Other specifically northern aspects were added to the site. Kajiura, the 'shrine adjutant' discussed above, made a deliberate effort to plant as many Onko (Japanese Yew),[34] an evergreen tree characteristic of Hokkaido, as possible to make the site famous for them (Shimemura 1981, 582-3). In 1932, Kajiura along with Sukegawa, planned on transporting a rare fifteen-tonne stone of Kotan-ishi (green hyaloclastite) discovered in the nearby Ishikawa River to use as the shrine's purification basin. Kotan-ishi is found only at the site for which it is named, Kamui Kotan. The expense and power necessary prevented Kajiura and Sukegawa from immediately realizing their plan, but in 1941 a drought exposed the stone, allowing the stone to be raised and brought to the shrine (Shimemura 1981, 623-4).

The renovation and expansion of the site in the 1930s and 1940s were financed through wide donation campaigns. While residents close to Asahikawa donated the largest portion of money and labour, areas across Hokkaido took part in the effort. As donations financed a particular building, or took the form of natural resources like stone or wood, residents who donated could point to a particular structure as representing their area's contribution to the site. This mirrored the national volunteer labour efforts conducted by shrines like Kashihara Jingū discussed previously. But while those shrines were relevant to all Japanese subjects and thus drew donations from across the empire, Hokkaidō Gokoku Jinja was a site particular to the north, and thus drew donations from Hokkaido. This fundraising was largely conducted by the Seventh Division in conjunction with the civil government. Due to this, it is possible that some Hokkaido residents felt forced to donate, but the fact that the fundraising repeatedly surpassed its stated goal indicates that most Hokkaido residents were eager to support the site.

Perhaps the most significant influence *shōkon-sha* and later *gokoku* shrines had on the Japanese secularity was in affirming the national morality as promoted by Yasukuni Jinja. While war dead rites were not exclusively developed from Shinto traditions, Yasukuni Jinja pioneered a new conception of the war dead as public deaths to be mourned by the entire empire. Japanese secularity's ethics encouraged the Confucian values of loyalty and filial piety, with the entire nation being envisioned as a single expansive family (Jansen 2000, 492). The emperor, rather than a direct ancestor, stood as the founding father of the family. Likewise, the war dead, who died for the emperor, became the protectors of the nation. Thus *shōkon* rites were similar to ancestral ritual, but with the entire nation, rather than just blood relatives, owing the war dead reverence (Takenaka 2015, 87).

Hokkaidō Gokoku Jinja, as a northern Yasukuni, supported this modern conception of the war dead. In Hokkaido, a newly imperial land where many residents lacked an illustrious line of ancestors, this new conception which made all imperial subjects children of the emperor particularly had potential. Raising up Hokkaido into fully imperial land was consistently evoked when petitioning for a higher rank or permission to fundraise. For example, the prospectus for improvements to Hokkaidō Shōkon-jō in 1933 begins by invoking two imperial poems and 'our nation's beautiful virtue' of venerating the war dead before introducing its petition for conducting fundraising activities (Shimemura 1981, 574). The incorporation of distinctly Hokkaido elements such as Onko trees and Kotan-ishi stones into the site transformed by association Hokkaido's previously 'foreign' landscape into a local version subsumed within the broader category of Japan. It positioned Hokkaido and its residents as a member of a single, but diverse, Japanese family.

Furthermore, the long-time distinction between *shōkon* sites and shrines contributed to the understanding of Shinto as a universal form of ritual, not exclusive to shrines. The ritual practiced at *shōkon* sites was based upon shrine practices but also included elements adopted from the West such as military music and moments of silence. Shinto practices were enthusiastically adopted by Buddhists (Victoria 2006, 137). The Catholic Church, too, encouraged its members to take part in Shinto ritual, particularly at Yasukuni Jinja, as an expression of patriotism.[35] This embrace of *gokoku* shrines as universal sites for venerating the war dead can be seen by the diverse groups that contributed to Hokkaidō Gokoku Shrine during its improvement project starting in 1940. In addition to contributions by newspapers, merchants, veteran groups, community groups and individuals, volunteer labour by members of an Asahikawa branch of Tenrikyō, a religious Sect Shinto group, was particularly enthusiastic. The shrine's history also lauds fifty members of the Nichiren Buddhist temple Myōhō-ji, who practiced winter austerities for a month to raise money for Hokkaidō Gokoku shrine (Shimemura 1981, 618–19). The enthusiastic participation by a variety of religious groups suggests that supporters of Hokkaidō Gokoku Jinja saw its ritual as serving a universal purpose.

Hokkaidō Gokoku Jinja and religion

The transformation of the Seventh Division Shōkon Ritual Site into Hokkaidō Gokoku Jinja demonstrates the changing concerns the Japanese government had with secularism. While *shōkon* rites were originally neither legally religious nor shrine-related, they were embraced by the military and then the civil government as a public method for commemorating the war dead and building a national identity. While two rare exceptions were made for Yasukuni Jinja and Kenkō Jinja in Taiwan, *shōkon* sites with their connection to the recent dead were kept separate from Shinto shrines. As the government became less concerned with instilling the system of secularism into the populace and more concerned with building up a sense of patriotism and national identity in Japanese subjects, the line drawn between *shōkon* sites and shrines began to weaken.

The changing names of Hokkaidō Gokoku Jinja demonstrate this. The site began as a temporary ritual site for the military. In 1910, it became the Dai-Nana Shidan Kan Shōkon-sha, a permanent site connected to the military but used equally by the civil government. The 1916 change of name to Hokkaidō Shōkon-jō indicated the site's public character, but also that it was a site where the war dead are only temporarily present, bringing it in line with national terminology. The 1935 change to Hokkaidō Shōkon-sha indicated it was now a site where the war dead are in permanent residence, bringing it closer to the nature of a shrine. Aligning with this, the site gained its first connection to a Shinto ritualist as well. The name change to Hokkaidō Gokoku Jinja in 1939 made the site officially into a shrine and gave it its own full-time Shinto ritualist. Despite this, it was still distinguished from standard shrines by having a separate ranking system. Ironically, the site did not become indistinguishable from Shinto shrines until the post-war, when the Occupation forces banned the term *gokoku* from shrine names. Thus in 1946 the site became Hokkaidō Jinja and its official purpose in its registration as a religious organization made no reference to the war dead.[36] Thus as the character of the war dead became increasingly public and the government's concern with separating shrines from the other world decreased, *shōkon* sites were folded into the category of shrines (*jinja*).

However, as seen above at Shinonome Shi in Sapporo, the popular conception of ritual sites did not always precisely align with the government's legal definition. As previously discussed, the Seventh Division's *shōkon* site was early on seen as a *yōhai* site – not technically a shrine but closely connected to them. In the 1930s, supporters of the site like Kajiura clearly considered it as a shrine, so much so that a ritualist's residence was constructed at the site, despite the lack of such a ritualist at the time. In some ways this resembles Tōkyō Shōkon-Sha's conversion into Yasukuni Jinja: supporters of the site desired a Shinto ritualist, but the only way to gain a ritualist was to become a shrine. The unusual situation of *gokoku* shrines like Hokkaidō Gokoku Jinja also demonstrates how 'Shinto' and 'shrines' were conceived not as equivalent terms, but rather separate categories on different taxonomic levels. Shintō/Kami no Michi, often equated with the Way of the Kami (*kannagara no michi*) or the Imperial Way (*kōdō*), was conceived as a broad category governing all of life. Shrines (*jinja*, including *jingū* and *taisha*), on the other hand, referred to secular institutions charged with conducting rites of the state. Thus a broad variety of institutions – Sect Shinto sites, *shōkon* sites, Buddhist patriotic rituals, school ceremonies surrounding the Imperial Rescripts – might be called Shinto, but remain distinguished from shrines, or Shrine Shinto.

Furano Jinja: Local settler communities

The shrines examined so far have been large shrines with significant government involvement. But smaller shrines also embraced a modern conception of Shinto shrines. Furano Jinja (Figure 3.3), a small shrine in the Furano Basin at the geographic centre of Hokkaido, is an example of this. Although Furano Jinja was established and run with relatively little government encouragement, the shrine's local community largely embraced, and adapted, the modern conceptions of shrines and *shōkon* rites, allowing settlers to locate their land and themselves within the larger Japanese sphere.

The Furano Basin is a mountain-encompassed plain approximately an hour south from Asahikawa and two hours north-east of Sapporo by train today. Opened to settlement by migrants from the Home Islands in 1898, it developed along a common pattern seen in Hokkaido, with a mix of small independent farms, large farms employing tenant farmers and the experimental farm and forest land belonging to the Tokyo and Hokkaido Imperial Universities.[37] As the community grew and divided into several different towns, each area set up their own small ritual site, sometimes by erecting a miniature shrine building but other times utilizing only a stone monument or pillar. These early shrines were

Figure 3.3 Furano Jinja today. (Author's photograph.)

set up at the migrants' volition and without permission from the government (*mugan jinja*). This was typical of Home Islander migrants not only in Hokkaido but also in other overseas areas.

The residents of Lower Furano quickly set up a small Shinto site by the Zunashi River, but in 1907, they relocated it to what was then the edge of town, not far from the wide Sorachi River. Around the same time, Furano residents decided to petition the government for legal recognition of their shrine. In 1912, the central government recognized Furano Jinja as an unranked shrine. This recognition meant Furano Jinja was allowed a Shinto ritualist, if only one sent down from Asahikawa on festival days.[38] In 1919, Furano Jinja gained the rank of village shrine, which afforded it its own dedicated ritualist, Nishikawa Gensai. Gensai was a rural intellectual from Tokushima Prefecture, who, like many Japanese of his age, was deeply interested in the world beyond Japan. After migrating to Hokkaido, Gensai first tried farming before enrolling at the Hokkaido branch of the Classics Institute to become a Shinto ritualist (Furano Jinja 2004, 6).[39] In 1940, Furano Jinja was raised to the rank of district shrine, positioning it as the protector shrine of the entire Furano area (Furano Jinja 2004, 1–2).

Although Furano Jinja was founded without government involvement, the shrine's community saw it as a public institution and actively sought out government recognition. But gaining government recognition was not an easy process. Permission to exist as an unranked shrine took over four years to obtain. In preparation for gaining the rank of village shrine, Furano residents had to construct a new larger shrine building, as well as a residence for the future dedicated ritualist. While recognition entitled the shrine to offerings from the local government, this supplied more status than financial support (Hardacre 2017, 417). Nishikawa Gensai, Furano Jinja's first dedicated ritualist, had no experience as a 'religionist', but had studied Western medicine and served as the mayor of his town in Tokushima. He, and his son Nishikawa Ni'noshin who succeeded him, trained to be ritualists at the Classics Institute, the secular government organization discussed previously in this chapter. The kami enshrined were also of a public nature: Ōkunitama-no-kami, Ōnamuchi-no-kami and Sukunahikona-no-kami, the 'ancestral kami of developing and protecting the national land' (Furano Jinja 2004, 2). In other words, they were the same Three Pioneer Kami as Sapporo Jinja.

The shrine also served as a site for celebrating national and local events related to governance. Even before recognition as an unranked shrine, a ritual was held for Emperor Meiji's poor health in 1912. The establishment of a local government in Furano in 1915 was commemorated with the planting of about fifty trees (thirty-eight of them cherry blossom trees) on the shrine grounds. In 1912, Emperor Taisho ascended to the throne and Japanese citizens from Tokyo to Hawai'i celebrated the occasion. This included Furano Jinja's community, who planted a 'German Spruce' tree at the shrine in commemoration (Furano Jinja 2004, 14). Furano Jinja, like Kashihara Jingū and Sapporo Jinja, also served as a public site for leisure. In commemoration of the Crown Prince's visit to Hokkaido in 1922, Gensai along with several shrine supporters constructed a small park, including a pond, decorative bridge and lawn on the public land behind the shrine. The shrine and the park served as a venue for not only cherry blossom viewing but also the performance of a brass brand and other entertainment (Furano Jinja 2004, 22).

Local shrines often came to represent the community as a whole, leading both the local government and residents to devote significant resources towards the shrine. In Furano the shrine's community had already once constructed a new shrine building and residence in 1921. But in 1933, the shrine's supporters again began making plans for expanding and improving the shrine. A committee to manage this was put together, with the mayor of Furano, Matsuzaki Shinajirō, being elected as committee president by the 120 members in attendance. The cost of improvements was 25,000 yen, an enormous amount for a small town. The local government contributed half this amount, with the rest being raised by the community through fundraising. Once the improvements were completed, Furano had a chance to show off its new shrine facilities. Over twenty ritualists from across Kamikawa district came to assist at the ritual to transfer the kami, while over 7,000 people attended the rite (Furano Jinja 2004, 22). Thus Furano Jinja served as a visual representation of the growing prosperity of the community.

The importance of the shrine to the community's status is demonstrated by the competition that occurred between Furano Jinja in Lower Furano and Kami Furano Jinja in Upper Furano. Today, the name 'Furano' alone refers to what used to be Lower Furano, while Upper Furano sounds like a sub-village of the main city of Furano. Contrary to this image, Upper Furano was settled early, gained access to modern technology like trains earlier and originally had a greater population than Lower Furano. Until 1903, the Furano area was considered a single administrative unit with the town hall located in Upper Furano. As the population increased, the area divided into Upper and Lower Furano. Both communities had established unrecognized shrines, but residents of Lower Furano were first to petition for legal recognition of their Furano Jinja, and thus were first to claim the name.

The name changes of Hokkaidō Gokoku Jinja have already shown the importance of a Shinto site's name in indicating its character, and the same was true for Furano. The name Furano Jinja positioned the shrine as relevant to the entire Furano area, while the name Kami Furano Jinja limited the shrine's community only to the area of Upper Furano. By the time Upper Furano petitioned for recognition of their Furano Jinja as an unranked shrine in 1920, Lower Furano's shrine had already been granted the rank of village shrine. Each raise in rank was accompanied by physical improvements of the shrine, as well as attention and offerings from the regional government. While Kami Furano Jinja was quickly raised to the same rank of village shrine as Furano Jinja in 1923, Furano Jinja again outpaced Kami Furano Jinja when it was raised to the rank of district shrine in 1940. By this time, Lower Furano had clearly overtaken Upper Furano in importance, which was seen in other areas, such as when Shimo Furano station was renamed to simply Furano Station, while Upper Furano retained its Kami Furano Station.[40] While Furano Jinja's rank was only one of many factors which influenced Lower Furano's local predominance, the shrine served as an important physical representation of the Furano community.

If Furano Jinja represented the larger Furano community, the shrine's location in the larger network of the modern shrine ranking system reflected Furano's location in a Japanese metageography. As a modern shrine established after the Meiji Restoration, Furano Jinja lacked ties to pre-modern shrine systems such as Yoshida Shinto. Furthermore, as an unrecognized shrine it began outside of the new state system. Many shrines such as Kami Furano Jinja continued to function as unrecognized shrines.[41] But since the modern shrine ranking system was aligned with geographic administrative districts, Furano Jinja's recognition located it and its community both vertically and horizontally within the metageography of the Japanese secularity. Above Furano Jinja was the leading shrine of the Kamikawa district, Kamikawa Jinja (Figure 3.4), and above that, shrines that were relevant to the entire prefecture, including Sapporo Jinja and Hokkaidō Gokoku Jinja. Finally above them were the imperial shrines relevant to the entire empire, such as Ise Jingū and Kashihara Jingū.

As Furano rose in rank, it was positioned above other shrines in the Furano area, including Kami Furano Jinja as discussed above. These relationships were reinforced by the recycling of shrine buildings and the practice of ritualists assisting at the major festivals of other shrines. After the rebuilding of Furano Jinja's shrine buildings in 1933, for example, the old main building was donated to Torinuma Jinja, an unrecognized shrine in the Furano area (Furano Jinja 2004, 206). Thus the recycling of buildings, such as how the imperial palace donated

Figure 3.4 A postcard of Kamikawa Jinja: The shrine building, completed in 1924, remains largely unchanged today. (Author's collection.)

its old shrine buildings to Kashihara Jingū and Ise Jingū donated its old building to Sapporo Jinja, was also repeated among small shrines. In a similar manner, all ritualists from the Kamikawa district assisted at Furano Jinja's transfer ritual in 1933, while in reverse Nishikawa assisted at Hokkaidō Gokoku Jinja's festival in 1940. Thus Furano Jinja and its community were positioned in a series of concentric circles expanding from the local to the national. This concentric metageography was also seen in the administration system, but Shinto shrines were physical reminders of these vertical relationships.

As a public institution located as a part of the larger empire, Furano Jinja played a role in communicating a modern Japanese secularity to its community, much as larger shrines like Sapporo Jinja did. Furano Jinja celebrated the annual ritual cycle mandated by the Ministry of Home Affairs that largely aligned with the national holidays. Its own annual festival (*reisai*) was first held on 15 September, but was shifted to 25 August in 1930 to avoid the busy harvest season. While all Hokkaido residents celebrated Sapporo Jinja's festival as a holiday, Furano Jinja's festival was celebrated as a public holiday within Furano. The shrine was also a site for *yōhai* rites towards the Home Islands. The shrine held a grand celebration for the 2600th anniversary of Jinmu's enthronement, and held a popular class teaching Urayasu-no-mai, the *kagura* dance written especially for the occasion (Furano Jinja 2004, 72–5). Furthermore, Nishikawa

Ni'noshin received the 2600th Anniversary Celebration Memorial Medal for his participation in the Tokyo celebration.

The shrine's ritualists were an active part of Furano's cultural society. Nishikawa Gensai was an intellectual educated in both Western learning and the Japanese classics, while his son, Ni'noshin, became well known as a writer of Japanese poetry, in addition to his work as a ritualist. He also served as secretary for the Furano Area Debate League in 1928. Ni'noshin's wife, Aida Fusae, was accomplished in cultural activities, and taught flower arrangement and tea ceremony at the shrine. In recognition of these activities, they, along with their son Kunihide, were listed in the Who's Who of Furano, published to commemorate the 100th anniversary of the Furano government (Furano-shi Jinbutsu Jiten Henshū Iinkai 2004, 282–4).

Furano Jinja affirmed a new sense of space, time and ethics in a manner similar to that seen at larger shrines, if on a smaller scale. But did it have any connections to *shōkon* sites dedicated to the war dead? Furano residents constructed a stele-type cenotaph (*chūkon-hi*) dedicated to the local Furano war dead in November 1918, after the First World War. While local elites such as Kanematsu Tamekichi were involved in both shrine activities and the construction of the cenotaph, there was no direct connection between the shrine and the cenotaph (Furano Jinja 2004, 19). The cenotaph's inscription was written by the previously mentioned Lt. Gen. Ōsako Naotoshi, who in 1918 had retired from being the Head of the Seventh Division of the Imperial Army. The cenotaph was located in the school yard of Furano Normal and Higher Primary School, and remained there for ten years. However, the school principal requested the Furano Veteran's Association that it be removed due to disrespectful behaviour towards it by the students. Thus in 1928, the Veteran's Association moved the site to the garden of Furano Jinja.

Although the cenotaph was located in the shrine garden, it was not formally a part of the shrine. Since it was a cenotaph rather than a *shōkon-sha*, the site was not converted into a shrine like Hokkaidō Gokoku Jinja. In 1942, as the shrine's garden lacked space and was inappropriate for the storing of physical remains of the war dead, Furano residents began constructing an obelisk-shaped war memorial (*chūrei-tō*) on the summit of nearby Asahigaoka Hill. The stone was granite transported from Ibaraki Prefecture, with an inscription by Prime Minister Tōjō Hideki (Takamatsu 1984, 210). The construction suffered delays, including the collapse of a bridge under the weight of the stone that sent both the monument and people into the rain-swollen Sorachi River. However, the first *shōkon* rite at the completed site was held on 15 June 1944 (Okabe 1984, 224). After the rite, the remains of the war dead were stored at the site using Buddhist ritual.[42]

The case of Furano again demonstrates the ambiguous position of *shōkon* sites. While the shrine garden eventually served as the site of the cenotaph, Furano residents did not consider it an ideal location. Furthermore, ritual for the war dead was not solely based on Shintō rites, but also included Buddhist rites for the treatment of the physical remains, and Western elements in the choice of an obelisk for the war memorial. The use of Shinto rite in a non-shrine context positioned it as a form of universal etiquette, but the inclusion of legally religious Buddhist rites suggests that Furano residents did not conceive of strictly separated secular and religious spheres as promoted by the Meiji government.

Shrines in Karafuto

When Japan established the Colonization Commission in 1869 to govern Hokkaido that included the island of Karafuto (Sakhalin). In 1870, Karafuto was briefly given its own Karafuto Colonization Commission, but in 1875 Japan relinquished its claims on the island in favour of Russia. In 1905, Japan regained the southern half of Karafuto as a spoil of the Russo-Japanese war. Karafuto was set up as its own colonial territory under the Ministry of Colonial Affairs, and migration from Hokkaido and the Home Islands was encouraged. By 1941, over 400,000 Japanese (including Korean-Japanese) resided in Karafuto alongside 425 people of indigenous tribes and 305 foreigners (Yamada and Maeda 2012, 14). When the Ministry of Colonial Affairs was converted into the Ministry of Greater East Asia in 1942, Karafuto was reclassified as a part of Japan's inner territory, legally becoming a part of the Home Islands.

Shrines in Karafuto were established following the same pattern that had been used in Hokkaido. Permission to establish Karafuto Jinja – the island's general protector and only greater imperial shrine – was given in 1910, with its enshrinement rite held the next year. The shrine was located to the east of the new capital city of Toyohara (today Yuzhno-Sakhalinsk) on a mountain overlooking the city, much like how Sapporo Jinja overlooked the city of Sapporo from Mt. Maruyama.[43] The site enshrined the same Three Pioneer Kami as Sapporo Jinja, with its annual festival falling on the same day as Karafuto's Dominion Day holiday. The festival was designated a prefectural holiday, with government officials and school children having the day off and residents expected to fly the national flag to celebrate (Tetsudō-shō 1943, 41). The shrine received visits from Emperor Taisho and other imperial family members, who planted indigenous pine trees in the shrine's garden (Yamada and Maeda 2012, 218). The local flora of Karafuto (lit. 'birch-plump') was also invoked through the shrine's official crest representing a three-leafed sprig of birch (Yamada and Maeda 2012, 278). The shrine was also a site for modern leisure activities, with scenic points built into its garden and night-illuminated ski slopes constructed to its north. Thus Karafuto Jinja was established with the same public conception as other modern shrines and utilized the pioneer theology developed in Hokkaido.

Karafuto Jinja was the first shrine to be granted official permission, but unofficial shrines had existed in Karafuto since at least the mid-1800s. The travel diaries of Japanese explorers record that many of these early Shinto sites were dedicated to Benten, the Shinto-Buddhist amalgamatory kami associated with maritime safety and prosperity (Yamada and Maeda 2012, 23-4). After the Russo-Japanese war, Japanese migrants to Karafuto set up new Shinto sites, often dedicated to Amaterasu Sume-Ōmikami.[44] Toyohara Jinja was one of these. Toyohara Jinja was first set up by Ban Yūzaburō – an instructor of Kurozumi Sect Shinto – as a *yōhai* site towards the Ise Jingū in 1908. Despite this, the site wasn't given official permission as a shrine until August 1910, half a month after Karafuto Jinja received permission. By 1928, it had gained the rank of prefectural shrine, making it the protector shrine of the entire Toyohara district. Ban also constructed a *shōkon* site within the shrine's grounds. In 1925, he successfully petitioned Yasukuni Jinja for a 'divided spirit' to enshrine at the site. In 1935, however, the *shōkon* site was moved from Toyohara Jinja to a site of its own next to Karafuto Jinja (Yamada and Maeda 2012, 436). It thus became an independent *shōkon-sha* similar to Hokkaidō Shōkon-sha. In 1939, like other *shōkon-sha*, it was transformed into Karafuto Gokoku Jinja, venerating all those 'glorious spirits' of Yasukuni who had connection to Karafuto. By the end of the war, there were at least 127 shrines in Karafuto.[45]

Conclusion

Shrine communities in Hokkaido and Karafuto, from the small Furano Jinja to the eminent Sapporo Jinja and Karafuto Jinja, largely embraced a secular conception of shrines. Furthermore, these shrines helped communicate the new Japanese secularity to their area's residents. These shrines played a significant role in positioning the new land of Hokkaido within a Japanese space and time, a Japanese metageography and History. However, as Shinonome Shi, Hokkaidō Gokoku Jinja and the *shōkon* sites in Kamikawa demonstrate, the relationship between the recent dead and shrines was often ambiguous, particularly for the average resident. The Japanese government considered Hokkaido's transformation into imperial land successful, and the Colonization Commission was abolished in 1882. This was followed by the establishment of the Hokkaido government in 1886,[46] incorporating the island as an integral part of the Home Islands. While Hokkaido is rarely considered a colonial space in the popular imagination today, its success as a modernization/colonization project was a successful trial for Japan's future colonial efforts in Karafuto and elsewhere. In the next chapter, we travel south to the 'outer lands' of the Japanese empire to look at how the lessons of the experiment of Hokkaido's shrines were applied to Japan's 'colonial triumph',[47] Taiwan.

4

A model colony: Taiwan at the far periphery

28 October 1895, 7:15 AM. Prince Yoshihisa at last began his 'return to the Capital' (Taiwan Jinja Shamusho Hensan 1935, 39). Only six months ago, Taiwan had passed from Qing administration to Japanese through the Treaty of Shimonoseki. Prince Yoshihisa and the Imperial Guardsmen under his command rushed from China to establish Taiwan's defences. They faced burning days reaching 138 degrees, suffered from a lack of food and were prevented from sleep by hordes of mosquitoes, but Prince Yoshihisa greeted these hardships with no more complaint than a bitter smile. A man versed in both martial and literary arts, his quick southern progress from Taihoku to Tainan was accompanied by Chinese poems expressing his journey. Even as he lay deathly ill upon a rough military stretcher, he gathered the energy to stay abreast with the occupation of Tainan. When the last of the Qing loyalists fled, the mood of the Japanese camp should have been jubilant. But a sombre pall hung over them: the prince was near death. It is said that Prince Yoshihisa spent his final breath raised in one last banzai to the emperor. His body was returned in state to the Capital of Japan. Yet Prince Yoshihisa's selfless devotion to the nation and the welfare of its subjects continued to shed light upon this once-foreign land.[1]

Prince Yoshihisa, or Kitashirakawa-no-miya Yoshihisa Shinnō, spent little more than half a year in Taiwan, but his southward journey from Keelung to Tainan became a trail of monuments and shrines in the following fifty years of Japanese rule. In 1901, he was enshrined as a kami with the establishment of Taiwan Jingū: the second Shinto shrine established by the Japanese on Taiwan. In the following years, shrines dedicated to him sprang up across the island, and Prince Yoshihisa was the most common Shinto kami enshrined there. Although Taiwan Jingū was not established until six years after Taiwan became Japanese territory, Shinto shrines became one of the most potent symbols of Japanese rule.[2]

A common depiction of shrines' roles in Japanese colonialism is to see shrines as a part of a Shinto religion to which the local populace was forcibly 'converted'.[3] This chapter will complicate that depiction by demonstrating how Taiwan Shintoists – those shrine ritualists, government officials and resident elites involved in supporting shrines – did not necessarily aim for assimilation to the customs of the Japanese Home Islands, but rather saw shrines as an integral part of modern civilization suited to Asia. This was partially due to the double or even triple 'transplantation of cultural dependency' (Allen 2012, 96) to which Taiwan was subjected. Japan brought a layered colonial modernity that was an amalgamation of a Western secularity adapted to the Japanese case. Taiwan provides a fascinating example of how shrines worked to not only communicate this new Japanese secularity to imperial subjects, but also how Japanese Shintoists subsumed Taiwanese customs into a modern Shinto-based social imaginary.

Although sixty-eight shrines had been built in Taiwan by the end of the Second World War, four shrines stand out as especially significant. The first was the most prominent shrine in Taiwan, Taiwan Jingū. Taiwan Jingū served not only as the general protector shrine of Taiwan, but also had an outsized influence on other Taiwan shrines. This was because a majority of later shrines were largely built as miniature copies of Taiwan Jingū. Like the greater imperial shrines in the Home Islands and Hokkaido, Taiwan Jingū served as a public, historical and modern site. Taiwan Jingū also demonstrates how shrines helped incorporate the newly imperial land of Taiwan into the metageography of the empire and helped foster a Japanese ethic into Taiwan residents. At the same time, differing pressures influenced Taiwan Jingū's relationship with the concept of religion.

Kaizan Jinja and Kenkō Jinja, on the other hand, stand out as two very unusual shrines. Kaizan Jinja was the very first shrine recognized in Taiwan, but was atypical in that it originated as a Taiwanese mausoleum (*byō*) dedicated to the Japan-born hero Koxinga. Kenkō Jinja was unusual in that it was dedicated to the 'glorious spirits' (*eirei*) who died in the service of Japanese Taiwan, and its architecture replaced the Shinto-style common in the Home Islands with a combination of Western and Chinese influenced architecture. These two shrines demonstrate how the definitions of 'shrine' and 'kami' were contested by Shintoists in Taiwan and how Taiwanese customs could be subsumed into a Shinto framework that legitimized Japanese-rule of Taiwan while legitimizing some Taiwanese customs as Japanese and thus civilized.

Taiwan Gokoku Jinja was another shrine dedicated to the 'glorious dead'. As the trend towards treating Taiwan the same as the Home Islands grew in popularity, the non-standard nature of Kenkō Jinja led to criticism that it was unsuitable for serving as the main war memorial of Taiwan. Furthermore, with the move in the Home Islands towards converting *shōkon-sha* war memorials into Shinto shrines, the colonial government felt the need to construct a similar facility. Taiwan Gokoku Jinja shows how government policy moved away from treating Taiwan as a special case. Yet Taiwan Gokoku Jinja was established only in 1942 – three short years before the end of the war – and the lack of other shrines' pre-modern associations beyond that of 'sites of state ritual' allowed the Taiwan Governor-General to mobilize all shrines in the service of militarism, perhaps even more so than in the Home Islands.

Finally, there was a variety of Shinto sites in Taiwan that were not official shrines. The activities of official shrines in Taiwan were mostly focused on Home and Taiwan Islanders. Shinto ritual was seen as an important tool for civilizing the indigenous Takasago tribes, but their relatively lower level of 'civilization' meant Japan rarely set up formal shrines in their villages. Furthermore, while smaller shrines usually followed the same pattern as Taiwan Jingū, there was a much more diverse selection of Shinto sites in Taiwan, including pre-shrines (*sha*), *yōhai* sites, *shōkon* sites and unrecognized shrines.

Taiwan's layered colonialism

The earliest inhabitants of Taiwan were not Taiwan Islanders,[4] but a variety of Austronesian-speaking tribes referred to by the Japanese as the Takasago tribes, using an old poetic name for the island. By the 1600s, however, a transient population of merchants and pirates had begun taking up residence in Taiwan. In 1623, the Dutch East India Company began colonizing the island and, despite violent resistance from the Austronesian tribes, built two forts in southern Taiwan to serve as their bases. Shortly after, the Spanish also established a colonial outpost on the island. During this period, many migrants from Fujian in Southern China began settling in Taiwan. The Dutch and Spanish colonies fared poorly, plagued by conflict with both the Takasago tribes and each other. In 1642, the Dutch drove the Spanish from the island, and in 1661, the merchant-pirate Koxinga drove the Dutch from Taiwan. Koxinga (Jp. Tei Seikō, Ch. Zhèng Chénggōng) was the son of the famous Ming pirate Zheng Zhilong (Jp. Tei Shiryū) and Tagawa Matsu, the daughter of a Japanese samurai family. While he spent his early years in Japan with his mother, Koxinga later moved to Fujian and joined the civil service of the Ming Dynasty. When the Ming were defeated by the Qing, Koxinga fled to Taiwan, driving out the Dutch and establishing his own kingdom there. After Koxinga's death, his son surrendered the kingdom to the Qing dynasty.

During this period, more migrants from southern China settled in Taiwan, although the different migrant groups often clashed. In the mid-nineteenth century, Taiwan was subject to punitive campaigns by the British in 1841, the Americans in 1867, the Japanese in 1874 and then the French in 1884. This convinced the Qing to attempt to set up formal administration of the island as a province (Ts'ai 2009, 34). In 1885, the Qing established Taiwan as a formal province and relocated the seat of governance from its historical location in the South to the newly established city of Taihoku (Taipei) in the North (Allen 2012, 24). However, the fierceness of the Takasago tribes prevented the Qing from establishing direct administrative control over the whole island. In 1895, the Qing ceded Taiwan to Japan as a spoil of the Sino-Japanese war. The Treaty of Shimonoseki not only transferred Taiwan to Japan but also forced the Qing to recognize Korea's independence and pay indemnity to Japan.[5] While there continued to be unrest during the early years of Japanese rule, the six months of Prince Yoshihisa's campaign introduced above were spent cementing Taiwan as a formal Japanese territory, as imperial land.

While the expense of pacifying and modernizing Taiwan was not immediately greeted with enthusiasm by the Japanese Diet, Taiwan became Japan's first internationally recognized colony.[6] Japan set up the Taiwan Governor-General to administer the island, maintaining the yet sparsely populated Taihoku city as its capital. The first few years of Japanese rule were dominated by military force to pacify the populace, but in 1889, the fourth Governor-General of Taiwan, Kodama Gentarō, along with the civilian Chief of Home Affairs Gotō Shinpei, set a new precedent of carrot-and-stick rule. This transformed the island from a drain on Japan's treasury to an economically self-sufficient region, able to supply the Home Islands with resources such as rice, lumber and sugar.

Sai, in his study of Taiwan religious policy during Japanese rule, has divided Taiwan's Japanese history into three periods (Sai 1994, 10). The first period, beginning with the start of Japan's rule and continuing until the Xilai Temple Incident in 1915, was characterized by a government more interested in economic stability than the ideological transformation of the populace. While the incorporation of Taiwan as a territory equal to the Home Islands was not ruled out, the twenty-first Imperial Diet ruled in 1905 that Taiwan was a colony and thus privileged to separate laws from the Home Islands. The laws of the Home Islands were to be considered the model, but the Governor-General had enormous leeway in adapting his method of rule to established traditions in Taiwan. Although the Takasago tribes were treated as racial 'brothers' by the Japanese in the early years, as economic concerns took priority, the

Governor-General's policy towards them quickly changed to one of ruthless military suppression, especially against the fierce 'raw barbarians'.[7] During this same period, many of the colonial elite recognized a shared classical Chinese heritage in the ethnic Chinese living in Taiwan. For these Chinese residents, contemporarily referred to as Taiwan Islanders or just Islanders in contrast to Japanese Home Islanders, the Governor-General co-opted the traditional neighbourhood watch (Jp. hokō, Ch. baojia) system and left alone those customs considered perhaps superstitious, but not harmful (Sai 1994, 16). This lack of interest in influencing Taiwan residents' social imaginary was reflected by the relatively few shrines founded during this period. Only twelve shrines had been established by 1915, and most of those by Home Islanders[8] (Sai 1994, 21).

The second period, from 1915 until 1931, was marked by the development of government offices to oversee both temples and shrines. In 1915, a group of Taiwan Islanders revolted against Japanese rule by attacking multiple police stations in what became known as the Xilai Temple Incident. The incident began at the Taiwanese Buddhist Xilai Temple and included elements of folk religion and millenarism. This provoked the colonial government into conducting a major survey of Taiwanese temples. This in turn led to the establishment of the Shrines and Temples Bureau in 1918, which was demoted to the Shrines and Temples Division under the Culture and Education Bureau in 1924. It was not until 1923 that Shinto shrines and religious organizations (Buddhist and Taiwanese temples) began to be governed under separate laws.[9] The shrines and pre-shrines established during this period included a few dedicated to popular Japanese kami set up by migrants from the Home Islands, but a majority were in the lineage of Taiwan Jingū, dedicated to the Three Pioneer Kami and Prince Yoshihisa. This would hold true until the end of Japanese rule, with Taiwan Jingū setting the standard for all shrines on the island. The lack of popular financial support for shrines also led the Governor-General to develop a new legal category of Shinto sites called pre-shrines (sha). For a site to be legally recognized as a Shinto shrine, it had to fulfil strict criteria which included possessing at least 1.5 hectares of land and a variety of facilities. Building a shrine, thus, required significant financial resources. The new category of pre-shrine, based on the pre-shrines (shinshi) developed by the Chōsen Governor-General,[10] functioned the same as full Shinto shrines but required less land and fewer facilities (Sai 1994, 78). As this meant pre-shrines were cheaper to build than full shrines, this would allow the Governor-General to sponsor the rapid building of Shinto sites across Taiwan.

The worldwide trend towards democracy inspired by American president Woodrow Wilson's 'National Self-Determination' during this period also affected Taiwan. Taiwan Islanders protested against the discriminatory treatment they received in comparison to the Home Islanders, and a movement towards treating outer territories like Taiwan the same as the Home Islands grew. While previously the colonial government had been relatively unconcerned about the lifestyle patterns of Taiwan Islanders, equal treatment as the Home Islands meant Islanders were also expected to conform to Home Islands standards of behaviour. During this assimilation period, mandatory visits to Taiwan Jingū by religious leaders became standard, but without causing social unrest (Sai 1994, 79).[11] These political trends were reflected in a shift in the role of Shinto shrines as well. Sapporo Jinja in Hokkaido had established the Three Pioneer Kami as most suitable kami for developing new imperial land. However, Amaterasu Ōmikami as ancestress of the imperial house and thus the Japanese, rather than the Three Pioneer Kami, began being considered just as suitable for new imperial lands as she was for the Home Islands (Suga 2014, 137).

Sai's last division runs from the Manchurian incident in 1931 to the end of the Second World War. As Japan descended into militarism and mobilized for war, in Taiwan policies such as the Citizen Cultivation movement and later the Imperialization movement aimed to transform Taiwanese residents into good imperial subjects. Many policies during this period aimed to assimilate Taiwan Islanders to Home Islands customs. The Seichō (Ch. Zhèngtīng) Improvement (Seichō Kaizen) and Temple Reorganization (Jibyō Seiri) movements, for example, encouraged Islanders to replace their Chinese-style ancestral tablets with Japanese Buddhist ones, and encouraged Taiwanese Buddhist temples to 'reform' into branches of Japanese Buddhism or else face the danger of being denounced as superstitious. The policy towards the Takasago also changed during this period to focus on imperialization projects that eventually succeeded in transforming them into 'modern ethnic minorities' (Barclay 2018, 120).

Shintoists in Taiwan, however, were more interested in fostering a patriotic spirit of reverence for the kami and (imperial) ancestors – a task not yet wholly completed even in the Home Islands – than having Islanders replace their Chinese customs with Home Islands customs. This was the period when serious effort began being devoted to instilling a Japanese secularity into Taiwan residents. The construction of shrines greatly increased during this period, with the Governor-General aiming to build a shrine in every village. This mirrored the Shrine Reorganization movement that lasted from 1906 to 1912 in the Home Islands and which aimed to limit each village to one shrine (Hardacre 2017, 416; Kaneko 2018, 77). While in the Home Islands that policy had meant merging the plethora of small shrines into a single shrine for each district, and

A Model Colony 95

in Hokkaido it had meant restricting which shrines were granted official shrine status, in Taiwan it meant increasing the number of shrines. These efforts aimed to form an imagined community for each village around its protector shrine, realigning the community to match the administrative districts drawn by the Japanese government. However, there was little financial enthusiasm from the local populace in Taiwan. Thus a majority of these new shrines were top-down projects by the government, or merely the recognition of an already existing pre-shrine as an official unranked shrine. Even when the government financed the building of a new shrine, Taiwan Islander community life largely continued to revolve around the many Taiwanese temples.

Taiwan Jingū: Pioneer theology

The first shrine recognized in Taiwan was Kaizan Jinja, but the first shrine constructed, and the second formally founded, was Taiwan Jinja (Figure 4.1), on the outskirts of Taiwan's capital, Taihoku. A movement to commemorate Prince Yoshihisa with a special imperial shrine was first introduced to the Japanese Diet by Negishi Takeka and Kitahara Nobutsuna in 1896 (Sai 1994, 20). This initial effort developed into a plan to build a greater imperial shrine enshrining the

Figure 4.1 A postcard of Greater Imperial Shrine Taiwan Jinja: Its name was changed to Taiwan Jingū in 1944. (Author's collection.)

Three Pioneer Kami and Prince Yoshihisa to serve as the general protector of Taiwan. On 27 October 1901, six years after Taiwan was ceded to Japan, Taiwan Jinja held its enshrinement ritual, and on the 28th held its first annual festival, on the sixth anniversary of Prince Yoshihisa's death. The shrine's annual festival became an island-wide holiday.

The visit of the Crown Prince – the future Emperor Showa – to Taiwan in April 1923 led to a flurry of renovations in preparation, the most significant being the renovation of the newly named Imperial Messenger Highway, a grand three-lane Haussmanian boulevard forming the main approach of the shrine from central Taihoku. In 1940, the celebrations for the 2600th anniversary of the Japanese empire again provided an impetus for major renovations to Taiwan Jinja. In 1942, Taiwan Gokoku Jinja was added to the grounds adjacent to Taiwan Jinja. Finally, in 1944, in anticipation of Taiwan's eventual rise from colony to an integral part of Japan, the imperial ancestress Amaterasu Ōmikami was scheduled to be enshrined at Taiwan Jinja. The transfer ritual began on 23 October, but a plane crash and fire interrupted the ritual. Although it is unclear if the ritual to enshrine Amaterasu was ever fully completed, Taiwan Jinja began to be referred to as Taiwan Jingū,[12] an appellation reserved for those shrines venerating a direct imperial ancestor (Kaneko 2015, 12, 2018, 35).

A public site

Taiwan Jingū, like Kashihara Jingū in the Home Islands and Sapporo Jinja in Hokkaido, was treated as a public site. In 1896, the Imperial Diet passed a resolution to fund the construction of an imperial shrine in Taiwan from the national treasury (Sai 1994, 20) to protect the newly imperial land of Taiwan. The Diet leaned towards enshrining Prince Yoshihisa, in order to soothe his 'glorious spirit' as well as to protect Taiwan. This would have given the site the character of a patriotic monument. However, the imperial ancestress Amaterasu Ōmikami and the Three Pioneer Kami were also raised as suggestions. Amaterasu Ōmikami would have indicated Taiwan was an integral part of Japan, while the Three Pioneer Kami would have emphasized Taiwan's still unfinished state of 'civilized' development. In the end, the Imperial Diet took the suggestion of the Governor-General of Taiwan, Kodama Gentarō, and two seats at the shrine were established: the Three Pioneer Kami in the first and Prince Yoshihisa in the second. Furthermore, the construction and maintenance of Taiwan Jingū was amply funded by the national government (Sai 1994, 20–4).[13] Thus the shrine was publicly conceived and funded.

Taiwan Jingū as a public site shared many similarities with Sapporo Jinja. Taihoku, like Sapporo, was laid out on the rational grid-structure of the ancient capitals. The original plan for Taiwan Jingū called for it to be built in a Maruyama Park to the north of the city so that the shrine might face south looking towards the city.[14] However, the shrine's site was shifted a little further north across the Keelung River to be perched at a higher vantage point on Mt. Jiantan.[15] The shrine was connected to the city centre by rail service, the Imperial Messenger Highway and the Western-style Meiji Bridge. Like at many other greater imperial shrines, Taiwan's outer garden and surrounding park area were continually expanded, eventually including a variety of public facilities, from an extensive forest and lakeside, to a sports arena, a 'training institute for national spirit', and a zoo (Aoi 2014, 107).

The Taiwan Governor-General also worked to make Taiwan Jingū into a communal site. One method was 'encouraging' students and community groups to volunteer their labour in renovating or beautifying the shrine to give them a sense of ownership. By 1935, at least nineteen different volunteer groups were donating their time regularly to Taiwan Jingū. These groups included neighbourhood youth groups, employee clubs and elementary and common school student groups (Taiwan Jinja Shamusho Hensan 1935, 123). Similarly the shrine displayed lanterns, statues and trees donated by both individuals and groups. The practice of displaying the donor's name on the item allowed people to point out the specific part of the shrine they contributed.[16] Like at Sapporo Jinja, the shrine grounds were planted with native cherry blossom and evergreen trees to create a public park ideal for cherry blossom viewing. The lakes, sports arena, baseball diamond and swimming pool in the east of the outer garden also positioned the shrine as a public facility (Aoi 2014, 107).

Finally, the annual festival of the shrine became a holiday celebrated by the entire island. Many smaller shrines shared this day as their annual festival. That government officials participated in Shinto ceremonies both at the shrine and at the government office indicated that shrine ritual was a type of public ceremony. The Governor-General and Taiwan Jingū were able to emphasize shrines' role as a public patriotic site. Taiwanese Islanders, who had previous experience with Qing state ritual and few associations with Shinto shrines outside of a state context, had little reason to reject this conception. Shintoists like Yamaguchi Tōru, chief ritualist of Taiwan Jingū, tried to utilize this Chinese conception of state ritual to explain Shinto shrines, writing, 'Shinto shrines are historically for rituals of the state, and shrine mausoleums (Jp. *shibyō*, Ch. *címiào*) are for the same ritual of the state' (Sai 1994, 27).

An Historical site

Taiwan Jingū was originally conceived as a monument to Prince Yoshihisa, a recent historical figure. While the more abstract Three Pioneer Kami were also enshrined, it was Yoshihisa that attracted the most attention. For example, the Record of Taiwan Jinja dedicates a mere seven pages to the Three Pioneer Kami, but devotes thirty-two pages including illustrations to Prince Yoshihisa (Taiwan Jinja Shamusho Hensan 1935, 2–40). Prince Yoshihisa's widow was invited to the shrine's enshrinement ritual, clothing worn by the prince was displayed in the shrine's treasure house and his relatives planted multiple trees in the shrine's garden. In many ways, Prince Yoshihisa was related to Taiwan as Emperor Jinmu was related to the wider Japanese empire: his death marked the completion of Taiwan's pacification, bringing the island under Japan's control and ushering it into the story of Japanese progressive History.

Much as historical sites related to Emperor Jinmu were commemorated to create a 'national topography' (Ruoff 2010, 67), sites related to Yoshihisa formed a Japanese topography for Taiwan. Taiwan Jingū may have been the grandest monument to Yoshihisa, but it was far from the only one. Stone monuments were erected at many of the sites where the prince had spent the night on his journey south to Tainan, and local houses at where he had boarded were preserved as historical assets. Eventually some of these sites would be turned into shrines,[17] but shrines as monuments to Yoshihisa stood within a network of historical monuments dedicated to him and the pacification of Taiwan. While Taiwan Jingū focused on Yoshihisa, the Three Pioneer Kami were also treated as distant historical figures. The shrine's ritualists recognized that the legendary exploits of the kami were difficult to take at face value, but still argued that the acts of the kami in the 'so-called ancient myths' should not be judged by current standards of common sense (Taiwan Jinja Shamusho Hensan 1935, 1). This location of shrines as historical monuments aligned with older ideas in Taiwan about revering great historical figures at mausoleums (*byō*). The conception of mausoleums as a lesser version of Shinto shrines was adopted by the colonial government and Shinto ritualists in Taiwan.

A modern site

Taiwan Jingū was constructed as an instrument of modernity in Taiwan. Like Sapporo Jinja, Taiwan Jingū enshrined the Three Pioneer Kami. Taiwan was seen largely as *terra nullius* that was still in need of development (colonization) and the pioneer narrative was common across Governor-General's policies.[18] The specific rationale for enshrining the Three Pioneer Kami, instead of Amaterasu Ōmikami or only Prince Yoshihisa, was that they could watch over the development and modernization of Taiwan (Sai 1994, 22-3). In other words, Taiwan Jingū utilized the pioneer theology that had begun at Sapporo Jinja. This process of modernization was portrayed as a continuation of a progressive narrative extending back to the legendary days of Ōnamuchi and Sukunahikona. In the classics, Ōnamuchi was an earthly kami charged with administering the land, who later passed that administration to the descendants of Amaterasu. Sukunahikona, on the other hand, was a kami who 'came from across the seas' and aided Ōnamuchi by bringing civilized technology such as agriculture and brewing to the Japanese isles. This pair – a native Japanese kami and a foreign kami working together – served as an example for the layered colonialism that Japan brought to Taiwan. The selected Western customs supplemented Japanese civilization, following the precedent set by Sukunahikona aiding Ōnamuchi. Furthermore, Sukunahikona, as a kami from across the seas, had a natural connection to overseas territories like Taiwan (Taiwan Jinja Shamusho Hensan. 1935, 2-6). This narrative did not deny the reality of foreign kami existing, but at the same time it suggested both that the Shinto-style of reverence was the most civilized and that foreign kami could become Japanese.

Most Taiwan residents had little exposure to complex discussions of the exact nature and history of the Three Pioneer Kami like the above. But the integral connection between Taiwan Jingū and modernity was communicated through less intellectual means as well. The construction of the shrine itself was a display of modern technology. Massive trees from Mt. Ali (Jp. Ari), pillars of granite from the Home Islands and bronze sculptures were transported by rail and sea to Taihoku to build the shrine. The Meiji Bridge on the shrine's main approach, which was first constructed from iron and then rebuilt in stone in 1933 (Tomita 2005, 84), was lauded as a triumph of modern engineering and appeared on postcards and travel guides.[19] The shrine was connected to central Taihoku by train – visitors could alight at Miyanoshita (lit. 'Below Shrine') Station – while the main approach of the shrine was widened to accommodate automobiles in 1923. Walking up the approach, visitors could admire the electric lanterns donated by patrons from both Taiwan and the Home Islands. Cannons captured as spoils from the First Sino-Japanese War and Russo-Japanese War provided displays of Japan's modern military strength (Taiwan Jinja Shamusho Hensan 1935, 78). Bronze statues, a technique adopted from the West, were especially popular in Taiwan, with bronze horses and bulls being donated to Taiwan Jingū.

The shrine's garden and sports facilities provided a centre for engaging in modern leisure and fitness activities. The rites themselves often mixed modern technology and dress. In short, Taiwan Jingū was as modern as any other greater imperial shrine in Hokkaido or the Home Islands.

An affirmation of Japanese space

Taiwan Jingū, like Sapporo Jinja, located Taiwan within the broader metageography of Japan. How Taiwan Jingū served as an historical landmark in the national topography has been discussed, but its rank as a general protector and greater imperial shrine gave it a parallel connection to other shrines of the same status across the empire. This was particularly significant as the empire continued to expand, creating parallels with other new imperial territories. Just as Taiwan had Taiwan Jingū and Hokkaido had Sapporo Jinja, Karafuto had Karafuto Jinja, Korea had Chōsen Jingū, Micronesia had Nan'yō Jinja and Kantō had Kantō Jingū: all greater imperial shrines and all general protectors of their respective geographic territories. Likewise, other shrines in Taiwan were arranged hierarchically under Taiwan Jingū according to their geographic location. The one-village, one-shrine movement by the government in the 1930s aimed to standardize shrines as a public facility essential to a village. Lack of resources prevented this effort from being accomplished (Sai 1994, 140), but it demonstrates that the colonial government aimed to link each geographic administrative district with a shrine. In this manner, each village in Taiwan was also organized by its shrine into a hierarchy spanning the entire empire.

Yōhai, as discussed in previous chapters, was also a common practice in Taiwan. On Taiwan Jingū's annual festival, Taiwan residents were expected to visit the shrine or perform *yōhai* towards it if too far away, physically directing their bodies towards Taiwan's centre. *Yōhai* towards the Home Islands on national holidays such as Foundation Day and the Emperor's Birthday was also practiced by Taiwan Jingū and by residents of Taiwan directly (Sai 1994, 92). So while Shinto ritual affirmed a concentric metageography with Taiwan Jingū as a regional centre, it did not establish a hierarchy that prevented imperial subjects from directly facing towards the emperor and his ancestors.

Taiwan did not have a one-way view looking towards the centre. Imperial visits meant the centre looked towards Taiwan as well.[20] From 1901 to 1935, Taiwan Jingū received twenty-seven visits by imperial household members, including the Crown Prince, Korean imperial household members and multiple visits by relatives of Prince Yoshihisa. These visits were usually commemorated by the dignitary planting a tree at the shrine. These trees were marked with signposts and featured in photographs, meaning the visit would not easily be forgotten. Japanese nobles, government officials and military officers also hand-planted trees at the shrine, while more trees were donated, but not necessarily physically planted, by other citizens. While some of these trees were typical of the Home Islands, a majority were trees native to Taiwan. For example, Prince Naruhisa, a relative of Yoshihisa, planted a 'Home Islands pine' at the shrine in 1917, but the Crown Prince (the future Emperor Showa) during his visit in 1923 planted Aburasugi, an evergreen that is rarely found in Japan, but native to Taiwan and South China (Taiwan Jinja Shamusho Hensan 1935, 83–9).[21] The vocabulary of colonialism in Japanese often invokes the idea of planting[22] and the imperial household members were literally breaking the ground and planting trees at Taiwan Jingū. These trees, representative of the island, became part of the national ecology.

An affirmation of Japanese time

Following the same pattern previously seen at Kashihara Jingū and Sapporo Jinja, Taiwan Jingū affirmed a new sense of modern Japanese time. As seen in Chapter 2, Emperor Jinmu's enthronement was chosen as the start of Japanese progressive History. Prince Yoshihisa's southern progress echoed the pioneer spirit ascribed to Jinmu, enduring battles and hardships to bring order to the land. Jinmu was the first pioneer in his Eastward expedition from Himuka to Yamato. Shima Yoshitake as the Pioneer Magistrate had made his northern journey from Hakodate to Ishikari to found the northern capital of Sapporo. And Prince Yoshihisa began Japan's southern advance by travelling from Keelung to Tainan. The occupation of Tainan and the death of Yoshihisa marked, if not the island's entry into History, then at least into modern 'civilization'.

The imperial calendar counting linear time from Jinmu's enthronement was, like in the rest of Japan, used in Taiwan. This calendar was issued through the Jingū Hōsaikai but was distributed by Taiwan Jingū and local shrines. While it was useful thanks to its listing of official government holidays, it was unpopular with many Taiwan residents since it omitted marking the 'superstitious' auspicious and inauspicious days traditionally used. In 1914, the Taiwan Jinja Shin'en-kai, a semi-governmental organization associated with Taiwan Jingū, began publishing the Taiwan Folk Calendar. This calendar was largely based on the Jingū calendar, but added in only the auspicious days as 'harmless' superstitions (Sai 1994, 195). But it failed to gain significant popularity among Taiwan residents. It was not until 1932 that the Jingū calendar, paired with the Jingū *taima*, began to be strongly pushed by Taiwan Shintoists. While the Jingū calendar never gained mass popularity in Taiwan, the 2600th anniversary of Jinmu's enthronement and the start of linear time were occasioned by major renovations utilizing volunteering labour at Taiwan Jingū. Furthermore, many of the events held as a part of the 2600th anniversary celebrations involved shrines, such as the passing of a sacred flame received from Kashihara Jingū from shrine to shrine in Taiwan (Kaneko 2018, 312). So even if Taiwan residents lacked a Jingū calendar, they would be made aware of Japanese linear time by visiting the shrine.

Besides linear time, Taiwan Jingū and other shrines reinforced a new sense of cyclical time. The colonial government's yearly cycle of holidays, like in the Home Islands, utilized the solar calendar and was based around shrine and imperial ritual. This was an important break from the pre-modern lunisolar calendar marked with local temple festivals that was standard previous to Japanese rule. The yearly cycle of holidays united Taiwan's measurement of time with the Home Islands. However, two festivals were added into this cycle: Dominion Day (Shisei Kinenbi) and the Taiwan Jinja Festival (Taiwan Jinja-sai). Dominion Day, which commemorated the start of Japanese rule on 17 June, formed a fifth 'season', added to the 'four seasons' (*shidaisetsu*) celebrated in the Home Islands (Sai 1994, 194).[23] Taiwan Jinja Festival on 28 October marked the shrine's annual festival. These two new holidays – one shrine-based and the other rule-based – were both celebrated with government and shrine ceremonies, which communicated little distinction between shrine and civic rites. Taiwan Jingū's festival also placed Taiwan on the imperial calendar (Figure 5.2). Just as 15 June was marked as Sapporo Jinja's festival day, 28 October was marked as the festival day of Taiwan Jingū on the Jingū calendar, issued across the empire. Thus Taiwan was included into the empire's cycle of time.

Finally, Taiwan Jingū helped instil a new sense of time. Like other government institutions, Taiwan Jingū operated on a strict clock-based schedule. But Taiwan was differentiated from the Home Islands by the creation of a new time zone. When Japan took possession of Taiwan, the time zone Western Standard Time was created to govern Taiwan and Western Okinawa, while Standard Time was renamed Central Standard Time.[24] Thus the periphery literally defined the centre. Although Taiwan was aligned with the Japanese linear and annual cycle of time, it was not aligned with the Home Islands to the minute. The practical benefits of matching daily time with solar noon aligned with the early priorities of the Governor-General of focusing on economic concerns and separating Taiwan from the Home Islands as a colony. But this changed in

1937 when priorities shifted towards incorporating Taiwan as an integral part of Japan. Not coincidentally, this was also when the Tokyo government began promoting mass 'rule-by-time' practices, including timed *yōhai*.[25] While the government and Taiwan Jingū had long used *yōhai* to promote a new sense of Japanese space, its use of *yōhai* to promote a central Japanese time began only in the late 1930s.

An affirmation of Japanese ethics

Taiwan Jingū promoted a new sense of Japanese ethics to Taiwan residents. This was especially complicated because of the layered nature of Japanese morality. As Japan's role as leader of Asia was often rationalized by invoking its shared culture and language, Japanese administrators could not dismiss the entirety of Taiwan's Chinese culture as antiquated or barbaric like European colonialists could (Allen 2012, 8).[26] Modern Japanese ethics heavily drew from Confucian ethics and, as discussed below, Shinto ritual shared many similarities with the ritual of Taiwanese shrine-mausoleums.[27] Taiwan Jingū, while maintaining Shinto as the most civilized form of ritual, did not attempt to stamp out all Chinese customs. The shrine's *komainu* statues were done in a Chinese, rather than Japanese, style[28] and a look at its enshrinement ritual and first annual festival in 1901, attended by approximately 65,000 people over the two days, further reveals the inclusion of Chinese elements at the shrine. Formal attendees include those in Chinese formal wear. Baron Matsudaira gave a speech in formal Chinese. Chinese poems were also offered to the shrine. Furthermore, chief ritualist Yamaguchi usually composed Chinese language summaries of the shrine's major ceremonies, which were included in the mainly Japanese language Record of Taiwan Jinja (Taiwan Jinja Shamusho Hensan, 1935, 49–66).

Taiwan Jingū often utilized Chinese concepts to explain modern Japanese morality not as a foreign imposition, but as an evolution of classical morality. The Record of Taiwan Jinja's editors reinterpret the Warring States period 'Roots-Leaves Flower-Fruit' theory to explain Shinto as the root of morality, a sort of 'higher state' (Josephson-Storm 2017, 93), while allowing for Confucianism to serve as the branches and leaves. They also attributed the Taiwan Islanders' excellent civic obedience, such as demonstrated by religious leaders' attendance at shrine rites, to the island's Confucian culture (Taiwan Jinja Shamusho Hensan 1935, 5–7).[29] Taiwan Jingū also set the standard for shrines as sites for venerating heroes of the state. A majority of shrines in Taiwan enshrined the same kami as Taiwan Jingū. By aligning Shinto shrines as the equivalent to mausoleums, it emphasized Shinto's connection to the state. This kept Shinto shrines' position tightly tied to state ritual.

Like at Kashihara Jingū, Taiwan Jingū became a major site for 'hands-on citizenship training' (Ruoff 2010, 5). Not only did the successive renovation projects of Taiwan Jingū require significant donations and volunteer labour, but at least in 1924, nineteen different community, work or school groups were making monthly or bimonthly visits to clean the shrine, perform reverence and listen to lectures. Another eleven groups helped with the preparations before festivals (Taiwan Jinja Shamusho Hensan 1935, 123-4). As the general protector of Taiwan, Taiwan Jingū was the most prominent example of this, but volunteer service at one's local shrine was common across Taiwan for school children. Thus Taiwan Jingū took an active role in adapting Taiwanese Confucian traditions to make Shinto shrines more understandable to Taiwanese Islanders in addition to serving as a moral training ground like shrines in the Home Islands.

Taiwan Jingū and religion

Many modern shrines began with a connection to the semi-religious Shinto sects born from the Great Promulgation Campaign. Kashihara Jingū was connected to the Unebi Kashihara Kyōkai. Sapporo Jinja's ritualists conducted rituals for Jingū-kyō and the Shinto Secretariat. By the time Taiwan Jingū was established, the concept of religion and the location of shrines into the legally secular sphere had already been established. Taiwan Jingū's chief ritualist, Yamaguchi, like Sapporo Jinja's chief ritualist Ōnuki, held a licence as a teacher of Jingū-kyō. But the sect had already been disbanded by 1901 when the Taiwan Jingū was founded. So Taiwan Jingū lacked the early connections to the Great Promulgation Campaign many modern shrines in the Home Islands did.

The introduction to the Record of Taiwan Jinja, first written in 1921, specifically differentiates shrines from religion. It explains that shrines surpass religiousness. It argues that Westerners may have defined Japan's ritual as 'religion' (*rerijon*) previously, but then cites two Western scholars[30] who by studying Shinto realized that Shinto's spirit lay in filial piety and national spirit. It backs up this argument by describing religion (*shūkyō*) as international, while shrines remain inseparable from the Japanese state (Taiwan Jinja Shamusho Hensan 1935, 3). The foundation of Taiwan Jingū and most other shrines in Taiwan in a top-down manner by the government, and the close connection between shrines, Shinto ritual and state ceremonies supported the definition of shrines as exclusively patriotic sites.

However, the relation of Taiwanese temples and mausoleums to the Japanese secular state had yet to be resolved. Half a century earlier, the Meiji government began dividing up the pre-modern traditions of Japan into the spheres of the secular, religious and superstitious, and by 1890, Japan had been established as a secular nation-state. After Taiwan became a Japanese colony, the Japanese government was faced with the similar task of reorganizing Taiwan's pre-modern traditions into those same three categories. However, it was not until the 1930s, when the movement towards treating Taiwan by the same standards as the Home Islands began, that efforts to change the daily customs of Taiwan Islanders started in earnest. This began with the National Customs Promotion Council (Minpū Sakkō Kyōgikai), but the government policies that left the deepest impression were the Seichō Improvement and Temple Reorganization movements beginning in 1934. Taiwan Jingū did not have a direct part in these movements, but its ritualists were members of or in discussion with the government's Shrine and Temple Division. So it is helpful to look at Shintoists' part in these movements.

The imperialization movement is often described as the forced assimilation of Taiwan Islanders to Home Island customs. But for Taiwan Shintoists, the goal was to create good imperial subjects, something that was not yet entirely accomplished even in the Home Islands. Taiwan Islanders traditionally maintained a ceremonial table called the *seichō* in their homes that served as the equivalent to Home Islanders' *kamidana*, and *butsudan*, where Shinto *taima* and Buddhist ancestral tablets are kept, respectively. In Taiwan, the family's ancestral tablets, statues of the kami and buddhas and offerings were arranged on the *seichō*, with picture scrolls hung up behind it. The *seichō* improvement movement began in 1934 with local governments encouraging or forcing families to remove Chinese elements from the *seichō*. In place, the *seichō* would be used as a *kamidana* and *butsudan*. The move to include patriotic scrolls and add the Jingū *taima* to the *seichō* was relatively successful, but the Seichō Improvement movement was unpopular among Taiwan Islanders. Although Shintoists were open to including Taiwanese kami into Shinto and thus allowing them to be kept on the *seichō*, many local governments advocated the ceremonial burning of all the statues due to their Chinese appearance (Sai 1994, 207).

The treatment of ancestral tablets is of particular interest. The aim of local governments was to rid the *seichō* of Chinese elements; thus, the tablets needed to be converted into a Japanese style. Most families who converted chose a Japanese Buddhist style. But the Shrine Ritualist Association promoted a 'national-style' of ancestral tablets, that is, a Shinto style (Sai 1994, 213). After the 1870s, shrine ritualists were forbidden from conducting funerals, and association with the recent dead was reserved for the religious sphere. Yet the patriotic dead were slowly incorporated into the domain of shrines, from the establishment of the special imperial shrine category in 1872, to Yasukuni Jinja's conversion into a shrine in 1879, to the eventual transformation of all *shōkon-sha* into shrines in 1939. In Taiwan, the location of the patriotic dead at shrines occurred early on. Prince Yoshihisa was enshrined as a kami only a few years after his death, and Kenkō Jinja, which enshrined Taiwan's patriotic dead, was established in 1928. Thus Taiwan Shintoists were more ready to concern themselves with matters concerning the recent dead. The 'national-style' of ancestral tablets divided ancestors into the categories of pre-Japanese rule and post-Japanese rule. Those in the pre-Japanese rule category were subjects of the Qing, and did not owe their loyalty to the Japan. But those in the post-Japanese rule category were Japanese subjects. This suggested that all imperial subjects – living and dead – were ideally patriotic supporters of the state.

In 1937, the Temple Reorganization movement began. It began as initiatives from local governments. Although the Governor-General issued guidelines cautioning prudence in late 1938, it treated the movement with implicit approval. The head of the Shrines and Temples Division, Kamura Masaharu, also wrote up guidelines for the movement. In it, he argued that Taiwanese mausoleums are the Chinese equivalent to Shinto shrines and suggested consolidating them into a single mausoleum or temple per village, much as the Meiji government had attempted during the Shrine Reorganization movement in the Home Islands. As a colonial official, he was not going so far as to defend local Taiwanese temples, but felt that converting them into shrines – rather than destroying them – would be more effective in cultivating good imperial subjects. Despite this, Kamura's proposal was not looked upon kindly by the Governor-General and he was dismissed from his post soon after submitting it (Sai 1994, 252).

In conclusion, the position of Taiwan Jingū and other official shrines in the secular sphere was accepted without much controversy in Taiwan. The government kept strict control of what sort of Shinto sites were recognized as shrines, and Taiwan Islanders, lacking pre-modern exposure to shrines, had little reason to contest the government's definition. Taiwan Shintoists also saw the recent dead and Taiwanese mausoleums as potentially within the same sphere as Shinto shrines. However, Shinto-style ancestral tablets were not popular among either Taiwan or Home Islanders, while inclusion of Taiwanese mausoleums as Shinto shrines became increasingly controversial as anti-Chinese sentiment arose among Taiwan's central and local governments in the 1930s. The next section looks at Kaizan Jinja, the only Taiwanese mausoleum to become an official shrine.

Kaizan Jinja: Taiwanese kami as Japanese kami

The legend of Prince Yoshihisa, which told of a son of Japan driving a foreign power from Taiwan, only to perish from malaria in Tainan shortly after victory, bore resemblance to another Taiwanese legend. Two hundred years earlier, Koxinga was born in Hizen Province (now Nagasaki Pref.) to a Japanese mother and Chinese father (Figure 4.2). As a young man, he became an official under the Ming dynasty, but was forced to flee to Taiwan after the Ming were deposed. In 1662, Koxinga drove the Dutch from Taiwan and established the Kingdom of Tungning in southern Taiwan. Four months later, Koxinga died of malaria.

Figure 4.2 Koxinga: A statue of Koxinga in Ming period dress remains enshrined at Koxinga Shrine (former Kaizan Jinja). (Author's photograph.)

Kaizan Jinja, the first shrine officially recognized in Taiwan, traces its history back to the mausoleum Koxinga's followers established for him, Kāitái Shèngwáng Miào (Jp. Kaitai Seiō Byō). After a mere twenty years, the Kingdom of Tungning surrendered to the Qing dynasty and the shrine was renamed Kāishān Wáng Miào (Jp. Kaizan Ō Byō). In 1875, the Qing incorporated the site into its state ritual, renaming the site Yánpíngjùn Wáng Cí (Jp. Enpeigun Ō Shi) (Yamada 1915, 9). In 1896, after Japan took control of Taiwan, the new Japanese governor of Tainan, Isogai Seizō, immediately requested that the site be recognized as a Shinto shrine. Isogai requested the shrine be called Kaitai Jinja (lit. 'Opening-Taiwan Shrine') and be ranked a national shrine. Although the national government granted Isogai's request to recognize the site as Taiwan's first Shinto shrine, it rejected his suggestions for name and rank. Instead, the site was called Kaizan Jinja and it was given the middling rank of a prefectural shrine.

The typical site chosen for a modern shrine was on virgin land located in a majestic natural location, particularly a site overlooking the town the shrine was to protect. Shrines might also be founded upon the site of a significant event in the life of its enshrined kami, such as Kashihara Jingū at the site of Emperor Jinmu's palace, or Tainan Jinja at the site of Prince Yoshihisa's death. So why did the Japanese government recognize this site as a shrine? Kaizan Jinja was likely recognized for two main reasons. First, Taiwanese mausoleums shared a significant number of similarities with shrines, encouraging Taiwan Shintoists to see them as already a sort of Shinto facility. Second, Kaizan Jinja was a popular site among Taiwan Islanders and the legend of Koxinga could be utilized to bolster the legitimacy of Japanese rule.

Taiwan Shintoists saw Taiwanese mausoleums as sharing the same character as Shinto shrines. Yamaguchi Tōru, chief ritualist of Taiwan Jingū from 1901 to 1938, expected Taiwan Islanders to respect shrines and likewise Home Islanders to respect shrine-mausoleums. Furthermore, he wrote in 1934 that shrines and shrine-mausoleums were based on the same 'oriental morality'. The Governor-General of Taiwan seems to have acted on this view. Government officials made formal visits to some shrine-mausoleums and the government provided monetary offerings to mausoleums dedicated to Confucius (Sai 1994, 44). In 1934, the semi-governmental Taiwan Shrine Ritualists Association recommended that since the folk kami aid the Japanese kami, the veneration of local kami should gradually be converted into the Japanese style (Sai 1994, 203). Meanwhile, the previously mentioned Kamura Masaharu, who was Head of the Shrines and Temples Section from 1930 to 1938 and a board member of the

Taiwan Ritualists Association, wrote that 'Temple-mausoleums (Jp. *jibyō*, Ch. *sìmiào*) are the shrines of the ethnic Han who came to this island, and shrines are the temple-mausoleums of the ethnic Japanese' (Sai 1994, 250). In 1942, the governor of Chūreki District in Shinchiku (Hsinchu) Prefecture, Miyazaki Naokatsu, advocated that the kami of temple-mausoleums are not superstitions (*inshi jakyō*),[31] but that much like how Taiwan residents became Japanese citizens when Japan started governing Taiwan, Taiwanese kami became Japanese kami (Sai 1994, 265–6).

As Inoue Nobutaka has noted, East Asia shares a 'Chinese religio-cultural sphere' (Inoue 2003, 7), and thus shrines and shrine-mausoleums share many similar customs. The terms 'small shrine' (*shi* or *hokora*) and 'mausoleum' (*byō*) are both used in Japan to refer to Shinto facilities. During this period in the Home Islands, *hokora* usually referred to small Shinto shrines unrecognized by the government. The term 'mausoleum' was used less in the Home Islands, but some shrines had historically used the term.[32] And as will be seen in Chapter 6, the term 'mausoleum' was also used in the puppet state of Manchukuo to refer to its main Shinto facilities. Beyond vocabulary, shrines and shrine-mausoleums shared customs, including the issuing of talismans and the parading of the kami annually through the streets of its domain in a palanquin. While Shintoists and colonial officials generally saw Chinese customs as less civilized than modern Shinto customs, shrines and shrine-mausoleums were seen as located within the same category. This was in contrast to temples and churches which venerated the buddhas or worshipped the Christian God.

In Hokkaido, the Japanese government was particular about which Shinto sites they allowed the status of shrine. *Sorei-sha*, *shōkon-sha* and Sect Shinto churches (*kyōkai*) were all Shinto sites, but not Shinto shrines. The term 'shrine' (*jinja*) did not apply to just any Shinto site of kami-veneration, but only those which could fulfil certain criteria (Sai 1994, 132). And more was required of a shrine the higher it was ranked within the shrine ranking system. Taiwan's definition as a mere colony perhaps caused the government to be less strict in the early years, but the impetus to allow Kaizan Jinja to be ranked not just as a shrine, but as a *prefectural* shrine, was likely the advantages of transforming a popular site into a place for Japanese state ritual. The site had previously been designated a site of Qing state ritual. Japanese elites in Taiwan often admired high Chinese culture, even while claiming a more civilized status (Allen 2012, 102). So the renaming of Enpeigun Ō Shi to Kaizan Jinja drew a line of continuity between the state ritual of the Qing and the state ritual of Japan. A history of the shrine written in 1915 repeatedly emphasized that the site had been included within Qing state ritual

(Yamada 1915). Thus Shinto shrines were positioned as a more civilized version of something with which Taiwan Islanders were already familiar.

The legend of Koxinga also formed a mythic narrative that helped legitimize Japanese rule of Taiwan. Koxinga was already a popular hero of Taiwan. Koxinga and his mother, Tagawa, were known in both Taiwan and Japan for their loyalty to the vanquished Ming dynasty, with Tagawa said to have committed suicide rather than surrender. Furthermore, Koxinga was lauded for driving out the Dutch colonists from Taiwan and starting Taiwan's development (Kaneko 2018, 118). In 1909, when Diet representative Sasaki Yasugorō criticized the Taiwan Governor-General on its brutal policy against the Takasago, he invoked Koxinga as a model example of good governance (Barclay 2018, 104). Photobooks including the shrine described Koxinga as the founding father of Taiwan's colonization (Yamazaki 1939, 39), and the 1915 history of the shrine praises Koxinga for implementing the farmer-soldier system of colonization in Taiwan, the same system which formed such a significant part of the colonization narrative of Hokkaido. While not directly compared, the similarities between the legends of Koxinga and Prince Yoshihisa united the two figures. Indeed, a shrine dedicated solely to Prince Yoshihisa – Tainan Jinja – was erected only a few blocks from Kaizan Jinja, on the site of the prince's death.

Kaizan Jinja, as a pre-existing shrine-mausoleum that was recognized as a Shinto shrine, was not typical. The site's Fujian-style buildings were not replaced; the Chinese-style statue of Koxinga that served as the central object of veneration was not removed. For the first year, Zhèng Fútián (Jp. Tei Fukuda) – the monk who had looked after the shrine since the Qing incorporated it into state ritual – continued to serve at the shrine, now as chief ritualist. Despite this, both the new Home Islander residents of Tainan and the central government in Tokyo recognized the site as a Shinto shrine. While in the early years physical changes to the shrine were few, efforts were made to modernize the shrine's activities. The fruit market run by the shrine was ended for 'sanitary reasons', and the shrine stopped accepting the payment previously given for personal prayers (Yamada 1915, 37). The economic support system for the site was also modernized. In the Qing period, the shrine's festival expenses were supported by the six neighbourhoods nearby the shrine, and it kept only periodic festivals. But as a prefectural shrine under the modern shrine ranking system, the site incurred a plethora of new costs, including regular festivals and the support of a full-time ritualist. Its former six-neighbourhoods system was replaced by a shrine board, made up of three Taiwan Islanders and three Home Islanders, while the gratitude money was replaced with funds from the government and donations drawn from not only the traditional six neighbourhoods but also the entire Tainan prefecture.

Despite these modernization efforts, Kaizan Jinja still included many Taiwanese elements. Dedicatory performances at the shrine's major festivals included local-style theatre and martial arts. Furthermore, film footage of the shrine's '270th Anniversary' in 1930 shows the kami paraded along the street in a Japanese-style palanquin, preceded by formally dressed Shinto ritualists and attendants in historical Japanese dress. But as the procession continues, the solemn beat of the taiko drum is replaced by the cacophony of traditional Taoist music while Taoist-style floats, a Taoist-style palanquin and Chinese banners form the bulk of the parade (University of South Carolina 2019). This incorporation of Taoist/Chinese customs into the Shinto ritual at Kaizan Jinja was a visible example of how Shinto was the modernized form of 'oriental morality'.

This also helped transform Taoist/Chinese customs from being foreign superstitions that need to be stamped out into local variations subsumed within the broader tradition of Shinto. In other words, Kaizan Jinja worked to 'Shintoize' these non-Home Island customs. The construction of 'Shinto' as a system has a long history of incorporating previously disparate elements into shrine life (Breen and Teeuwen 2010, 221). The pre-eminence of local traditions at shrines, even after they were united into a single system, has also been a characteristic of Shrine Shinto (Kasulis 2004, 54–6). But modern shrines were in the position to not only Shintoize the Taiwanese customs they incorporated, but to 'imperialize' them. By their veneration at a prefectural shrine, the Taiwanese kami of Kaizan Jinja did not merely become Shinto kami, they became Japanese kami.

As discussed in Chapter 1, there was a significant shift in the conception of overseas shrines beginning in the 1910s from a pioneer theology to a universalized theology (Suga 2014, 141–5). This shift influenced the development of Kaizan Jinja. The first major change to Kaizan Jinja was in 1915, when the site underwent a major renovation project. The site until now had remained unchanged from 1875, when the Qing rebuilt the site using the Fujian style of architecture typical in Taiwan (Kaneko 2018, 118). The renovation project repaired these buildings, keeping the original architecture. It also added a purification basin and a ritualist's residence, as well as expanded the garden to evoke the more typical layout of a Shinto shrine. But perhaps the most significant change was the addition of a Japanese-style pavilion in the centre of the shrine's courtyard, where ritual could be performed. Many postcards of Kaizan Jinja featured this pavilion, which, framed by trees, largely obscures the Fujian-style building. However, other postcards featured the front of Kaizan Jinja, with a view of the Fujian-style

Three-Rivers-Gate. Sometimes the Japanese-style *torii* is also in frame. Thus until 1936, Kaizan Jinja seems to have included a significant amount of both Home Islands and Chinese elements at it. The film of Kaizan Jinja's annual festival mentioned previously was filmed in 1930. It included Japanese taiko drums, traditionally dressed Shinto ritualists and a drunkenly weaving Japanese-style palanquin, even while a majority of the procession featured cheerful Taoist-style music, multiple bouncing Chinese palanquins, Taoist-style effigies and Chinese flags.

However, Kaizan Jinja's heavy Chinese influence did likely prevent the government from raising the shrine's rank from one of the various shrines to a national or imperial ranked shrine. The Tainan prefectural government's desire for an imperial or national shrine was instead fulfilled with the construction of Tainan Jinja. This new shrine, located a few blocks from Kaizan Jinja, was constructed on the site of Prince Yoshihisa's death. It was granted the exceptional permission to venerate solely Prince Yoshihisa, as opposed to the usual combination of the prince along with the Three Pioneer Kami. Tainan Jinja was given the high rank of intermediate imperial shrine and designated the protector shrine of Tainan.

In 1936, the same year the imperialization movement started in Taiwan, Kaizan Jinja began a major renovation project to transfer the shrine to a Home Islands–style site. The Fujian-style shrine was preserved as a part of the shrine's garden, but an entirely new Home Islands–style shrine was built next to it. Completed in 1941, the shrine used the *nagare*-style typical of Shinto shrines in the Home Islands (Aoi 2014, 109; Kaneko 2015, 136). Although the Japanese government was earlier open to including Chinese style customs at Shinto shrines, and thus legitimizing them as permissible in the public sphere, the anti-Chinese trend in the late 1930s began rejecting these customs as inappropriate in the public sphere, to be discouraged as uncivilized.

Kenkō Jinja: Dying for Japanese Taiwan

Kaizan Jinja was not the only shrine in Taiwan to display Shinto as something not limited to Home Islands customs. While Kaizan Jinja was generally treated as other Shinto Shrines, Kenkō Jinja, founded on 14 July 1928, was often remarked upon for its unusual style. Postcards pointed out its 'distinctive architecture' (Kaneko 2018, 105), while the British Japanologist Richard Posonby-Fane wrote that no one 'would suppose it to be a shrine' and that it 'resembles somewhat a mosque' (Allen 2012, 165).

Kenkō Jinja traces its origin back to 1902. That year a *shōkon* ritual was held in Tainan to honour the 'glorious spirits' who had died for the sake of Japanese Taiwan. Six years later, in 1908, another *shōkon* ritual was held, this time in Taihoku, the capital of Taiwan, and the tradition of an annual *shōkon* ritual in both Tainan and Taihoku began (Taiwan Sōtokufu 1928, 1). The Governor-General began making plans to build a permanent *shōkon-sha* in 1925, to commemorate thirty years of Japanese rule. A general protector shrine and a *shōkon-sha* were both seen as essential parts of a modern Japanese capital. Money for the site was included within the Governor-General's budget in 1926 and a site within the Taihoku Botanical Garden was designated. On 30 April 1926 – commemorating the date of the annual Taihoku *shōkon* ceremony – ground was broken for the site. Despite this, construction stalled and it was not until 1928 that the cenotaph was completed, now officially ranked not as a *shōkon-sha*, but as a shrine (*jinja*).[33]

Kenkō Jinja was unusual in three main ways. First, the site was planned as a *shōkon-sha*, but was ranked as a shrine. As discussed in Chapter 3, *shōkon-sha* had become permanent sites utilizing Shinto rites to venerate the war dead, a ritual which had evolved from the new custom of temporarily inviting the spirits of the war dead to pacify them. *Shōkon* sites' close connections to the recent dead and the only temporary residence of the spirits originally differentiated them from shrines. *Shōkon-sha* were merged into a special category of *gokoku* shrines only in 1939. At the time of Kenkō Jinja's foundation in 1928, Yasukuni Jinja was the only *shōkon-sha* that had been transformed into a shrine. The Taiwan Governor-General's desire to venerate a wide variety of people who had contributed to Japanese Taiwan, in addition to the war dead, is probably why a shrine was decided on over a *shōkon-sha*. Taiwan was also a colony, not yet subject to the same standards and rules as the Home Islands. Furthermore, a close connection between shrines and relatively recent heroes (rather than kami from antiquity) had previously been established in Taiwan. Thus it is likely that all three of these factors contributed to the unusual circumstance of establishing Kenkō Jinja as a shrine dedicated to the collective recent dead. While Yasukuni Jinja was given the rank of special imperial shrine – a new category of shrines specifically for those who had died for the emperor – Kenkō Jinja was only recognized as a shrine. It was not given a specific rank, but left as an unranked shrine.

Second, the enshrined kami of Kenkō Jinja included not only the war dead such as was standard at Yasukuni Jinja and Home Islands *shōkon-sha*, but was expanded to include all who 'gave their life for this island's communal good' (Taiwan Sōtokufu 1928, 2). While the largest category of kami at the time of the shrine's foundation was army personnel, also enshrined were civil officials, government officials and educators. Members of neighbourhood watch associations, usually Taiwan Islanders, were also included as a specific category eligible for enshrinement. Thus the kami of Kenkō Jinja included not only Home Islanders but also Taiwan Islanders and Takasago.

Third, and perhaps most commented upon, was the shrine's architecture (Figure 4.3). The site, like many other government buildings, was designed by Ide Kaoru, chief architect for the Taiwan Governor-General. He aimed to create a combination of Western and Asian architecture styles that was suited to Taiwan's particular social and geographic position. It was built of ferroconcrete to withstand termites and evoke the grandeur of Western stone buildings, with a Chinese-style tiled roof and an Indic mausoleum dome.[34] The *torii* gate was also adorned with a tiled roof that evoked traditional Chinese gates (Jp. *haibō*, Ch. *páifāng*) more than the *shinmei* gates popular at Shinto shrines during this period. The inside of the main shrine kept to a 'pure Japanese-style' of architecture (Taiwan Sōtokufu 1928, 2), although contemporary photographs make this description debatable. While Ide's design was controversial, he argued that the unusual nature of the kami of Kenkō Jinja warranted the multicultural design (Kaneko 2015, 21).

Kenkō Jinja provides an example of the 'European-Japanese hybridity' (Allen 2012, 96) that typified the Japanese secularity. At Kenkō Jinja, Home Islands norms were not forced upon Taiwan residents. Rather, the shrine was an effort to promote a modern Japanese method of venerating the glorious dead that, to paraphrase the Meiji government's Charter Oath of 1868, amalgamated the best of elements sought from throughout the world.[35] Thus the shrine would be suitable to the local situation while remaining universal to all imperial subjects. Kenkō Jinja did this by expanding the definition of what a Shinto shrine could be. It provided an example of a shrine that used Western and Chinese architecture, and that venerated kami who, although imperial subjects, were not necessarily from the Home Islands. Similar to how Kaizan Jinja expanded the definition of Shinto shrines to include Chinese customs, Kenkō Jinja incorporated Chinese, Indic and Western elements as legitimate variations within Shinto. Kenkō Jinja's focus on a multiethnic empire, rather than strict assimilation to Home Islands customs, is an example of how the Governor-General and Taiwan Shintoists did not necessarily equate Home Island customs as the one-and-only method for being Japanese.

The broadening of Shinto's definition at Kenkō Jinja also worked to subsume a Taiwanese identity into the broader identity of Japanese as a local variation. That is, 'Taiwanese' was treated as a category within the broader category of

Figure 4.3 Kenkō Jinja: Designed by Ide Kaoru, its architecture was designed as a mix of Western, Chinese and Japanese styles. (Taiwan Sōtokufu Kōtsū-kyoku Tetsudō-bu 1935, 57.)

'Japanese'. Kenkō Jinja was a Japanese shrine, located within the empire-wide hierarchy of the shrine ranking system. But its architecture and kami made it distinctly a Taiwanese-Japanese shrine. The glorious dead enshrined there were also of Chinese, Takasago and Home Islander descent, with the home town of each kami recorded along with his name and occupation in the shrine record. The shrine record in 1928 lists all the kami by name, but as the number of kami increased, the key organizational information became the home town of the enshrined (Kenkō Jinja Shamusho 1940). Despite this, the Home Islands are not given precedence: the list is organized geographically from north to south, starting with Hokkaido. In other words, Taiwan-born kami are listed as a type of Japanese kami, undifferentiated from those born in Tokyo or the Home Islands. Likewise, the Chinese architectural elements of the shrine became a type of Japanese architecture, just as the Imperial Crown Style of architecture transformed originally Western architectural elements into a type of Japanese architecture.[36]

Kenkō Jinja, as a cenotaph, also promoted a modified morality, based on Taiwanese precedents, but adapted to serve the imperial state's purpose. The Confucian virtues of loyalty and filial piety were upheld, but the family state with the emperor at its centre was cast the object worthy of that devotion. While Kaizan Jinja anachronistically transformed the Taiwanese hero Koxinga into the pioneer Japanese liberator of Taiwan, Kenkō Jinja raised up the everyday residents of Taiwan who helped solidify Japanese rule into national heroes, aiding not necessarily the war effort, but rather the colonial project in both its military and civil aspects. This provided role models to which current residents could aspire, and the list of the enshrined was continually added to throughout the shrine's existence.

Taiwan Gokoku Jinja: Dying for Taiwanese Japan

Kenkō Jinja, whose enshrined kami included the war dead, had similarities to the public *shōkon-sha* found in the Home Islands. But its unusual features and lack of defined rank separated it from the standard system of war dead commemoration in Japan. After the national government incorporated *shōkon-sha* into the shrine system in 1939 by ordering them to convert into *gokoku* shrines, the Taiwan Governor-General took this opportunity to set aside a budget for a new *shōkon-sha*. An 8.6-hectare site, later expanded to 12.7 hectares, to the east of Taiwan Jingū was chosen (Kaneko 2018, 107). The national treasury contributed 200,000 yen while the shrine's semi-governmental supporting organization collected another 2600,000 yen in donations to finance the shrine's construction. On 23 May 1942, the enshrinement ritual, witnessed by 500 government and military officials including Governor-General Hasegawa Kiyoshi and a thousand bereaved relatives, enshrined 9,226 war dead.[37]

The decision to build Taiwan Gokoku Jinja, rather than renovate Kenkō Jinja, is another example of the gradual shift from a pioneer theology to a universalized theology. This shift was not exclusive to shrines, but was a part of a wider trend towards treating the outer territories by the same standards as the Home Islands. Particularly as the Second Sino-Japanese war dragged on and Taiwan became a key area for Japan's southern advance, antipathy towards Chinese customs grew even while the necessity of gaining Taiwan residents' support for the war increased. This led to increasing rights for non–Home Islanders, but also lowered the toleration for non–Home Island customs. Kenkō Jinja, controversial from its foundation for its use of Chinese and Western visual elements over Home Islands-style shrine architecture, appeared increasingly out of line.

A comparison between Taiwan Gokoku Jinja and Kenkō Jinja is enlightening. First, while both sites were conceived as *shōkon-sha* venerating the glorious dead, they had different ranks. Kenkō Jinja was unranked, leaving it without clear connections to other shrines within the ranking system, but Taiwan Gokoku

Jinja was a *gokoku* shrine. As discussed in the previous chapter, *gokoku* shrines were equated with the shrine ranking system, but formed their own category distinct from, but equivalent to, the various shrines. Since Taiwan was legally a colony, Taiwan Gokoku Jinja could not be a nationally designated *gokoku* shrine like Hokkaidō Gokoku Jinja, but it was designated by the Governor-General. Thus Taiwan Gokoku Jinja was connected horizontally to other *gokoku* shrines across the empire, and vertically within the shrine ranking system as equivalent to prefectural shrines. Furthermore, as the unusual Western-Chinese-Japanese style of Kenkō Jinja's architecture made the site distinctive of Taiwan, Taiwan Gokoku Jinja's architecture, *myōjin torii* gate and *nagare*-style buildings followed the standard pattern of *gokoku* shrines across the empire. The shrine's seal – a stylized cherry blossom embedded with the character *tai*, for Taiwan – also followed a common pattern among *gokoku* shrines.

Second, the eligibility of the 'glorious dead' to be enshrined at Kenkō Jinja and Taiwan Gokoku Jinja differed. While Kenkō Jinja included a wide variety of recent dead including civilians such as educators and specifically Taiwanese categories such as neighbourhood watch members, the enshrined kami of Taiwan Gokoku Jinja was limited to the local war dead already enshrined at Yasukuni Jinja. This did not specifically exclude non-Home Islanders. However, as Taiwan Islanders were banned from combat until 1942, very few non-Home Islanders could be enshrined. Of the almost 10,000 kami enshrined at Taiwan Gokoku Jinja's foundation, not a single one was a non-Home Islander. While at least one Takasago was enshrined there later (Sai 1994, 153), this is a significant difference from Kenkō Jinja.[38] Although new glorious dead continued to be added to Kenkō Jinja, the construction of Taiwan Gokoku Jinja specifically for the war dead also communicated that, among those who died for the emperor, those that died as soldiers and as a part of war were of particularly high moral value.

The connection of Taiwan Gokoku Jinja to Yasukuni Jinja and the larger network of *gokoku* shrines also made the enshrined kami less local and more national. At Kenkō Jinja, those enshrined were those perceived to have died for Japanese Taiwan. Thus they were praised for their direct aid to the (perceived) improvement of Taiwan, while this only indirectly improved the whole of Japan. But at Taiwan Gokoku Jinja, the enshrined kami most often died in the Sino-Japanese and Pacific wars. These wars were not a part of directly benefitting Taiwan as an island (and were often directly negative for Taiwan), but were part of the national ambition of Japan. In other words, Taiwan Gokoku Jinja venerated those who as a part of Taiwan died for Japan, while Kenkō Jinja venerated those who died for Taiwan as a part of Japan. Thus while both sites venerated patriotism, Taiwan Gokoku Jinja gave significantly less room for a local identity, even if subsumed within a larger national identity.

Although Taiwan Gokoku Jinja was incorporated into the national *gokoku* shrine network, its location in new imperial territory required broader eligibility criteria for enshrinement, as it did in Hokkaido. Typically the enshrinement of the glorious dead was limited to those war dead enshrined at Yasukuni Jinja whose registered home town was in that prefecture. But in Taiwan, like in Hokkaido, the large settler population meant many of the war dead who had resided there kept their registered home town within the Home Islands. This was compounded in Taiwan due to the ban on Taiwan Islanders and Takasago joining the imperial military as soldiers which was lifted only in 1942.[39] Thus Taiwan Gokoku Jinja enshrined not only those Yasukuni war dead whose registered home town was in Taiwan, but also those whose domicile was in Taiwan at the time of death, or those who, like Prince Yoshihisa, may have not lived in Taiwan, but died there.[40]

Third, it is significant that the site for Taiwan Gokoku Jinja was located directly adjacent to Taiwan Jingū. As seen in the previous chapter, shrines were required to avoided connection to the recent dead from the 1880s, but the patriotic dead were slowly incorporated as legitimate objects of veneration at shrines over the first half of the twentieth century. In Taiwan, however, shrines had a connection to the recent dead and the military – through the enshrinement of Prince Yoshihisa – from the foundation of Taiwan Jingū. Furthermore, by the 1940s the location of war memorials at Shinto shrines was no longer unusual. Neither was the construction of *gokoku* shrines adjacent to normal shrines unprecedented.[41] While Taiwan Gokoku Jinja's location was not unprecedented, the sandwiching of Taiwan Gokoku Jinja between Taiwan Jingū and its outer garden's sports arena practically combined them into one large site (Aoi 2014, 107). Thus Taiwan Gokoku Jinja took part in how Taiwan Jingū helped affirm a new sense of Japanese space and time and utilized the same methods. Furthermore, Taiwan Gokoku Jinja added emphasis to the Japanese morality that saw the pinnacle of the Confucian virtues of loyalty and filial piety exemplified in the war dead who died not merely for Japanese Taiwan but for the Empire of Japan as a whole.

Shinto beyond shrines

The four different shrines examined in this chapter each venerated a different kami. Taiwan Jingū was Taiwan's general protector shrine, venerating the Three Pioneer Kami and Prince Yoshihisa. Kaizan Jinja was originally a shrine-mausoleum dedicated to Koxinga while Kenkō Jinja and Taiwan Gokoku Jinja were established as *shōkon* style shrines venerating separate, but overlapping, groups of glorious dead. But these four shrines perhaps give an overly diverse impression of shrines in Taiwan. The vast majority of shrines were in practice miniature, local versions of Taiwan Jingū. They largely enshrined the same kami, utilizing the same architecture and celebrating the same festivals as Taiwan Jingū. Of the sixty-eight official shrines in Taiwan, just four of them – the three mentioned above in addition to Taihoku Inari Jinja – did not enshrine the Three Pioneer Kami and/or Prince Yoshihisa (Kaneko 2018, 385). The aim to establish a shrine systematically for each geographic administrative district, in combination with the trend for shrines in Taiwan to be established in a top-down manner by the local government, meant that shrines were less varied than in Hokkaido. This was even more true when compared to the Home Islands.

As discussed previously, the modern shrine ranking system organized Shinto shrines into a vertical and horizontal network, but the main enshrined kami formed another concentric hierarchy connecting shrines. The Three Pioneer Kami, as a newly named kami, meant that Sapporo Jinja was the first and parent shrine of the many shrines in Hokkaido which elected to enshrine the same kami. In a similar manner, Prince Yoshihisa (combined with the Three Pioneer Kami) was newly named as the kami for protecting Taiwan when he was enshrined at Taiwan Jingū. Thus nearly all shrines throughout the prefectures of Taiwan were connected back to Taiwan Jingū, located in the capital of Taiwan, as their parent shrine. These smaller shrines seemed to have largely followed the same practices that Taiwan Jingū used in communicating new senses of time, space and ethics to their communities.

The lack of variety in shrines in Taiwan, as compared to Hokkaido and the Home Islands, was due to a combination of reasons. First, the government had strict guidelines on what was necessary for a site to qualify as a shrine. When the Governor-General began its one village, one shrine policy in 1934, it also issued standards to preserve the dignity of sites that qualified as shrines. Thus a shrine was to be furnished with at least an oratory and main building, a purification basin, a shrine office and a *torii* gate, on approximately 1.5 hectares of land, amply planted with trees (Sai 1994, 132–3). Towns in Hokkaido often vied to improve their local shrines and thus raise the rank of both their shrine and village. But village life among Taiwan Islanders remained centred around Taiwanese temples and mausoleums. While donation drives in Hokkaido often exceeded their goal, local governments in Taiwan had considerably less success in drumming up financial enthusiasm for shrines. Thus the second and third reasons were a lack of financial resources and a lack of popular enthusiasm. Finally, the fourth reason was a lack of personnel. The Taiwan Shrine Ritualist Association made efforts to foster the education and training of Shinto ritualists, as well as average citizens, in Shinto rites, but this was not enough to solve the chronic ritualist shortage.

But Shinto was not limited to shrines. While Shinto shrines might have been the ideal site of state ritual, a wide variety of Shinto sites were established in Taiwan. Kaneko suggests that if we include shrines, *yōhai* sites, pre-shrines and unrecognized shrines, there may have been up to 500 such Shinto sites in Taiwan (Kaneko 2018, 383). Thus Shinto permeated many areas of daily life, from Shinto rituals at school, to Shinto sites located at sugar or sake factories where many residents worked, to the *yōhai* and *kamidana* rites performed at community centres (Sai 1994, 92), to commemorative sites for victims of work accidents, to popular sites for praying for maritime safety like Kotohira-sha. In other words, Shinto's role in Japanese Taiwan was far from limited to shrines. Shinto ritual was one essential part of learning to be a modern Japanese citizen, rather than rarefied conduct restricted to shrines.

Furthermore, the variety of Shinto facilities is one reason the subsumption of Taiwanese mausoleums into Shinto could be thinkable. There might be quite a difference between an official shrine and a shrine-mausoleum, but if Shinto is understood as a broad category that encompasses a spectrum of sites from grand *jingū* shrines to cenotaphs for the war dead to unrecognized factory shrines, the inclusion of shrine-mausoleums as Taiwanese-type Shinto sites is not difficult to imagine.

Shrines in the Takasago villages

Most shrines in Taiwan were positioned in communities made up of Home Islanders and Taiwan Islanders. These groups had a shared cultural heritage based on classical Chinese culture and had already experienced being ruled by a state, whether that was Japan or the Qing. In contrast until the twentieth century, the majority of Taiwan's mountainous landscape where the original Austronesian inhabitants of Taiwan, the Takasago, resided had remained outside of state control. Japan, however, was determined to bring the entire island under its rule. The Governor-General divided the Takasago into the two groups of 'raw barbarians' and 'mature barbarians', based on the historical Chinese view. This dividing line between raw and mature barbarians was largely defined by whether or not they were governable by the state (Barclay 2018, 212; Scott 2009, 28). The raw barbarians had successfully kept the Qing at arm's length and expected a similar relationship with the Japanese state. This led the Governor-General to set up a separate administration for governing the Takasago, which treated them as primitive peoples not yet ready for the rights of normal imperial subjects, and not yet able to fulfil normal subjects' duties like tax-paying.

The Taiwan Governor-General ended up having two contrasting views of the Takasago, and official policy seems to have slid between these two views as the priorities of the government changed. One view, held by officials such as Ministry of Civil Affair's councillor Mochiji Rokusaburō,[42] saw the Takasago as little better than animals who were obstacles standing in the way of properly extracting the island's natural resources (Barclay 2018, 222). The other view, held by officials such as the colony's first Chief of Civil Affairs Mizuno Jun, saw the Takasago as 'children of the emperor ... our brothers' and 'ethnic affines' to the Japanese (Barclay 2018, 83, 152): pure-hearted innocents who were often taken advantage of by unscrupulous Chinese merchants (Barclay 2018, 166). Modern shrines often embraced the idea that there existed a pure antiquity when people and kami lived in harmony. That idealized past had been corrupted over time, but Japan was evolving towards a return to that perfect past: towards an idealized modernity. If the Takasago were seen as ethnic affines of the Japanese who still maintained much of that antiquity's purity, they could relatively easily be taught to be good imperial subjects through 'the sacred virtue of brotherly love' (Kaneko 2018, 386), even while they needed protection from the corrupting influence of the 'greedy' Chinese residing in Taiwan.

Shinto shrines were seen as having an integral role in the project of modernization/imperialization, but the precise role shrines were to have in civilizing the Takasago was debated. Establishing a Shinto shrine, after all, was expensive. As discussed previously, a shrine (*jinja*) must have a full set of facilities along with an appropriately sized garden to preserve its dignity as a site for state ritual. Towns which could not afford to build a shrine could instead build a subsidiary shrine associated with its closest full shrine, or they could construct a pre-shrine. Pre-shrines were Shinto sites that resembled shrines except that they lacked the full facilities of one. In addition to serving as a less expensive version of a shrine, many Shinto sites located at schools or factories were recognized as pre-shrines rather than full shrines (Kaneko 2018, 384). In the case of the Takasago villages in the late 1930s, pre-shrines became a method for providing the civilizing influence of shrines for half of the cost. These pre-shrines, like most full shrines in Taiwan, usually venerated the same kami as Taiwan Jingū (Three Pioneer Kami and Prince Yoshihisa), although Amaterasu or other kami were sometimes enshrined in addition to or instead of these kami.

How were these pre-shrines to aid the 'civilizing' of the Takasago? Even the Japanese who considered the Takasago brothers saw them as a primitive, superstitious people. While stamping out those superstitions was the ideal, harmless superstitions could be allowed to continue or even utilized to foster a Japanese sense of morality. For example, in 1939, a Home Islander connected to the police suggested, under the pen name Haimenbō, that since the Takasago are innately superstitious, they would naturally attribute the benefits of modernity like good crops and no malaria to their veneration of the kami (Kaneko 2018, 387). In other words, while the Takasago may yet be too barbaric to understand the importance of state ritual at shrines, a new sense of Japanese morality could be fostered in their hearts by emphasizing the perceived intrinsic connection between the civilized method of kami veneration at shrines and the other benefits of civilization such as malaria vaccination and high-yield agricultural methods.

Although Japanese administrators saw the Takasago as barbaric, they also acknowledged that they had a natural sense of respect for the kami. No doubt due to difficult language translation situation, Japanese administrators felt verbal exhortations to respect the kami were ineffective (Barclay 2018, 141). Civil administrators were also aware that merely imposing a foreign ritual upon the Takasago was unlikely to produce actual changes in their social imaginary. Instead, they expected that the physical incorporation of Shinto rites into the indigenous ritual life of the Takasago would then foster a change in their intellectual attitudes. Thus the combination of indigenous rituals such as the *ilisin* harvest festival, Shinto shrines and folk customs was seen a stepping stone towards true civilization.[43] Haimenbō, previously mentioned, also advocated including a large courtyard at pre-shrines constructed in the Takasago villages. Creating a convenient place for ritual would encourage the Takasago to hold their important agricultural rituals at the shrine, turning the shrine into the centre of village life. Inducing residents to add Shinto aspects to their indigenous rituals would provide a method for eventually subsuming that rite as a local variation of Shinto. As the Takasago became more civilized, the more 'superstitious' aspects could be suppressed, leaving a Shinto ritual that was satisfactorily modern and loyal to the state, while theoretically remaining an intimate part of life rather than being something imposed on them from above. In this manner, Japanese administrators in Taiwan hoped that shrines could be used to bring the Takasago into a Japanese modernity without it feeling like a colonial imposition, much in the same way Kashihara Jingū worked to bring Home Islands residents into modernity without it feeling like a Western imposition.

Conclusion

In an effort to make Taiwan into a model, the Japanese government devoted significant resources to modernizing the island, and this included the construction of shrines. Shrines in Taiwan shared many similarities with shrines in the Home Islands. Furthermore, they were based on the pioneer theology the government had utilized in Hokkaido. However, Taiwan's particular situation as a colony with a significantly sized population of Taiwan Islanders also led to differences from the Home Islands and Hokkaido.

Shrines in Taiwan were treated as secular sites. Perhaps even more so than in the Home Islands, shrine and government rituals were conducted with little distinction between the two. Shintoists in Taiwan drew on the precedent of Qing state ritual in explaining the significance of shrine ritual to the populace, but shrines acted as agents of modernization. Shrines served as public sites with plentiful facilities for modern forms of leisure, while the kami reverenced at shrines were historical persons or portrayed as such. As secular sites, shrines communicated the new Japanese secularity to their communities. This included fostering changed senses of time, space and ethics in Taiwan residents, but shrines had an especially important role in locating Taiwan as new imperial land within Japanese space and time, as they had in Hokkaido.

Particularly during the first half of Japanese rule, these processes included drawing on Taiwan and Japan's shared 'Chinese religio-cultural sphere' in order to subsume Chinese or Taiwanese customs into the broader framework of a Japanese secularity. Kaizan Jinja and Kenkō Jinja were the two most prominent examples of this, but it also occurred on a more subtle level across the island. In this sense, many Taiwan Shintoists like Taiwan Jingū's chief ritualist were more interested in the imperialization of Taiwan residents, which aimed to transform them into modern imperial subjects, rather than their assimilation which aimed to transform them into copies of Home Islanders. The pioneer theology originally formulated for Sapporo Jinja and then chosen as the basis for Taiwan's shrines provided room for the incorporation of select non-Home Islands customs into shrine ritual as local variations. However, as a trend towards treating Taiwan less as a distinct colony and more like the Home Islands occurred, a shift towards a universalized theology began. This included the expectation that Taiwanese would be held to the same standards as Home Islanders.

Shrines were utilized as sites of state ritual with relatively little protest from Taiwan residents, even if the enthusiasm of Taiwan Islanders did not match the Governor-General's high expectations. However, this was not true in all of Japan's colonies. We now move north-east to Korea, which was annexed by Japan fifteen years after Taiwan became a Japanese colony.

5

Of the same lineage: Korea as annexed territory

5 January 201 AD.¹ After three years of campaigning in Korea, the Empress Consort Jingū returned to the shores of Tsukushi and gave birth to Hondawake-no-mikoto, future emperor Ōjin. She embarked on this journey when her husband Emperor Chūai died, struck suddenly ill after refusing to listen to the oracle of the kami. To fulfil her husband's dying wish, Jingū first chastised the Kumaso bandits to the south. Listening to the words of the kami, she then set their gentle spirit upon her person, and their rough spirit guided her ship as she sailed to the land of Silla. Still pregnant with the imperial child, she wrapped stones within her sash to prevent him from being born until she would be able to return. Upon Jingū's arrival in Korea, the king of Silla met her with fear and trembling and fell prostrate before her. The kings of Koguryŏ and Paekche, hearing of her power, also sent her tribute. She planted her staff at the king of Silla's gate and settled the rough spirit of the Great Kami of Sumiyoshi there to protect that land. Only then did she return to Tsukushi to birth her son. Empress Jingū ruled as regent for 69 years, living until the age of 100.²

Like Emperor Jinmu, Empress Jingū was usually treated as a real historical figure in the nineteenth and early twentieth centuries, despite her contested historicity today. Although removed from the official lineage of emperors in the Meiji period, Empress Jingū was a popular figure in the imperial mythology. She, along with her 'prime minister' Takenouchi-no-Sukune, featured in popular *ukiyoe* prints, including Tsukioka Yoshitoshi's *Short Illustrated History of Great Japan* (#15) and *Mirror of Famous Generals of Japan* (#2), both published in the 1870s. They were also depicted as warrior dolls (Figure 5.3), displayed by households on the holiday of Children's Day. The Bank of Japan featured her on the 1-yen banknote in 1881, while from 1908 her image was used on the 5- and 10-yen stamps. She was venerated at shrines across Japan, sometimes along with Takenouchi and/or her son.³ The tale of her conquest of the three Korean kingdoms (*sankan seibatsu*) would become evidence of the ancient connection between Japan and Korea and provide justification for the Japanese rule of Korea, much like Koxinga's Japanese birth helped legitimate Japanese rule of Taiwan. Although a more famous imperial ancestress – Amaterasu Ōmikami – was enshrined at Korea's first greater imperial shrine, a second greater imperial shrine dedicated to Jingū was planned in 1940. Taiwan had been a territory merely dropped into Japan's lap as a spoil of the Sino-Japanese war, but influence over Korea was a long-desired and hard-fought for gain of Japan's after the Russo-Japanese war. The annexation and colonization of Korea, then, was an endeavour optimistically and enthusiastically embraced by Japanese society.

This chapter examines how the particular circumstances of annexed Korea helped universalize and religionize shrines over the first half of the twentieth century, even as select indigenous customs were subsumed into Shinto. It begins by looking at Korea's general protector shrine, Chōsen Jingū. All the general protector shrines of Japan's new territories – Sapporo Jinja, Karafuto Jinja and Taiwan Jinja – had so far venerated the Three Pioneer Kami. Chōsen Jingū, however, broke this precedent and enshrined Amaterasu Ōmikami and Emperor Meiji instead. The debate around this enshrinement demonstrates how Amaterasu, first conceived as an ethnic kami exclusive to Home Islanders, began to be incorporated into a universalized theology. The example of Chōsen Jingū also reveals a shift among Shintoists in the 1920s and 1930s from a flattened conception of religion to a hierarchical one. Although Chōsen Jingū continued to be treated as a secular site, its ritualists increasingly saw Shinto shrines as the highest form of religion, rather than as sites separate from religion.

Next, the chapter explores the examples of Keijō Jinja and Heijō Jinja, both lesser national ranked shrines. Keijō Jinja, located next door to Chōsen Jingū on Mt. Namsan, demonstrates how space was created for subsumed Korean customs by pairing the kami Kunitama with a universalized Amaterasu. This dual enshrinement of Amaterasu with Kunitama would be followed at all the shrines subsequently given the rank of lesser national shrine. Heijō Jinja, located in the city of Heijō (Pyongyang), demonstrates the conflict that grew between shrines and Christians. In the first decade of Japan's rule, the Governor-General attempted to use religious groups, including Christians, to help foster patriotism in colonial subjects. This effort failed to produce satisfactory results, and from the 1920s the government began relying more on shrines to produce patriotic subjects loyal to the state. This, combined with the growing popularity of the idea of Shinto as the True religion, led to some Christians refusing to participate in the shrine visits increasingly required by the state. The most significant of these refusal incidents occurred at Heijō Jinja.

Finally, the chapter delves into how Korean history and customs were legitimized as a part of Shinto by looking at Fuyo Jingū, the shrine which venerated Empress Consort Jingū. The proliferation of pre-shrines in the late 1930s brought partially Koreanized Shinto sites to villages, but it was with the construction of Fuyo Jingū in 1940 that Korea's Japanese history was most visibly commemorated. Planned as Korea's second greater imperial ranked shrine, the site provides an example of how the Governor-General invoked an idealized past that subsumed a Korean past into imperial Japan's History, while using the rhetoric of assimilation.

A history of colonial Korea

Chinese sources record the mythic origins of Korean civilization as beginning with the foundation of the ancient Chosŏn (Jp. Chōsen) kingdom by the legendary king Tan'gun in the third millennium BC (Cumings 2005, 23). Evidence of Japan's relationship with the Korean peninsula is more easily found during the Three Kingdoms era (57 BC to 668 AD), with Japanese classics like the Kojiki and Nihon Shoki referring to a regular exchange of people and goods between the two areas. During this period, the Korean peninsula was divided into the three kingdoms of Koguryŏ (Jp. Kōkuri), Silla (Jp. Shinra) and Paekche (Jp. Kudara). Paekche, in particular, had an active relationship with the early Japanese state. These ancient eras continued to be harkened back to by successive rulers of the Korean peninsula. The Chosŏn dynasty (1392–1897), Japanese-ruled Korea (Kr. Chosŏn, Jp. Chōsen) (1910–45) and post-war North Korea (Kr. Chosŏn Minjujuŭi Inmin Konghwaguk, Jp. Chōsen Minshushugi Jinmin Kyōwakoku) invoked the semi-mythical age of the ancient Chosŏn era (traditional dates: 2333 BC–108 BC) by using the ancient name Chosŏn, while the Empire of Korea (Kr. Taehan Jeguk, Jp. Daikan Teikoku) (1897–1910) and post-war South Korea (Kr. Taehan Min'guk, Jp. Daikan Minkoku) invoked the Three Kingdoms (Kr. Samhan, Jp. Sankan)[4] by using the term *han* in Taehan.

The Korean peninsula had been largely unified by Silla in 668. Silla was supplanted by the Koryŏ dynasty, founded in 918, which became formally a Yuan Chinese vassal state. In 1392, this dynasty was overthrown following the disintegration of the Yuan dynasty in China. It was replaced by the Chosŏn dynasty, which was given the blessing of the Ming emperor. Diplomatic exchange and trade became especially active during this period, while the Imjin War (1592–98) saw the Japanese warlord Toyotomi Hideyoshi unsuccessfully invade the Korean peninsula twice. The first shrine in Korea, Ryūtōsan Jinja, was established during this period in 1676 at the Japanese trading post in Pusan. This shrine was dedicated to Kotohira Daigongen, a kami known for protecting sea voyages. Later in 1765, Tenman Tenjin and Sumiyoshi-no-Ōkami were also enshrined, followed by Amaterasu Ōmikami in 1865 (Kondō 1943, 48).[5]

The Chosŏn dynasty, like the Shogunate in Japan, was forced to face the prospects of modernization and imperialism starting in the mid-nineteenth century. Chosŏn attempted to maintain an isolationist policy in the face of the colonial threat, but, like Taiwan, suffered multiple punitive expeditions, including the French in 1866 and the United States in 1871. Caught geographically between the powers of Japan, China and Russia, Chosŏn tried to maintain its sovereignty by playing these powerful states' competing interests off one another (Caprio 2009, 20). Japan, eager to cement its influence over Korea before the Western nations, imposed a Western-style Treaty of Amity on Korea in 1876. This treaty declared Korea an independent nation and required the establishment of two open ports for trade, which started an influx of Japanese settlers in Korea (Henry 2014, 30).[6] This Japan–Korea treaty was quickly followed by similar unequal treaties with the Western powers. This led to Chosŏn becoming divided into a pro-Japan faction interested in modernization and a pro-China conservative faction (Cumings 2005, 111).

Japan's victory over China in the First Sino-Japanese War (1894–5) gained it not only the island of Taiwan as a colony but also a dominating influence in the affairs of Korea. In 1894, Chosŏn undertook the Kabo reforms. These reforms were aimed at transforming Korea into a modern state, but they also placed it more firmly under Japan's influence. In 1897, King Kojong of the Chosŏn dynasty established the Korean Empire, becoming Emperor Kwangmu. It was during this period that Japanese settlers founded Nanzan Daijingū, the shrine which would later become Keijō Jinja. In 1904, increasing Russian interest in Korea led to the Russo-Japanese war (1904–5). Japan's victory made it possible for Japan to claim Korea as a protectorate, and in 1910 it formally annexed Korea with the Japan–Korea Treaty of 1910. Although this loss of sovereignty was a blow to many Koreans who saw themselves as more civilized than the Japanese, Western nations largely approved of Japan's rule of Korea (Cumings 2005, 141, 130).

Japan's annexation of Korea was contrary to its earlier arguments for Korea's independence from China. But part of Japan's justification for its change of view on Korea's right to independence was based on the Same Ancestor theory (*dōsoron*).[7] Broadly this discourse invoked Japan and Korea's ancient history, especially the stories of Susanoo-no-mikoto and Empress Jingū as recorded in the Japanese classics, to argue that Korea and Japan were a single nation which had been tragically split apart in ancient times. In this narrative, Empress Jingū's ancient conquest of the Three Kingdoms and imperial Japan's modern annexation of the Korean Empire were both attempts to reunite a once-whole nation. Koreans, through their ancient shared heritage with Japan, would be innately capable of becoming proper Japanese once they were under right governance. This was in contrast with the Chinese-descended islanders of Taiwan who were seen as a separate race.

Japanese rule of Korea can be broadly divided into three periods. From its annexation in 1910 until the 1 March incident in 1919, Korea was governed under military rule. The Governor-General was required to be affiliated with the military and worked to centralize and modernize the government, while a gendarmerie was set up to police the colony. The laws governing shrines in Korea were also established during this period. At first, the shrines and temples that had been founded by Japanese settlers before annexation were placed under the same regulations, issued in 1915.[8] However, these regulations removed shrines but not temples from the administration of the Religion Section under the Educational Bureau and placed them under the jurisdiction of the Regional Section under the Interior Bureau. In 1917, the legal category of pre-shrines (*shinshi*) was established as a holding category for Shinto sites already established by Home Islander settlers that could not yet meet the physical criteria for full shrines, but intended to eventually do so.[9] Although invented as a temporary category, the category of pre-shrines later provided a legal mechanism that allowed the government to finance the rapid building of Shinto sites across Korea. As seen in the previous chapter, the category was also adopted by the Taiwan Governor-General for the latter purpose. Despite the establishment of these shrine regulations, there was no serious effort to establish a general protector shrine like Karafuto Jinja and Taiwan Jinja at this time and shrines mainly remained the enclaves of Home Islanders.

The second period, from 1919 to 1935, begins with the 1 March incident. Contrary to the predictions of Same Ancestor theory, Koreans did not easily accept Japanese rule. In 1919, Korean activists drew up a declaration of independence and on 1 March staged public readings and marched in protest of Japanese rule. The Chōsen Governor-General reacted severely to this movement, which led to criticism from both the Japanese Home Islands and abroad (Peattie 1984a, 21). Count Hasegawa Yoshimichi, Governor-General at the time, was forced to step down, with Viscount Saitō Makoto taking his place. This led to a new policy of 'cultural rule', which allowed non-military officials to serve as the

Governor-General[10] and replaced the gendarmerie with a civilian police force. It also heralded in policies permitting looser control over the use of the Korean language and customs. This cultural rule policy was underpinned by the rationale of slowly incorporating Korea into Japanese Home Islands by giving colonial subjects more of both the rights and responsibilities of full Japanese citizens and by encouraging closer integration between Home Islanders and Koreans (Caprio 2009, 118, 123, 128). This latter aim was perhaps most significantly symbolized by the marriage of Crown Prince Yi Un of Korea to Princess Nashimoto-no-miya Masako of Japan. Furthermore, the Japanese government approved the plan to build a greater imperial shrine in 1919, although it wasn't until 1925 that the shrine, Chōsen Jingū, had its formal enshrinement rite (*chinza*). The Governor-General also began attempting to incorporate Shinto ritual into the lives of rural Koreans during this period. In 1932, the Governor-General welcomed the agriculturalist Yamazaki Nobuyoshi to Korea and based on his ideas began the Agricultural Village Promotion (Nōson Shinkō) movement. This movement's stated aim was to increase the self-reliance of rural villages, but it included some attempts to centre village life around an unofficial shrine dedicated to local deities (Jp. *kami*, Kr. *shin*) or the Jingū *taima* talisman.

During the third period, 1935–45, the Chōsen Governor-General increasingly aimed to mobilize Korean sentiment in support of Japan, and saw shrines as one of the key institutions for facilitating this aim. In 1935, the Heart-field Development (Shinden Kaihatsu) movement was born out of the Agricultural Village Promotion movement. This effort enlisted a wide variety of social elites from priests and Confucianists to teachers and social workers to promote its three aims. These were 'to clarify the concept of the body politic (*kokutai*)', 'to foster a spirit of gratitude and independence' and, most importantly to shrines, 'to cultivate the theory of, and a faithful heart for, respecting for the kami and the venerating ancestors (*keishin sūso*)'. In 1936, the Governor-General began a revision of the shrine system and started designating a lesser national-ranked shrine for each prefecture. Although individual efforts by prefectures began earlier, in 1939 the Governor-General gave formal approval of prefectures' efforts to build one shrine in each village to serve as the village's centre of community. Encouraged by Koreans being newly allowed to serve in the Japanese military, it also began planning the eventual construction of Korea's two *gokoku* shrines (Caprio 2009, 146). In 1944, as the war front in China increasingly deteriorated, the construction of shrines in Korea was halted. By the end of the war, a total of two greater imperial shrines, eight lesser national shrines, two *gokoku* shrines and seventy regular shrines had been built in Korea (Tsuda et al. 2006, 289).

Chōsen Jingū: A universalized theology

In Hokkaido, Karafuto and Taiwan, an imperial shrine dedicated to the Three Pioneer Kami was established within six years of Japanese rule to support the transformation of these new territories into productive imperial lands. Korea shared a similarity with Hokkaido in that Japan had long been interested in the area and migrants from the Home Islands had previously settled there. But Korea differed from these three areas in that it was formally annexed by Japan through treaty, rather than claimed by right of *terra nullius* or as a spoil of war. Korea also differed in that it took a lengthy fifteen years after annexation before Korea's greater imperial shrine, Chōsen Jingū, was formally established.

Despite this late start, Chōsen Jingū, like other overseas general protector shrines, would become extremely influential on other shrines in Korea, including those predating it. As Korea's main greater imperial shrine, it served as a model for lesser shrines in Korea. The chief ritualist of Chōsen Jingū was given the power to appoint other ritualists in Korea. Lower-ranking ritualists of Chōsen Jingū were often promoted and sent to serve as the chief ritualists of shrines in the prefectures and in the 1930s a training institution was established at Chōsen Jingū. This meant new ritualists trained at Chōsen Jingū were sent to shrines in not only Korea but across the empire (Hiura 2013, 176). In other words, the establishment of Chōsen Jingū had wide-reaching implications for shrines in Korea and more broadly on overseas Shinto shrines.

The Chōsen Jingū enshrinement debate

The enshrinement of the Three Pioneer Kami at overseas shrines had become an established precedent at overseas shrines. But Chōsen Jingū rejected this trend. Instead, Amaterasu Ōmikami and Emperor Meiji became its enshrined kami. The Same Ancestor theory, which argued that Japanese Home Islanders and Koreans descended from the same historical ancestors, is essential for understanding this change. The Same Ancestor theory continued to be widely supported by Japanese intellectuals in the 1920s. For example, Chōsen Governor-General Hara Kei who initiated the 1919 Culture Rule reforms, as well as historians such as Kita Sadakichi and Kurosaka Katsumi, saw Japanese and Koreans as sharing the same ethnic origins (Caprio 2009, 83–4, 121; Chen 1984, 250). Even historian Kume Kunitake, who became infamous for arguing that Shinto was an outdated custom, believed that Korea and Japan were a single nation previous to the days of Emperor Jinmu (Caprio 2009, 53).[11]

The kami suggested as the most appropriate for Korea has included many choices over the twentieth century: Amaterasu Ōmikami, Amaterasu's younger brother Susanoo-no-Mikoto, Okunitama-no-kami alone of the Three Pioneer Kami, the legendary founder of the Korean nation Tan'gun, and the Emperor Meiji. The idea for enshrining Amaterasu at a major shrine in Korea was broached as early as 1906, when the National Shrine Ritualists Association suggested Amaterasu and Tan'gun be enshrined in Korea. Amaterasu would be enshrined as the founder of the Japanese nation, while Tan'gun would be identified with her younger brother Susanoo and enshrined as the founder of the Korean nation (Suga 2010, 54). This conception of Amaterasu aligned with that adopted by many Home Islander migrants to Hokkaido, pre-annexation Korea, Hawai'i and beyond, which saw Amaterasu as a kami who could represent a national Japanese identity (Aono 2015, 11). The legends about Susanoo in the classics, meanwhile, depicted him variously as Amaterasu's unruly younger brother and as a kami who came from across the sea to settle the Izumo region of Japan (Grayson 2002, 467). Susanoo's sixth-generation descendent Ōkuninushi – the main kami of Izumo Taisha and identified with Ōnamuchi of the Three Pioneer Kami – was the one to transfer the land (*kuni yuzuri*) to Amaterasu's grandson, Ninigi-no-Mikoto. However, these early calls for a major Korean shrine dedicated to Amaterasu and Susanoo went nowhere.

During the construction of Chōsen Jingū, debate erupted over which kami should be enshrined there. Korea, unlike previously obtained territories, was not considered *terra nullius*, but was a recognized independent empire that was being 'reunited' with Japan through formal annexation. This made the Three Pioneer Kami less appropriate to Korea as they had been for Taiwan. Amaterasu again became a popular choice. Under the assumptions of the Same Ancestor theory, Amaterasu was not merely the ancestress of Home Islanders, but also of Koreans, meaning there was no need for Tan'gun as the founder of a separate Korean nation. But many Shintoists still argued that Tan'gun should be enshrined (Suga 2010, 54). Some, like Ogasawara Shōzō who wrote extensively about shrines in Korea, argued that Tan'gun should be enshrined instead of Amaterasu, whom ought to be exclusively enshrined at the Ise Jingū. Others argued that Korea's Kunitama-no-Kami should be identified with Tan'gun and enshrined under the name Chōsen Kunitama (Suga 2010, 56).

At the conclusion of these debates, both Tan'gun and Kunitama were rejected. Amaterasu Ōmikami and Emperor Meiji became the kami of Chōsen Jingū. The original proposal planned to include the title 'Imperial' (Sume) for Amaterasu, as was typical at *daijingū* shrines founded by Home Islanders. *Daijingū* shrines, such as Nanzan Daijingū (Keijō Jinja) in Korea's capital city, were part of the network of shrines connected through their subsidiary relationship to the Ise Jingū. For shrines in this network, Amaterasu usually served as an ethnic kami relevant to all Home Islanders, regardless of their prefectural origins. Sometimes *daijingū* shrines were seen not as full shrines but rather as *yōhai* (veneration from afar) sites. But the use of 'Imperial' at Chōsen Jingū was rejected by the Home Ministry. Instead, Amaterasu's title was written only with the characters for 'great kami' (Ōkami),[12] distinguishing Chōsen Jingū from *daijingū*-type shrines. Amaterasu Ōmikami's ancient 'achievements and goodness' and Meiji's 'unparalleled benevolence for the Korean masses' made them the 'most appropriate kami' for Korea (Chōsen Sōtokufu 1927, 4). In this way, Amaterasu's relevance ceased being limited to Home Islanders and was expanded to include Koreans as a part of the same Japanese race.

Chōsen Jingū as a secular shrine

Although Chōsen Jingū did not venerate the Three Pioneer Kami, it was conceived and operated as a public, historical and modern site like the shrines discussed in previous chapters. At the shrine, the chief ritualist's main duty was to 'conduct rituals of the state' (Aono 2015, 47). Its first chief ritualist, Takamatsu Shirō, had been especially interested in building connections between shrines and school students in the Home Islands and also devoted effort to this at Chōsen Jingū.[13] Achiwa Yasuhiko, who became the shrine's second chief ritualist in 1931, continued this effort, convincing Governor-General officials from the Education and other bureaus to attend Chōsen Jingū's festivals in person (Hiura 2013, 49). Furthermore, in the late 1930s, Chōsen Jingū and other shrines became sites for public displays like the recitation of the Imperial Subject's Pledge and public services like food rationing (Caprio 2009, 109, 161).

Chōsen Jingū, like Taiwan Jingū in Taiwan, commemorated Korea's Japanese history. Amaterasu was the ancestress of both Home Islanders and Koreans according to the Same Ancestor theory, and Emperor Meiji had enabled Japan and Korea to be 'reunited'. In this way, Chōsen Jingū venerated and commemorated historical persons and located Korea within the broader scope of Japanese history. The role of shrines as historical sites was affirmed by a directive in 1935 which prohibited statues unrelated to public heroes or the kami being erected at shrines (Hiura 2013, 176).

Chōsen Jingū also served as a site where both Home Islanders and Koreans could encounter a Japanese modernity. Chōsen Jingū's construction was a massive architectural project and the modern technology of the train and cars provided access to the shrine. The shrine's rituals were broadcast across the colony on radio, while the trappings of modern patriotism such as flying the national flag and erecting triumphal arches made their appearance at Chōsen Jingū and Keijō Jinja (Henry 2014, 83). The shrine also hosted radio gymnastics, patriotic projection movies and modern leisure activities such as ice skating (Hiura 2013, 120).

Although Chōsen Jingū positioned itself in the secular sphere as a public, historical and modern site, it was less concerned with maintaining a strict divide between shrines and arguably religious elements. Older shrines like Sapporo Jinja and Kashihara Jingū undertook an effort to clearly distance themselves from religious elements such as funerals and the religious Shinto sects in the late 1800s. Ritualists at these earlier shrines often had connections to the semi-religious organizations birthed by the Great Promulgation Campaign which then had to be cut. All three chief ritualists[14] of Chōsen Jingū were trained at Kōgakkan, the secular successor to the Jingū-kyō sect's training institution. But they were also all born in the 1870s, receiving their training after the urgency of separating shrines from religion had passed. Without directly experiencing that urgency, the ritualists at Chōsen Jingū felt less pressure to keep religion entirely separated from shrines.

Chōsen Jingū also worked to instil new senses of space, time and ethics in Home Islanders and Koreans. The geography of Chōsen Jingū affirmed the concentric conception of space that located Korea within the larger Japanese empire. Built above Keijō Jinja on Mt. Namsan, Chōsen Jingū literally watched over the capital city and the new Chōsen Governor-General building.[15] In the late 1930s, when school children and their parents were increasingly encouraged to make regular visits to the shrine, the physical height would have been impressed on them by the long stair climb up the shrine's main approach and the impressive views of the city gained from the top of the shrine (Figure 5.1). In 1935, Chōsen Jingū was also compared to the Ise Jingū: as the Ise Jingū protected and watched over the Home Islands, so Chōsen Jingū protected and watched over Korea (Aono 2015, 46).

Regular physical visits to Chōsen Jingū were mostly limited to residents of Keijō, but the shrine was in charge of distributing the Jingū *taima* to the peninsula. *Taima* distribution jumped significantly in the latter half of the 1930s, rising from less than 50,000 in 1934 to over 1.25 million in 1940.[16] Despite this significant increase, as few as 5 per cent of Korean households may have had a Jingū *taima* by 1939 (Henry 2014, 193).[17] In contrast, almost 60 per cent

Figure 5.1 The stone stairs of Chōsen Jingū's main approach (c. 1930s): This postcard, one of a set of three, came wrapped in a paper envelope emblazoned with the shrine's crest and detailing the basic facts and history of the shrine. (Author's collection.)

(59.6 per cent) of households in Taiwan maintained a Jingū *taima* by 1937 (Sai 1994, 184). Chōsen Jingū was also a site of *yōhai*. In 1937, the government formulated a three-article Imperial Subject's Pledge for Koreans and Chōsen Jingū included it with the ethics textbooks it passed to students. As a part of the process of reciting the pledge, schools instructed students to venerate the *taima* and perform *yōhai* towards the imperial palace (Hiura 2013, 226). Chōsen Jingū became a particularly important place for this rite in 1939, when the Imperial Subject's Pledge Tower was constructed within its garden.

Like other shrines, Chōsen Jingū also worked to instil a new sense of time in residents of Korea through festivals, calendars and regular shrine visits. Chōsen Jingū's annual festival was held on 17 October on the national holiday of Kanname-sai, when the first fruits of the year are offered at the Ise Jingū. The shrine also began holding more popularly oriented festivals such as celebrations for Boy's Day and Girl's Day. Although these festivals were based on Japanese folk traditions, the dates they were celebrated on were based on the modern solar calendar rather than the traditional lunisolar calendar. Chōsen Jingū also distributed, and was listed on, the Imperial calendar (Figure 5.2). After 1937, modern clock time was affirmed through strictly timed *yōhai* and rituals

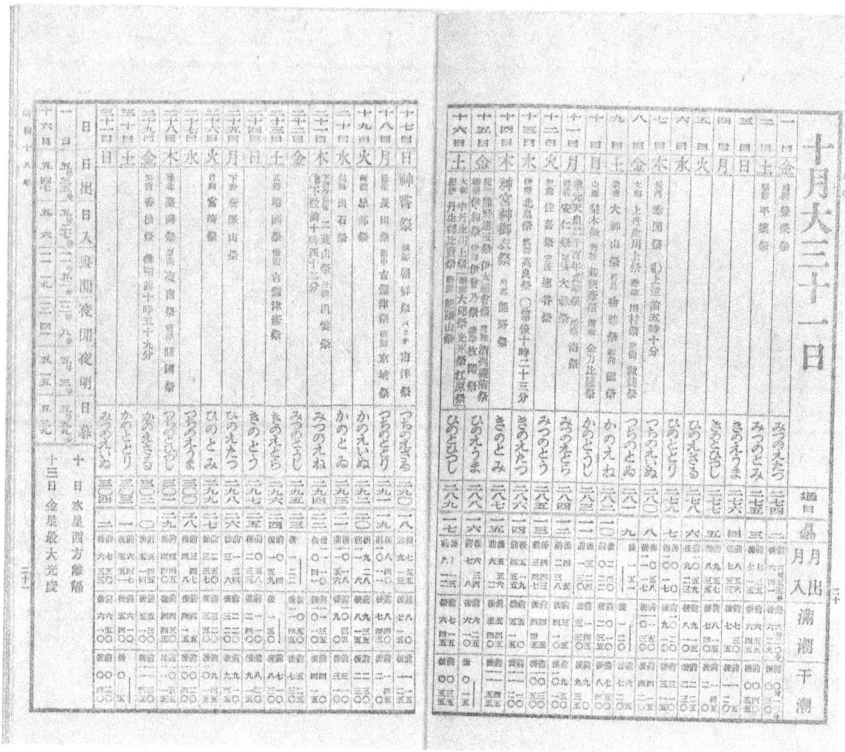

Figure 5.2 Calendar of October, Showa 18 (Imperial Year 2603, Western Year 1943): The national holiday of Kanname-sai is listed in large characters on the 17th, followed by the festivals of Chōsen Jingū and Nan'yō Jinja (Palau) in smaller characters. Five other major Korean shrines' festivals are listed on their respective days in October, as well as Taiwan Jingū and Tainan Jinja's festivals on the 28th. (Author's Collection.)

for military success (Henry 2014, 184). The shrine also began a campaign to encourage children to visit the shrine every Sunday, associating the start of the modern seven-day week with shrines (Hiura 2013, 107). Neither was the importance of the 2600th anniversary of Jinmu's enthronement rite ignored in Korea (Hiura 2013, 229). Commemorative projects were planned across the peninsula, including the installation of the sacred torch from Ise Jingū which had been run through the imperial territories as a part of the sacred torch relay (Henry 2014, 175).

Finally, ethics took on a significant role at Chōsen Jingū. The shrine's chief ritualists were especially interested in fostering a connection between children and the shrine. In 1926, Chōsen Jingū began a ritual to announce the shrine's distribution of ethics textbooks to local Japanese public schools. In 1932, after Achiwa became chief ritualist, this ritual was revised into a public festival attended by the head of the Education Bureau, while in 1934 it was renamed the Kangaku-sai. Private schools in the area started to attend, while the shrine started also distributing ethics textbooks for Korean school children. In 1933, the Chōsen Shrine Ritualists Association Bulletin wrote that shrines 'provided students with a living ethical education and produced a beautiful civic morality' (Hiura 2013, 51). The shrine also started stamp rally campaigns to promote individually motivated – rather than group-based – shrine visits by students during two months of the summer in 1936 and on Sundays in 1937 (Hiura 2013, 128, 140). In 1937, the shrine's annual report wrote that shrine visits 'opened the hearts of especially Korean children to the wordless sermons of the kami' (Hiura 2013, 124).[18] Although Chōsen Jingū's efforts were limited to schools in the area and less than 5 per cent of students participated in the stamp rally campaigns, other shrines copied Chōsen Jingū's example. This would lead to conflict between Christian schools and the colonial government which required them to participate in these and other Shinto rituals.

Shinto as the True religion

Even into the late 1930s, the Chōsen Governor-General's official view of shrines remained that they were secular sites of patriotic state ritual and civic displays of filial respect (Henry 2014, 74). The 1937 ethics textbook, for example, illustrated the national anthem with an image of children in Korean dress attending Chōsen Jingū (Hiura 2013, 60). However, the popularity among Shintoists in Korea of what Aono (2015) has called the 'logic of State Shinto' undermined the legitimacy of this secular view of Shinto. Based on the theories of Japanese intellectuals like Kakei Katsuhiko, Ozaki Hotsumi, Katō Genchi and Kawatsura Bonji, this logic adopted a hierarchical conception of religion which replaced Christianity with Shinto as the most True religion. Collapsing respect for the kami and ancestor veneration into one, it argued that actions such as *misogi* and gymnastics could mystically reunite people with their divine ancestors. Tensei-kai, the support organization for Chōsen Jingū founded in 1926, probably derived its name from Kakei's teachings (Aono 2015, 130), and the incorporation of activities like *misogi* and a focus on internal 'reunion' with the ancestral kami in shrine publications and by government officials called into doubt the sincerity of the Governor-General's insistence that shrines were only sites of patriotism.

Achiwa, chief ritualist at Chōsen Jingū from 1931, was one of those who adopted a hierarchal idea of religion. He felt Shinto shrines deserved as much as or even more enthusiasm than people demonstrated for religions like Shinshū Buddhism or Tenri-kyō[19] (Hiura 2013, 86). He believed that it was not enough for Japanese subjects to perform loyalty with the body, but that it must also be from the heart (Hiura 2013, 13). His efforts to encourage students and their families to visit shrines on summer mornings and on Sunday were motivated by a desire to convince people to visit the shrine on their own volition, rather than out of a sense of duty.

Other sections of the government also adopted a hierarchical religious view of Shinto. For example, Ikeda Kiyoshi, as an official of the Home Islands' Shrine Bureau from 1924, kept to the government's official line that shrines were not religious. But after he became head of the Police Bureau of the Chōsen Governor-General in 1931, Ikeda helped Achiwa found the Chōsen Misogi-kai, and had his police officers perform *misogi* purification as a part of their work (Aono 2015, 134–5). He also wrote an enthusiastic introduction to Oyama Fumio's 1934 book *Jinja to Chōsen* (*Shrines and Korea*) that argued that Shinto shrines, as well as other religions, reflected the same universal Truth (Hiura 2013, 75).

The ancient Shinto which the Same Ancestor theory had held up as proof of Japan and Korea's shared ancestry was expanded into a universal religious Truth. The concerns Japanese Christians and Shinshū Buddhists had about being required to take part in 'religious' elements such as purification rituals and receiving talismans at shrines in 1930 – a debate about which Ikeda presided over as head of the Shrine Bureau – were dismissed in Korea. Achiwa and other Shintoists in Korea felt shrines should not only be given veneration (*sūkei*), but even more so 'the [religious] faith (*shinkō*) that goes along with veneration' (Hiura 2013, 80).

Furthermore, in 1935 Governor-General Ugaki Kazushige started the Heart-field Development effort, which aimed to start a 'religious revival' within Korea. While the term 'religious revival' was soon dropped from the government's discourse, the Heart-field Development movement aimed to use religions, shrines and other social institutions to instil a patriotic loyalty in the populace that reached their innermost being. Although a divide in vocabulary between shrines and religion was maintained in the movement's stated goals, both institutions were largely grouped together in the enactment of the plan. The vocabularic divide was further muddied by the continued use of pre-modern terms like 'lewd rites and evil teachings' indicating the hierarchal view of religion, alongside more modern terms like 'superstitions' and 'false religions' suggesting the flattened view of religion (Aono 2015, 156).

Around the same time the hierarchal view of religion was growing in popularity, the East Asia Ethnicity discourse – which saw all of greater East Asia as sharing the same cultural heritage – was also gaining ground. The ritualists of Taiwan Jingū had explicitly separated shrines from religion by arguing that shrines were inseparable from being a Japanese subject, in contrast to religion which was universal. But as Korea Shintoists adopted a hierarchal view of religion, a universalized theology expanded to include not just Koreans but all East Asians, with Amaterasu and shrines untethered from the Japanese state and expanded into the 'Greater East Asian religion'[20] (Kondō 1943, 334).

Keijō Jinja: The local at national shrines

As Amaterasu Ōmikami was universalized and untethered from the state, Kunitama – the kami once rejected as a candidate for enshrinement at Chōsen Jingū – took on the new role of representing the particular. In 1936, the Chōsen Governor-General began an effort to reorganize and rank shrines in Korea. The plan called for a shrine in each Korean prefecture to be raised to the rank of lesser national shrine. This raised the question of what kami were most appropriate for these newly promoted shrines. This section examines how Amaterasu and Kunitama were paired together at these lesser national shrines. The example of Keijō Jinja – one of the first shrines to be raised to that rank – demonstrates how Amaterasu's relevance continued to be expanded while the conception of Kunitama morphed into one signifying any local Korean kami.

The first shrines to be raised in rank to lesser national shrines were Ryūtōsan Jinja – the oldest shrine in Korea – and Keijō Jinja. Keijō Jinja, located on Mt. Namsan (Jp. Nanzan) right below Chōsen Jingū, had been the pre-eminent shrine of Keijō (Seoul) until Chōsen Jingū was built. Keijō Jinja was originally established as Nanzan Daijingū and dedicated to Amaterasu by Home Islanders in 1898, before Japan had annexed Korea. As discussed further in Chapter 7, Amaterasu was a common choice at migrant shrines and helped create a national, rather than prefectural, identity for Home Islander migrants.

After the enactment of shrine regulations in 1915, the Chōsen Governor-General began encouraging shrines in Korea to adopt a more secular conception. At Keijō Jinja, this included positioning the shrine as not exclusive to the Home Islander community, but also including both Koreans and some Korean customs into the shrine activities. Keijō Jinja was required to include Koreans as at least one third of its board of directors from 1916 (Henry 2014, 66), and it slowly began including more Korean elements into its main festival, such as drum-playing *kisaeng* entertainers. In 1919, the Government-General convinced the musicians of the Korean royal house to participate in Keijō Jinja's festival, and the shrine festival's procession was extended to include more of Keijō's Korean district (Henry 2014, 76–7). Although these changes were not welcomed by all Home Islanders, the Japanese media praised Keijō Jinja for its localism (Henry 2014, 183). When Chōsen Jingū was built directly above and overshadowing Keijō Jinja on Mt. Namsan, the two shrines were connected as a pair. The former was the solemn greater imperial shrine and general protector of Korea, while the latter remained a local shrine, restricted to the city of Keijō.

Keijō Jinja was originally founded as *daijingū* shrine to Amaterasu Sume Ōmikami, but the shrine added the Three Pioneer Kami to its kami after they were rejected as candidates for Chōsen Jingū. Keijō Jinja originally referred to Ōkunitama-no-kami of the Three Pioneer Kami using the term Chōsen Kunitama-no-kami, which interpreted Ōkunitama as the spirit of the land. However, the Shrine Bureau objected to this terminology and crossed out the term Chōsen, leaving Keijō Jinja's kami named Kunitama-no-kami.

In 1936 when Keijō Jinja became a lesser national shrine, Amaterasu Sume Omikami was changed to Amaterasu Ōmikami, while Kunitama-no-kami was changed to Kunitama-no-Ōkami. Both names were written with four characters meaning 'Amaterasu Great-Kami' and 'Kunitama Great-Kami', respectively, and Amaterasu and Kunitama were paired into a single seat. Although previously some Shintoists had interpreted Kunitama as Tan'gun, the government sent out a notice saying Kunitama was to be understood as a title (*shinkaku*) for any local Korean kami[21] and should always be enshrined with Amaterasu (Aono 2015, 166). The Governor-General never completed its plan to give each prefecture a lesser national shrine, but Ryūtōsan Jinja and the other shrines raised to the national rank all newly enshrined Amaterasu and Kunitama as a pair.[22] Amaterasu became a kami universally relevant to all East Asians, while Kunitama served as her local counterpart. These shrines, as national-ranked shrines and secular sites, were prohibited by law from conducting funerals. Despite this, Keijō Jinja continued to do so,[23] reflecting the lack of concern Korea Shintoists had about drawing a line between shrines and religion (Hiura 2013, 153).

Heijō Jinja: Christians at Shinto shrines

An essential element of the post-war narrative positioning 'State Shinto' as an oppressive state religion has been the hagiographic tales of Christians – Home Islanders and colonial subjects alike – facing social or real martyrdom for their refusal to venerate at Shinto shrines. From the late nineteenth century, both Christians and Buddhists influenced what elements were considered secular and religious in Japan. Where the exact line between those two spheres lay continued to be contested by these groups into the 1930s. Although significant lèse majesté incidents involving Christians began in the 1890s, it wasn't until the 1930s that serious incidents involving shrines occurred.

This section looks at how the increasingly common hierarchical conception of Shinto as the True religion, combined with the pressure for imperial subjects to prove their loyalty through shrine visits, led Christians into conflict with the state. Heijō (Pyongyang) was known as the centre of Christianity in Korea and it was at Heijō Jinja, a shrine that would be ranked a lesser national shrine in 1937, that perhaps the most well-known conflict between Christians and shrines occurred. But to understand the broader relationship between the Japanese state, shrines and Christianity, it is helpful to first review Christianity's earlier history in Japan and Korea.

When the Meiji Constitution established Japan as a secular state and guaranteed freedom of religion in 1890, that included the official legalization of Christianity along with Buddhism and Sect Shinto. Despite this, Christians continued to be seen as suspect of national loyalty and Japanese Christians asserted alternative ideas about what being loyal to the state meant (Anderson 2014, 7). In the 1890s, a series of lèse majesté accusations concerning Christians occurred. Perhaps most publicized were the Uchimura Kanzō incident in 1891 and the Okumura Teijirō incident in 1892. In both these incidents, Christian school teachers were accused of disrespecting not shrines, but the words of the emperor: the Imperial Rescript on Education (Anderson 2014, 28).[24]

Japanese Christians worked to prove their loyalty to the state, and they were eager to prove Christianity's usefulness when Japan annexed Korea by using it to 'civilize' and 'reunite' Koreans with Japan (Anderson 2014, 109). The Congregationalist Church set up a mission to Korea including these aims in 1911, and the Chōsen Governor-General provided financial support to it until 1921, when the mission was closed down. The government also aided the Mission's fundraising efforts and sent major officials to speak at its events (Anderson 2014, 145). Rather than being anti-Christian, the Chōsen Governor-General was actively supportive of *Japanese* Christianity.

At the same time, the Governor-General remained suspicious of Western-led Christian churches and schools. In 1911, the government accused American missionary George S. McCune along with Korean independence activists of plotting to assassinate the first Governor-General Terauchi Masatake in what became known as the 105 Man Incident (Kang 1997, 44). Charges against all but six of the Koreans were dropped after international outcry, but McCune would become the centre of controversy again in the Heijō Jinja incident in 1935. The differing attitude shown towards Japanese Christianity and Westerner-led Christianity mirrored the goals of both the Japanese government and Japanese Christians in the Home Islands for a Christianity independent from its missionary beginnings (Krämer 2011, 204). Despite the Japanese government's antagonist view towards foreign Christianity, most Western missionaries were supportive of Japan's annexation of Korea, and some complained that Korean Christians were more nationalistic than religious in their Christian faith (Kang 1997, 38).

In 1919, criticism over the Governor-General's overly harsh reaction to the 1 March independence protests led to the adoption of the new policy of 'cultural rule'. This corresponded with the decision to establish a greater imperial shrine for Korea. Although the government was already forcing some shrines like Keijō Jinja to include Koreans more, Shinto shrines had remained largely ethnic institutions for Home Islanders. But as seen previously, Chōsen Jingū's ritualists saw the shrine as an institution for both Home Islanders and Koreans. The Governor-General also started looking more towards shrines as institutions able to instil patriotism within colonial subjects as it grew disillusioned with the ability of Japanese Christians to influence Koreans. Although the government would later try to mobilize religious groups in fostering loyalty to the state with the Heart-field Development movement, the Governor-General stopped financially supporting the Japanese Congregationalist Church's mission in 1921.

The government was not yet requiring shrine visits by schools in the 1920s, but the first incident of students refusing to perform a shrine visit occurred in 1924, a year before Chōsen Jingū was established. Kōkei Public Normal School, a school for Korean students, performed a group visit to Kōkei Jinja in Chūsei-nan (South Chungchong) prefecture. A teacher and a student at the school refused to participate on the grounds of their Christian belief. As a result, the school asked them both to resign (Hiura 2013, 24–5). The incident at Kōkei Public Normal School was significantly earlier than the first major incident in the Home Islands involving Christian students refusing to visit a shrine: the Sophia University Incident. In 1932, the military training officer took students at Sophia University to venerate at Yasukuni Jinja. Two or three of the students refused on grounds of their Catholic beliefs. Although the army wished to withdraw its training officer from the school, the Ministry of Education refused and aimed to resolve the situation by clarifying to the archbishop of Tokyo that the shrine visit was not religious, but only to express patriotism. The Catholic archbishops accepted the government's explanation, but the army unofficially withdrew its military officer from Sophia while the mass media turned the incident into a sensation.

The pressure on Christian students to venerate at Shinto shrines began earlier in Korea than in the Home Islands, but in Korea the schools themselves put that pressure on students, rather than the central government as in the Sophia case. Furthermore, Kōkei Jinja was a relatively local shrine in comparison to Yasukuni Jinja, a special imperial shrine which in 1932 was nearly uniquely dedicated to the collective 'glorious dead'. However, there was an incident in Korea similar to the Sophia case in the same year that did not involve shrines. In 1932, the Heijō prefectural government planned a *shōkon* rite – which included both Shinto and Buddhist elements – to commemorate the war dead of Manchuria at Heijō's Loyal Dead Monument. Despite the prefectural governor's request for all schools to attend, those run by the Presbyterian Church declined. Although the Governor-General downplayed the incident, Veterans groups and then newspapers picked up the story and used it to fan rising anti-American sentiment caused by America's refusal to recognize Manchukuo as a legitimate state (Komagome 2005, 11). In these early 1930s cases, it was the refusal to venerate the war dead that outraged the public. While the civilian government attempted to resolve the issue quietly, pressure from the military or associated groups turned the incidents into media sensations.

In 1935, the Heart-field Development movement placed increasing pressure on schools and other organizations to demonstrate loyalty to the state through shrine visits, even as it continued to expect religious groups' cooperation with its aim of cultivating 'respect for the kami and veneration of the ancestors (*keishin sūso*)'. While participation in the school-related shrine visits had previously been left up to the school's principle, it now became expected of all schools.[25] This led to the Heijō Jinja incident.

Heijō Jinja, the most prominent shrine in Heian-nan (South Pyongan) Prefecture, was located in the prefectural capital, Heijō (Pyongyang).[26] Founded in 1913 by Home Island settlers, it was officially registered as a shrine in 1915, when the Governor-General established laws governing shrines. Like many early shrines in Korea, the shrine was originally a *daijingū*-type shrine dedicated to Amaterasu and focused on connecting the migrant community to the Home Islands. It also served as the protector shrine of the prefecture (Tetsudō-shō 1943, 349). In the 1930s, inspired by Chōsen Jingū, it began conducting the Kangaku-sai ritual when distributing ethics textbooks to schools. In 1937, Heijō Jinja was raised to a lesser national shrine. Kunitama, as a generic title for local kami, was enshrined in the same seat as Amaterasu, like at all lesser national shrines in Korea.

In 1935, Heijō Jinja was not yet a lesser national shrine, but prefectural Governor Yasutake Tadao was an enthusiastic supporter of shrines and asked all school principals to visit Heijō Jinja. Like they had done in the 1932 Loyal Dead Monument incident, Presbyterian missionary George S. McCune, the president of Union Christian College, along with Velma L. Snook of the Sungui Girls' High School, rejected this demand. The Bureau of Education quietly attempted to resolve this issue as it had in the Sophia University case: shrine visits were only expressions of patriotism and loyalty and it was permissible to instruct students that 'there were no "spirits (*rei*)" at shrines' (Hiura 2013, 81). These arguments, however, did not convince McCune, and this time the consequences for the Presbyterian school's refusal were more severe. In 1936 the government revoked McCune's teaching license, leading him to return to the United States and forcing the school find a new president to continue operation. After two years the Presbyterian Church chose to close the school rather than continue to compromise its principles by visiting shrines.

The Heijō Jinja incident brought to a head the conflict between the Japanese government's demand for total loyalty and the principles of the Western-affiliated Christian churches. In the following years, the Christian denominations in Korea were forced to decide between conducting school shrine visits and shutting down their schools down. In 1936, the Catholic Church issued the *Plures Instantique*, which allowed Japanese Catholics – including Korean Catholics – to visit shrines as a patriotic duty (Breen 2010). In 1937, Korean Methodists accepted the government's official interpretation of shrines as non-religious. Finally in 1938, the Presbyterian Church in Korea, under pressure from the police, voted to do so. This decision, however, caused a bitter split among Korean Presbyterians with repercussions that continued into the post-war period (Kang 1997, 65).

When the issue of refusing to venerate at shrines based on religious grounds came up in the 1930s, the Japanese government in both the Home Islands and Korea relied upon a secular understanding of shrines, which saw them as sites of patriotic state ritual. Although Christians were required to show physical reverence at shrines, the government's official stance was to maintain a freedom of belief that saw shrines as sites where no religious 'spirit' is present. However, this official viewpoint was undermined by both government and shrine officials who adopted a hierarchical view of religion. This is illustrated by the published reaction of Yoshida Sadaharu, Assistant Chief Ritualist at Chōsen Jingū, to the Heijō Jinja incident. While firmly acknowledging that shrines are indivisible from the state, he wrote, 'Shrines essentially include religious conduct, but [they are] more inclusive, sites which are rich in a universality that is above religion … Christianity and so on are at best narrow sects within Shintō' (Hiura 2013, 87). In 1937, when Heijō Jinja became a lesser national shrine, Yoshida became its chief ritualist. Shintoists like Yoshida understood shrines as both religious and secular, so it is unsurprising that McCune and other Christians had difficulty accepting the government's official explanation of shrines as purely secular.

Fuyo Jingū: Korea's Japanese history

Reviving the supposed ancient 'unity of the Home Islands and Korea' (*naisen ittai*) became a key goal and slogan for the Chōsen Governor-General, and in 1938, the Governor-General began planning a grand new shrine, one that would rival Chōsen Jingū or even Kashihara Jingū in the Home Islands. Ranked as greater imperial shrine, the new Fuyo Jingū would be the 'embodiment of *naisen ittai*', according to Governor-General Minami Jirō (Aono 2015, 228). Fuyo (Kr. Puyŏ), the ancient capital of Paekche, would not merely host the shrine, but be transformed into a 'kami capital (*shinto*)' (Henry 2014, 173). Despite the rhetoric of assimilation, the Fuyo Jingū project aimed to commemorate a particular Korean part of Japanese history. Although a universalized theology came to position Amaterasu as the kami relevant to all East Asians, space was also created for Korean customs subsumed within the broader category of Shinto. In contrast to a universalized Amaterasu, the four kami of Fuyo Jingū – Emperor Ōjin, Empress Saimei, Emperor Tenji and Empress Consort Jingū – would serve as kami particular to Korea. Fuyo Jingū shared similarities with shrines like Kaizan Jinja and Kenkō Jinja in Taiwan, and reflected a wider trend in 1930s Korea of incorporating selected Korean customs into shrines and pre-shrines.

The involvement of Koreans at Shinto shrines is often held up by current scholars as one of the colonial government's key assimilation efforts, along with the use of Japanese language and Japanese names.[27] But the inclusion of Korean elements and customs at shrines worked contrary to the goal of racial assimilation, rather than being one of the most egregious examples of it. Furthermore, Hiura has pointed out that the Chōsen Governor-General made it more difficult, rather than easier, for shrines to be established during the period when its major assimilation efforts were taking place (Hiura 2013, 178). Contrary to the Chōsen Governor-General's assimilation efforts, ritualists and local government officials' efforts in the 1930s to cultivate a sincerely felt connection between shrines and rural Koreans led to the incorporation of more Korean customs into Shinto, even while lèse majesté laws were increasingly used to punish Koreans suspected of disloyalty to the state. So while shrines continued to be a key part of Japanese colonialism, they were not always agents of Japanese assimilation.

Pre-shrines and Korean customs

Early in its rule, the Chōsen Governor-General suppressed Korean customs it saw as superstitious, such as Korean *kagura* dance and shamans (Jp. *fugeki*, Kr. *mukyŏk*) (Aono 2015, 254). But with the start of the Agricultural Village Promotion movement in 1933, the government began experimenting with ways of co-opting selected customs to achieve its aims. The Agricultural Village Promotion movement was based on the ideas of Japanese educator Yamazaki Nobuyoshi and aimed to increase harvest yields and build self-sufficiency in agricultural villages. The movement encouraged villagers to treat indigenous ritual sites (Jp. *tenchi shindan*, Kr. *chŏnji sindan*), understood as venerating all the kami of heaven and earth, as the centre of village life in a manner similar to how shrines in the Home Islands were. The movement also tried to reform village festivals (Jp. *dōsai*, Kr. *tongje*) by eliminating elements the authorities considered harmful superstitions, such as the services of itinerant shamans (Aono 2015, 59).[28]

The idea underpinning the Agriculture Village Promotion movement's encouragement of indigenous customs was that Korea and the Home Islands had once shared the same primitive form of Shinto. Just as shrines in the Home Islands had to be purified of Buddhist influences in the late 1800s, Korean Shinto also needed to be purified of Chinese influence. Oyama Fumio, in his 1934 book, *Jinja to Chōsen*, was a major Japanese advocate of this idea, but Koreans like Ch'oe Namsŏn (Jp. Sai Nanzen), who was imprisoned for authoring the Independence Declaration after the March 1st protests in 1919, argued that Korean customs, rather than those of the Home Islands, were the older and more authentic version of ancient Shinto. While Ch'oe continued to advocate for the primacy of Korean customs, he abandoned a strong nationalist stance, lecturing in 1935 that 'If we are incorporated into Japan, not only the people, but also the kami are comforted' (Aono 2015, 90).[29] Despite this favourable view of Japan, not all Japanese officials supported views like those of Oyama and Ch'oe. An article the same year in the Chōsen Shrine Ritualists Association's journal, *Torii*, for example, criticized 'certain intellectuals' and argued that 'Korean indigenous Shinto' was merely a primitive religion, which continued to be mixed with superstitious and Buddhist elements, in contrast to the 'perfected' Shinto of Japan (Aono 2015, 262).

As the Agricultural Village Promotion movement petered out, the Heart-field Development movement incorporated its aims, while laying more emphasis on fostering 'respect for the kami and veneration of the ancestors' through both shrines and religion. Kageyama Yoshikage, chief of the Agricultural Administration Section, for example, gave a radio broadcast in 1936 which advocated for reformed indigenous Korean village or agricultural Shinto sites (Aono 2015, 265). In 1937, the government-commissioned ethnographic survey of Korean village festivals by Murayama Chijun – *Village Festivals: Chōsen's Local Ritual* – was completed (Chōsen Sōtokufu 1942). Although Murayama concluded that village festival sites were not appropriate for recognition as shrines as the kami venerated were usually natural features rather than historical figures,[30] his survey affirmed that rural Korean festivals were the equivalent to village festivals in the Home Islands and thus a type of folk Shinto (Aono 2015, 280). As Shintoists in Taiwan saw shrine-mausoleums as the Taiwanese version of Shinto shrines, Murayama recognized indigenous Korean village shrine sites as Korea's version of Japanese Shinto shrine sites.

The government and scholars' interest in Korean indigenous festivals as a type of ancient Shinto motivated prefectural governors' ambitions to establish one shrine per village. In the early twentieth century, shrines had been reorganized and limited to one shrine per administrative district in the Home Islands and Hokkaido. In 1934, a similar effort in Taiwan to increase shrines to one per village began. In Korea, plans to build one shrine per village started in 1935. Governor Yasutake Tadao[31] of Heian-nan Prefecture, whose insistence on school shrine visits precipitated the Heijō Jinja incident discussed previously, constructed a plan for one shrine per village at which school principals could be trained to serve as the ritualist. In 1936, Yasutake was replaced as governor by Kamiuchi Hikosaku, who, while still a devout Nichiren Buddhist, was so enthusiastic about promoting Shinto that he became known as the 'Kamidana Governor'. He affirmed the former governor's one-shrine-per-village plan, but saw it as a longer-term goal. Kamiuchi believed that Korean and Home Islands shrines sprang 'exactly from the same root', and praised how Korean village festivals were already using Shinto-style rites (Aono 2015, 268). His plan for the prefecture was to 'revive' ancient Korean Shinto practices at newly established larger sites which could be eventually transformed into full-fledged shrines. Kōgen Prefecture's governor, Son Yŏngmok (Jp. Son Eiboku), inspired by Kamiuchi's plan, also made plans to 'restore' Korean ritual sites. Lamenting that the prefecture's 2,300 indigenous sites had declined into superstition, his restoration plan called for sites to clarify which kami they venerated and allowed for Korean or Home Islands ritual to be used (Aono 2015, 289).

The prefectures of Kōkai (Hwanghae), Keiki (Gyeonggi), Chūsei-hoku (North Chungcheong) and Chūsei-nan (South Chungcheong) made similar plans (Hiura 2013, 170). Major regional shrines, such as Kaishū Jinja in Kōkai Prefecture and the lesser national shrine Kōgen Jinja in Kōgen Prefecture, also adopted Korean elements (Aono 2015, 239). Both these shrines venerated Susanoo-no-Ōkami, in addition to Amaterasu, Kunitama and Emperor Meiji. Susanoo was often identified with Tan'gun, which probably influenced their choice to include Korea elements. Despite, or perhaps because of, this enthusiasm for transforming indigenous sites into eventual shrines, the Governor-General revised the law governing pre-shrines in 1936, making them more difficult to establish and adding a fine to punish unregistered shrine-like sites.[32] As a result, the following years saw a decreasing number of pre-shrines being established, with only nine new pre-shrines across all of Korea being registered in 1938 (Hiura 2013, 175).

Despite the stricter laws surrounding pre-shrines, Zenra-nan (South Jeolla) prefecture began a new one-shrine-per-village effort in 1938, becoming the only prefecture to succeed in completing that goal. In Zenra-nan prefecture, the majority of pre-shrines enshrined Amaterasu Ōmikami, either alone or with Emperor Meiji following Chōsen Jingū's example. The Governor-General issued a directive in 1936 that, like at the lesser national shrines, pre-shrines should use the title Ōmikami, dropping the character 'imperial' for Amaterasu (Aono 2015, 223). Kunitama, in contrast, was much less commonly venerated at pre-shrines. In Zenra-nan prefecture, 175 pre-shrines were dedicated to Amaterasu, with 106 of those including Emperor Meiji as well. In contrast, only seven of these pre-shrines – all in Junten District – also enshrined Kunitama (Aono 2015, 281).

The dominance of Amaterasu at pre-shrines, however, did not preclude the inclusion of Korean customs at the sites. Pre-shrine festivals included Korean customs from wrestling to theatre (Hiura 2013, 192). Furthermore, the lack of training for officiants and the interpretation of village festivals (*dōsai*) as a type of Shinto ritual suggest that the ritual conducted at pre-shrines included a significant number of indigenous practices. The registered representative of most of Zenra-nan prefecture's new pre-shrines was the village's Korean mayor, and a 1941 photograph of a Korean mayor from Jeju Island shows him dressed not as a Japanese Shintoist, but in Korean-style ritual dress (Hiura 2013, 181).

Zenra-nan Prefecture began its one-shrine-per-village plan without the blessing of the Chōsen Governor-General, but in 1939, the Governor-General officially endorsed the effort. This led a few other prefectures to increase their number of pre-shrines. But in contrast to Zenra-nan Prefecture's 247 pre-shrines,

Kōkai Prefecture and Keiki Prefecture came in second and third with 152 and 133 pre-shrines respectively. Over half of Korea's prefectures, furthermore, ended the war with less than fifty pre-shrines having been established (Hiura 2013, 175).

The Kami of Fuyo Jingū

Pre-shrines' liminal status gave them space to incorporate Korean customs into their festivals, but Fuyo Jingū was to be of the highest rank, a greater imperial shrine. The kami of Fuyo Jingū was not Amaterasu, either as an ethnic kami or as a universal kami, but four imperial kami who were seen as historically binding Korea and Japan together: Empress Consort Jingū, the mother of Emperor Ōjin and Empress Saimei, the mother of Emperor Tenji.[33]

Emperor Ōjin (Figure 5.3), often along with his mother, was a popular kami among Home Islanders when identified as the kami of Hachiman-gū and its many branch shrines. At Fuyo Jingū, however, he was venerated for his role in continuing the relationships his mother had started on the Korean peninsula. His connection to the Korean peninsula began while he was in his mother's

Figure 5.3 'Warrior Dolls': Empress Consort Jingū and her prime minister Takenouchi-no-sukune cradling the infant Emperor Ōjin, 1891. (Author's photograph.)

womb. As the chapter's starting vignette describes, legend says his mother, Jingū, bound stones within her sash to prevent Ōjin from being born until after she had received the submission of the three kingdoms of Korea. Empress Consort Jingū had frequently been treated as an empress prior to the Meiji period, but when the current succession of emperors was established, she was demoted to mere regent for her son. Jingū ruled for sixty-nine years while Ōjin ruled for the forty years after her death.

Empress Saimei, on the other hand, continued to be recognized as an empress in the Meiji period and ruled twice as the 35th[34] and 37th emperor of Japan. During her second reign in 660, she went to the aid of Paekche, who was under attack from the allied forces of Silla and Tang China. Her son, 38th emperor Tenji, continued to aid Paekche after her death. However, they suffered a severe defeat at the Battle of Hakusukinoe, which led to the end of the Paekche Kingdom and Yamato Japan's involvement on the peninsula. Plans for the Fuyo Jingū depicted these four kami as having historically helped bring peace to a war-torn peninsula and paralleled this ancient history with Japan's contemporary stated aim of creating peace through its war on the Asian continent (Sohn 2004, 303). Fuyo Jingū repositioned the ancient capital's history as a part of Japanese history and attempted to legitimize Japanese rule as a restoration of the area's historical relationship.

The plans for Fuyo Jingū were directly inspired by Kashihara Jingū. The construction of Fuyo was planned as one of the major projects celebrating the 2600th anniversary of Jinmu's enthronement rite, and its architecture of inner and outer oratory buildings surrounding a broad courtyard resembled that of Kashihara's renovations. Fuyo Jingū, like Kashihara Jingū, was seen as a sacred site (*seichi*) – a major historical landmark in the 'national topography' (Ruoff 2010, 86) of Japan. The historical legitimacy of the site was treated with the utmost importance. When deciding which kami to enshrine there, a debate over Jingū's historicity brought into question whether it was appropriate to include her among the shrine's kami. The government ruled that she was a historical figure and could thus be enshrined (Sohn 2004, 305). The plans for Fuyo also included the excavation and restoration of nearby historical sites of Paekche. For example, the five-tiered pagoda of Chŏngnimsa (Jp. Jōrin-ji), a temple of the Paekche period, was restored and a 32.7-acre park connecting it to Fuyo Jingū was constructed around it (Sohn 2004, 318). Fuyo Jingū, like Kashihara Jingū, included elements from both the wider empire and the local. Materials from across the empire, such as cypress from Mt. Ali in Taiwan, were transported to Fuyo. At the same time, the shrine was to be roofed in 130,000 tiles made from Korean *hoeryŏng* (Jp. *kainei*) ceramics (Inamiya 2020).

Fuyo Jingū's plans were on a grand scale that rivalled Kashihara Jingū's 2600th-anniversary renovations. The shrine's grounds were to cover approximately 70 hectares, with plans to expand it to over 100 hectares. The budget for the site was three million yen, half of which was supplied by the government and half raised through fundraising (Tetsudō-shō 1943, 347). In addition to donating money, the public also donated their time and labour. By 1943, 120,000 people ranging from government officials and bank managers to Christian pastors and students had helped in the construction of the shrine. Like at Kashihara Jingū, trips to volunteer at the shrine included a precisely timed schedule, the singing of the national anthem and participation in Shinto ritual. Particular to Korea was the inclusion of reciting the Imperial Subject's Pledge (Sohn 2004, 311). In other words, Fuyo Jingū's construction site functioned as a site for training Koreans into modern Japanese imperial subjects. Furthermore, the plans for Fuyo included not just the shrine, but the rebuilding of Fuyo as a Shinto capital (*shinto*). Probably inspired by a similar project to transform Uji-Yamada (Ise) City into a Shinto capital, volunteers at Fuyo were told to take pride in helping build one of 'Japan's only two Shinto capitals' (Sohn 2004, 307). Fuyo had grown into a small city of 2,238 households under Japanese rule,[35] and the Governor-General planned for its rapid growth with broad boulevards, open plazas and facilities like a district office, police station, two schools, as well as museums, hotels, an amusement park and train access (Sohn 2004, 315).

Fuyo Jingū, for all its planners' grand ambitions, was never completed. The deteriorating conditions of the war caused delays and in 1944 construction on all shrines was halted. The ritual to settle the kami at Fuyo – which would transform it from a mere monument into shrine – was never conducted. But Fuyo Jingū is an example of how, despite the Chōsen Governor-General's rhetoric of assimilation, the late 1930s and 1940s saw the greater incorporation of local customs into shrines and Shinto sites. At shrines, 'unity between the Home Islands and Korea' was not a one-way assimilation to Home Island customs, but the harkening back to an idealized past that subsumed selected Korean customs into an imperial Japanese History.

Conclusion

At shrines in Korea, a major shift occurred from a pioneer theology to a universalized theology. Factors influencing this shift were many, but the Same Ancestor theory and the idea of Korea as annexed territory reunited with Japan rather than as a colony of not-yet-civilized land was central to the choice of enshrining Amaterasu rather than the Three Pioneer Kami at Chōsen Jingū. Although settler-established shrines were encouraged to adopt a secular conception of shrines by the government, an idea of Shinto as a True religion based on the hierarchical idea of religion gained popularity in the 1930s. This, combined with increasing pressure in the late 1930s to demonstrate patriotic loyalty through shrine visits, caused conflicts with Christians, Shinshū Buddhists and other religious groups in both the Home Islands and Korea.

Adoption of the hierarchical view of religion led to Amaterasu being seen as a kami relevant to all East Asians, not only to those of the Home Islander and/or Korean race. However, this also opened up space for the subsumption of a distinctly Korean type of Shinto. Kunitama, as a generic title for any local kami, was paired with Amaterasu at major prefectural shrines, while a boom in pre-shrine construction provided more room for local customs to be legitimized as Shinto. This reached its zenith with the failed Fuyo Jingū, an imperial greater shrine which was intended to subsume a Korean identity into the broader identity of Japanese. Next, we move across Korea's north-western border, out of Japan's formal empire and into imperial Japan's attempt to build a new multiethnic state: Manchukuo.

6

A multiethnic empire: Manchuria and Asia outside of Japan

15 July 1940, 1:30 AM. In the quiet darkness of early morning, the silk of Japanese and Manchurian ritual dress whispers softly as the civil and military officials of Manchukuo – first among them Prime Minister Zhang Jinghui (Jp. Chō Keikei) – file across the jewelled gravel of the kami-mausoleum. The fires of the braziers flicker off the structure's white wood and copper roof, the half-light evoking a feeling of mystery. At 2:10, the ritualists and musicians take their places on the middle stair. At 2:27, Kwantung Army Commander-in-Chief Gen. Umezu Yoshijirō, led by the Ritual Council's Vice-head Shen Ruilin (Jp. Shin Zuirin), takes his seat upon the upper stair. Finally, at 2:30, His Imperial Majesty (kōtei heika) – resplendent in military uniform and led by the Ritual Council's Head Hashimoto Toranosuke – takes the highest seat. The lights extinguish. The room is wrapped in the 'clean darkness of ancient times' (Hashimoto 1941, 113) as Amaterasu Ōmikami settles into the National Foundation Shrine of Manchukuo. The tranquillity of the night is then broken by the emperor's voice and lamps flare into light again. The emperor and chief ritualist Hashimoto offer up their words to the kami, and strains of music echo through room. The song is Goshōraku, a melody from the ancient Tang Dynasty written to celebrate the five constant virtues of Confucius. Forgotten in China, it had been preserved only in Japan until now. At 3:50, as the heavens begin to whiten in the East, the enshrinement ritual finishes. With this act of filial piety, like Jinmu before him, His Imperial Majesty 'establishes the Way of the Kami as the basis of the state' (Nichiman Chūō Kyōkai 1941, front matter).[1]

Manchukuo, the Manchurian puppet state set up by the Kwantung Army of Imperial Japan in 1932, was supposed to be a 'paradise of the Kingly Way' (Jp. Ōdō rakudo). The new state took as its two founding ideals multiethnic harmony and the 'oriental morality' of the Confucian Kingly Way. Yet eight years later when Puyi, the deposed last emperor of the Qing Dynasty and new ruler of the state of Manchukuo, read out the imperial edict commemorating his second visit to Japan and subsequent founding of the Kenkoku Shinbyō (National Foundation Kami-mausoleum), he proclaimed that these early ideals were only fulfilled with the establishment of the 'Way of the Kami' (*Kannagara no Michi*) as the basis of state. With this, a universal Shinto no longer limited to Japanese imperial subjects was positioned as Manchukuo's ideological basis. This chapter examines this attempt in Manchukuo to establish a Shinto-based secularity outside of Japan's formal empire. It also looks at how the association of shrines with the Yamato 'model race' within a multiethnic Manchukuo – rather than with all Japanese imperial subjects regardless of race – eliminated the space for local customs that had been found at some shrines in colonial Taiwan and Korea.

Constructing the empire of Manchukuo

Japan first came to have a strong interest in Manchuria after the First Sino-Japanese war (1894–5). The war won Japan not only a dominating influence in Korea, but also included the ceding of the Liaodong Peninsula and island of Taiwan to Japan. While Taiwan became Japan's first formal colony, Russia, France and Germany organized the Tripartite Intervention, which forced Japan to return the Liaodong Peninsula to China. The humiliation of being forced to give back this war spoil was increased when Russia gained a lease on the peninsula only three years later. The expansion of Russian influence into Korea and Manchuria led to the Russo-Japanese war (1904–5). Japan's victory this time led not only to Japan's annexation of Korea and rule over southern Karafuto but also transferred Russia's rights over the Liaodong peninsula's Kwantung Territory (Jp. Kantō-shū) and the Southern Manchurian Railway zone to Japan.

In the Kwantung Leased Territory gained from Russia, Japan set up a military, and then colonial government largely controlled by the Kwantung Army and South Manchurian Railway Company. Japan was also given extraterritoriality over the S. Manchurian Railway Zone, an area of 62 metres along either side of the railway owned by the company. Japanese control led to increased migration to the Territory and Railway Zone, and the first shrines were set up by migrants settling in towns located along the Railway. The first shrine in Manchuria, Antō Jinja, was set up by such migrants in 1905 in Antō city on the Liaodong peninsula. As Japanese migration continued, shrines slowly increased. By 1932, thirty-eight shrines had been established, mostly within the Kwantung territory or in the towns along the S. Manchurian Railway. The vast majority of Manchuria shrines, however, would be built after 1932.

In 1912, the Qing Dynasty in China – ostensibly ruled by the two-year-old Emperor Puyi – was overthrown. A fledging Republic of China was set up, but Manchuria became ruled by various competing warlords. The Kwantung Army worked to protect Japan's interests with various alliances with and campaigns against the warlords and 'bandits' in Manchuria. In 1931, the Kwantung Army staged the Mukden Incident, and used it as a pretext for further occupying Manchuria. Then with the cooperation of its Chinese allies, the army set up Manchukuo as an 'independent', multiethnic state on 1 March 1932. Puyi was installed as the state's head, with his advisor and Qing loyalist Zheng Xiaoxu (Jp. Tei Kōsho) becoming Manchukuo's first prime minister. These actions by the army, unsanctioned by the central Japanese government, amounted to a power grab by the army not only for control over Manchuria but also for influence in politics at home (Young 1998, 115). Since the invasion of Manchuria had been done in contradiction to orders from the central government, the prime minister Inukai Tsuyoshi's cabinet refused to recognize Manchukuo as a legitimate state. However, Inukai was assassinated by naval officers in an attempted coup on 15 May and his successor Saitō Makoto – recently returned from serving as Governor-General of Korea – was quick to extend diplomatic recognition to Manchukuo as the Kwantung Army desired.

On the international stage, the League of Nations formed the Lytton Commission to determine whether Manchukuo should be recognized as an independent state or if it should be returned to China. The conclusions of its report ruled in favour of the latter, and Japan subsequently withdrew from the League in 1933. The League was able to do little about Japan's control in Manchuria, however, and the Kwantung Army continued to hold the reins of power in the state (Young 1998, 29, 41). As a defence policy, it began to encourage group migration of Home Islanders to the border regions of Manchuria, starting with the Iyasaka Pioneer Group in 1932. In 1934, Puyi was given a Chinese-style enthronement rite. At this point the Empire of Manchuria drew from a Chinese Confucian tradition, invoking ideals such as the Kingly Way and (ethnic) harmony among the people (Tsuda et al. 2007, 205). In April 1935, Puyi made his first visit to Japan. This became a major step towards adopting a Japanese secularity in Manchukuo, with the imperial edict issued after his return (Jp. Kairan Kunmin Shōsho, Ch. Huíluán Xùnmín Zhàoshū) declaring Japan and Manchukuo's perfect unity in spirit (*ittoku isshin*). In 1936, the Japanese central government embraced Manchurian migration as a pillar of national policy

(Young 1998, 307), leading to approximately 200,000 Japanese crossing over to Manchukuo as pioneers by the end of the war (Nakajima 2007, 159). This period also saw a rapid increase in the construction of Shinto shrines, with about a third of all shrines in Manchukuo being those built by pioneer groups (Tsuda et al. 2007, 206).

In 1937, the S. Manchurian Railway Company returned control of the Railway Zone to the Manchukuo government, and the Japanese government gave up its rights to exterritoriality in Manchukuo. This included ceding administrative control of Japanese religious institutions to the Manchukuo government, but the Japanese embassy retained control of military and educational issues concerning its subjects – including shrines both within and outside of the Railway Zone (Nakajima 2007, 154).[2] Manchukuo also introduced the 'New Educational System' for schools in 1937. This system began emphasizing the 'unity in spirit' between Japan and Manchukuo that had been proclaimed in the 1935 imperial edict (Miyawaki 2017, 15). This meant Manchukuo students regardless of race started being required to venerate Amaterasu at schools (Tsuda et al. 2007, 205). In July 1940, Puyi made a second visit to Japan to commemorate the 2600th anniversary of Emperor Jinmu's enthronement rite. Upon his return, he founded the Kenkoku Shinbyō and its subsidiary war shrine Kenkoku Chūreibyō. In the imperial edict issued to commemorate this major event, the Confucian ideology that had previously been invoked to legitimize the state was exchanged for the 'Way of the Kami' and the 'teachings of loyalty and filial piety'. At the same time, gaps began to reveal themselves between the aims of Shintoists in the Manchukuo government, Kwantung Army officials and Home Islander migrants.

Kenkoku Chūreibyō: Manchukuo's Yasukuni Jinja

In 1940, the Manchukuo government established two national mausoleums in the capital city of Hsinking (Jp. Shinkyō). Kenkoku Shinbyō enshrined Amaterasu and her the source of Manchukuo's founding principle of 'Way of the Kami'. The other, Kenkoku Chūreibyō, was a site for venerating the war dead and was officially designated a 'subsidiary mausoleum' of Kenkoku Shinbyō. Despite this, the planning for the sites can be traced back to 1935 to a single site where the war dead could be commemorated. The site began not as a Shinto shrine or Chinese mausoleum, but as a national *shōkon* ('spirit-inviting') site: a war memorial that would instil patriotism and a modern national identity in the fledging Manchukuo nation.

A Multiethnic Empire 157

Before looking at Kenkoku Chūreibyō specifically, it is helpful to understand the broader history of Japanese war memorials in Manchuria. There was a wide variety of war memorial sites. Many drew their inspiration from Western architecture, such as the obelisk-shaped 'Monument to Royal Dead'[3] in West Park, Shinkyō, the decorative Victorian stonework of Antō's 'Loyal Dead' monument, or the monolithic art deco architecture of Dairen's Chūrei tower. Other sites used Chinese-inspired architecture, such as Shinkyō's Chūrei tower. As seen in Hokkaido, Home Islander migrants did not always maintain a strict line between the recent dead and Shinto shrines. Shrine elements, especially *torii* gates, were used at some war memorial sites, while shrines might host a small cenotaph within their garden. There was also the establishment of 'ossuary shrines' (*nōkotsu jinja*) – visually no different from a standard shrine – on battlefield sites like Mt. Hakugyoku (Ch. Báiyù) in Port Arthur.[4] Some of these sites included the remains of the war dead, while others served as cenotaphs. Shrine priests were also called on to conduct *shōkon* rites for the war dead. For example, the head priest of Antō Jinja conducted a *shōkon* rite for the army at the ossuary site on Mt. Chinkō (Ch. Zhènjiāng) (Sagai 1998, 27). Although this was not typical, in 1912 Ryōyō Jinja also enshrined the war dead of Yasukuni alongside with its other kami (Sagai 1998, 40).[5] Thus, although war memorials and *shōkon* sites in Manchuria drew on a wide variety of Eastern and Western commemorative traditions, the inclusion of Shinto elements at these sites was not unusual.

In 1935, the Kwantung Army's chief military advisor to Manchukuo, Sasaki Tōichi, suggested the idea of building a *shōkon* site that could serve the state in the same manner as Yasukuni Jinja did in Japan. In the Home Islands, the character of the war dead had become increasingly public, and this year also marked the start of the process of folding *shōkon* sites into the category of shrines as *gokoku jinja*. Although Sasaki's original plan called for the use of Shinto *shōkon* ritual, it was not imagined as a Home Islands *shōkon-sha*, but rather as a Chinese-style mausoleum. In April 1936, construction started at the chosen location in Shinkyō. As a national site, it was expected to be a place where students and government officials would visit and pay their respects. Accordingly, the construction ritual was attended by dignitaries such as Prime Minister Zhang Jinghui and Tōjō Hideki, at this time commander of the Kwantung Army's military police. The site was to use 'oriental' architecture and be decorated in a colourful Chinese style which would 'attract the veneration of the citizens' (Tsuda 2008, 73–6). Although the details of who would be enshrined and what type of ritual would be used were still not agreed upon, the name of the site was changed from the first suggestion of Gokoku-byō (lit. Nation-Protecting Mausoleum) to Kenkoku-byō (lit. Nation-Founding Mausoleum). Despite the fact that construction had already started, in August 1936 the direction of the building was shifted from facing the Northern border of Manchukuo to facing east towards the Ise Jingū.[6] This decision necessitated the purchase of more land in order to accommodate the change, and suggests a significant change in conception about the site (Tsuda 2008, 73). While a north-facing *gokoku* site would have ritually protected Manchukuo's vulnerable border from the Soviets, the east-facing 'state-founding' site looked towards to the Ise Jingū in Japan as its source.

In 1937, the Second Sino-Japanese War broke out, which slowed progress on the project. Sasaki was transferred from Manchukuo to southern China, where he would take part in the Nanking Massacre. Tsuda argues that Sasaki modelled his idea on the Chinese Fuling and Zhao Tombs,[7] which ensepulchered the Qing dynasty founders Nurhaci and his son Hong Taiji (Tsuda 2008, 81). After Sasaki's transfer, a Shintoization of the *shōkon* site occurred. Terminology used to describe the site shifted from Chinese to Shinto terms and distinctly Shinto elements such as a purification basin were added to the site.

From July 1938, a system of volunteer labour – much like that which was used to renovate Kashihara Jingū in the Home Islands and construct Fuyo Jingū in Korea – was enacted for 'Kenkoku-byō' (Tsuda 2008, 74). The issue of who would be enshrined at the site, however, was still not resolved. The Kwantung Army wanted to enshrine not only the national 'glorious spirits' (*eirei*) in a manner similar to Yasukuni Jinja but also Amaterasu. The idea of enshrining Amaterasu not merely overseas but in the same seat as glorious spirits was out of the question for most Japanese Shintoists, with organizations like the Tōa Minzoku Kyōkai protesting this suggestion (Zushi 2003, 223). In February 1940, the Ise Jingū and the Home Islands' Bureau of Shrines were consulted and the issue was cursorily resolved by splitting Kenkoku-byō into two (Tsuda 2008, 74). The current site would enshrine the glorious spirits in its Chinese-style building and be renamed Kenkoku Chūreibyō (Figure 6.1). Another site, as yet unplanned and whose enshrined kami was not yet determined, would be built within the Manchukuo imperial palace. This other site would become Kenkoku Shinbyō, discussed in the next section.

Although Kenkoku Chūreibyō was the original site, it was designated as a subsidiary mausoleum to the new site (Nichiman Chūō Kyōkai 1941, 93). Kenkoku Chūreibyō's enshrinement ceremony[8] was held on 18 September 1940, which coincided with the anniversary of the Mukden Incident, while

A Multiethnic Empire 159

建 國 忠 靈 廟 ― 新 京

Figure 6.1 A postcard of Kenkoku Chūreibyō (1940s): Venerating the 'glorious spirits' who helped found Manchukuo, the site utilized Chinese-influenced architecture. (Author's collection.)

Kenkoku Shinbyō was hastily constructed in less than three months so that its enshrinement ceremony could occur earlier on 15 July (Tsuda 2008, 74).

Kenkoku-byō began as a military-led project to instil patriotism and a modern sense of identity in Manchurian subjects. The conception of the project shifted over the five years it took to construct it, starting with a single *shōkon* site deeply influenced by Qing dynasty tombs and ending with two geographically separated sites using Shinto architecture and ritual. The need to construct two separate sites demonstrates the gap between the Kwantung Army's conception of Shinto sites and that of Japanese Shintoists. While the army had no issue with incorporating kami into the modern practice of venerating the war dead, Home Islander Shintoists remained reluctant about eliminating the divide between glorious spirits and kami. This gap was never fully resolved, and in Kenkoku-byō's case necessitated the creation of a pair of sites. One reflected the Shinto-based veneration of the war dead as practiced at Yasukuni Jinja and the *gokoku* shrines in Japan, while the other was modelled on the Ise Jingū and Japanese imperial palace's Kashikodokoro. In the 1940s, this pairing came to be mirrored in most of Japan's colonies by enshrining Amaterasu at each area's general protector shrine along with building a *gokoku* shrine, often next door to the general protector shrine. Kenkoku Chūreibyō may have been the first planned and built, but it was designated as the subsidiary of the two. It was Kenkoku Shinbyō that issued into existence a new type of Shinto site, and marked a major change in the ideology underpinning Manchukuo's contested legitimacy as a state.

Kenkoku Shinbyō: Manchukuo's Ise Jingū

The ideology leading to the foundation of Kenkoku Shinbyō aimed to expand a Shinto-based secularity beyond the bounds of the formal Japanese empire by adopting a multiethnic, but universalized, theology centred on Amaterasu. As such, the relationship between Manchurian subjects and Emperor Puyi mirrored the relationship between subjects and emperor in Japan, but at the same time this ideology maintained Japan's superiority by positioning the Manchurian emperor as the 'little brother' of the Japanese emperor.

Kenkoku Shinbyō's foundation began with Emperor Puyi's second visit to Japan. On 22 June 1940, Emperor Puyi began his 19-day trip to Japan (Nichiman Chūō Kyōkai 1941, 81). On this trip, Puyi offered his respects and congratulations to Japan and its imperial house for the occasion of the 2600th anniversary of Emperor Jinmu's enthronement rite. Puyi visited not only with the Japanese imperial family but also paid his respects at major shrines, including Meiji Jingū, Yasukuni Jinja and Kashihara Jingū. Most important to the foundation of Kenkoku Shinbyō, however, was his visit to the Ise Jingū. The record of Puyi's trip and subsequent founding of Kenkoku Shinbyō, *Manshū Teikoku Kōtei Heika Gohōnichi to Kenkoku Shinbyō Gosōken*, repeatedly mentions the extreme respect Puyi felt for the Japanese imperial house and its imperial ancestress, Amaterasu. It cites how he requested to eat alone before his visit in order to prepare himself for his visit on 3 July to the Ise Jingū, and how he offered a long silent prayer at the shrine after presenting a tree branch using standard Shinto ritual. It was there, the record says, that the 'Great Way of the Kami – the essence of Japanese spirituality which shines its light upon East Asia – was brought home to him' (Nichiman Chūō Kyōkai 1941, 69). Although not mentioned in the record, it was also there where the most sacred object of Kenkoku Shinbyō, the 10-inch cupronickel mirror 'spirit proxy', was ritually purified (Zushi 2003, 222).

Only five days after Puyi's return, the enshrinement rite for Kenkoku Shinbyō was held. The top officials of both Manchukuo and the Kwantung Army were in attendance, with Puyi personally taking part in the ritual – a fact much lauded by the record. Hashimoto Toranosuke, former commandant of the Kwantung military police and from 1937 vice-head of the Manchurian Privy Council, became head of the newly established Ritual Council which was charged with performing the enshrinement rite and other state ritual at the kami-mausoleum.[9] While it was often described as Manchukuo's Ise Jingū, Kenkoku Shinbyō was located within the imperial palace.[10] This made it more similar to the Kashikodokoro, the shrine venerating Amaterasu Ōmikami within the Japanese imperial palace in Tokyo at which the Japanese emperor sometimes directly performs rites (Sagai 1998, 13; Tsuda 2008, 71).

The Kenkoku Shinbyō enshrinement debate

Kenkoku Shinbyō venerated Amaterasu Ōmikami as the source of Manchukuo's 'founding spirit', but she was not the only choice suggested for the site during its planning stages. Manchukuo was founded as a multiethnic state, but it was nominally ruled by Puyi, the last emperor of the Qing dynasty, and had drawn on Qing pageantry for his enthronement rite. Thus the founding father of the Qing dynasty Nurhaci (1559–1626), perhaps under the generic title of Kunitama, was one suggestion raised for the kami-mausoleum. Jinmu, the founding father of Japan, and Meiji, who had been enshrined at Chōsen Jingū, were also considered (Sagai 1998, 219; Zushi 2003, 223). The Kwantung Army, however, pressed for enshrining Amaterasu at its earlier plans for 'Kenkoku-byō'. Amaterasu would be enshrined alongside the 'glorious spirits' (war dead) at the same site, and the army hoped that the Ise Jingū would provide a 'divided spirit' for the site, essentially making the Manchukuo site into a child shrine of Japan's Ise Jingū.

Both these suggestions were beyond the pale for many Japanese Shintoists. Ise Jingū, set uniquely above all other shrines through the shrine ranking system, did not technically issue 'divided spirits'. Shrines that officially venerated Amaterasu either were *daijingū* shrines – officially a type of *yōhai* ('veneration from afar') site – or were not formal shrines but merely shrine-like sites for storing and venerating the Jingū *taima*. This was one of the reasons the decision to enshrine Amaterasu at Chōsen Jingū in Korea was contested. Although Amaterasu was enshrined directly at Chōsen Jingū and not with a divided spirit from Ise, many felt she should be exclusively enshrined at the Ise Jingū.[11] Furthermore, the transformation of war cenotaphs into *gokoku* shrines had been completed only in 1939 and many Shintoists were still uncomfortable with the association of shrines with the recent dead. As discussed above, the idea that Amaterasu would be enshrined at the same site as 'glorious spirits' was untenable.

Negotiations between the Kwantung Army representing Manchukuo and the Institute of Ritual (Jingi-in) in Japan led to Amaterasu being enshrined at Kenkoku Shinbyō within the imperial palace, while the glorious spirits were enshrined at the geographically separate site of Kenkoku Chūreibyō. The difficulties over reaching this compromise between the Kwantung Army's desire and the objections of Home Islander Shintoists overshadowed possibility for alternative kami to be considered (Sagai 1998, 269). Citing that it would be inappropriate for the national shrine in a foreign country like Manchukuo, the Ise Jingū refused to provide a 'divided spirit' (Sagai 1998, 81), although it did ritually purify the mirror that became Kenkoku Shinbyō's spirit proxy (Zushi 2003, 222). As a result of Ise Jingū's refusal, Amaterasu, like at Chōsen Jingū, was settled directly at the kami-mausoleum as the foundational kami (Jp. *genshin*, Ch. *yuánshén*) of Manchukuo (Figure 6.2). The debate and conflict that surrounded this choice was papered over in public by attributing the idea to the Manchurian emperor and his deep respect for the Japanese imperial family (Nichiman Chūō Kyōkai 1941, 8).

Kannagara no Michi: The Way of the Kami

When Manchukuo was established in 1932, the Kingly Way and ethnic harmony were cited as the foundational principles of the state. Kenkoku Shinbyō, however, served as an attempt to shift the ideology underpinning Manchukuo from these principles to the Way of the Kami (*Kannagara no Michi*). The Kingly Way, drawn from Confucian tradition, positioned the king as a mediator between heaven and earth (Young 1998, 285). The Japanese state also relied on the Confucian ethics enshrined within the Imperial Rescript on Education – especially filial piety and loyalty – to form a national morality and Confucian kinship obligations were utilized to imagine a family of empires, with Japan as the parent empire and Manchukuo as the child empire (Young 1998, 370).[12] The principle of ethnic harmony prevented Manchukuo from being a nation-state for only ethnic

A Multiethnic Empire   163

Figure 6.2 Kenkoku Shinbyō (1940): Emperor Puyi in military dress is purified before the site's enshrinement rite. Note the imperial crest of the noble orchid and sorghum on the gate's curtain. (Author's collection.)

Manchus, and justified the inclusion of Yamato migrants as legitimate citizens of the new state. After the enshrinement ritual of Kenkoku Shinbyō however, Puyi issued the Imperial Edict Establishing the Pillar of the State (Jp. Kokuhon Tenjō, Ch. Guóběn Diàndìng). This new edict redescribed Manchukuo's 'founding spirit'. It announced the establishment of the Way of the Kami as the Pillar of the State and affirmed loyalty and filial piety as the state's principles (Zushi 2003, 224).

The record of Kenkoku Shinbyō's foundation includes three essays to illuminate Manchurian subjects on the meaning of the new imperial edict.[13] The first, 'The Foundation of Kenkoku Shinbyō and the Imperial Edict on Establishing the Pillar of State', is by Ritual Council Head Hashimoto. After repeating a description of Kenkoku Shinbyō's enshrinement rite, Hashimoto makes four main points. First, Kenkoku Shinbyō and the Pillar of the State edict are an expression of Manchukuo's 'foundational spirit'. Second, the Way of the Kami – which is a part of the Imperial Way – expresses the 'teachings' of the state. Third, the 'spiritual reunion' between the races encompasses and supersedes the mere 'ethnic harmony' invoked at Manchukuo's founding in

1932. Fourth, the unity between Japan and Manchukuo is contrasted positively with the division among Western nation-states (Hashimoto 1941). The second essay, 'The Way of the Kami is Here Complete', is also by a member of the Ritual Council, Yatsuka Kiyotsura. His essay attempts to define the Way of the Kami by describing it as 'the way opened up by the kami' and 'the way taught by the kami'. The kami here is specifically understood as the ancestral kami Amaterasu whose 'heavenly work' was continued through Emperor Jinmu and the Japanese empire. He explains the Way of the Kami as a universal principle that fully encompasses the Kingly Way and principle of ethnic harmony upon which Manchukuo had originally been founded. For Yatsuka, then, the establishment of the Way of the Kami was the fulfilment of Manchukuo's original founding principles (Yatsuka 1941).

As might be expected of Shinto ritualists, these two essays emphasize the importance of the Way of the Kami, how it supersedes the previously established state principles of the Kingly Way and ethnic harmony, and its position as a 'universal truth (*uchū no shinri*)' (Yatsuka 1941, 119). The last essay, in contrast, is written by army major Kanzaki Osamu. Titled the 'Manchukuo Foundational Spirit', it makes no mention of the Way of the Kami which the two previous two essays held up as so dear. Kanzaki's essay begins by lauding how the new Manchurian foundational spirit – based on Japan and Manchukuo's spiritual unity and achieving ethnic harmony by following the Kingly Way – has created a 'new Manchuria'. He continues by contrasting Manchuria favourably with China and Western countries. Manchukuo's principle of ethnic harmony, he writes, is different from American president Woodrow Wilson's principle of national self-determination because Wilson's principle has not led to a true peace. Manchukuo's principle of ethnic harmony, however, is based on Japan's spirit of 'universal brotherhood' (*hakkō ichiu*), articulated by Jinmu and centred around the heavenly descended (*tenson*) race. Japan's, and thus Manchukuo's, principle of ethnic harmony, Kanzaki insists, will lead to a true peace. Manchukuo's Kingly Way, likewise, is different from the Kingly Way of the China of old. The old Kingly Way saw the will of heaven as embodied by the masses who could overthrow a dynasty, but Manchukuo's Kingly Way was based on Japan's Imperial Way, which was sustained by the unbroken succession of the imperial line extending back to Jinmu. Kanzaki spends the rest of the essay explaining that Manchukuo's 'new government structure' – the Concordia Association – was the 'government's spiritual mother' and that it differed from Western political systems like democracy, Nazism and fascism (Kanzaki 1941, 134–5). The essay ends with a call for mass Japanese migration and the development of

Manchuria's natural resources as a 'policy for enacting the foundational spirit' (Kanzaki 1941, 136-9).[14]
Kanzaki, as a militarist, continued to trumpet the two principles of the Kingly Way and ethnic harmony, while reinterpreting them to place Japan at the centre. In contrast, the ritualists Hashimoto and Yatsuka saw the Way of the Kami – now a 'universal truth' – as subsuming and superseding Manchukuo's older principles of the Kingly Way and ethnic harmony. This illustrates the gap between the Kwantung Army and Manchukuo's state ritualists. While the former was focused on the practical aspects of government for mobilizing the Manchukuo state for war, the latter were more interested in much grander project: the construction of a new secular basis for the state. Thus the gap between military and state ritualists revealed itself not only in the geographic separation between Kenkoku Shinbyō and Kenkoku Chūreibyō, but also in the ideological arguments put forth by the two groups. Despite this, the division between the two was not always clear: the ritualist Hashimoto, after all, belonged to the Kwantung Army longer than he served in Manchukuo's Ritual Council.

Kenkoku Shinbyō as a secular site

Kenkoku Shinbyō was not a Shinto shrine (*jinja*), but it served as the Manchurian parallel to the Ise Jingū or Kashikodokoro. This meant it was conceived in the same manner as Shinto shrines as a public, historical and modern – that is, secular – site. First, Kenkoku Shinbyō's main purpose within the imperial palace was as a site for the ritual of the state. This included commemorating Manchukuo's public holidays there with Shinto ritual, often by the emperor himself. The site did not venerate Puyi's ancestors – which could be interpreted as a private act – but venerated the 'state's foundational kami' Amaterasu (Kobayashi 1944, 126). Public schools also started incorporating Shinto-based morality. After 1940, Shinto sites for storing the emperor's words and/or venerating Amaterasu as enshrined at Kenkoku Shinbyō were constructed at some schools. In 1943, the government declared that education in Manchukuo was to be based upon the Way of the Kami, and school curriculum included teaching about Amaterasu as the founding kami (Miyawaki 2017, 15-16).

Kenkoku Shinbyō, like shrines such as Sapporo Jinja and Taiwan Jingū, was a new historical site within Manchukuo's national geography, and was subsumed into Japanese history by paralleling Puyi as Manchukuo's first emperor with Jinmu as Japan's first emperor. The establishment of Manchukuo was positioned as continuing the 'expansion of the heavenly work' that started with Emperor

Jinmu and Puyi's visit to Japan in honour of the 2600th-anniversary celebrations was inextricably linked to the story of Kenkoku Shinbyō's foundation. Even in the lead-up to 1940, tourism campaigns about Manchuria's 'sacred' sites mirrored the media attention given to Jinmu's sacred sites (Young 1998, 266). The battleship upon which Puyi sailed from Manchuria to Japan was the *Hyuga* (*Himuka*), not accidently named after the ancient province from whence Jinmu started his Eastern Expedition. During the trip, Puyi was treated to lectures about Jinmu's place in Japanese history and when the ship sailed past Takachiho – identified as where Amaterasu's grandson descended to earth from the High Heavenly Plain – Puyi performed *yōhai* veneration (Nichiman Chūō Kyōkai 1941, 33–6). Once in Japan, Puyi's itinerary heavily featured shrine visits, including Kashihara Jingū and Jinmu's tumulus on 4 July. Kenkoku Shinbyō's record repeatedly insisted on the historic nature of its foundation, and in it Hashimoto drew an explicit parallel between Jinmu's enthronement rite followed by his 'great filial rite' on Mt. Tomi seven years later and Puyi's enthronement rite in 1934 followed by his own great filial rite – the establishment of Kenkoku Shinbyō – in 1940 (Hashimoto 1941, 114–16).

Furthermore, Kenkoku Shinbyō was a part of Japan's effort to 'sponsor Japanese-style modernization' (Young 1998, 433) in Manchuria by making a Japanese secularity the basis of the Manchurian state. Unlike at Puyi's enthronement rite, Kenkoku Shinbyō's enshrinement rite did not dress him in Chinese or Japanese dress, but in a modern Western-style military uniform (Figure 6.2). The kami-mausoleum's building itself was done in the Japanese style; it was located within the broader oriental-modern architecture of the imperial palace, complete with electricity poles behind its stone walls.

Public holidays provide an interesting example of how Kenkoku Shinbyō was involved in establishing new senses of time, space and ethics in the Manchukuo populace. In September 1940, two months after the kami-mausoleum's enshrinement rite, the Manchukuo government issued imperial ordinances #226 and #227, establishing a new annual cycle of holidays for the state.[15] The holidays were divided up into three categories. The first two – celebratory days (*keishuku-jitsu*) and festival days (*sai-jitsu*) – resembled Japan's holiday categories.[16] All but one[17] was fixed to a date on the modern solar calendar, and most were celebrated with ritual at either Kenkoku Shinbyō, Kenkoku Chūreibyō, or both. The third category, made up of six minor Seasonal Days, in contrast, lacked Japanese precedent and retained their lunisolar calendar date. The designation of both Japan's Foundation Day (11 February; Jinmu's enthronement rite) and Manchukuo's Foundation Day (1 March) positioned Manchukuo within the

A Multiethnic Empire 167

longer History of Japanese linear time. Cyclical time, meanwhile, was affirmed through the use of both Japanese and Manchukuo's regnal years and the holidays of both the Japan and Manchukuo emperors' birthdays (29 April and 6 February, respectively).

Space was affirmed through practices like nation-wide *yōhai* towards Kenkoku Shinbyō on the celebratory day of 'Foundational Kami Festival Day' (Genshinsai-setsu), which commemorated the Kenkoku Shinbyō's foundation (Kobayashi 1944, 135–9). Finally, all eleven of the celebratory and festival days were connected to Japan's Shinto-based secularity. Three of the holidays overlapped official Japanese holidays (New Year's Day, Japanese Foundation Day, Japanese Emperor's Birthday), while a further four were Manchurian versions of Japanese holidays (Manchukuo Foundation Day, Manchukuo Emperor's Birthday, Kikoku-sai and Jōshin-sai). Two more celebrated the spring and autumn festivals of Kenkoku Chūreibyō. The final two (Hōnichi Senshō Kinenbi and Genshinsai-setsu) commemorated the two major edicts issued by Puyi after his two trips to Japan: the Edict on Instruction to the People Upon Return and the Edict on Establishing the Pillar of the State. In contrast, although the six Seasonal Days based on Chinese customs were retained as holidays, they were given less significance on the national calendar. Thus Kenkoku Shinbyō and its subsidiary Chūreibyō functioned as secular sites and attempted to instil new Japanese-based senses of time, space and ethics in Manchukuo.

A multiethnic Shinto secularity

Kenkoku Shinbyō demonstrates how Shinto was universalized beyond the formal Japanese empire. Amaterasu was venerated as the foundational kami and her Way of the Kami was not exclusive to Japanese imperial subjects, but was a 'universal truth' that was applicable across East Asia. In the late 1930s, Shintoists argued that Manchukuo as a multiethnic nation should also have multiethnic Shinto shrines. In April 1938, the semi-governmental Kaigai Jinja Mondai Kenkyū-kai (Research Council on the Overseas Shrine Issue) put forward guidelines for shrines in Manchuria and China. Its suggestions included both cultural and practical adaptions for making shrines suitable for their overseas location. For example, the Council suggested using the elaborate *gongen*-style of shrine architecture historically associated with Buddhist temple complexes, rather than the popular *shinmei*-style of architecture that was associated with Amaterasu. It also suggested that purification using incense – a custom common at Buddhist temples, but not shrines – could replace water purification basins in areas of extreme winter cold. The Council's plan further argued that, while Home Islanders remained Manchukuo's 'model race', non-Japanese should not be divided into the separate category of venerators (*sūkeisha*) at shrines, but rather all ethnicities should be considered familial members (*ujiko*) (Tsuda et al. 2007, 230).

The vast majority of shrines in Manchukuo did not adopt the Council's recommendations. The Japanese embassy in Manchukuo complained that Japanese migrants saw shrines as exclusive to their race, excluding even ethnic Koreans who were legally Japanese subjects (Tsuda et al. 2007, 230). But there were a few Shinto sites which incorporated local or non-Home Islands elements. One shrine, for example, performed weddings where the Japanese migrants wore the new 'Concordia dress',[18] rather than Japanese dress. This shrine, Gojō Jinja, was named after the five constant virtues (*gojō*) of Confucianism and was the only one in Manchuria to enshrine Kunitama along with Amaterasu and Emperor Meiji. This suggests its community was more interested in adapting to the local environment in comparison to other shrines (Sagai 1998, 202).

Shinton Jinja was another shrine that incorporated local elements. It was established in 1938 by the Manchurian Minister of Justice, Zhang Huanxiang (Jp. Chō Kanshō), in his hometown of Shinton (Ch. Xīntún). The shrine venerated not only Japan's first emperor Jinmu with a divided spirit from Kashihara Jingū but also Nurhaci, the founder of the Qing dynasty (Sagai 1998, 218). It is impossible to know how much this shrine incorporated Chinese customs in its ritual, but the description of the enshrinement rite at a different Shinto site, Tai-gū, deliberately details the multiethnic customs it incorporated. Like Shinton Jinja, Tai-gū venerated not only Japanese kami but also a Manchurian personage: Zheng Xiaoxu (Jp. Tei Kōsho), the first prime minister of Manchukuo. Zheng had been pressured out of his position as prime minister in 1935 by the Kwantung Army and died shortly after. Ōta Toyō, a Home Islander migrant who had personally admired Zheng and regularly commemorated him at his grave site, founded Tai-gū in 1940. Tai-gū included Chinese elements within its architecture, while its enshrinement rite included Japanese, Chinese and Arabic language addresses. Participants also wore what Ōta called '*hakkō ichiu* dress', an amalgamation of Japanese, Chinese and Western sartorial styles (Sagai 1998, 215).

Gojō Jinja, Shinton Jinja and Tai-gū demonstrate that there was precedent for incorporating multiethnic customs into Shinto sites in Manchukuo. Kenkoku Shinbyō also adopted some localized elements, although not as obviously as at Kenkoku Chūreibyō. Kenkoku Shinbyō's building, for example, was constructed in the *gongen* style of architecture, despite the *shinmei* style being more typical for shrines dedicated to Amaterasu. Furthermore, the limited number of contemporary photographs of the site which have been preserved does not immediately evoke a Home Islands-style shrine. Kenkoku Shinbyō's enshrinement rite used both of Manchukuo's official languages (Japanese and Chinese), while Western-style military dress was used by Puyi and other officials during the rite. The kami-mausoleum also took as its crest the imperial seal of Manchukuo, which featured Puyi's favourite flower, a five-petalled noble orchid, and ears of sorghum, an essential grain in Manchukuo (Figure 6.2). Although Kenkoku Shinbyō did localize to a certain extent, it was unmistakably a Shinto site. Ritualists like Hashimoto wore Japanese Shinto dress and offered up standard Shinto goods like five bolts of coloured silk. Although built in the *gongen*-style, the kami-mausoleum forwent the use of bright paints in the continental style and included a *shinmei*-style *torii* gate. In comparison to Kenkoku Chūreibyō, Kenkoku Shinbyō largely lacked obvious Chinese influence (Tsuda 2008, 83).

In Taiwan, Shintoists had argued that shrines were the Japanese version of Taiwanese mausoleums, while the Taiwanese mausoleum to Koxinga was transformed into the shrine, Kaizan Jinja. In Manchukuo, the opposite occurred. Instead of an older local site being turned into a Shinto shrine, a new Shinto site was turned into a localized kami-mausoleum. Kenkoku Shinbyō, the Manchukuo version of Japan's Shinto shrines, was also the expansion of the 'Way of the Kami' beyond the formal Japanese empire. The site adopted a type of universalized theology centred on Amaterasu that was applicable to all ethnicities. At the same time, like other major overseas shrines, Kenkoku Shinbyō's main function was as a public, historical and modern site for conducting state ritual.

Shinkyō Jinja: Japanese shrines in Manchuria

The Japanese embassy may have hoped that Manchukuo's Shinto shrines would embrace a multiethnic conception, but the Home Islander migrants who founded and supported these shrines had different ideas. Shinkyō Jinja, the largest Shinto shrine in Manchukuo's capital, demonstrates how shrine communities often embraced a secular conception of Shinto shrines, but also saw them as ethnic Japanese sites and tried to maintain them as sites exclusive to Home Islanders. The vast majority of Manchukuo shrines were founded after 1932, although starting with Antō Jinja in 1905 a slow trickle of shrines was established earlier in the Kwantung Leased Area and the towns along the S. Manchurian

Railway.[19] Shinkyō Jinja was one of these earlier shrines, established as Chōshun Jinja in 1915. Chōshun (Ch. Chángchūn) was the northernmost town on the S. Manchurian Railway Company's lines, and the Japanese migrants living in Chōshun – most of them connected to the railway company in some way – first applied to Kwantung government for permission to establish a shrine in 1911. This request was denied, but like many other shrines,[20] the migrants were able to gain permission in honour of Emperor Taisho's enthronement rite in 1915. Amaterasu, Meiji and Ōkuninushi were formally enshrined the next year. Like Keijō Jinja in Korea, Chōshun Jinja was first conceived as a *daijingū*-type shrine, with Amaterasu chosen as an ethnic kami relevant to all Home Islanders regardless of prefecture.

In 1932, Manchukuo was established and Chōshun designated the new state's capital city. The city's name was changed to Shinkyō (Hsinking, lit. 'New Capital'). Chōshun Jinja also changed its name to Shinkyō Jinja, following the standard pattern of shrine names established under the concentric geographic conception of shrines. In 1937, Japan gave up its extraterritorial rights in Manchukuo. This included passing its control over Japanese religious organizations to the Manchukuo government. However, Japan did not relinquish its control over educational organizations, which included Shinto shrines. Instead, the administration of shrines passed from the S. Manchuria Railway Company to the Japanese embassy (Nakajima 2007, 160). Shinkyō Jinja, as the largest shrine in the capital, continued to expand its influence across Manchukuo. It held training seminars for the many unofficial ritualists who looked after rural shrines across Manchukuo, and at the war's end, the Japanese embassy directed those communities abandoning their shrines to bring their spirit proxies to Shinkyō Jinja for safekeeping (Sagai 1998, 72, 291).

As the shrine developed, Shinkyō Jinja's community embraced a modern public conception of shrines. The shrine was founded in honour of Emperor Taisho's enthronement rite and only after receiving official permission from the Kwantung government. The community also chose to enshrine the recently departed Emperor Meiji as one of its kami. They marked national Japanese events with major renovations projects, such as rebuilding its shrine buildings in honour of Emperor Showa's enthronement in 1929 (Tsuda et al. 2007, 241). The shrine was designated to receive official offerings from S. Manchurian Railway Company, which largely functioned as the government within the Railway Zone. The Railway established standardized guidelines on when and how great an offering was to be given to each shrine. Shinkyō Jinja was among the highest ranked, receiving 10 yen on the national holidays of the New Year

A Multiethnic Empire 171

and Niiname-sai, and 20 yen for its spring and autumn festivals (Nakajima 2007, 155).²¹ The shrine also adopted modern elements. It was built of ferroconcrete and boasted a pair of bronze dedicatory horse statues (Tsuda et al. 2007, 241, 218). The city tram announced the shrine when passing Shinkyō Jinja and all passengers, regardless of ethnicity, were expected to take off their hats to express respect (Zushi 2003, 205). In this way, the Japanese community in Shinkyō expected the shrine to 'evoke the feeling of civil reverence', as one postcard's caption expressed (Tsuda et al. 2007, 246).

Shinkyō Jinja utilized some elements of the concentric geographic conception of shrines. Its name reflected its position as protector of the city, and the shrine received treasures handed down from the Ise Jingū, deepening its connection to the Japanese centre (Sagai 1998, 74). Shrines like Shinkyō Jinja were also the site of *yōhai* rites, where participants physically bowed in the direction of Ise, Kashihara or the imperial palace.²² However, Shinkyō Jinja did not follow the common shrine custom of being built on virgin land overlooking its city. Although the S. Manchurian Railway Company planned out the cities surrounding its stations, it did not originally allocate land for shrines. This contrasts with other colonial cities such as Sapporo and Taihoku. Likewise, the relatively flat geography of Manchukuo led to shrines being built in a central city park, rather than on a nearby hill overlooking the city (Tsuda et al. 2007, 232–3).

Although shrines like Shinkyō Jinja embraced many elements of the secular conception of shrines, they also rejected the multiethnic conception of Shinto proposed by the Japanese embassy and sites like Kenkoku Shinbyō (Tsuda et al. 2007, 231). Ideas for adapting shrines to the local circumstances, such as those put forth by the Research Council on the Overseas Shrines Issue, were rarely adopted. For example, Shinkyō Jinja used concrete to help withstand the cold winters of Manchukuo, but also hid most of it with wood to give the impression of shrine architecture more suited for the humid Home Islands (Figure 6.3). Likewise, Shinkyō Jinja had a water purification basin, despite the fact it would be frozen and unusable for half the year. Although all residents were expected to show respect for shrines when passing, non-Japanese residents were often specifically prohibited from visiting shrines (Tsuda et al. 2007, 229, 231–3).²³ Even when shrines did allow non-Japanese residents to become a shrine member, an ethnic divide was maintained by designating Japanese residents 'familial members' (*ujiko*) and non-Home Islanders – sometimes including Korean-Japanese – mere 'venerators' (*sūkeisha*) (Zushi 2003, 213). The Japanese embassy and some shrine priests complained that Japanese migrants saw shrines

Figure 6.3 A postcard of Shinkyō Jinja: The shrine's architecture makes it indistinguishable from a shrine in the Home Islands, complete with the water purification basin added in 1935 on the right. (Author's collection.)

as exclusive to Japanese and did not understand the true purpose of shrines, but did little to resolve the issue (Tsuda et al. 2007, 230).

Urban shrines like Shinkyō Jinja rejected the government's conception of multiethnic shrines, and an even larger gap formed between this idea and the shrines set up by the pioneer group settlements. The migrants that made up these groups were recruited and trained through what Louise Young has called the 'migration machine' (Young 1998, 352). This training included months or even years at training centres in the Home Islands and Manchuria. The most significant was Uchihara Training Centre in Ibaraki prefecture. Opened in 1938, it spent seven years preparing Home Islander migrants for their new life in Manchuria. The centre was run by Katō Kanji, sometimes called the 'father of Manchurian migration'. He was deeply influenced by Kakei Katsuhiko's ideas about Shinto. Kakei's ideas, which we have already seen were influential in Korea, were based on a hierarchical conception of religion and promoted an internal 'reunion' with the ancestral kami through activities like *misogi* and gymnastics. On Kakei's advice, Katō enshrined not only Amaterasu and all the historical emperors, but also the 'pioneer kami', 'economy kami', 'glorious spirits of pioneering' and 'spirits of the meritorious' at Uchihara's Iyasaka Jinja. Unlike the

A Multiethnic Empire 173

Three Pioneer Kami of the Sapporo, Karafuto and Taiwan shrines, the 'pioneer kami' of Iyasaka Jinja was a generic title that did not include Ōkunitama as the spirit of the land. The combination of these six kami, especially the combination of Amaterasu with 'spirits' at the same shrine, was considered unorthodox among most Shintoists in Japan (Sagai 1998, 98).

Trainees at Uchihara were taught to do *yōhai* daily towards the imperial palace, to practice Kakei's gymnastics (*yamato-bataraki*) and to cheer the Japanese emperor from afar using the *iyasaka* chant developed by Kakei (Sagai 1998, 90). Before leaving for Manchukuo, pioneer groups would often visit the Ise Jingū to receive a Jingū *taima* that would serve as the centre of their new village shrine. Once in Manchukuo, many groups continued to practice the Kakei-influenced activities they had learned in training. These groups rarely included a formally trained ritualist, so the village shrine's caretaker might also attend seminars held by the immigration company or Shinkyō Jinja. The Manchurian migration scheme encouraged strong links between the 'parent town' in the Home Islands and the 'child town' in Manchukuo. Migrants often enshrined a kami from their hometown shrine in addition to Amaterasu, and imitated the architecture of that shrine (Nakajima 2007, 162). Thus the shrines set up by these pioneer groups were largely removed from the supposedly multiethnic ideals of Manchurian harmony. Instead, Home Islander migrants relied upon Kakei's Shinto practices for psychological support and aimed to recreate their hometown shrine traditions as much as possible. Shinto shrines were first and foremost for helping the 'Yamato race' 'spiritually reunite' with the kami, with the inclusion of Manchukuo's other races only a vague future goal (Nakajima 2007, 161).

To summarize, the Japanese-controlled Manchukuo government utilized a universalized conception of Amaterasu to construct a vision of a multiethnic Shinto-based secularity that could apply outside of the formal Japanese empire. This vision was Japan-centric and relied upon the idea of a parent–child relationship between Japan and Manchukuo, but it constructed an ideological framework for utilizing shrine-like institutions as the basis for a non-Japanese state. Japanese migrants in Manchukuo, however, almost entirely rejected the idea of shrines as multiethnic sites and instead protected them as enclaves exclusive to Home Islanders. While urban shrine communities adopted a modern secular conception of shrines, the rural shrines of the pioneer groups were deeply influenced not only by the premodern traditions of their hometown shrines but also by Kakei's theories which took a hierarchical, rather than flattened, view of religion.

Shrines in the Asia-Pacific

The establishment of shrines on the Asian continent was not limited to Manchukuo. In 1922, shortly after the military government of the Kwantung Leased Territory was reorganized into the Kwantung Office, the Office issued Ordinance 78 to establish regulations for shrines within the Territory and S. Manchurian Railway Zone. Although these areas were legally temporarily leased areas, Japan treated them as colonial acquisitions that would be permanently retained. As Japan expanded into the Asian continent economically and militarily, civilian migrants and military members set up shrines in China and South-East Asia. In 1936, shrines in China and Manchukuo were briefly put under the same regulations until next year, when new regulations by the Ministry of Colonial Affairs put shrines in both Manchukuo proper and Kwantung Leased Territory under the administration of the Japanese embassy (Nakajima 2007, 160). By the end of the war at least 51 shrines had been built in China (Nakajima 2013, 18), with 113,682 Jingū *taima* being distributed there in 1943 (Zushi 2003, 260).

Shrines in the Kwantung Leased Territory and China largely followed the same pattern as in Manchukuo, commonly enshrining Amaterasu and focusing on the Japanese migrant community. Dairen Jinja, for example, began as a *daijingū*-type shrine in 1907 for the Home Islander community in Dairen (Dalian). As it grew to become the leading shrine in the Kwantung Leased Territory, its community increasingly adopted a secular conception of shrines. At the same time, it remained focused on Home Islanders rather than the other ethnicities living in the city (Nitta 1997, 101). Outside of Kwantung, shrines like Hokkyō Jinja in Hokkyō (Beijing) (Zushi 2003, 207) and Fukushū Jinja in Fukushū (Fuzhou) (Watanabe 2016) also followed this pattern. For example, Hokkyō Jinja included non-Japanese within its community, but like shrines in Manchukuo separated them as 'venerators' rather than 'familial members'. Fukushū Jinja, meanwhile, was built next to the Japanese elementary school in the foreigner's quarter of the city. The name of Toyokawa Inari Daimyō Jinja, which Kondō (1943, 320) cites as located somewhere in South East Asia, also suggests it was founded by Home Islanders, likely with geographic and cultural connections to Toyokawa Inari Temple (Myōgon-ji) in Aichi prefecture.

The Japanese military also supported grand shrine projects in areas it occupied. In Kwantung, the army pushed for a greater imperial shrine to be established in Port Arthur, the seat of the Kwantung government. Through the Kwantung Office, it negotiated with the Home Ministry in Japan for a shrine equivalent to Chōsen Jingū in Korea. Although the Home Ministry was against the enshrinement of Amaterasu and Emperor Meiji together, and argued that the choice to do so in Korea was a controversial, special case, the Kwantung Office ended up winning its way (Zushi 2003, 215-18). In 1944, Amaterasu Ōmikami and Emperor Meiji were enshrined at the newly established Kantō Jingū. The army was also involved in building Nankyō Jinja in Nankyō (Nanking). Plans for the shrine, which enshrined Amaterasu in 1943, originally included a cenotaph, but through urging of the military, this was transformed into a subsidiary *gokoku* shrine located within the shrine's garden (Li and Matsumoto 2016, 68). This demonstrates another example of the 1940s trend seen in Taiwan, Korea and Manchukuo of not only Shintoizing cenotaphs but also connecting them ideologically and geographically to the area's general protector shrine. Also in 1943, the army undertook the building of Shōnan Jinja in Singapore. Again dedicated to Amaterasu, it was built on a grand scale intended to rival officially established greater imperial shrines. The army used not only its own soldiers to provide the labour for building the shrine but also the labour of Australian and British prisoners of war (Zushi 2003, 235).

Furthermore, shrines like Mōkyō Jinja were set up in subsequent Japanese puppet states like Mengkiang (Jp. Mōkyō) in Mongolia. Mōkyō Jinja followed patterns similar to those seen at Kenkoku Shinbyō and Kantō Jingū, with its 1941 enshrinement ritual including participants from the Mengkiang government, Japanese government and Kwantung Army. Somewhat unusually, Mōkyō Jinja enshrined not only Amaterasu and Meiji but also Kunitama-no-kami and Prince Kitashirakawa-no-miya Nagahisa Shinnō (Zushi 2003, 245). The choice of Kunitama was influenced by the idea of venerating national founders at shrines. While arguments for venerating Tan'gun at Chōsen Jingū and Nurhaci at Kenkoku Shinbyō had failed, at Mōkyō Jinja the Mongolian founder Genghis Kahn was venerated if only under the generic title of Kunitama. On the other hand, Prince Kitashirakawa-no-miya Nagahisa Shinnō, the grandson of Prince Yoshihisa who was venerated so widely in Taiwan, had died in a plane crash during his military duties in Mengkiang. He was likely chosen for a similar mix of reasons as his grandfather had been in Taiwan. Sites like Kenkoku Shinbyō and Mōkyō Jinja were positioned as symbols of Japanese 'friendship' with its puppet states. Although a small shrine on a different scale than the sites above, Nagamasa Jinja in Thailand was another example of this. The shrine venerated Yamada Nagamasa, a Japanese adventurer who facilitated international trade relations between Japan and Ayutthaya Kingdom in the early 1600s. The shrine's *torii* gate featured a shield emblazoned with the Japanese and Thai flags as a symbol of 'Japan-Thailand friendship' (Kondō 1943, 320).

Japan also built shrines on the Micronesian islands it governed under the South Seas (Jp. Nan'yō) Mandate. Like the Kwantung Leased Territory, Japan's South Seas Mandate was not intended to be a permanent colonial possession, but given over by the League of Nations only temporarily to Japan's stewardship after the First World War. These islands had previously been colonial possessions of Germany and before that of the Spanish. Japan quickly began taking advantage of the economic opportunities in the islands. Starting in 1922, a class of military and civil officials set up on the islands while the South Seas Development Company, often compared to S. Manchurian Railway Company in terms of its huge influence, encouraged mass migration of Japanese – especially Okinawans – to Micronesia to work on its sugar cane plantations.

As Japanese migration increased, some Shinto shrines were established, but by 1937, this had amounted to only twelve shrines (Tomii et al. 2004, 246). At this point, shrines in Micronesia were not official recognized by the government. Rather, as Japan had been charged with 'the well-being and development' of the local people as 'a sacred trust of civilization' by the League of Nations, the Japanese government encouraged both Japanese and Western religious groups to set up or continue their mission in Micronesia. In the 1920s, this included financially supporting Christian groups working to educate the locals, including Japanese Congregationalists – whom the Japanese government had also supported in Korea – and the Spanish Catholic mission (Peattie 1992, 84). The government also largely tolerated indigenous shamanistic practices, but supressed Modekngei, a new religion that developed around 1915 in Palau[24] (Mita 2009, 15).

By the late 1930s, Japan had withdrawn from the League of Nations and began to see Micronesia as a permanent colonial possession. In 1939, a wave of shrine building began, with nine shrines being established that year alone. In 1940, a series of ordinances applying to both Karafuto and South Sea shrines were issued by the Ministry of Colonial Affairs (Yamada and Maeda 2012, 279–314), and in November the greater imperial shrine Nan'yō Jinja was established as the general protector shrine of the South Seas.[25] Shrines in Micronesia until then had been set up as protector-type shrines focused on Japanese migrant villages or specific sugar plantations and coal mines. Furthermore, all these shrines had been unofficial, located outside of the state's shrine ranking system. Nan'yō Jinja, however, was an official shrine of the highest rank, dedicated to Amaterasu Ōmikami. The shrine was located above the capital city of Koror, facing West over the island. Furthermore, local Micronesians and Japanese migrants were enlisted in donating their labour to construct the expansive shrine grounds.

Micronesian elders were invited to participate in the shrine's enshrinement ceremony while shrine visits became a standard activity for Micronesian school children (Kanpei Taisha Nan'yō Jinja Hōsankai 1941, 16).

During the same period, the Japanese government began persecuting Christian ministers who refused to place the emperor above all else – Japanese and Spanish alike. In some cases, Christian ministers gave into government pressure and performed *yōhai* rites towards the imperial palace at their churches (Mita 2009, 165, 195), but those who did not were arrested and treated severely (Mita 2009, 74). Micronesian school children during this period, most of whom practiced Catholicism and/or indigenous beliefs, repeatedly recall feeling conflicted by the dual pressures from their Japanese school teachers – who required them to visit Nan'yō Jinja – and the Catholic fathers – who sometimes forbid them from visiting on pain of withholding Holy Communion (Mita 2009, 228). Schools also had students perform *yōhai* rites north towards the Japanese imperial palace at the morning assembly. This was part of a larger civic ritual which included raising the Japanese flag, singing the Japanese national anthem and reciting a three-article vow to become 'splendid Japanese', similar to that which was recited by school children in Korea.

Despite the conflict between Catholicism in Micronesia and visiting Nan'yō Jinja, the practice of northern *yōhai* became common among locals. School children taught it to their parents and friends, and during the 1940s they continued to practice morning *yōhai* even when there were only other Micronesians around (Mita 2009, 181, 164). This suggests that Shinto practices like *yōhai* and visits to Nan'yō Jinja that focused on the emperor were often perceived as a non-religious practice. As one Micronesian former student recalled, 'I understood that the emperor was not the deity, but something like a president' (Mita 2009, 195). In 1941, shrines in the South Seas Mandate were officially incorporated into the shrine ranking system, with all but Nan'yō Jinja being given the 'unranked' status. At the war's end in 1945, there were twenty-seven recognized shrines in Micronesia.

Conclusion

In Manchukuo, a universalized theology was utilized to construct a new framework for a multiethnic Shinto-based secularity that could apply outside of the formal Japanese empire. However Japanese migrants, while often adopting the secular conception of shrines, almost entirely rejected the idea of shrines as multiethnic sites and worked to preserve them as enclaves exclusively for Home

Islanders. This latter pattern was broadly followed on the wider Asian continent, with migrants embracing Amaterasu but focusing on their own expatriate communities. Furthermore in the 1940s, the war dead were increasingly Shintoized and linked geographically and ideologically to shrines in both Manchukuo and wider Asia. The Kwantung Leased Territory and South Seas Mandate were not legally permanent Japanese territories, but they were treated as such in the 1940s and greater imperial shrines based on the universalized theology developed in colonial Korea were established there. The Home Islanders who settled in all these areas enjoyed the high status and economic benefits of belonging to the colonizer class, but next we travel to a Pacific island 2000 kilometres north of the equator, where Japanese migrants did not have that privilege: the Kingdom, and then American Territory, of Hawai'i.

7

A distant land:
Hawai'i on the East-West border

July 1892. Kōshi Kakuta had left everything behind to sail for weeks towards a foreign land. Japan was rapidly changing, and its expanding population meant some must set forth as pioneers for new lands and opportunities across the sea. Rather than face the freezing winters of Hokkaido, Kōshi chose to try his luck in Polynesia, where the balmy climate was more similar to that of his home prefecture of Kumamoto. Kōshi signed a three-year contract as a sugar plantation worker, bade farewell to his wife and son, and set sail across the Pacific Ocean to the tiny island nation of Hawai'i. After three and a half years of gruelling labour on the plantation, he made the decision to settle in the thriving metropolis of Hilo. There he drew the local Japanese community together to construct a shrine and on 3 November 1898, the emperor's birthday, the kami of Japan migrated to Hawai'i to settle at the newly built Yamato Jinsha, with Kōshi as the shrine's chief ritualist. From that day onwards, shrines continued to spring up in Hawai'i, giving proof that truly, as the Japanese poem printed to commemorate the Yamato Jinsha's 21st anniversary said, 'The kami watch over the peace and tranquillity of all our brothers, even in distant lands.'

The 'cult of the pioneer', in which Emperor Jinmu played such an important role, not only encouraged Japanese citizens to settle in new Japanese colonies like Hokkaido, Taiwan and Korea but also encouraged them to cross over to foreign countries as migrant workers (Ruoff 2010, 154-6). Likewise, Shinto shrines were not limited to imperial territory, but also sprang up in those foreign countries where communities of Japanese migrants settled. This included not only the Asian continent, where the Japanese government often had a controlling influence, but also across the Pacific Ocean in Brazil, the United States and Hawai'i. Hawai'i, in particular, had a special relationship with Japan. In the nineteenth century, the monarchy of Hawai'i felt a kinship with the Japanese as a 'cognate race' (Kotani 1985, 14), although in the twentieth century Hawai'i became a territory of the

United States. Positioned geographically, economically and culturally between these two world powers, Hawai'i had the unusual circumstance of being ruled by a white American government, while its majority population consisted of imperial subjects of Japan.

Like in Japan's colonies, Shinto shrines in Hawai'i helped communicate a modern Japanese secularity to imperial subjects. Located outside of Japanese rule, shrines in Hawai'i were not restricted by the regulations that prohibited many Shinto facilities in Taiwan and Korea being designated 'shrines', but like in Hokkaido, Japanese migrants in Hawai'i often embraced the modern idea of Shinto and ran their shrines on the same model as found within Japanese territory. Furthermore, Japanese in Hawai'i faced the difficulties of translating Shinto shrines not only into a different language, but into a different secularity. After briefly situating Shinto shrines within the broader background of Hawai'i and the international stage, this chapter examines Hilo Daijingū, originally called Yamato Jinsha and the first shrine established in Hawai'i, to see how Hawai'i-Japanese largely embraced a secular conception of shrines in a manner similar to migrants in Japan's colonies. Then, it complicates the situation by examining how four separate Shinto sites on O'ahu negotiated the space between pre-modern, Japanese secular, Japanese religious and American religious conceptions.

Hawai'i in-between

Hawai'i is a chain of islands located in the middle of the Pacific Ocean approximately equidistant from Japan and the United States.[1] While waves of Polynesian explorers had come and settled within the archipelago since the thirteenth century, the islands were not discovered by the West until 1778. The islands' isolated location made it a vital spot for refuelling ships and planes, and this incorporation into the international economy led to rapid changes in Hawai'i's society and government. Beginning in 1782, the chief of Kona, Kamehameha the Great, unified the major islands under his rule and adopted the trappings of a Western-style Kingdom, while his successor, Kamehameha II, led the royal house in converting to Protestant Christianity. During this period, the native population had been decimated with introduced diseases. The Hawaiian islands also lacked the natural resources important to developing modern military technology such as metal, coal and oil reserves. Thus the Kingdom of Hawai'i had limited military strength and relied upon the goodwill of, and competition between, the Great Powers surrounding the islands for maintaining her independence from colonization.

In the late nineteenth to early twentieth centuries, the United States and Japan were both adding to their colonial possessions. Hawai'i, located between these colonial powers, was well aware of her precarious independence. The United States quickly became the dominating influence in the islands. In 1881, concern over this situation prompted the monarch of Hawai'i, King Kalākaua, to ask for a protectorate-style relationship with Japan (Hazama and Komeiji 2008, 14). Japan declined, but agreed to send migrants to work on the sugar plantations in Hawai'i. However, within six years, King Kalākaua was forced to sign the Bayonet Constitution, a document which placed power into the hands of the American-controlled legislature. When King Kalākaua's successor, Queen Lili'uokalani, attempted to replace the Bayonet Constitution, the Committee of Safety – a group largely composed of Americans and advocating the annexation of Hawai'i by the United States – overthrew the Hawaiian monarchy with the support of US troops. Repeated requests by this new government in Hawai'i led to the annexation of the islands by the United States in 1898, a decision pushed through by the acquisition of the Philippines as a colony (Bell 1984, 33-4).

The Japanese government formally protested the annexation of Hawai'i and the Japanese public were outraged (Stephan 1984, 18-19). While the Japanese government had no choice but to accept an American-controlled Hawai'i, the location of the islands and the high percentage of Japanese subjects there meant Japan continued to take an interest in them. The Japanese Consulate took an active role in supporting Japanese education for local Japanese (Asato 2006, 20) and the Hawai'i-Japanese were interested followers of news from Japan. They continued to send remittances back to Japan, including donations to support the Sino-Japanese wars (1894-5, 1937-45), while the Grand Congress of Overseas Compatriots, an event organized in 1940 to celebrate the continuing expansion of the Japanese sphere, included almost 200 participants from Hawai'i (Ruoff 2010, 161; Stephan 1984, 49). The same year, plans drawn up by the Japanese Imperial Navy explicitly included Hawai'i within the middle sub-sphere of Greater East Asia (Stephan 1984, 136). Although Hawai'i was an American territory, Japan did not see it as an integral part of the United States and increasingly considered it part of Japan's sphere of influence.

The position of Hawai'i between two great powers led to an unusual ethnic situation there. Even during the later years of the Hawaiian monarchy, political power was held by a white American elite while a separate, but related, group of mostly white American sugar plantation owners controlled Hawai'i's economy.

The dethroned Queen Lili'uokalani was unable to prevent annexation, despite widespread anti-annexation feelings among native Hawaiians. But by the first decade of the twentieth century, the majority of the population of Hawai'i was not white nor native Hawaiian, but made up of migrants from various countries. The Japanese comprised the largest percentage, making up nearly 40 per cent of the population in 1900, with this number increasing; full- and part-native Hawaiians made up about 26 per cent, and non-Portuguese Caucasians,[2] who largely held the political and economic power, made up less than 6 per cent of the population the same year (Adams 1924, 9).

This power imbalance in relation to population and the differing motivations between annexationists and plantation owners had significant effects on the Japanese community. Since Americanized migrants were more likely to demand higher wages and participate in cross-ethnic union strikes, plantation owners often encouraged migrants to maintain their cultural values and form ethnic enclaves (Asato 2006, 22). Meanwhile, advocates of annexation and eventual statehood saw the total Americanization of migrants as the only way to allay fears of granting the large second-generation population of Hawai'i voting rights (Bell 1984, 96). Thus Japanese migrants were under conflicting pressures from the white elite to retain a Japanese identity and to Americanize. The strength of these pressures often depended on the location of the Japanese community, with urban migrants in Honolulu, the seat of the territorial government, feeling more pressure to Americanize and rural migrants working on sugar plantations on the outer islands feeling more pressure to retain an ethnic identity.

Migrants and immigrants

The experience of the Japanese in Hawai'i is often compared with that of Japanese migrants to the American continent. While these groups sometimes overlapped, and shared the common element of living under American rule, they also faced significant differences in their situation. Furthermore, the Hawai'i-Japanese shared significant similarities to the Japanese migrants who settled in new Japanese territories, such as Hokkaido and Taiwan. First, Hawai'i was not an integral part of the United States politically until it became the fiftieth state in 1959. Hawai'i was recognized as an independent nation until annexed in 1898, and remained an American territory for a majority of the twentieth century. Although Japan was uninterested in Hawai'i as a possible territory in the 1800s, the expansion of the Japanese empire into Micronesia brought Hawai'i into

Japan's sphere of interest during the Second World War. Second, Hawai'i is located in Oceania rather than on the North American continent. Geographically and culturally, Hawai'i has shared more with the Asia-Pacific than the United States. Third, Japanese made up nearly half of Hawai'i's population (42.7 per cent) in 1920. In comparison, Japanese made up a mere 2 per cent of the population in California, the US state then with the largest Japanese population (Kanzaki 1921, 9). This high percentage of Japanese resembles Japanese colonies more than foreign migration destinations such as the United States and Brazil. Fourth, it was more likely in Hawai'i than on the mainland that Japanese residents did not possess American citizenship, but retained only their Japanese citizenship. Fifth, it has been argued that, despite the Japanese government never ruling Hawai'i, the Hawai'i-Japanese should be considered a form of settler colonialism, similar to what occurred in Korea and Taiwan (Fujikane and Okamura 2008). This suggests that the experiences of Japanese in Hawai'i merit their own research for comparison with the experiences of Japanese migrants not only in the United States but also in Japanese overseas territories.

How did Buddhism and Shinto specifically fit into Hawai'i's unusual political and international situation? Although the first Japanese came in 1868, large-scale migration from Japan to Hawai'i began in 1885 as a result of the migration treaty arranged by King Kalākaua. These migrants were generally required to come on contract as sugar plantation labourers, and were intended to return to Japan. Buddhism quickly followed the migrants and the first temple, belonging to Shinshū Buddhism's Nishi Hongwanji (the largest sect in Hawai'i), was established in Hilo in 1889. Buddhist priests often presented Buddhism as a modern universal religion capable of instilling temperate values in rowdy plantation labourers and preventing conversion to Christianity. The founder of Hawai'i's first temple, Kagahi Sōryū (1855–1917), argued controversially that Amida Buddha should be identified with the Christian God. Imamura Yemyō (1866–1932), an advocate of pan-Asian Buddhism who arrived in Hawai'i in 1899, argued that Buddhism promoted democratic Americanism and rewrote Buddhist gathas into Christian-style hymns (Tanabe and Tanabe 2013, 10–11). This inclined plantation owners to support the establishment of temples in plantation settlements (Hazama and Komeiji 2008, 80; Tamura 1994, 16). The annexation of Hawai'i in 1898 opened up migration to all occupations. During this period, many Japanese began settling down in Hawai'i and the first shrine, Hilo Daijingū, was established in 1898. Growing anti-Japanese sentiment in the United States led to the Gentleman's Agreement of 1907 that limited Japanese migration to the United States, including to Hawai'i, to relatives of current residents. Japanese schools in Hawai'i also began to increase, with nearly 98 per cent of Japanese children in Hawai'i attending them in 1920 (Asato 2003, 15).

The pressure on Hawai'i-Japanese to Americanize continued to grow, and in 1941 the Pearl Harbor attack led to martial law in Hawai'i. The entire territory was put under curfew and free mobility was curtailed. Community leaders and other suspect Japanese such as newspaper men and priests were sent to internment or prisoners-of-war camps. The Japanese remaining in Hawai'i moved to demonstrate their American patriotism and rid themselves of anything that might indicate loyalty to Japan. Temples, shrines and schools were shut down and later their assets confiscated by the government under the Trading with the Enemy Act. After the end of the war, Buddhist temples were usually reopened by their communities as religious buildings, but shrine assets were put up for auction by the government until a legal battle ruled that shrines were also religious. This treatment reflects how temples and shrines were perceived differently in pre-war Hawai'i.

Hilo Daijingū: A modern Shinto shrine

Hilo Daijingū was the first Shinto shrine to be established in Hawai'i. Although Japanese migrants in Hawai'i treated Hilo Daijingū in a manner similar to shrines within Japanese territory, they also embraced more doctrinal-type Shinto organizations. Furthermore, the location of Hawai'i shrines within American territory required a translation of Shinto shrines into the American secular sphere.[3]

Yamato Jinsha (Hilo Daijingū) was founded in 1898 in the thriving plantation city of Hilo on the eastern side of Hawai'i Island.[4] Hilo, while located away from the political centre of Honolulu on O'ahu Island, was an important port of call for ships and had a significant concentration of Japanese migrants. The main figure behind the shrine's foundation was a contract labourer from Kumamoto Prefecture, Kōshi Kakuta, introduced in this chapter's opening. Having left his family in Japan, Kōshi likely intended to return once his contract was completed, but he instead felt inspired to found a shrine for the Hilo community. While a labourer, he began collecting donations and on 3 November, Yamato Jinsha was established with Kōshi serving as its first ritualist. The main kami was the 'dual kami of Ise', Amaterasu and Toyouke. In 1903, the name of the shrine was changed to Hilo Daijingū (Maeda 1999, 104). The shrine was forced to move twice when the long-term leases on the land were terminated, first in 1912 and then in 1928.

By 1928, the shrine community had grown, allowing them the ability to buy land. Despite growing tensions between the United States and Japan, 1940 was a year of expansion for Hilo Daijingū. Branch shrines were established across the island, while a women's auxiliary and maiden's group were formed to support shrine activities. This prosperity was not to last. After Japan's attack on Pearl Harbor on 7 December 1941, Hawai'i time, the authorities swiftly arrested the shrine's ritualist, while the US Army confiscated the shrine's land and assets. Without ritualist or assets, and under martial law, the shrine community ceased all activities until years after the war.

Hilo Daijingū as a secular site

Like the Japanese who settled in Hokkaido, many migrants who decided to reside long-term, if not permanently, in Hawai'i adopted a conception of Shinto shrines as public sites relevant to all Japanese subjects, regardless of their individual home prefectures or religion. This was suggested by the first name chosen for the shrine, Yamato Jinsha. As seen in previous chapters, it was most typical for modern shrines to be named after the geographic area which the protected: Furano Jinja, Taiwan Jingū, Chōsen Jingū, Keijō Jinja and Shinkyō Jinja are some examples of this. The choice of Yamato, however, emphasized not the location, but the demographic: this shrine was relevant to all ethnic Japanese, not only those of a certain prefecture or residence. The foundation date of the shrine, the Japanese national holiday of the emperor's birthday, was also a date significant to all Japanese subjects. The importance of the shrine as a public site for all Japanese is supported by an article in the Honolulu Japanese-language newspaper, Yamato Shinbun, announcing the shrine's foundation. Noting that the kami Amaterasu Ōmikami,[5] Lord Katō Kiyomasa and Hachiman-gū would be venerated, its headline happily announced that the 'myriad kami of Japan' were at last coming to Hawai'i (Maeda 1999, 100).

This choice of kami also indicates that the shrine was conceived as a universally relevant, rather than particularistic, site. Amaterasu Ōmikami, as the imperial ancestress, was seen as a kami relevant to all Japanese, but Lord Katō and Hachiman-gū were especially popular among people from Kyushu, such as Kōshi.[6] Yet regardless of the newspaper's announcement, officially the main kami of the shrine became the dual kami of Ise (Amaterasu and Toyouke), which emphasized the universal nature of the shrine over a prefectural identification. This is particularly significant in light of the strong prefectural bonds that typically characterized Japanese society in Hawai'i. In the early years of the Meiji period, national identity was still in the process of being formed, particularly in the rural villages from where many migrants came. Domain-focused or prefectural identities remained strong. Among the Hawai'i-Japanese, prefectural associations were a major support network, connecting migrants with others from their home villages in Japan. But Yamato Jinsha subsumed this prefectural identity by promoting the dual kami of Ise, to make the shrine a public site for an imagined community including all Japanese.[7]

Contrasting this with Buddhist temples in Hawai'i is enlightening. It was not uncommon to have more than one Buddhist temple, each belonging to a different sect, within a single plantation camp or town. While there was cooperation among Buddhist denominations in Hawai'i, especially between West and East Hongwanji, Hawai'i-Japanese mainly looked only to their own family's temple for services. In contrast, while shrines dedicated to different kami – say a shrine to Kotohira and one to Amaterasu Ōmikami – might be located in the same geographic area, their supporters were not divided by denomination, but by function.

This was especially true for *daijingū* shrines, who potentially had the ability to distribute the Jingū *taima*. The enshrinement of the Jingū *taima* in the home was promoted by the Japanese government as an essential part of being a good Japanese subject. Kōshi, as Yamato Jinsha's chief ritualist, sought official recognition and permission to distribute the Jingū *taima* from the Jingū Hōsaikai, the semi-governmental organization charged with distributing the Jingū *taima* and calendar (Hilo Daijingū 1928, 10). In 1899, he was given permission to distribute the Jingū *taima* across the entire territory of Hawai'i, but as more shrines began to be constructed in the territory of Hawai'i, Hilo Daijingū's domain was limited to the island of Hawai'i.

In 1902, Kōshi Kakuta's son Jikkō (Jitsuo), who had grown up in Japan, took over as chief ritualist of the shrine and a year later the name of the shrine was changed to Hilo Daijingū (Maeda 1999, 104). Adding Hilo to the name emphasized the shrine's location in Hawai'i, and specified its community as all those Japanese living in Hilo. But perhaps more importantly, the new name brought the shrine in line with the standard terminology of Shrine Shinto in Japan. *Daijingū* was a shrine designation limited to shrines that had received permission from the Jingū Shichō to venerate the kami of Ise. As explained earlier, the Japanese government strictly controlled the use of vocabulary to separate legally religious Sect Shinto sites (*kyōkai*) from legally non-religious shrines. Shrines in Hawai'i, outside of Japan's legal jurisdiction, were not bound to use this vocabulary, but Hilo Daijingū's community still sought to conform their shrine to the standards of modern Shrine Shinto.

Thus Hilo Daijingū had an ambiguous position. It was treated largely the same as shrines within Japan – public, factual and modern – despite its inability to be officially designated a shrine. In some cases, it continued using elements from the heady days of the early Meiji period, when Shintoists still hoped for a major position for shrines within the government structure. For example, Jikkō is still referred to as a 'kami official' (*shinkan*) in the 1930 edition of the Hawaii Jinmeiroku – a Who's Who of Hawai'i-Japanese – even though the official term for Shinto ritualist had been demoted to 'kami personnel' (*shinshoku*) in 1894.

Hilo Daijingū also had public recognition in the form of a talisman (*goshinsatsu*) and offerings from the Jingū Shichō, a government organization. Kōshi Kakuta and his son Jikkō were licensed by the Jingū Hōsaikai to distribute Jingū *taima*, and the shrine celebrated the same festivals as shrines in Japan. Despite this, Hilo Daijingū was not under Japan's legal jurisdiction and thus was not officially included in the modern shrine ranking system. It might be helpful to compare Hilo Daijingū's situation with smaller shrines in Hokkaido and Taiwan. For example, Hilo Daijingū shares similar beginnings to Furano Jinja. They both began as unrecognized shrines and then slowly grew along with their communities. While in Furano, the growth of the shrine and town was matched with an increasing shrine rank, Hilo Daijingū could not be recognized as a Japanese shrine due to its location outside of Japanese domain. In Taiwan, on the other hand, shrines were largely founded by the government in top-down initiatives. Furthermore, the colonial government was hesitant to give the status of 'shrine' to any Shinto site that was not sufficiently grand enough. Thus many of the Shinto sites in Taiwan founded by Home Islanders, and whose origins more closely resemble Hilo Daijingū and Furano Jinja, never became shrines, but remained mere Shinto sites (*hokora*) or pre-shrines.

Besides the community of Hilo Daijingū going through great lengths to set up the shrine as a public site similar to shrines in the Home Islands, it also served as a general community centre. In 1904, Jikkō, who had worked as a school teacher in Japan, set up an elementary school (Kokumin Shōgakkō) at the shrine. The shrine also served as a site for an obelisk-shaped First World War memorial (*chūkon-hi*), commemorating those who had died in the siege of Tsingtsao. Further community events, beyond the yearly cycle of shrine ritual, were also conducted by the shrine, such as week night sumo practices (Kobayashi and Nakamura 2008, 57) and civic events such as the Keirō Iankai held in 1924, where nearly seventy elders of the community enjoyed music and theatre for the evening (Maeda 1999, 109). In 1928, after the shrine community was able to purchase land, a Western-style community hall was constructed next to the shrine to provide a more sufficient space for holding these events and festivals.

However, an important difference between Hilo Daijingū and many modern shrines is that the physical location of the shrine was given relatively less importance. Many modern shrines were founded upon an historical site: Kashihara Jingū at Jinmu's palace, Tainan Jinja at the death spot of Prince Yoshihisa and Kaizan Jinja at the historical site of Koxinga Shrine. In the case of shrines founded in new imperial land still lacking 'History', the location of shrines was carefully picked to be on a hill in order to literally watch over the village: Sapporo Jinja, Taiwan Jingū and Chōsen Jingū are examples of this. But in Hawai'i, migrants usually had to lease land in ten-year periods, and when they could afford to buy land, they rarely had the pick of the area. Thus Hilo Daijingū, like many shrines in Hawai'i, moved to multiple different locations. The first two locations were on leased land, and the third location was on land the community bought.[8] As will be discussed more below, the necessity to move the shrine regularly weakened the site's suitability as a historical site within a Japanese metageography.

Japanese space, time and ethics

Although outside Japanese legal jurisdiction, Hilo Daijingū connected its community to the Japanese centre and positioned it within a larger conception of the Japanese sphere. This affected Japanese migrants' perception of reality. This resembled the role of shrines within the Japanese empire, but the lack of coercion by the Japanese government makes Hawai'i an interesting case. This section first looks at how Hilo Daijingū helped locate its community informally and formally within the national network of Shinto shrine, and then how it helped foster a Japanese sense of space, time and ethics.

As it was not under the Japanese government's jurisdiction, Hilo Daijingū was under no legal obligation to follow the standard shrine rites mandated by the government, nor did it belong to the modern shrine ranking system. However, adopting the metageography of the Japanese secularity allowed Hawai'i-Japanese to locate themselves within the wider Japanese sphere and to legitimize American or Hawaiian customs as local variations within the Japanese order rather than as foreign customs compromising the migrants as less than Japanese. This latter process resembled how shrines like Kashihara Jingū legitimized ideas originating from the West or how Kaizan Jinja legitimized Chinese customs.

The choice of venerated kami, the distribution of Jingū *taima* and rites like *yōhai* demonstrate how Hilo Daijingū positioned its community within the larger network of Shinto shrines. The main kami of Hilo Daijingū was the dual kami of Ise Jingū, and the shrine received a talisman and offerings from the Jingū Shichō. This located the Hilo Daijingū hierarchically as a recognized local shrine in the Ise lineage, below Ise Jingū but above the four other *daijingū* shrines on Hawai'i Island. Hilo Daijingū was also given permission to distribute Jingū *taima*. This gave the shrine a role similar to that of the various shrines (*shosha*) in the shrine ranking system, which served as protector shrines to their individual geographic communities.[9] The Jingū *taima* was sent from the Ise Jingū in the centre of Japan to shrines in the periphery. These shrines in turn distributed them to their branch shrines which then distributed them to their community members. This process affirmed Japan as the centre of Japanese space and allowed shrine members in the periphery to enshrine a piece of the Japanese centre within their homes. Over 18,000 Jingū *taima* were distributed in Hawai'i in 1940 (Kondō 1943, 324).[10]

Hilo Daijingū's location in relation to shrines in Japan was also communicated through the rites it conducted. In addition to the rites that mirrored Japanese national holidays, Hilo Daijingū regularly conducted *yōhai* rites. *Yōhai*, as discussed previously, broadly refers to Shinto-style veneration towards a distant place, with peripheral shrines sometimes being seen less as individual shrines but as *yōhai* site towards their ideological parent (Kihara 1935, 213; Suga 2010, 66). Mass, timed *yōhai* rites became an important tool in uniting the Japanese empire by bringing together imperial subjects to bow towards the empire's centre.

Similar to shrines within the Japanese empire, Hilo Daijingū conducted annual *yōhai* rituals towards the imperial palace on the equinoxes and towards Emperor Jinmu and Emperor Meiji on their respective anniversaries.[11] It seems likely that the festivals on Kigensetsu (Foundation Day) and Tenchōsetsu (Emperor's Birthday) also included *yōhai*. While the etiquette of *yōhai* was Shinto, the ritual was considered an act of reverence and patriotism suitable for all within the Japanese sphere. In Hawai'i, *yōhai* rites were also performed at community centres, Japanese schools and plantations such as on the occasion of Emperor Taisho's funeral (Tsuchiya 1927). These events used the Shinto rite of *yōhai* as the universal etiquette in the Japanese sphere for expressing reverence. Being able to participate in this ritual along with the entire Japanese sphere despite their distant geographic location helped instil a feeling of being, in the words of Ozaki Otokichi, a Hilo poet and a fellow war internee of Hilo Daijingū's third ritualist Kudō Isamu, 'one of us one hundred million loyal subjects of the emperor' (Honda 2012, 78).

The ritualists of the Hilo Daijingū also helped connect the Hawai'i-Japanese in the periphery to the Japanese centre. All of the ritualists grew up in Japan and seem to have been well versed in Japanese scholarship. Kōshi Kakuta was described in a biography as reciting the poems of Ga Chishō (He Zhizhang, 659–744) while strolling down the street, and his son Jikkō was a schoolteacher (Maeda 1999, 99). The ritualists' understanding of Shinto reflected intellectual trends in Japan, and this affected their dress. Jikkō's portrait shows him in the flowing Heian-style court dress typical of Shrine Shinto ritualists and adorned with a *magatama* jewel necklace, evoking the necklace worn by the famous Meiji era geographer Matsuura Takeshirō.[12] His successor, Kudō, wore a simple black robe and cap in his portrait, an outfit similar to the uniform of judges in Japan and favoured by pan-Asianists like Okakura Kakuzō (Watanabe 2000, 11).[13] This uniform was based on the dress of Shōtoku Taishi, who helped establish the Ritsuryō state of classical Japan, to which Meiji-period ideologists looked back as a model for uniting Shinto ritual with state governance (Hachijō 1999). Furthermore, the shrine facilitated direct interactions between Hawai'i-Japanese and visitors from Japan, with sumo tournaments between Japanese naval ship crews and local Japanese becoming popular at Hilo Daijingū (Kobayashi and Nakamura 2008, 57).

The drawing of the centre into the periphery was returned by legitimization of local practices as Japanese, rather than foreign. Local resources like lava rocks were incorporated into Hilo Daijingū's architecture while local plants such as palms, plumeria and Norfolk pines adorned shrine grounds (Figure 7.1). The kami of Hawai'i (*ubusuna no kami*) were incorporated as a local, yet still legitimate, part of the Japanese sphere. This extended to other customs at the shrine like flying the American flag beside the Japanese flag. Rather than being a sign of potential disloyalty to Japan, this action incorporated an American identity as a local custom within the broader Japanese sphere, a topic which is discussed more below in relation to Hawaii Daijingū.

Hilo Daijingū also helped affirm a Japanese sense of linear and cyclical time in its community members. The imperial calendar counted linear time from the enthronement rite of Emperor Jinmu, rather than the birth of Christ and Hilo Daijingū had permission to distribute the Jingū calendar, which used the imperial calendar. The festival of Kigensetsu at the shrine, celebrating Jinmu's enthronement rite, also raised consciousness of the imperial calendar in contrast to the Western calendar. Cyclical time was also measured by the

A Distant Land

Figure 7.1 Commemorating Hilo Daijingū's fortieth anniversary (1939): The new hall stands centre, entrance decorated with palm fronds and flags. The oratory stands to the right and tropical plants adorn the shrine grounds. (Courtesy of Hilo Daijingū.)

Hawai'i-Japanese by celebrating national holidays at the shrine. The shrine did not start this; some plantation owners gave their Japanese labourers national holidays such as the emperor's birthday off work and that likely contributed to why Hilo Daijingū was founded on that day (Kihara 1935, 213; Maeda 1999, 101). But, shrines like Hilo Daijingū affirmed Japanese time even as pressure to assimilate to Western/Christian customs increased in Hawai'i. This also affected the non-Japanese community in Hawai'i who could not help but notice when a majority of students did not attend public school on Japanese holidays.

Finally, Hilo Daijingū played an active part in promoting a Japanese sense of ethics. American ethics descend from Western civilization's basis in classical philosophy and Christian theology (Smith 2008, 156). The state in Japan, while incorporating many elements of Western secularism, formed its legitimacy around the Confucian-style family model which emphasized the paternal benevolence of the emperor. Hawai'i-Japanese felt it was possible to embrace both Japanese and American 'ideologies' and 'lifestyles', but saw many elements as contrasting: honour versus wealth, family versus married couple, respect for elders versus equality (Watanabe 1930, 386). The most famous summation of these Meiji period ethics was likely the Imperial Rescript on Education. The shrine community of Hilo Daijingū was devoted to enacting the virtues of the Rescript and formed a *shidōkai* ('Society of the Way Set Forth') with that aim in 1912. The school and community groups run at the shrine, in addition to its festivals and events, provided situations in which Japanese ethics were expected and affirmed.

Religion at Hilo Daijingū

Although Hilo Daijingū was treated in a manner similar to the secular shrines within Japan by its community, Hilo Daijingū also established a connection to Shintō Honkyoku, one of the legally religious Shinto sects in Japan. This was not uncommon among shrines in the 1880s. Sapporo Jinja in Hokkaido, for example, had an early connection to more doctrinal forms of Shinto through the Shinto Secretariat (Shintō Jinmukyoku, an umbrella organization for Shinto-based instructors from the Great Promulgation Campaign) and Jingūkyō. Shintō Honkyoku was formed in 1884 out of the Shinto Secretariat. As Shinto groups broke off and gained recognition as independent religious sects, Shintō Honkyoku became an official religious sect in its own right. The 1941 summary of Hilo Daijingū states that the Hawai'i Branch Office of the sect was established at the shrine and the Kami of the Three Palace Sanctuaries were enshrined in 1910 (Maeda 1999, 111). Hilo Daijingū's association with both the secular Jingū Shichō and Hōsaikai and the religious Shintō Honkyoku may seem odd. However, the Shintō Honkyoku's focus on the 'national teachings' of the Great Promulgation Campaign gave it a less sectarian cast than other religious sects, and the connection to both organizations does not seem to have caused conflict. The Shintō Honkyoku maintained the ambiguous character the Campaign possessed before the categories of religion and the secular were clearly established in Japan. While many new Shinto sects took on the Protestant-like aspects of religion – a revered founder, written doctrine, salvational teachings and a single 'god' esteemed above all others – the Shintō Honkyoku did not develop these aspects and enshrined the Kyūchū Sanden no Saishin (Kami of the Three Palace Sanctuaries), which collectively includes all the kami of heaven and earth (*amatsukami kunitsukami*).

Furthermore, as the name of the sect, 'Shintō Honkyoku' and after 1886 'Shintō', indicates,[14] the sect positioned itself not as an exclusive and independent religion but as the doctrinal branch of Shinto in general. Association with both the secular Hōsaikai and the religious Shintō Honkyoku could then be interpreted as embracing both doctrine and rite as two sides of the same coin. In late-nineteenth-century Japan, the legal distinction between doctrinal Shinto as religious and shrines as secular continued to widen. Shintō Honkyoku became religious while the Jingū Hōsaikai became non-religious. Likewise, shrines were forced to cut ties with these newly religious organizations and ritualists like Wakabayashi Yoshimichi at Sapporo Jinja had to choose between secular shrines and religious Sect Shinto. But in Hawai'i, since both shrines and Sect Shinto sites were legally religious under American law, Hilo Daijingū and its chief ritualists could unproblematically maintain a connection to Sect Shinto while remaining a shrine.

Hilo Daijingū also likely performed personal rites for this-worldly benefits. It maintained a subsidiary shrine for Inari, a kami associated with agriculture and business success. Petitions for business success and other this-worldly benefits were personal acts but not private acts (Reader and Tanabe 1998, 181–2). The granted benefit was seen as profiting not only the individual but the entire community and nation (Reader and Tanabe 1998, 104–5). However, as will be discussed later, the larger shrine community in Hawai'i sanctioned shrines who focused on 'superstitious' personal rites at the expense of public ritual. This reflected the situation in Japan, where the government prohibited otherworldly-focused activities at shrines such as funerals, but accepted rites for this-worldly benefits as permissible. Still, the lack of legal imperative in Hawai'i to divide activities into secular versus religious acts allowed shrines the flexibility to position part or all of their activities as religious or non-religious depending on the context. This can be seen as a characteristic of shrines in Hawai'i. Since both shrines and Shinto sects were considered legally religious under American law, shrine communities had more freedom to keep elements from the pre-modern period as well as doctrinal aspects from the Great Promulgation Campaign. American secularism sanctioned against acts considered superstitious and pre-modern, much as Japanese system of secularism did. But there was no need to keep doctrine and connections with the other world strictly separated from shrines in Hawai'i.

Translating Hilo Daijingū

Finally, Hawai'i-Japanese dealt with the gap between American and Japanese secularities by talking about Shinto in a different way in English than in Japanese. Translation is a useful analogy for this. While direct translation between related Western languages can often produce sensical text, translation from Japanese to English cannot be done word-for-word and produce a text that makes sense. In a similar manner, Japanese traditions including both Shinto and Buddhism could not be directly translated into the American religious sphere without significant mangling of their premodern form. Japanese Buddhists could draw upon the already established form of so-called original Buddhism as 'discovered' by the West, but Shinto lacked a European background like this.

Hawai'i remained in-between the concepts of Japanese secularism, which categorized Shrine Shinto as a secular practice, and American secularism, which assumed all Shinto was religious at best or superstitious at worst. Hilo Daijingū, as an institution established for and by the Hawai'i-Japanese, conducted its affairs mainly within the framework of Japanese secularism and the Japanese language. But the growing prejudice against Japan in the 1930s made a translation of the shrine necessary not only into English, but also into the framework of Western secularism. This translation involved the re-categorization of shrine practices considered secular in Japan as religious in America, rather than the adoption of elements modelled on American religious practices such as the hymn-writing and theological innovations seen in some Buddhist temples in Hawai'i. Thus the shrine could become religious in the English-language context of American secularism, while remaining mainly secular within a Japanese secularity.

As discussed earlier, a Japanese vocabulary was developed that distinguished between Shrine Shinto and religious organizations. The Hawai'i-Japanese largely adopted this vocabulary in Japanese. For example, the Nipponjin Jinmeiroku compiled by Watanabe Shichirō (1930, 24), a Hawai'i-Japanese, lists Buddhists as 'missionaries', 'monks' or 'religionists', while Shinto ritualists like Kōshi Jikkō are referred to as 'kami officials'. This variety of Japanese terms was translated into English terms possessing an entirely different set of connotations. Buddhist and Shinto ritualists both became 'priests', aligning them with Catholic priests, or 'ministers', which associated them with the more positively viewed Protestant minister. Thus the distinction in Japanese between Buddhists as 'religionists' and Shintoists as 'kami officials' was lost in English.

Likewise, Hilo Daijingū's ritualists attempted to keep their leadership roles at the shrine and in the Shintō Honkyoku separate in Japanese, but conflated them in English. This can be seen in Jikkō's calling card. The Japanese text on the card gives him two titles – ritualist of Hilo Daijingū and head of the Shinto Hawai'i Branch Office. But in the English text, he becomes only 'Reverend'. This is reminiscent of how Ōnuki Maura served as a shrine ritualist, the head of the Sapporo Shinto Secretariat, and an instructor of Jingū-kyō at the same time, even while seeing these roles as distinct from one another. Yet like in Hokkaido, the shrine ritualists in Hawai'i were probably more aware of these distinctions than the local community was.

Shinto shrines and Buddhist temples were also lumped together as temples. 'Temple' is a religious term associated with 'pagan' or 'primitive' religions, in contrast to Christian churches or even the mosques and synagogues of monotheistic Islam and Judaism.[15] This negative association is a remnant of the hierarchical fourfold categorization of religion that was standard in early-nineteenth-century Europe. Some shrines and temples adopted Christian terminology like 'church' and 'mission', perhaps to distance themselves from that negative association. Hilo Daijingū, located on an outer island peripheral to the territorial government, was somewhat insulated from the need to simplify complex Shinto concepts into the limited vocabulary of English, but the current practice of referring to the shrine as a 'church' in English suggests Hilo Daijingū was translated this way prior to the war.

The way shrines translated themselves into English had consequences for their legal categorization. As Josephson (2012, 260) has argued, the legal category of religion both regulates and protects the groups that fall into it while superstition is seen as something that should be stamped out. The property and assets of Hilo Daijingū were seized by the American military in 1941 and returned only in 1955 after the court ruled that shrines were legitimate religious organizations. Thus recognition as a religious organization – rather than as sites of secular 'Mikadoism' or of foreign superstitious practices[16] – provided protection for shrines within the system of American secularism. Similar to how bilingual Japanese newspapers in Hawai'i did not directly translate their articles, but rather converted the inspiring rhetoric of their Japanese articles into more detached translations favoured by English-language reporters (Stephan 1984, 27), it seems shrines in Hawai'i were fitted, however clumsily, into the American framework of religion even while they maintained the ambiguous non-religious framework of shrines in Japan in a Japanese-language context.

Buddhist temples in Hawai'i also underwent this process of translation, but there were significant differences in their experience. Before Japan began undertaking the process of modernization, an 'original' Buddhism had been 'discovered' and reinterpreted into a world religion by the West (Masuzawa 2005, 131). Thus Buddhist temples had an established Western-style framework of Buddhism as a religion within which to position themselves. The pan-Asian Buddhist movement, which aimed to create an international Buddhism based on this perceived original Buddhism, was popular in Hawai'i (Tanabe and Tanabe 2013, 20–2). Many Buddhist temples made efforts to remould their traditions in the American religious models (Ama 2011, 3). Although Buddhist temples in Hawai'i sometimes engaged in secular activities such as celebrating Japanese holidays – a practice which was severely criticized as engaging in 'Mikadoism' by Americans in Hawai'i – they usually remained sites for their specific community of members. Furthermore, while Shinto rites such as *yōhai* were considered universal and appropriate to conduct anywhere by the Hawai'i-Japanese, the performance of Buddhist rites such as sutra reading were prohibited at Shinto shrines by the Meiji government's orders requiring the separation of kami and buddhas.

Examining Hilo Daijingū has shown some of the ways migrants located between two colonial powers adapted to the conflict between differing secularities. Unlike shrines in Japan, Hilo Daijingū formed connections with doctrinal Sect Shinto while maintaining its position as a shrine without suffering legal repercussions. Instead, as Sect Shinto conformed better the Western framework of 'religion' than Shrine Shinto did, having a connection to Sect Shinto benefitted the shrine by giving the community more options when trying to explain the shrine to the surrounding American society. The Hawai'i-Japanese smoothed over the contrasting conceptions of religion in Japanese and American secularisms by translating shrine activities from the Japanese secular sphere into an American religious sphere. At the same time, they saw Hilo Daijingū as a public institution relevant to all Japanese, that is, along the same lines as a secular shrine in Japan, and were able to position their peripheral community as a legitimate part of the Japanese sphere. This not only allowed the Hawai'i-Japanese to legitimize foreign customs as Japanese but also became the framework through which many Hawai'i-Japanese interpreted their reality.

Ishizuchi Jinsha and Hawaii Daijingū: Shamanism to patriotism

Hilo Daijingū was the first shrine established in Hawai'i, but it was far from the only one. Maeda Takakazu has traced at least fifty-nine named shrines in historical sources, although very few were able to revive after the war (Maeda 1999, 7). This section looks at two shrines – Ishizuchi Jinsha and Hawaii Daijingū – established by women and located in the area of Honolulu, the capital of Hawai'i. Shinto has a long history of women serving important roles at shrines, including as ritualists. However, when the Meiji government reformed and standardized shrines into single system, it prohibited women from the role of ritualist on the basis that women should not serve in a public role (Odaira 2009, 226).[17] Despite or perhaps due to this, the founders of some Sect Shinto organizations were women, especially those who had experienced spirit possession. Activities such as spirit possession and faith-healing, however, were considered superstitious by the Japanese government and thus shrines as public institutions needed to distance themselves from such practices. The government oppressed those Shinto-based new religions which engaged such 'superstitious' activities, and its inability to stamp out 'superstition' led the government to regulate them through the recognition of some organizations as religion (Sect Shinto). In Hawai'i, shrines were not required to follow modern shrine standards, but as explained above, the Japanese migrants usually did. The following two shrines, which incorporated premodern folk traditions, had to manage life under the American secularity, which discouraged superstitious activities, but categorized both Shinto shrines and Sect Shinto churches (*kyōkai*) as religion.

Hawaii Ishizuchi Jinsha was a branch of Ishizuchi Jinja, a shrine in Aichi Prefecture, Shikoku. The parent shrine Ishizuchi Jinja was ranked a prefectural shrine in the modern shrine ranking system. With a tradition extending back to at least 685 AD, it was influenced by both pre-modern Buddhist traditions and the folk tradition of mountain veneration. Hawaii Ishizuchi Jinsha was founded by Mitaku Shina in 1913 after she experienced an episode of possession by Takayama no Takagami, who she determined to be Ishizuchihiko no Mikoto of Ishizuchi Jinja. After travelling back to Japan and bringing a 'spirit proxy' from Ishizuchi Jinja, she served as Hawaii Ishizuchi Jinsha's chief ritualist until 1927. Mitaku engaged in 'superstitious' activities, which brought criticism from other ritualists in Hawai'i. Although the shrine's spirit proxy was received from a Shinto shrine, Mitaku quickly registered her shrine as a religious organization with the Hawai'i Territorial government, becoming the first shrine to do so in Hawai'i. In 1927, Mitaku returned to Japan, and Kimura Tomiji, who had trained at Ishizuchi Jinja in Japan, took over as the shrine's second chief ritualist. Kimura remained the shrine's ritualist until 1941, when he was one of the first Japanese to be arrested and then interned by the American government.

Hawaii Daijingū, also known as the Honolulu Daijingū, venerated Amaterasu Ōmikami and Toyouke no Ōmikami, the same kami venerated at Hilo Daijingū. Hawaii Daijingū traces its foundation back to sometime between 1903 and 1906 after Chiya Matsue, a migrant from Kochi prefecture, came to Hawai'i. Chiya held qualifications as teacher in Ontake-kyō, a Shinto sect formed from pre-modern pilgrimage traditions focused on Mt. Ontake. She became well known among other migrants for her spiritual powers and faith healing abilities. She seems to have started Hawaii Daijingū as an unofficial recruiting office for members of the Jingū Hōsaikai, due to the popularity of Ise Jingū among the Hawai'i-Japanese. However, the shrine needed a proper ritualist to gain legitimacy. In 1907 Kawasaki Masakuni (Ritarō), also from Kochi prefecture, arrived in Hawai'i. He had a licence from the Classics Institute Tosa Branch and, thus, became Hawaii Daijingū's first official ritualist. The shrine rapidly expanded under Kawasaki. In 1920, the shrine registered itself with the Territorial government as a religious organization and formed a connection to the Japanese religious Shinto sect, Shintō Honkyoku. When the war broke out, Kawasaki was stranded in Japan during a trip, but his son Kazoe, along with several other leaders of the Daijingū community, was arrested and eventually repatriated to Japan.

These shrines both developed from pre-modern style shrines that engaged in popular kami traditions into modern Shinto shrines following the same pattern as secular shrines in Japan. They at first engaged in pre-modern activities that were increasingly seen as 'superstitious'. There was a popular demand for such services within the Hawai'i-Japanese community, and esteemed members of society, such as future US senator Spark Matsunaga, were involved in them (Matsunaga 1978, 73–5). However, their performance at shrines, or by shrine ritualists, was seen as unbecoming by other ritualists in Honolulu. Although Hawaii Daijingū was popular under Chiya's care, there were rumours (reported post-war in the 1950s) that she secretly venerated foxes (Oinari-san)[18] and had associations with prostitutes and other unsavoury characters (Hansen 2010, 74). Later in 1915, both Chiya and Mitaku were publicly accused in a newspaper of engaging in 'lewd rites and evil heresies' (*inshi jakyō*) (Maeda 1999, 124). The same year, Hawaii Daijingū, now with Kawasaki as chief ritualist, engaged in a newspaper debate with Hawaii Izumo Taisha's Miyaō Katsuyoshi and Katō Jinsha's Sakaki Shigejirō over Hawaii Daijingū's lack of qualifications to distribute the Jingū *taima*. This public discourse put pressure on shrines to gain legitimate qualifications from Japan and avoid the overt practice of those pre-modern activities seen as superstitious. In other words, the social pressure of the wider Shinto community in Hawai'i forced shrines still operating in a pre-modern style to reform themselves into a modern Japanese style of shrine.

Hawaii Daijingū also serves as an example of how shrines expressed patriotism. It promoted Japanese patriotism by popular demand, but later pivoted to utilize the same framework to promote American patriotism by necessity. Although the shrine was established by Chiya who was connected to Sect Shinto, its first official ritualist Kawasaki was trained by the secular Classics Institute, which gave the shrine more legitimacy. Like Hilo Daijingū's ritualist Kōshi, Kawasaki sought and gained a connection to the Jingū Hōsaikai, and thus gained official permission to distribute Jingū *taima* to all of O'ahu. As Jingū *taima* were considered essential for good imperial subjects, many Hawai'i-Japanese desired to obtain one. The shrine was active in welcoming Japanese citizens and sailors to Hawai'i, and it began venerating the popular Admiral Tōgō Heihachirō after his death in 1934. Furthermore, the shrine described itself as a place for 'citizens' ritual' in a postcard (Zushi 2003, 133), stated its 'equivalent rank' in the modern Shinto shrine ranking system and held *yōhai* ritual towards Kashihara Jingū (Maeda 1999, 132).

However, the pressure to Americanize grew in Hawai'i, especially on O'ahu. Advocates of assimilation particularly saw the presence of Japanese language and elementary schools, which were attended by most Japanese children, as especially dangerous. These schools, often run by temples or shrines, became the subject of controversy in the 1920s and were charged with teaching 'anti-Americanism' and 'Mikadoism'. The opponents of temple-run schools often saw Christianity as integral to Americanization, and arguments against Japanese schools included the accusation that Buddhist temples – which celebrated Japanese holidays and used government-published textbooks – were 'patriotic' entities that used religion as a cover for teaching Japanese patriotism (Asato 2006, 39; Hazama and Komeiji 2008, 85). Buddhist temples often excised secular elements such as holiday celebrations and emphasized the religious nature of Buddhism in order to protect themselves from charges of anti-Americanism.

In contrast, the Honolulu Shintō Renmei, an alliance of ritualists in Honolulu established in 1920, formulated the 'Stars and Stripes Shinto' effort. Hawaii Daijingū enacted this effort by mirroring its veneration for the imperial ancestress Amaterasu Ōmikami with the veneration of American national leaders and heroes. The founder of a unified Hawai'i, King Kamehameha the Great, and the founder of the United States, President George Washington, were enshrined as kami and venerated in a similar manner to which Amaterasu was (Hansen 2010, 78; Maeda 1999, 131). This Shinto framework was not limited to shrines and affected how the Hawai'i-Japanese displayed their loyalty to the United States in other settings as well. For example, Japanese children across the territory were taught to bow before the portrait of George Washington in the mornings (Tamura 1994, 153). In other words, Hawaii Daijingū did not express its American patriotism by emphasizing Shinto as one religion among many within a multi-religious American society. Instead, it applied Shinto ritual to the American state as a secular method for displaying reverent patriotism. The incorporation of American patriotism as a local variation of shrine life further helped ease the tension between the potentially conflicting identities of being both an American citizen and a Japanese subject.

Hawaii Kotohira Jinsha: A shrine for migrants

In Hawai'i, shrines were founded by the Japanese migrants based on their desire for the support of kami. In the case of the Hilo and Hawaii Daijingū, the migrants chose universal kami that would appeal to all Japanese, while Ishizuchi Jinsha was founded based on the experience of spirit possession. However, another popular kami venerated in Hawai'i shrines was the kami of Kotohira. The parent shrine in Japan, Kotohiragū, is known for the this-worldly benefit of maritime safety. Located in Kagawa prefecture in Shikoku, it was popular among the many migrants to Hawai'i who came from there. As Hawai'i-Japanese finished their contracts on the plantation, they often moved into the towns and cities, taking up fishing for a living. Thus in the 1920s, many small shrines to Kotohira sprang up in the shoreline settlements on O'ahu and the outer islands.

Hawaii Kotohira Jinsha was founded by its chief ritualist Hirota Hitoshi. Hirota was a migrant from Hiroshima who came with his family in 1917 to serve at Hawaii Izumo Taisha. Since he was licensed both as an instructor in Izumo Taisha-kyō and as a shrine ritualist, he decided to open up a Kotohira shrine in Hawai'i after his retirement, in response to the requests from the local community. Hirota and four compatriots went to Japan to bring a 'divided spirit' from Kotohiragū back to Hawai'i, and the shrine was formally founded on 3 November 1920 (Figure 7.2).[19] The shrine gained recognition as a legal religious organization from the Territorial Government in 1924. Hirota suddenly passed away in 1925, leaving the shrine without a ritualist. Ritualists from Katō Jinsha and Hawaii Daijingū – both members of the Honolulu Shintō Renmei along

Figure 7.2 Hawaii Kotohira Jinsha today: A second shrine, Hawaii Dazaifu Tenmangū, was added to the site in 1952. (Author's photograph.)

with Kotohira Jinsha – filled the gap until another ritualist, Okazaki Donkai, could be called from Hiroshima. However, after two years Okazaki transferred to Nawiliwili Daijingū on another island, leaving Hawaii Kotohira Jinsha without a ritualist again.

In 1928, Isobe Misao from Yamaguchi Prefecture came to serve as Kotohira's third ritualist. The 1930s were particularly a period of expansion for the shrine. In 1930, Shirasaki Hachimangū and Ōtaki Jinja were added as subsidiary shrines to Hawaii Kotohira. The shrine was able to buy land in 1931, and that was followed by the construction of a *torii* gate, purification basin, hall, martial arts centre, archery range, theatre, sumo ring, kendo hall, *komainu* statues and *tōrō* lanterns. The attack on Pearl Harbour in 1941 and the subsequent martial law saw Isobe arrested and eventually repatriated back to Japan. Although Kotohira Jinsha's community tried to continue some shrine activities, by 1945 the shrine community decided to temporarily close the shrine.

The Meiji period saw the separation and reorganization of Buddhist temples and Shinto shrines into new legal categories. Hawaii Kotohira's parent shrine also underwent this process. Thal, in her case study on Kotohiragū, showed how Kotohiragū was transformed from a Shingon Buddhist inflected site to a national Shinto shrine, and how its ritualists translated the shrine's 'miracles' into 'the language of secular, scientific progress' (Thal 2005, 216). It eventually was given the rank of intermediate national shrine. Hawaii Kotohira Jinsha was founded because the local community desired its this-worldly benefits, but this included adopting Kotohira in its new modern form as a secular shrine. It engaged in public activities like other Hawai'i shrines, including the welcoming of Japanese navy and mercantile ships. However, Kotohira Jinsha also gained recognition as a religious organization from the Territorial government within five years of its foundation. The shrine's ritualist Hirota, although holding a ritualist licence, had come to Hawai'i not as a ritualist, but as an instructor in Izumo Taisha-kyō. Thus Hawaii Kotohira Jinsha, like other shrines in Hawai'i, drew from pre-modern, Shrine Shinto and Sect Shinto traditions as the local situation warranted.

In the case of the *daijingū* shrines, the shrine community was united around their nationality, but in Kotohira Jinsha's case, the community's occupation as fishermen and sailors was a key uniting factor. The shrine was established less due to efforts of an enthusiastic ritualist, but due to the strong desires of the local community. Shrines like Hilo Daijingū tended to keep the shrine in the family, with Kōshi's son, and then grandson-in-law serving as successive ritualists and central figures at the shrine. When Kōshi's grandson-in-law was arrested and interned, the shrine community ceased all activity. While the chief ritualists also played an essential role at Hawaii Kotohira Jinsha, the shrine continued to function when lacking a ritualist such as when Okazaki left in 1927, or when Isobe was arrested and interned during the Second World War. So community identity was especially strong at Kotohira Jinsha.

As explained previously, prefectural and village identity continued to play an important part in Hawai'i-Japanese lives. At Hilo Daijingū, prefectural identity was celebrated through the enshrinement of Lord Katō and Hachiman-gū, who were important in the heritage of Kumamoto. But the inclusion of shrines based on the ancestral villages of different groups of Hawai'i-Japanese was even more prominent at Kotohira Jinsha. Isobe, the third ritualist of Kotohira Jinsha, had previously served at Shirasaki Hachiman-gū in Yamaguchi Prefecture before he came to Hawai'i in 1928. In 1930, he and the Hawai'i-Japanese Komeya Miyozo, also from Yamaguchi, received a divided spirit from that shrine. The enshrinement of this divided spirit in Hawai'i and the forming of a supporting organization established a Shirasaki Hachimangū as a subsidiary shrine of Hawaii Kotohira Jinsha. The same year, a similar process led to the establishment of an Ōtaki Jinja as another subsidiary shrine, with its supporting organization led by Sugimoto Teiichi, a Hawai'i-Japanese from Ōtaki.

Both of these shrines were brought over from villages from where many of Kotohira Jinsha's community had come. The Shirasaki Hachiman-gū had 1,200 families in its supporting organization, all from Yamaguchi, while Ōtaki Jinja had 600 families, all from the city of Ōtaki in Hiroshima. These shrines had festivals on particular days when the migrants from those villages or prefectures would gather. Around these shrines, imagined communities based on hometown affiliations could be sustained. However, Shirasaki Hachiman-gū and Ōtaki Jinja remained subsidiary shrines. They reflect a social geography that positioned the Hawai'i-Japanese as members of their ancestral villages within the larger category of Japan, since Kotohira-gū was a national shrine. Thus Hawaii Kotohira Jinsha's community was geographically connected to Japan through two paths. One was through their ancestral villages, based on the position of the Hawai'i-Japanese as migrants temporarily residing in Hawai'i but with the intention of returning to their birthplace. The other was through their location in the Hawai'i-Japanese community, connected to Japan as a branch of the national shrine Kotohira-gū.

Hawaii Kotohira Jinsha provides an example of a shrine which was universal less through national symbol and more through occupation. Shrines like this were not uncommon, with shrines dedicated to Ebisu (fishing) and Inari-san (commerce/agriculture) also common in Hawai'i. Although Kotohira Jinsha often acted as a public site, its popularity came from its ability to provide this-worldly benefits and its community drew on religious strategies to establish its place under American law. Kotohira Jinsha also demonstrates how prefectural and village identity could be sustained among migrants to Hawai'i by attaching branches of their local ancestral shrines to shrines with more universal appeal. In this way, the location of Hawai'i-Japanese in the concentric geographic organization of Japanese space could be affirmed and maintained.

Hawaii Izumo Taisha: A Shinto church

Shrine Shinto and Sect Shinto were largely conceived and treated differently from each other in Japan. Furthermore, scholars have divided the thirteen official Sect Shinto religions into four broad types based on characteristics (Hardacre 2017, 382–4). The most well-known Sect Shinto groups are those based on the revelation of founders, such as Tenri-kyō, Konkō-kyō and Kurozumi-kyō. There were also groups which largely aimed to carry on the work of the Great Promulgation Campaign; this includes Shintō Honkyoku, which Sapporo Jinja's Wakabayashi joined in order to carry out funerals and with which the Hilo and Hawaii *daijingū* formed associations. The veneration 'churches' formed around Emperor Jinmu's tumulus, although never legal religious organizations, might be categorized as this type as well. There were also Sect Shinto groups based on earlier mountain veneration associations, such as Ontake-kyō, from which Ishizuchi Jinsha's Mitaku had a licence. Finally there were two groups that were formed as the doctrinal branches of Japan's two most prominent shrines: Jingū-kyō supporting the Ise Jingū and Izumo Taisha-kyō supporting Izumo Taisha. Jingū-kyō quickly reformed into the secular organization Jingū Hōsaikai charged with distributing the Jingū *taima*, and shrines like Sapporo Jinja, Hilo Daijingū and Hawaii Daijingū formed associations with it. Izumo Taisha-kyō, however, continued as a religious organization.

Hawaii Izumo Taisha, or, more formally, Izumo Taisha-kyō Mission of Hawaii (Hawaii Izumo Taisha-kyō Hawai Bun'in), was not a shrine (*jinja*), but a church of the Shinto sect Izumo Taisha-kyō. Despite this, it was treated more like a shrine such as Hilo Daijingū than like a revelatory Sect Shinto group in Hawai'i. Looking at Hawaii Izumo Taisha first as a Sect Shinto church, and then as a Shinto shrine, this section examines how the site's relationship to the categories of religion and the secular was fluid. Furthermore, it examines how this fluid relationship was made possible due to the circumstances of its parent shrine in

Japan, as well as due to the American situation where both shrines and churches were considered legally religious.

The history of Hawaii Izumo Taisha (Figure 7.3) goes back to 1906, when a migrant from Hiroshima named Miyaō Katsuyoshi came to Hawai'i as a plantation labourer. Miyaō had come from a shrine family in Japan, studied at the Classics Institute and then served as a ritualist at his family's shrine. However, when he decided to come to Hawai'i, he determined that religious Shinto, rather than Shrine Shinto, was more appropriate for Hawai'i as a foreign land. He gained a licence as an instructor in Izumo Taisha-kyō. By 1907, a year after Miyaō came to Hawai'i, a temporary building for Hawaii Izumo Taisha had been constructed. In 1909, the Izumo Taisha-kyō organization in Japan recognized the Hawai'i organization as an official church site (*kyōkai*) and in 1918, it was raised to the level of a mission (*bun'in*). It was a year after this that the site gained legal recognition as a church from the Hawai'i Territorial government. In 1935, Miyaō Katsuyoshi passed away and the mission was taken over by his son Miyaō Shigemaru, who had been raised in Japan and was also licensed as a ritualist. The Izumo Taisha-kyō Mission was popular in Hawai'i and formed branches on the outer islands. When war broke out, Miyaō and his family were arrested and

Figure 7.3 Hawaii Izumo Taisha (1923): The head of Izumo Taisha-kyō, Senge Son'yu, stands centre in this photograph. (Courtesy of Izumo Taishakyo Mission of Hawaii.)

interned. Meanwhile the mission's property was 'donated' to the city government while the Mission was dissolved, bringing an end to the Mission's activity until after the war.

Although Miyaō was a Shinto ritualist, he chose to gain qualification as an Izumo Taisha-kyō instructor. This practical choice makes sense if the origin of Izumo Taisha-kyō is examined. The failure of the Great Promulgation Campaign was a significant reason for establishing Japan as a secular state with shrines as sites for state ritual. The Pantheon Dispute which played a significant part in the Campaign's demise especially made the Japanese government wary of delving into the matters of a Shinto doctrine. This Dispute began when Senge Takatomi, chief ritualist of Izumo Taisha, argued that Ōkuninushi no Ōkami – who was the kami given domain over the other world in the classical myths – should also be venerated by the Campaign. The Campaign already venerated the kami of creation (*zōka sanjin*) who were described as the first kami to appear and start the creation of the world in the classical myths. Furthermore, it venerated Amaterasu Ōmikami, the main kami of Ise Jingū. This debate was eventually brought before the emperor, but instead of pronouncing a doctrinal ruling on the matter, the imperial house left the matter standing (Zhang 2016, 188). The demise of the Great Promulgation Campaign and the prohibition against shrine funerals meant that Izumo Taisha, as a shrine, was no longer allowed to conduct funerals or teach a doctrine about the other world. Thus in 1882, the shrine was divided into the secular shrine organization (Izumo Taisha) and a religious organization (Izumo Taisha-kyō). Thus Izumo Taisha-kyō, although a Sect Shinto group, was not conceived as an independent new religion such as the revelation-based Sect Shinto groups, but rather as the doctrinal branch of the shrine Izumo Taisha, one half of a whole.

Hawaii Izumo Taisha was legally recognized by Japan's Izumo Taisha-kyō organization as a branch, Miyaō held a licence as an Izumo Taisha-kyō instructor and the organization had doctrine about what happens after death. This provided the Hawaii organization with more 'religion'-like elements. As a church, it had an eschatological doctrine that could be believed in, and it was active in conducting rites like weddings and funerals that were historically not the prerogative of shrines. It also quickly registered as a religious organization with the Hawai'i Territorial government. So legally in both English and Japanese, Hawaii Izumo Taisha-kyō Hawaii Bun'in was a religious Sect Shinto church. Despite this, the popular treatment of Hawaii Izumo Taisha did not always align with its official status as religious. Instead, its community often spoke about it in Japanese as a shrine and it acted more like other shrines in Hawai'i than like Sect

Shinto groups. Although technically the site was a 'church' and then a 'branch institute', and not a shrine, it was referred to as a 'shrine' in newspapers. This is reminiscent of how Hokkaidō Gokoku Jinja was conceived as a *yōhai* site and then shrine (*jinja*) by members of the Seventh Division even before it became a shrine.

Likewise, although Miyaō had been a shrine ritualist in Japan, he was officially the 'director' of the Mission in Hawai'i. Despite this, he was often referred to as a ritualist. As previously mentioned, Miyaō was also one of the ritualists who raised concerns over Hawaii Daijingū's qualifications for distributing Jingū *taima* in 1915. It seems likely that his high education and then training as both a ritualist and Taisha-kyō instructor made him more aware of the debates occurring within Japan about shrines' position within the system of secularism. Furthermore, Hawaii Izumo Taisha associated with other Shinto shrines in Honolulu, and became a founding member of the Honolulu Shintō Renmei, an organization that included Hawaii Daijingū, Kotohira Jinsha, Katō Jinsha and, later, Ishizuchi Jinsha. While occasionally other Shinto sects would join with shrines in social movements – both Konkō-kyō and shrines united to support workers during the 1920 sugar plantation strikes – shrines were less prominent in social issue debates when compared to Buddhist temples and Sect Shinto.

Hawaii Izumo Taisha thus provides an example of how the popular conception of a Shinto site did not always align with its official legal status, much like how the popular conception of Shinonome-shi, the funeral hall in Hokkaido previously discussed, did not necessarily match its designation by the national government. But located outside of Japanese rule, Hawaii Izumo Taisha had considerable leeway when manoeuvring between acting like a shrine and acting like a Sect Shinto church. Hawaii Izumo Taisha is also an example of how Shintoists were aware of Shinto sites' complicated relationship to the legal categories of secularism. The community supporting a Shinto site could draw upon a diversity of kami-related heritages – Shrine Shinto, Sect Shinto, pre-modern traditions and/or non-Shrine Shinto customs – in an effort to promote or preserve the site. Shintoists often did not see secular and religious aspects as conflicting opposites, but rather as two parts of a greater whole, to be emphasized or de-emphasized as circumstances demanded. Depending on the situation, a community could shift which aspects of the site it promoted in order to argue for its secular or religious nature. This ability would decide life or death for the organization after the Second World War.

Shrines on the American continents

Beyond Hawai'i, the American continents also saw significant Japanese migration. The United States and Brazil were the target of the bulk of these migrants, together making up around 80 per cent of the Japanese population in the Americas in 1930.[20] Japanese migrants to the Americas, however, faced a very different demographic situation. While the Japanese population in Hawai'i quickly exceeded 40 per cent of the area's total population, in the Americas they remained only a tiny percentage. Especially in the United States, Japanese migrants often lived dispersed across a wider geographic area, rather than residing in mono-ethnic communities on plantations. This relative isolation increased the pressure on migrants to assimilate, especially as anti-Japanese sentiment increased during the early twentieth century. Controversy over Japanese-language schools, inspired by the concerns in Hawai'i, also arose on the West Coast of the United States. In light of these political circumstances, the Japanese embassy took the position that Japanese-Americans should be subject to an American education, rather than a Japanese one, in order to avoid conflict with the United States (Asato 2006, 17). Thus the Japanese embassy did not actively encourage the construction of shrines. Furthermore, alien land laws in the United States made it difficult or impossible for Japanese migrants to own or even lease land, which also complicated any prospects of building a shrine.

Despite this, a few shrines were constructed on the West Coast of the United States. Kondō records that there was a Shinto site (*shinshi*) dedicated to Inari and a *daijingū* shrine in Los Angeles. He finds these small shrines especially significant since Los Angeles was 'the hometown of anti-Japanese sentiment' (Kondō 1943, 319). Ethnographic research among Japanese-Americans post-war mention at least two shrines located within the 'Japan town' of Seattle, Oregon, as well as a fishing-related shrine in Los Angeles, California. At least some Japanese migrants in the United States also maintained *kamidana* or small private Shinto sites on their farms (Abe and Imamura 2019, 6–7). Since none of these shrines were official and often treated as private sites, it is difficult to know how much migrants may have adopted a modern conception of shrines. The construction of the Inari shrine, which was connected to business prosperity, and the fishing shrine suggests migrant communities in the United States maintained the premodern tradition of relying on shrines for bestowing this-worldly benefits. At the same time, the establishment of a *daijingū* shrine also points to a desire by migrants to be connected to a larger Japanese sense of concentric space.

However, the statistics on Jingū *taima* distribution suggest Hawai'i-Japanese had a far greater interest in establishing a connection with the Japanese Home Islands through shrines. While Hawai'i-Japanese received 18,250 Jingū *taima* in 1940, only 2,520 *taima* were distributed in the Americas.[21]

The anti-Japanese sentiment in the United States led to the Gentlemen's Agreement in 1907 and then the Immigration Act of 1924, which restricted and then banned further Japanese immigration. In reaction, Japanese migration to Brazil started in 1908, especially flourishing after 1925 (Shoji 2008, 16). In contrast to Hawai'i and the United States, the Japanese embassy explicitly discouraged the construction of Shinto shrines in Brazil. Although not officially supported by the state, the Catholic Church was a strong influence in Brazil and Japan was keen to avoid creating conflict with it. Japan prohibited the migration of non-Catholic missionaries to Brazil, including Buddhist priests and Sect Shinto ministers (Watanabe 2008, 116). Despite the embassy's encouragement to assimilate into wider society, Brazil-Japanese often set up ethnic enclaves called colonia (Maeyama 1997, 156). These communities rarely established shrines, but set up schools which included some Shinto practices like veneration of the imperial portraits. Like in Hawai'i and the United States, schools set up by the migrants came under criticism and in 1938 laws aimed at such schools prohibited the use of Japanese in educational materials (Shoji 2008, 19).

There is evidence of very few shrines being established in Brazil. The oldest recorded shrine was Tōkyō Shokuminchi Jingū, established around 1918. Tōkyō Shokuminchi was a colonia set up by Japanese migrants in São Paulo. Tōkyō Shokuminchi Jingū, similar to shrines set up in the pioneer villages in Manchuria, was established by the leader of the settlement, Baba Nao. The site was a *daijingū*-type shrine, venerating Amaterasu Ōmikami. The shrine also took its name from that of the community, following the standard pattern followed by the protector shrine model. As Baba Nao was a Christian, it seems unlikely he was motivated by religious sentiment, but rather established the shrine as a patriotic Shinto site for connecting the colonia to the Japanese Home Islands. A secular conception of the site was also suggested by the shrine's location next to the community's elementary school and the fact the school's principal also served as the shrine's ritualist. Students of the school were charged with caring for the shrine grounds. The shrine's four annual festivals were treated as holidays by the entire community, with school children and adults taking the day off to take part in the festivals (Maeyama 1997, 157). Tōkyō Shokuminchi Jingū, Brazil's earliest and most significant pre-war shrine, followed the same secular pattern seen at shrines in Japan's formal colonies.

In 1918, another shrine in Brazil, Bogure Jinja,[22] was established. Unlike Tōkyō Shokuminchi Jingū, this shrine did not venerate a Japanese kami, but rather the ancestors of the indigenous tribe where Japanese migrants had settled. Uetsuka Shūhei, representative of the immigration company Kōkoku Takumin Kaisha and 'father of Brazil immigration', acquired land for a new colonia he called Uetsuka Dai-ichi Shokuminchi. When clearing the land for cultivation, the settlers discovered two earthen tumuli. Determining these were graves of the indigenous Bugre people, Uetsuka decided to erect a small Shinto shrine at the site dedicated to these indigenous spirits as the Kunitama-no-kami of the land (Kondō 1943, 319). The anniversary of the community's first day of settlement was chosen as the shrine's main festival, and Shinto ritual was conducted at the site. While the shrine's building and *torii* gate were built in the Japanese style, Uetsuka designated an indigenous water jar and clay flute as the shrine's sacred objects. The Japanese community also substituted local alcohol for Japanese sake as an offering at the shrine. Despite this, within a decade the shrine reportedly became neglected. A hive of bees took up residence within the building and the sacred objects were lost (Maeyama 1997, 159). Bogure Jinja differed from Tōkyō Shokuminchi Jingū in that it venerated a non-Japanese kami and incorporated local customs into its ritual. But both of these shrines were public sites treated as protector shrines by their Japanese communities.

Contemporary sources cite Tōkyō Shokuminchi Jingū and Bogure Jinja as the only two shrines in Brazil (Kondō 1943, 318). However, ten years after these first two shrines, there was another attempt to build a shrine. In 1921, the Shino Overseas Association was formed to facilitate group migration from Nagano prefecture to Brazil. The destination for these migrants was the newly formed Alianza Colonia (Ariansa Shokuminchi). The community consulted the Shintoist Ogasawara Shōzō, who travelled to Brazil and promoted the idea of building a shrine for the community. As members of the colonia were from Nagano prefecture – which hosted the greater imperial shrine Suwa Taisha – plans were made to establish a 'Suwa Jinja' as Alianza Colonia's protector shrine. In 1928, the site for the shrine was cleared and the groundbreaking ritual held. When the immigration office heard about this, however, they asked the community to refrain from constructing the shrine in fear of attracting backlash from wider Brazilian society. Concern about the issue spread to the wider Brazil-Japanese community, and the Alianza community was forced to abandon its plans for a shrine (Maeyama 1997, 163). Despite the previous example of Tōkyō Shokuminchi Jingū, the case of Suwa Jinja shows that by the late 1920s, political concerns over maintaining good relations with Brazil made the construction of public shrines impossible.

There was a private, company-type Shinto site constructed in Brazil. In Bastos, São Paulo, a Japanese community had sprung up focused on silk production. In order to study the latest in silk production at the prefectural silk factory in his home prefecture of Fukushima, a migrant named Yamaki Masao travelled back to Japan in 1938. While in Fukushima, he visited the prefectural factory's shrine and received a 'divided spirit' from it, as well as a ritual sake cup and poem composed by the empress. Upon his return to Brazil, he built a small factory shrine to mirror the one in Fukushima and enshrined the cup and poem in it (Maeyama 1997, 165). Called Tenso Jinja (lit. 'Silk Worm Ancestor Shrine'), this was not a public shrine like Tōkyō Shokuminchi Jingū, but an occupational Shinto site. It is likely due to its semi-private status within the factory that Yamaki was able to set up the site without attracting negative attention.

Although the Japanese migrants to the American continents, like those in Hawai'i, faced living under a dominating Western secularity, the lack of population density and accompanying greater pressure to assimilate from both the Japanese embassy and wider society meant comparatively very few shrines were constructed in the Americas. While migrants did build semi-private Shinto sites on their farms or in their factories, there were few opportunities for building shrines conceived and functioning as secular sites as they did in areas with greater Japanese migration.

Conclusion

Hawai'i had the unusual situation of Japanese subjects being the majority population, even while the territory was ruled by a white American elite. Thus the Hawai'i-Japanese had to navigate a space between pre-modern conceptions, the Japanese secularity of their homeland and the American secularity of the ruling government. Hilo Daijingū showed that shrines acted in a very similar manner to shrines in Japan, and thus influenced migrants' conceptions of space, time and ethics. However, Hawai'i shrines could also maintain connections with religious Shinto organizations unlike shrines in Japan, which gave them flexibility and allowed them to emphasis or de-emphasis aspects as required by the circumstances. Hawaii Daijingū and Ishizuchi Jinsha demonstrated that although migrants often brought pre-modern conceptions of Shinto with them, social pressure from the Hawai'i shrine community encouraged shrines to tone down those pre-modern elements and embrace the modern secular conception of shrines as in Japan. Hawaii Daijingū further demonstrated how a Shinto secular framework could be applied to not only Japanese patriotism but also American patriotism. Kotohira Jinsha showed how this-worldly benefits were an important function for shrines in Hawai'i, and that shrines offered an alternative protector model that affirmed the geographic ancestral identities of migrants within the larger framework of a Japanese metageography. Izumo Taisha demonstrated how the popular conception of the line between religious and secular Shinto often differed from legal definitions. Circumstances in Hawai'i changed depending on the location (on an outer island or in Honolulu) and on the international situation (the relationship between Japan and the United States), but Shinto sites could use the ambiguity of differing secularisms and lingering pre-modern conceptions to adapt to the circumstances as they changed. In contrast, the American continents had a lower Japanese population density and Japanese migrants faced even greater assimilation pressure from anti-Japanese sentiments than in Hawai'i. This made it difficult for communities in the Americas to establish shrines, and prevented the shrines that were established from adopting a modern secular conception to the same degree as in Hawai'i.

8

Conclusion

From Kashihara Jingū in the Home Islands to the shrines in Hawai'i and the Americas, modern Shinto shrines have had to negotiate between the modern categories of the secular and religion. Although overseas shrines are often separated into their own category,[1] this distinction is based on the post-war political situation that allowed shrines within Japan's post-war borders to 'actually' be religious sites misused by the government, while shrines outside those borders remained secular state sites and were thus abolished. But there was significant continuity between modern Shinto shrines across the Japanese sphere of influence, and three broad points have repeatedly appeared. First, after a period of confusion in the late nineteenth century, modern Shinto shrines came to be conceived and treated as secular sites, which functioned to affirm a new Japanese secularity in imperial subjects. Second, a pioneer theology focused on the local land itself was developed for use at shrines in new imperial lands. Over the course of the early twentieth century, this gave way to a universalized theology, which positioned Amaterasu as the kami relevant to all East Asians regardless of ethnicity. While the Japanese government often encouraged shrines in these new lands to subsume select local customs into their ritual, some Home Islander migrants worked to maintain their ethnic privilege by reserving shrines as sites exclusive to Home Islanders. Third, this universalized theology allowed for a Shinto secularity to be applied outside of the formal Japanese empire. Especially from the late 1930s, shrines began blurring the Meiji-period boundary that had been established between the secular and religion. In some cases, shrines adopted a hierarchal view of religion in order to raise shrine's status above other forms of patriotism, while in other cases, shrines used a flexible boundary as a tool in negotiating their precarious existence under a Western secularity.

Modern Shinto shrines as secular

Japan's process of modernization in the second half of the nineteenth century saw pre-modern categories redivided into the new spheres of the secular, religion and superstition. Over the course of decades, shrines were positioned into the secular sphere, and – as appropriate to a secular site – treated as public, historical and modern sites. This was not a straightforward or uncontested process. During the 1870s and 1880s, shrines often embraced both their role as sites for state ritual and the national doctrine of Great Promulgation Campaign, only to be forced to cut these ties later as conducting funerals and promoting 'doctrines' became unacceptable at shrines located in the secular sphere. Imperial-ranked as well as smaller migrant-established shrines became treated as sites for public ritual. They received government offerings according to their rank and were connected to public transport like other government offices. They relied upon donated labour and resources from the public at large to expand and maintain their grounds, making them shrines 'by the people, for the people' (Yamaguchi 2005, 201).

Shrines were also treated as historical sites – that is as sites of History – relevant to all imperial subjects, rather than sacred sites relevant only to 'believers'. Kashihara Jingū was especially important because it marked the government-designated site of Jinmu's enthronement rite, but shrines like Tainan Jinja, located at the death site of Prince Yoshihisa, marked more local historical sites. In new imperial lands, the shrines became new historical sites, inscribing a Japanese topography upon the land. The virgin land was formed into shrine gardens through practices like tree planting, while the shrines themselves collected and displayed historical artefacts and monuments related to the shrine's kami and history. The exception to this was shrines outside of Japanese rule such as in Hawai'i, where it was difficult for Japanese migrants to obtain land for a permanent shrine. Despite this, shrines established by these migrants did become at least temporary monuments where memorials could be erected and Japanese holidays could be celebrated.

Finally, shrines were modern sites returning to a higher version of the idealized past. Shrines became an integral part of a modern Japanese community, and technology was part and parcel of that experience, from trains to radio to electric lights. Despite this immersion into modern technology, shrines remained primarily sites for ritual based on the reconstructed rites of antiquity. Shrines' connection to antiquity could be a liability: shrine rite was sometimes seen by both Westerners and westernized Japanese elites as little more than primitive superstition. But Shinto shrines positioned their combination of ancient ritual and modern technology as a 'natural' return to a purer idealized past when humanity still remained in harmony with the kami. In this thinking, the rapid adoption of Western technology by Japan, including at shrines, served as evidence of Japan's closeness to the primal Truth.

Affirming a Japanese secularity

As secular sites, shrines had a role in affirming basic elements of reality – space, time and ethics – that underpinned the new Japanese secularity promoted by the government. The project of modernization in Japan meant the construction of a new metageography and a new national topography. Shinto shrines were allocated to each administrative district, from the general protector and *gokoku* shrines allocated to each territory to the concentrically arranged protector shrines watching over increasingly smaller administrative districts. Depending on the territory, this linkage of shrine to administrative district was achieved by merging shrines, by selectively recognizing new shrines or by building pre-shrines. In this manner, protector shrines and the shrine ranking system became an essential part of a modern Japanese community, with the shrine's status reflecting the status of the community as a whole. The shrine system thus connected the entire empire vertically and horizontally into a single metageographic network. The shrine ranking system did not apply outside of the formal Japanese empire, but equivalent or informal systems were adopted by shrine communities in the Asia-Pacific. Furthermore, practices like *yōhai* physically oriented imperial subjects in the periphery towards the geographic centres of the empire, while the distribution of Jingū *taima* brought the centre into the periphery.

Modern Shinto shrines also affirmed a new sense of time. Kashihara Jingū, as the site of Emperor Jinmu's enthronement rite and the 'birthplace' of Japan, had an especially important role in marking the beginning of Japanese linear, progressive time. The national holiday of Foundation Day on 11 February became its main festival date, celebrated by all shrines in and outside the empire. The 2600th anniversary of Jinmu's enthronement saw many projects and celebrations planned to commemorate this landmark in Japanese linear time. Furthermore, the annual ritual cycle of modern shrines was aligned with the state's new calendar of national holidays, helping instil a sense of the new annual cycle of time based on the solar, rather than lunisolar, calendar. General protector shrines added their own annual festival as a public holiday in their geographic areas. These festivals used the same vocabulary as national festivals and were attended by local or national government officials as suitable to the shrine's rank, thus merging national holidays and shrine festivals into the same category. This new sense of linear and annual time was codified by the Jingū calendar. These calendars were distributed along with the Jingū *taima* by Shinto shrines across the Japanese sphere. National and imperial shrines' annual festivals were all noted on the Jingū calendar, allocating colonial territories each a day in the national cycle of time.

From the late 1930s, the practice of mass timed *yōhai* also began to gain in popularity. These events, timed to the very minute, raised awareness in Japanese subjects of modern time as measured by the clock instead of the sun. By 1937, the entire formal empire counted noon as it was in Tokyo, regardless of the local area's actual solar noon, which fell significantly earlier or later in Taiwan and Hokkaido. Timed *yōhai* also occurred on a smaller scale, with imperial subjects bowing towards their local, *gokoku* or general protector shrines. Thus shrines had a significant role in promoting a modern sense of Japanese time: linear, cyclical and clock time.

Shrines also promoted a new sense of ethics. Although based on Confucian and Western ethics, this new sense was framed within the Shinto-based legitimacy of the imperial house. Shrines as historical sites promoted national heroes, from imperial family members like Emperor Jinmu and Prince Yoshihisa, to subsumed local founders such as Koxinga, Kamehameha and the unspecified Kunitama-no-kami of Korean shrines, to the war dead venerated at *gokoku* shrines. Shrines were also sites where Japanese subjects enacted their citizenship. School visits, community events and even personal visits provided evidence of subjects' devotion to 'the way here set forth' in the Imperial Rescript on Education. The large-scale volunteer campaigns seen at major shrines also gave Japanese subjects opportunities to enact their citizenship in a structured way at a delineated time and place, while smaller shrines served as community centres where Japanese migrants held war memorial ceremonies and local celebrations.

Pioneer theology to universalized theology

When the Meiji government came to power in the mid-nineteenth century, it developed a pioneer theology to transform new territories like Hokkaido into part of the Japanese empire, that is, into imperial land (*kōdo*). This ideology focused on enshrining the spirit of the land itself (Ōkunitama) and two classical kami associated with development (Ōnamuchi and Sukunahikona) in a greater imperial shrine to watch over the entire territory and aid the development of the land into a productive colony. When the land and its people were deemed fully developed, the territory was incorporated into the Home Islands. This ideology was used at the general protector shrines of Hokkaido, Karafuto and Taiwan, although only the former two were legally incorporated into the Home Islands before the end of the war.

After the annexation of Korea in the early twentieth century, however, there was a shift away from a pioneer theology to a universalized theology. The focus on the development of the land was replaced with a focus on the transformation of people. While Amaterasu had been imagined as the ancestress of the imperial house and Yamato race especially at *daijingū*-type shrines, she was universalized to become the founding ancestress (*genshin*) of all East Asians. The general protector shrines of Korea, the Kwantung Leased Area and the South Seas Mandate all enshrined Amaterasu Ōmikami, while the general protector shrine of Taiwan – a territory not yet considered part of the Home Islands like Hokkaido and Karafuto – added Amaterasu to the Three Pioneer Kami already enshrined. This new universalized conception of Amaterasu was also utilized at Kenkoku Shinbyō in Manchukuo in an attempt to construct a Shinto-based secularity for the puppet state. Manchukuo's older founding principles of the Kingly Way and ethnic harmony were superseded by and subsumed into the Way of the Kami as a universal truth equally applicable to Manchukuo as to Japan.

The pioneer theology, with its focus on the local land, made space for selected local and indigenous customs. It created room for a local identity subsumed into a broader multiethnic identity as a Japanese imperial subject. Shrines adopted local elements into their architecture and practices, Shintoizing previously foreign elements as a localized variation of being Japanese. This included the veneration of indigenous kami often under the generic titles of *ubusuna* or *kunitama*, the performing of local dances during festivals, and the planting and use of local trees at shrines. Thus, although shrines were reorganized into a single system in the Meiji period with a standardized ritual cycle established by law, individual shrine traditions continued to be an important source of identity and pride for shrines and their community.

With the shift towards a universalized theology, the space for subsumed local customs was displaced from the general protector shrines to lesser-ranked shrines. *Kunitama* became a generic title for any local kami and, especially in Korea, was enshrined with Amaterasu to create a new model of pairing the local and universal. This localization, however, was not a rejection of a shrine's Japanese nature, and those many local customs considered beyond the pale could not be incorporated in shrines. Most overseas shrines, whether inside the formal Japanese empire or without, kept to the model ideal of Shinto shrines by celebrating Japanese national holidays, following prescribed dress, and utilizing Japanese-style shrine architecture. Furthermore, many Japanese migrants aimed to preserve their privilege as the 'model race' by maintaining shrines as exclusive ethnic sites. By replicating the architecture and customs of the Home Islands and excluding both local people and customs, they rejected the vision of a multiethnic Shinto.

A Japanese secularity and a Japanese religion

As the political system of secularism was established in Japan, Shinto shrines became located on the secular side of the religion-secular divide. In the second half of the nineteenth century, shrines built and then cut ties to the doctrinal groups of the Great Promulgation Campaign. They had been forced to invent Shinto style funerals and then they were prohibited from performing them. The distinction between shrine rites as secular and Shinto rites such as funerals as religious was not always wholly adopted by Japanese subjects. Likewise, when shrine visits and *taima* distribution became increasingly required as proof of patriotism in the 1930s, Christians and Buddhists contested where the line between secular patriotic ritual and religious ritual exactly lay.

As Japan gained national prestige and military strength on the international stage, the need to establish a clear line between shrines and religion lost its former urgency. Although the government's official position – that shrines were secular sites strictly distinct from religion – remained unchanged, the growing adoption of a hierarchal conception of religion among some Shintoists allowed the idea that shrines were also religion to gain popularity. This blurring of the boundary between shrines and religion made the Shintoization of the war dead easier too. Despite the fact that shrines had earlier been careful to distance themselves from funerals and the recent dead, in 1939 cenotaphs were transformed into *gokoku* shrines as the causalities of war mounted. In many cases, the new *gokoku* shrines were built next to general protector shrines in the colonies, linking the veneration of the war dead to shrines in a way more firmly than before.

A blurred boundary between the secular and religion also helped Japanese migrants navigate the differing position of Shinto shrines in Japanese and

Western secularisms through a process of translation. In areas outside of Japanese rule, shrines could adopt the secular shrine vocabulary of the Home Islands in Japanese while maintaining distinct their relationships with religious Shinto sects. But when shrines were translated into a Western language context, shrines' relationships with these two separate categories were collapsed into the single category of religion. This translation became vital after the Second World War, when the continued existence of shrines hinged on their ability to translate themselves into the American religious sphere.

Shinto shrines post-war

In 1945, after Japan agreed to unconditional surrender in the Second World War, the Allied Forces led by the United States occupied Japan. One of the tasks the Occupation was charged with was the establishment of 'freedom of religion', despite the fact that pre-war Western scholars and missionaries assured English-language audiences that 'religious freedom was safe in Japan' (Thomas 2019, 102). In order to establish 'real' religious freedom, the post-war occupation had to invent the concept of Shinto as a state religion, so that they could eradicate and then replace it with a new 'religious freedom as universal ideal' (Thomas 2019, 144). To this aim, the Occupation issued the Shinto Directive on 15 December 1945. This Directive did not prohibit Shinto as a religion, but abolished 'State Shinto', which the Directive defined as 'that branch of Shinto (Kokka Shinto or Jinja Shinto) which by official acts of the Japanese Government has been differentiated from the religion of Sect Shinto (Shuha Shinto or Kyoha Shinto) and has been classified a non-religious cult' (Allen 1960, 88). Shinto shrines, then, could continue to exist, but only providing they became religious sites divorced from the state, legally undifferentiated from other religious sites such as the churches (*kyōkai*) of Sect Shinto.

Despite this, the factor that determined whether a shrine remained secular and was thus shut down, or was religionized and thus allowed to continue as a private religious organization was not the closeness of the shrine's connection to the Japanese government or military. Instead, it was whether or not the location of the shrine fell within Japan's post-war borders. In the Home Islands, Hokkaido and Okinawa, shrines were able to reform into legal religious organizations (*shūkyō hōjin*), most joining the newly formed Jinja Honchō (Association of Shinto Shrines), an umbrella organization that worked to keep shrines united into a single system. The process of becoming a legal religious organization required submitting a request to the Occupation, outlining the shrine as a religious institution stripped of connections to the state or the war dead, regardless of how important those connections may have been to shrines pre-war. The shifting of shrines into the religious sphere also allowed the category of shrine (*jinja*) to absorb the wide variety of Shinto sites (*shōkonsha, soreisha, mugansha*, etc.) that had existed pre-war.

Shrines' transformation into religious institutions also changed the manner in which shrines promoted a Japanese secularity. Concerning time, the imperial calendar still lingers on shrine-published calendars and most shrines continue to celebrate largely the same cycle of yearly rites as they did pre-war. But shrine visits to mark the cultural yearly rites (*nenchū gyōji*), along with personal rites of passage (*jinsei girei*), have become far more prominent in shrine activities today. Likewise, the modern shrine ranking system was abolished as a part of State Shinto, but former imperial and national shrines remain important sites in the 'Japanese' topography. Even if the stated purpose of the visit has shifted from patriotic to cultural, most of these formerly high-ranked shrines continue to receive many visitors. In a similar vein, while some shrines post-war still embrace the ethics of the Imperial Rescript on Education and the Great Teachings to some extent, they have become more likely to emphasize their role as preservers or representatives of ethnic Japanese culture, rather than patriotism or universal Truth. Despite shrines' transformation into legal religious organizations, the line between religion, shrines and Shinto practices continues to be contested.[2] Some have found this controversial under the post-war constitution's call for a strict separation between religion and state, while others have argued for a looser interpretation of the constitution to allow for government officials' involvement if their intention is customary (*shūkan*) rather than 'religious'. The exact definitions of what 'counts' as religious – and shrines' relationship to that question – are still being contested in the Japanese courts and wider society.

Shrines within post-war Japan's borders may have been allowed to religionize, but shrines outside of those borders were largely shut down, destroyed or handed over to the area's new government as public property. In many cases, the Japanese government did not attempt to preserve the shrines in its former colonies as religious organizations. Even in cases when there was local interest in taking over the shrine post-war, the Japanese government advocated disenshrining the kami. The lands and assets of major shrines, as state property, were then usually handed over to the new government of the former colony and reused for a new public purpose.[3] In areas which had never been a part of Japan like Hawai'i, the US government still treated shrines as secular property of the Japanese government post-war and confiscated their lands and assets. It was only through the energetic protests of the shrines' local communities that a limited number of pre-war shrines were able to revive in the post-war era.

Kashihara Jingū and the Home Islands

Kashihara Jingū in the Home Islands was the centre of national attention in the early Showa period, but it lost its national significance after the Second World War. One reason for this was that it is located in the minor city of Kashihara, rather than in Tokyo like Meiji Jingū and Yasukuni Jinja, both of which had also been the object of mass *yōhai* practices in the 1940s. But perhaps even more significantly, the shrine's association with the 'world under one roof (*hakkō ichiu*)' ideology attributed to Jinmu and used so prominently to justify Japanese expansion seems to have tainted the shrine's image. In the photo book issued by the shrine in commemoration of the 2650th anniversary of Jinmu's enthronement rite, Yamada Tadashi, then chief ritualist of Kashihara Jingū, lamented the removal of Emperor Jinmu from the school curriculum and how the past forty years of post-war had 'negated the traditions' of Japan (Kashihara Jingū-chō 1989). Today, the shrine itself has legally become a religious organization (*shūkyō hōjin*), while the public facilities in its outer garden were given over to the secular administration of the city government. The shrine largely continues the same cycle of rituals as it did pre-war, if on a smaller scale. Kashihara Jingū is a part of the Jinja Honchō and, although it remains a significant shrine in Nara Prefecture, it is overshadowed in popularity by older shrines like Kasuga Taisha. Although the public relations materials issued by Kashihara City feature the shrine prominently, it is not for its status as the birthplace of Japan, but for the many forested hiking trails that cross the shrine's garden and Mt. Unebi behind it. Kashihara Jingū, like the majority of shrines within the Home Islands, was allowed to reinvent itself as a private religious site, while the many public facilities associated with it remained administered by the secular government.

Hokkaido and Karafuto

Sapporo Jinja in Hokkaido, like Kashihara Jingū, became a religious organization and joined the Jinja Honchō, while its outer garden was turned into a municipal park. However, the shrine also gained benefit from the removal of government control post-war. Despite petitions starting from the 1930s, the pre-war government repeatedly denied the shrine permission to add Emperor Meiji as an enshrined kami. The removal of government control post-war meant the shrine could go forward with this enshrinement. Thus in 1964, Sapporo Jinja was renamed Hokkaidō Jingū, an appellation that both gives it status as a *jingū* shrine and reflects the shrine's pre-war designation as the general protector of all Hokkaido. Today, its forested grounds and Japanese architecture have made it a popular attraction for not only Japanese tourists but also group tours from Asia.

Hokkaidō Gokoku Jinja was required to remove the word *gokoku* from its name during the Occupation, but it reverted to the name Hokkaidō Gokoku Jinja in 1951. It also joined the Jinja Honchō and continues to hold rituals for its enshrined war dead, which include martial aspects such as marching band music in its ritual. However, its beautiful grounds and facilities have also made it a popular place for weddings. Furano Jinja, too, joined the Jinja Honchō. The Occupation's land reforms damaged the shrine's financial basis by stripping it of the rental properties that had previously formed a major source of its income. Over the post-war its role in the secular sphere has gradually been curtailed: local students no longer get Furano Jinja's festival off from school, and the city's annual *shōkon* ritual was converted into a Westernized 'secular' ceremony unconnected to the shrine. Despite this, the shrine's yearly cycle and style of ritual has remained largely unchanged from the pre-war period. Likewise, it is still common for local government figures to take part in or give offerings at all of these Hokkaido shrines on major festival days.

The entirety of Karafuto (Sakhalin), in contrast to Hokkaido, was given over to the Soviet Union's administration post-war. In the last days of the war, the island was invaded by the Soviet Union, so the prefectural government made urgent plans to transfer the proxy spirits of outer-lying shrines to Toyohara Jinja or Karafuto Jinja within the capital city. As the Soviets advanced, the government started making arrangements to transfer the proxy spirit of Karafuto Jinja itself to Sapporo Jinja in Hokkaido. However, the haste of the wartime evacuation made this impossible, and the government resorted to ritually burning the proxy spirit (Yamada and Maeda 2012, 103–18). Most of the now-empty shrine buildings were destroyed by the Soviet Army, but some shrine sites were reused for new purposes by the Soviets.[4] In the case of Karafuto Jinja, the site was first transformed into a clubhouse for the communist party, but later became the site for a business office. The site of Toyohara Jinja, meanwhile, was utilized as a mortuary, while the site of Karafuto Gokoku Jinja was turned into the site for a municipal hospital (Nakajima 2013, 35). Although the kami of Karafuto Jinja were not able to be ritually transferred to Sapporo Jinja, in 1973 the Karafuto Pioneer Memorial was built on the grounds of the shrine. Every year on the date of old Karafuto Jinja's annual festival, 23 August, Hokkaidō Jingū (Sapporo Jinja) holds a ritual at the monument for remembering the dead of Karafuto.

Taiwan and Korea

Shrines in Taiwan and Korea faced an entirely different future post-war than those in the Home Islands. In both these places, the Japanese government did not even try to argue that they were religious sites which should be allowed to continue. After the spirit proxies of the shrines had been ritually disposed of, the shrines' resources and buildings were given over to the new ruling government. In Taiwan, the new ruling Republic of China tore Taiwan Jingū down and replaced it with the distinctive Grand Hotel Taipei (Jp. Maruyama/Enzan Daihanten, Ch. Yuánshān Dàfàndiàn) built in an extravagant Northern Chinese style. Despite this, the shrine's *torii* gate and *komainu* statues were kept and still frame the approach to the hotel today. Nearby Taiwan Gokoku Jinja, which commemorated the Japanese war dead, many of whom had died fighting the Republic of China, was turned into Taiwan's leading National Martyr's Shrine. Like the Japanese *gokoku* shrines which proceeded them, Martyr's Shrines are sites for state ritual where the war dead – the mostly mainland Chinese soldiers who had died fighting the Japanese – are venerated. The Republic of China commonly transformed Shinto shrines into Martyr's Shrines in both the Chinese mainland and Taiwan. In Taiwan Gokoku Jinja's case, the Shinto shrine building itself was used as the Martyr's Shrine until 1966, when it was torn down and replaced with a Chinese-style building.

The building of Kenkō Jinja, with its multicultural architecture, still remains today, albeit in a modified form. From 1955 to 1986, the ROC government used the building as the Central Library, but today the building houses a national museum. Kaizan Jinja, on the other hand, was transformed into a Chinese religious site (Jp. *byō/shi*, Ch. *miào/cí*). Although the ROC government tore down both the Japanese and Southern Chinese buildings and replaced them with Northern Chinese buildings, it remains a site dedicated to the veneration of Koxinga. The veneration is conducted in the Taoist style, but ritual implements from the site's Japanese period are preserved and the shrine's Taoist talisman wrapped in a Shinto-style amulet pouch can be obtained from the small shop on location.

The Japanese government took the same stance towards shrines in Korea as in Taiwan. Concerned about anonymous calls in Korea to burn down Chōsen Jingū and Keijō Jinja, the Chōsen Governor-General quickly applied to the American authorities for permission to shut down the shrine and destroy its main buildings. Home Islander members of Keijō Jinja opposed its destruction and hoped to continue its activities as a religious site post-war. Despite this, the American authorities sided with the Governor-General's argument that the shrines were secular sites not subject to protection under the principle of religious freedom. Chōsen Jingū and Keijō Jinja were dis-enshrined and their main buildings destroyed. In the late 1940s and 1950s, Christians in Korea began celebrating Easter on the former shrine's site[5] and for a short time, the Presbyterian Theological Seminary met at the site. However, the site was soon reverted to being used for political purposes. In 1955, the president of the new South Korean government Rhee Syngman erected a 28.4-metre statue of himself at the former site of Chōsen Jingū. Although this statue was torn down in 1960, a statue of An Chung-gun – the Korean who had assassinated the first Governor-General of Korea – was erected at the site by the third president Park Chung-hee in 1967 (Henry 2014, 206–8). In 1970, a museum about An was added to the site. The site's wider garden became a public park and is probably more famous now for the panoramic view of the city that can be had from the park's Seoul Tower.

The buildings of Heijō Jinja were burned down the night of Japan's surrender. Less than a year later, the massive neoclassical Moranbang Theatre was constructed on the former site of the shrine, while the entire mountain area has been designated a public park (Nakajima et al. 2015, 178). The construction of Fuyo Jingū, on the other hand, was never finished, and the site never underwent an enshrinement rite. In 1957, the Korean-style Samchungsa shrine was built at the planned site of the Shinto shrine. This new shrine was dedicated to three Paekche Kingdom loyal retainers belonging to the same era as Fuyo Jingū's intended kami, and reused construction supplies left at the site originally meant for Fuyo Jingū (Sohn, 320–1). The Paekche period pagoda of Chŏngnimsa (Jp. Jōrin-ji) that had been restored as a part of Japan's plan to turn Fuyo into a 'kami capital' was preserved and has been registered as a UNESCO World Heritage Site in 2015 as a part of the Baekje Historic Area. Thus in Taiwan and Korea, major shrine sites have continued to be secular sites, often used by the new ruling government for public facilities or for memorials dedicated to the new regime's national heroes.

Manchukuo and the Asia-Pacific

In Manchukuo during the last days of the war, the Manchurian emperor along with other government elites fled from Shinkyō in hopes of making their way to safety in Japan. They took with them the cupronickel mirror that served as the spirit proxy of Kenkoku Shinbyō. During this flight, the emperor was captured by the Soviet Army. It is unknown what happened to Kenkoku Shinbyō's mirror, but one story is that it was secretly brought to Shinkyō Jinja by Okada Minoru, a member of Manchukuo's Ritual Council (Sagai 1998, 285). Post-war, the emperor's palace was turned into the 'Illegitimate Manchukuo Imperial Palace Museum' by the People's Republic of China. The ruins of Kenkoku Shinbyō's foundations in the museum's garden are all that can still be seen of the mausoleum today. In contrast, the buildings of Kenkoku Chūreibyō remain almost entirely intact, most likely due to the Chinese, rather than Japanese, style of the buildings. Although the land on which the mausoleum stands is now owned by a school of the People's Liberation Army Air Force, the site has largely been abandoned to the forest (Inamiya and Nakajima 2019, 52–5).

The many Shinto shrines founded by Japanese migrants in Manchukuo suffered a similar fate to those in Karafuto. The Japanese embassy directed that Japanese evacuating in the face of the Soviet invasion should transfer their shrine's spirit proxy to Shinkyō Jinja, but very few managed to do so. More commonly, the shrine and its important objects were ritually burned or merely abandoned. After the end of the war, Shinkyō Jinja was subjected to looting, while the shrine office was turned into a temporary home for war orphans (Sagai 1998, 284–5). In 1946, the ritualists of the shrine secretly conducted the shrine's spring festival. The same year in July, the orphans were repatriated back to Japan and the shrine's spirit proxy may have been brought back with them. Today, the shrine buildings still stand, but have been renovated for use as a public preschool (Tsuda et al. 2007, 241).

Shrines in other areas of China and South East Asia suffered a similar variety of fates. The reuse of former shrine sites often depended on the government to which they were handed over. For example, Nankyō Jinja and Nankyō Gokoku Jinja were first passed into control of the Republic of China, which transformed the site into a Martyr's Shrine, as they did to shrines in Taiwan. After the People's Republic of China took over the area, however, the shrine buildings were torn down and the area turned into a sports arena (Li and Matsumoto, 69–72). The People's Republic of China also turned the site of the greater imperial shrine

Kantō Jingū into part of a base for People's Liberation Army Navy (Nakajima 2013, 88). Other shrines were turned into public parks, sometimes with a memorial erected at the former shrine's site. A war memorial was built at the site of Mōkyō Jinja in China, while the site of Nagamasa Jinja in Thailand has a small monument dedicated to Japan-Thailand friendship (Inamiya and Nakajima 2019, 87).

Shrines on the islands of Japan's former South Seas Mandate were largely abandoned to the jungle or turned into public park areas at the end of the war. A few sites, however, were transformed into Christian shrines, such as the former site of Izumi Jinja on Tinian Island (Nakajima 2013, 68). From the 1980s, a trend began towards rebuilding some of these Shinto shrines, with six shrines, including Nan'yō Jinja, being rebuilt on a small scale. The reason for this trend is likely a combination of friendship initiatives between Japan and the states in Micronesia as well as the economic benefits the sites bring as tourism spots (Tomii et al. 2004, 255).

Hawai'i and the Americas

In post-war Hawai'i, the US government treated Hawai'i shrines as a part of 'State Shinto', and seized their properties and assets under the Trading with the Enemy Act after the Second World War. Hawai'i shrines responded, beginning with Kotohira Jinsha, by arguing in court that all the shrines in Hawai'i were religious organizations connected to Sect Shinto, not Shrine Shinto, and thus subject to freedom of religion. Hawai'i shrines' connections to Sect Shinto and their registration as religious organizations under the Territorial government were brought up as points of evidence. Despite legal victory in court, anti-Japanese sentiment continued in Hawai'i. While some shrines engaged in theological innovations in their effort to religionize (Hansen 2010), most Hawai'i shrines had difficulty reviving as American religious institutions and ceased their activities or were merged into larger shrines. Today, there exists approximately eight shrines, but only half of these can afford to employ a ritualist. Although the shrines are classified legally as religious organizations, there continues to be a divide – like in Japan – between Shrine Shinto shrines and Sect Shinto sites in Hawai'i. Hawaii Izumo Taisha remains an exception. Just as it belonged to the Honolulu Shinto Renmei and acted in concert with shrines which traced their lineage to Shrine Shinto in the pre-war period, Hawaii Izumo Taisha acts and is treated as a shrine today, rather than a Sect Shinto site (*kyōkai*). However, the site's ability to draw upon the support of both Izumo Taisha and Izumo Ōyashiro-kyō

(Izumo Taisha-kyō) in Japan, in addition to its position in downtown Honolulu, has made it a successful shrine today. Like shrines in Japan, Hawai'i shrines have occasionally been involved in public activities such as the Shinto groundbreaking blessing given for Hilo Airport. But the only 'Shinto' related activity that seems to have involved significant complaints was the installation using public funds of the Hiroshima to Honolulu Friendship Torii, a monument unconnected to a shrine (Perez 2001).

In contrast, almost no Shinto shrines in the Americas managed to revive post-war. While the leaders of Japanese society in Hawai'i, including Shinto ritualists, were interned and often repatriated by the American government during the Second World War, nearly all Japanese-Americans in the United States proper suffered internment. Abe and Imamura suggest that the lingering effects of internment, including the inability of many Japanese-Americans to return to their pre-war communities and the loss of their homes and possessions that the internment caused, made it difficult practically to revive or reconstruct Shinto shrines. Furthermore, the anti-Japanese racism and stigma, as well as general greater pressure from mainstream American society post-war, meant many Japanese-Americans lacked a personal desire to revive shrines (Abe and Imamura 2019, 8). In Brazil, Bogure Jinja had already been abandoned by the late 1920s, while Tōkyō Shokuminchi Jingū was slowly abandoned as the colonia it had been built to protect depopulated. On the other hand, Maeyama records that Tenso Jinja continued its yearly festival post-war, even though the community's economic dependence on silk production decreased (Maeyama 1997, 166).

Conclusion

The Shinto shrines in this book were a part of Japan's project of modernization. By adapting the Western political system of secularism, Japan was able to formulate its own Japanese secularity built upon a foundation of modern science and Shinto myths. Post-war, Shinto shrines were able to utilize the ambiguity of the line between the secular and religion, and maintain a significant role in society today contrary to many predictions. But the construction of secularism and the communication of a new secularity to citizens have not been unique Japan. Japan directly attempted to establish a Shinto-based secularity in its puppet states, while Shinto shrines influenced the construction of public sites like the Martyr's Shrines of the Republic of China. Although this book has focused on Shinto shrines, the framework of creating a new system of secularism deserves application to areas beyond the Japanese empire. Japan's modern Shinto shrines serve as a comparative model for how other non-Western states worked to adapt (or not) their own pre-modern traditions to the political system of secularism. Kondō Yoshihiro said in his 1943 study of overseas shrines that the mission of founding Shinto shrines undertaken by the imperial government was 'the creation of the grand myth of birthing the state' (Kondō 1943, 358). The secularisms that birthed other states are also 'grand myths' that deserve to be examined more closely.

Notes

Chapter 1: Introduction

1. The definitions of religion, worship and faith according to the *English Oxford Dictionary*:
   religion: 1. The belief in and worship of a superhuman controlling power, especially a personal God or gods.
   1.1 A particular system of faith and worship.
   1.2 A pursuit or interest followed with great devotion.
   worship: 1. The feeling or expression of reverence and adoration for a deity.
   faith: 2. Strong belief in the doctrines of a religion, based on spiritual conviction rather than proof.
2. Nongbri gives a similar definition: 'religion is anything that sufficiently resembles modern Protestant Christianity' (2013, 18).
3. The difference in the conception of shrines between Japan and the English-speaking West can still be seen today in how vocabulary is used. While the West tends to focus on 'Shinto' as a single religious system, Japanese speakers are more likely to refer to 'shrines' specifically. Another example is the term 'Shinto shrines'. The English term narrows the broad term 'shrine', which can refer to structures belonging to any religion or even to a secular memorial, by modifying it as belonging specifically to a system called 'Shinto'. But in Japanese, Shinto shrines are called *jinja*, and are structures that predate any historical system/religion that can be called Shinto.
4. Primitivism, or the 'religion' of preliterate societies, is no longer a politically correct term, but the category remains largely the same, grouping cultural traditions of vastly disparate peoples under a single term like 'indigenous', 'folk', 'primal' or 'tribal'. Cf. Masuzawa (2005, 42–4).
5. Confer Masuzawa (2005, 282–91) for a discussion of this in relation to Hinduism.
6. The difference between the concept of the One True Religion versus Secularity is that the concept of heresy allowed for other religions or people to contain elements of Truth, but merely lack the full truth. Secularity, on the other hand, sees 'religion' as contestable. It is confined to the private sphere because it is not seen as truth, even if it is not quite delusion.
7. For example, some sects imagined God as an active creator while others saw Him as a clockwork Creator. Likewise, the necessity of sacraments was considered debatable.

8   The Amendment reads: 'Congress shall make no law respecting an establishment of religion, or prohibiting the free exercise thereof.'
9   Massachusetts, the last state to have a state church, disestablished it in 1833.
10 Cf. Ama (2011) on how Shinshū Buddhists in the United States and Hawai'i also worked to broaden the concept of religion in America in the late eighteenth and early nineteenth centuries.
11 Bellah's 'civil religion', then, falls in the secular sphere, not the religious sphere. Bellah (1991, 187) seems to be aware of this and notes that his use of religion includes more than the 'peculiarly Western concept of "religion"' that limits itself to exclusive sects. It is significant that Bellah (1991, 179) defines the 'American Shinto' of some critics as civil religion; that is, he equates American civil religion to a perceived American version of Shinto. However, to avoid confusion caused by the multiple definitions of 'religion', this book refrains from using Bellah's term. Furthermore, 'secularity' as used in this thesis has a broader meaning than 'civil religion'. It is not limited to the theocentric or hierocentric 'religious' elements in public life. It is perhaps more similar to Charles Taylor's 'modern social imaginary' (Taylor 2004), although secularity refers to the new sense of reality only as promoted under the political system of secularism.
12 For example, Kleine (2013) sees the transcendent as equivalent to religion and immanent as equivalent to the secular, and thus argues the divide between religion and the secular is not exclusive to the modern West. But defining religion by its transcendence is relying upon a hierocentric definition.
13 However, Buddhism was also allowed to keep some of its own terminology like *tera* ('temple').
14 Seager adds patriotism to the Colombian myth, which is something the Japanese government also embraced.
15 Contrasting linear and cyclical conceptions of History may echo Orientalist descriptions, but I do not argue that linear time is exclusive to the West. Rather, I argue that the new imperial calendar adopted by the Japanese government was an adaption of new ideas from the West about time and social evolution.
16 See Chapter 2 note 1.
17 A seven-continent geography is not the only one taught in Europe. For example, Southern Europe teaches a six-continent geography, but the continents combined are not Europe and Asia, but North and South America.
18 Metageography: 'the set of spatial structures through which people order their knowledge of the world: the often unconscious frameworks that organize studies of history, sociology, anthropology, economics, political science, or even natural history' (Lewis and Wigen 1997, ix).
19 In Meiji Japan, the world was divided up into three geographical continents (Eurasia-Africa, America and Australia), but six political-cultural continents (Asia, Europe, Africa, North America, South America and Australia or Oceania).

20 For instance, a prefectural or status identity was more prominent than a national 'Japanese' identity before the Meiji Restoration. One of the major tasks of modernization was to replace that older identity with a national identity as a Japanese subject. See Howell (2005) and Stegewerns (2006).
21 Also cf. Ruoff (2010).
22 For example, the Qing empire, in its struggle to maintain sovereignty at the start of the twentieth century, borrowed from the Japanese model, but utilized Chinese Confucianism as the basis of its state. Cf. Yang (2008).
23 See Boyle (2020) for more on Japan's early modern influence on Hokkaido.
24 For example, Okinawa was never given a greater imperial shrine. Its highest-ranking shrine – Naminoue-gū, founded possibly as early as the fourteenth century – was only ranked a lesser imperial shrine. Furthermore, this shrine was not newly established and did not enshrine either the Three Pioneer Kami or Amaterasu. Thus, although Okinawa can be classified as a colonial space similar to Hokkaido, its shrine system resembled the modernization of shrines in the Home Islands more than it followed the model of overseas shrines.
25 For an example of this, cf. Sugiyama (1922, front material).
26 Although the standard translation of *shingaku* – theology – is used here, the application of the English-language term outside of its Christian origins 'is applicable only to a very limited extent and in a very modified form' (Louth and Helmut 2014). What *shingaku* more specifically means here is theories about which kami's virtues are most appropriate for the circumstance.
27 Particularly in the case of Taiwan, Japan adopted the pre-modern Chinese terminology of 'raw barbarians' and 'mature barbarians' to categorize people as barbarians or semi-civilized. Cf. Scott (2009) for the relationship between state creation and this terminology.
28 To quote the English version of the Patriotic March (Aikoku Kōshinkyoku).
29 For a description of a similar idea in European intellectual thought around this same period, confer Abrams (1973, 183–7) and Josephson-Storm (2017, 86–9).
30 This included folklorists such as Yanagita Kunio and Origuchi Shinobu and Kokugaku scholars such as Hirata Atsutane and Motoori Norinaga.
31 For example, confer Ono (1962, 1).
32 'Article 28. Japanese subjects shall, within limits not prejudicial to peace and order, and not antagonistic to their duties as subjects, enjoy freedom of religious belief.' Unlike the Prussian Constitution upon which the Meiji Constitution was largely based, this article did not establish a state religion while allowing tolerance.
33 I use the term 'venerate' instead of the more common translation of 'worship' due to the strong connotation of worship to mean only 'adoration' (*latria*) in theological terms. Christianity traditionally differentiated between the adoration of God and the veneration of the saints and relics. The former (*latria*) emphasizes an internal

act, while the latter (*dulia* or *proskynesis*) is associated with physical acts, with the Eastern Orthodox term *proskynesis* originally referring to the Persian custom of protestation before a great person such as the emperor. While a variety of Japanese terms (*hairei, sūkei, sūhai, sanpai, matsuru*, etc.) are often translated as 'worship' in English, the custom followed at Shinto shrines is more similar to *proskynesis* than *latria* in that it originates as a custom for expressing reverence before those above, including kings. The term 'worship' can indicate both *latria* and *dulia/proskynesis*, but modern Protestantism (which is the model for the generic concept of 'religion') often does not differentiate between *latria* and *dulia*, and sees the 'worship' of saints and relics as a form of idolatry. Idolatry is the direction of adoration ('worship') towards something other than God. Thus using the term 'worship' in its common Protestantism-based meaning draws a false parallel between shrine practices and the Christian practice of adoration, when the term 'veneration' would be a much closer translation.

34 Although shrines were sometimes historically categorized on the immanent side of an immanent-transcendent divide theorized by Buddhist thinkers. Cf. Kleine (2013).

35 While the Japanese government stopped actively persecuting Christians in the 1870s, it officially became legal only in 1890 when the Meiji Constitution was enacted. Christianity, Buddhism and Sect Shinto became the three religions legally recognized in Japan.

Chapter 2

1 This was the first day of the first month of 660 BC on the lunisolar calendar. Today, it is more common for scholars to use CE/BCE (Common Era/Before Common Era) than AD/BC (Anno Domini/Before Christ). However, the substitution of 'Common' for 'Christ' is an example of how secularism can be more coercive than religious pluralism. While AD/BC are transparent about their particular Christian origins, 'Common Era' insists that counting time from the traditional birth of Christ is common to all people regardless of ethnicity or religious identity. Furthermore, the imperial calendar invented by Japan was a direct response to the AD/BC system used by the West. For these two reasons, I have chosen to maintain AD/BC dating in this book.

2 Adapted from Hajime no Tennō (Uta 1921).

3 This chapter incorporates material from Shimizu (2017).

4 Many scholars today consider Jinmu fictional (Antoni and Antoni 2017, 17–19), but during the period covered by this study Jinmu was depicted as a historical person.

5 The restored Council of Divinities was the highest organ of the Meiji government when it was first established, although it was gradually demoted and limited.

Cf. Hardacre (2017, 359–68) about the Council of Divinities and Imperial Palace Sanctuaries.

6   This system was established by Home Ministry directive issued 17 March 1887.

7   The kanji for *en* is generally used in connection with the gardens of a palace. Preceded by an honorific (*gyoen*) it refers specifically to the grounds of the imperial palace and can be divided into an outer garden, *gaien*, and inner garden, *naien*. If referring to a shrine's grounds, the term *shin'en* ('kami-garden') is used.

8   For example, Yasukuni Jinja and Meiji Jingū were also born from calls to establish monuments to the war dead and Emperor Meiji, respectively. Cf. Takenaka (2015, 3) and Yamaguchi (2005, 36). Heian Jingū also first began as monument (Van Goethem 2018).

9   For example in 1919, Chamberlain (1982, lxi–lxii) criticized the widespread acceptance of the Kojiki myths as accurate historical truth by Japanese and Westerners. His main complaint, however, is the early dates attributed to Jinmu, rather than his existence.

10 In particular, see Uta (1921, 1922, 1940).

11 This rite was equated with the Daijōsai and sometimes referred to as a part of his *gotairei*, which also includes his enthronement rite (*sokui*).

12 Tsukioka Yoshitoshi's 1880 print in his Dainippon Meisho Kagami is one example. See: http://www.yoshitoshi.net/series/generals.html.

13 A reprint of the scroll Ruoff discusses can be found in Kashihara Jingū-chō (1989).

14 This relies upon the idea of History as progressive, or what Francis Fukuyama in his popular work calls 'universal History' (Fukuyama 2006, xiv). This theory originated with Hegel and is still widespread in popular discourse today. For example, negatively perceived customs are commonly criticized as if they are outdated by a phrase like 'This is 2022!'.

15 For example, Kashihara Jingū performed rites about the annexation of Korea in 1910, the declaration of war with Germany in 1914, and the restoration of peace in 1920 (Uta 1981a, 506, 563, 772). It also received formal visits from the Manchurian emperor and representatives of the Empire of Manchuria (Uta 1981b, 586, 667).

16 In light of this, adopting the philosopher Thomas Kasulis's term 'fresh' might be more appropriate than 'new' when discussing shrines. For the idea is not to entirely innovate, but to renew, or make fresh again, the perfection of antiquity. Confer Kasulis (2004, 54, 168).

17 The exact rank and name changed over the years, but they were all under the Ministry of Home Affairs. From 1877, shrines were managed by the Bureau of Shrines and Temples. In 1900, shrines gained their own Bureau of Shrine Affairs. In 1940, this bureau was raised in status to become the Jingi-in.

18 Cf. Chapter 3 for the relationship between the recent dead and shrines.

19 'The Constitution of the Empire of Japan', translated by Ito Miyoji. Article 4. Accessed at www.ndl.go.jp/constitution/e/etc/c02.html.

20 As Kashihara Jingū explained it, 'From the standpoint of our national body, the imperial house and citizens are connected as the main family is to the branch family' (Uta 1981b, 32).
21 This contrast between shrine and tumulus can be more clearly seen in Emperor Meiji's case. The construction of Meiji Jingū was a massive public effort, while his tumulus at Momoyama was done as a project of the imperial house, without the sort of volunteer labour and donations involved at Meiji Jingū. Confer Yamaguchi (2005).
22 Confer Uta (1922) for examples.
23 Namely, Amenominakanushi no Kami, Takamimusubi no Kami, Kamimusubi no Kami, Izanagi no Mikoto, Izanami no Mikoto and Amaterasu Ōmikami.
24 Izumo Taisha relied upon Izumo Taisha-kyō, a legally religious Shinto sect, Kotohiragū formed a reverence association strongly influenced by the Great Promulgation Campaign, and Ise Jingū formed its own religious Shinto sect, Jingū-kyō, until it was dissolved in 1899 and reformed as a secular organization.
25 See Chapter 5 for more on this. Also, confer Kondō (1943, 334) for an example. Kondō, an ardent supporter of Shinto as universal to Asia, does not claim the idea as his own, but rather quotes a German scholar describing Shinto as the 'oriental religion'.
26 The term 'sacred' (*seinaru, shinsei*) frequently occurs in wartime ideology, but 'sacred' does not inevitably equal 'religion' within the context of secularism. Rather it is used within nationalism to place something as untouchable. Thus as the Imperial Rescript on Education and Kashihara Jingū were seen as sacred in the pre-war era, Americans have often spoken of the Constitution or Gettysburg Battlefield as sacred. Cf. Bellah (1991).
27 It developed its own unique character by adopting ritual elements directly related to the Jinmu legend, such as the Kume-mai (a revived *bugaku* dance Jinmu Tennō was said to have performed), Ōgi-no-mai (a new *kagura* composed to Emperor Meiji's poem about Kashihara Jingū) and Kuzusō-hōnō (an ancient custom of the Nara area) (Kashihara Jingū-chō 1989).
28 The common translation is 'worship from afar', but due to the common conflation of worship with adoration, the term 'veneration' is used here. The act of *yōhai* consists of bowing, often accompanied by clapping or a moment of silence, in the direction of the object of reverence.
29 For example, Tōkyō Daijingū began as a *yōhai* site for Ise Jingū and Hokkaidō Jingū Tongū began as a *yōhai* site to Hokkaidō Jingū before receiving a 'divided spirit' and becoming a subsidiary shrine in 1947.
30 Cf. Ruoff (2010, 86–97) on Miyazaki's campaign for recognition.
31 Hara (2011, 415) calls this in English 'Temporal Domination' (*jikan shihai*), although Ruoff's translation of 'rule by time' is perhaps more natural (Ruoff 2010, 57).

32 A current Western equivalent of a similar 'spellbound' moment of time might be the playing of the 'Colors' on American military bases every morning and evening. When the first notes of the bugle sound, everyone immediately stops what s/he is doing, faces towards the flag or music, and for a short, still moment of time salutes the American flag. This includes those driving in a car, who are required to pull over and get out in order to perform this patriotic ritual.

33 Thus Nitobe Inazō was inspired to write his famous book *Bushido* by a European friend's shocked query, 'No religion! How do you impart moral education?' (Nitobe 1905, 19).

34 An example of this can be found in Ōkawa Shūmei's popular 1939 *Nippon 2600 Nenshi*. Not only did the author feel the need to emphasize the importance of studying history during wartime in the prologue (Ōkawa 1940, 4), but the publisher also included an afterword justifying the 'Wartime System Edition' series as contributing to the war effort by 'fostering a firm backbone and will' and laying down preparations for the expected post-war 'renaissance of Oriental culture'.

35 Confer Ruoff (2010, 95-7) on tourism to Kashihara.

36 *Yōhai* also gave people a chance to practice punctuality, another virtue emphasized in morality textbooks.

37 This includes actions that contribute to personal good, because as Reader and Tanabe (1998, 105) have discussed, the good of individuals can contribute to the overall public good.

38 Confer Shimizu (2019, 14) for a table of overlapping national holidays and palace rites.

39 Ruoff (2010, 98) gives statistics for visitors to Nara prefecture the year of the 2600th anniversary, which included 18,000 from Korea, 7,000 from Manchuria and 1,000 from Taiwan.

40 Also confer Saaler (2016) on Jinmu monuments.

41 The top prefectures were Osaka (498,907 volunteers), Nara (410,671 volunteers) and Hyogo (126,036 volunteers).

42 Kashihara Jingū also incorporated distant places into itself as a centre by using their materials. Massive cypress logs, harvested from the mountains of Taiwan by the island's indigenous people, made up the numerous pillars of the shrine's buildings.

43 For more about this in English, confer Teeuwen and Breen (2018) on the Ise Jingū, Imaizumi (2013) on Meiji Jingū and Van Goethem (2018) on Heian Jingū.

44 Thal (2005, 203-19) provides an example of this at Kotohiragū.

45 For example, *daijingū* shrines all look to Ise as their parent shrine, *gokoku* shrines look to Yasukuni shrine, Izumo shrines look to Izumo Taisha and so on. See Chapter 7 on how shrine lineages played an important role overseas connecting the periphery to the centre.

Chapter 3

1. Based on Hokkaidō Jingū-shi Hensan Iinkai (1991, 25–31).
2. The word *kaitaku* can be translated a variety of ways, including 'pioneer', 'development' and 'colonization'.
3. Heian-kyō, capital from 794 AD to 1868 AD, is now Kyoto, although the city's original grid layout has largely been obscured. Fujiwara-kyō, in Kashihara, was the capital from 694 AD to 710 AD.
4. See Chapter 6 for more on the Kwangtung Army.
5. Confer Sasaki (2009, 177–80) for a case study on the modernization process of pre-modern shrines in one Hokkaido village.
6. Shima was executed in 1874 for his participation in the Saga Rebellion. However, he was posthumously pardoned by the Meiji government in 1889.
7. For examples, confer Suga (2014, 144) and Hokkaidō Jingū-shi Hensan Iinkai (1995, 665–81).
8. Kuroda served as vice-chairman of the Commission from May 1870 until August 1874. He acted as chairperson during the chairman's vacancy from October 1871, until being officially appointed as chairperson in August 1874 until February 1882.
9. Today, this tram line has been replaced by a subway system, which still provides public access to Maruyama Park and the shrine.
10. These can still be seen lining the approach to Hokkaidō Jingū today.
11. However, Fukutama's work could also be seen as an act of protest against what he saw as the central government's unfair dismissal of Shima. The act is then 'bimodel' (Josephson-Storm 2017, 268) affirming the central government's Hokkaido narrative while promoting an alternate version of that narrative that retains Shima as a hero.
12. For examples, confer Hokkaidō Jingū (1989).
13. These trips can be considered a form of 'rule by sight' (cf. Hara 2011). Photographs related to these visits can be seen in Hokkaidō Jingū (1989, 18, 28, 41).
14. This gate was constructed from volcanic tuff particular to the Sapporo area in 1895, and then replaced with copper-sheathed ferro-concrete in 1928.
15. Comparative maps of Sapporo in 1916, 1935 and today can be found online at 'Konjaku Mappu on the Web' (Tani 2017).
16. 'Abolish the Lunisolar Calendar and Circulate the Solar Calendar' (Taiin Reki wo Haishi Taiyō Reki wo Hankō Su), Dajōkan Proclamation #337.
17. In 1873, the festival was still celebrated on the 15th day of the sixth month on the lunisolar calendar (9 July on the solar calendar).
18. This also suggests that shrines were encouraging pan-Asian views like that of Miki Kiyoshi (Kim 2007, 158) and Rōyama Masamichi (Koschmann 2007, 190), which posited a broad Japanese sphere (Greater East Asia) within which each area could have a regional character.

19 I follow contemporary Japanese terminology here. See Chapter 4, note 4.
20 'A Matter on Shinto Ritualists Not Conducting Funerals' (Shinkan Sōshiki ni Kan Subekarazaru Koto).
21 The order was 'The Issue of Renaming Shōkon-sha as Gokoku Shrines, 1939 March 15 Ministry of Home Affairs Order #12' (Shōkon-sha wo Gokoku Jinja to Kaishō Suru no Ken Shōwa 14-nen 3-gatsu 15-nichi Naimushō Rei Dai 12-gō).
22 Hakodate Gokoku Jinja originated from the *shōkon-sha* founded in 1869 after the Battle of Hakodate to enshrine the imperial soldiers that died there, and served as their cemetery. Sapporo Gokoku Jinja developed from a cenotaph (*shōkon-hi*) set up in 1879 to commemorate the twenty-seven Hokkaido farmer-soldiers who died putting down the Satsuma Rebellion in 1877, but did not become a *shōkon-sha* until 1922. Hokkaido also had three non-designated *gokoku* shrines in Tokachi, Matsumae and Hiyama. Cf. Seaton (2016b, 162–6).
23 However, Gifu, Hyogo, Shimane and Hiroshima prefectures each had two designated *gokoku* shrines.
24 The term *gokoku* when adopted for *gokoku* shrines in 1939 may have drawn on the Shogunate's tradition of nation-protecting temples (*gokoku-ji*).
25 In 1878, Tōkyō Shōkon-sha argued that it should be allowed a Shinto ritualist (*shinshoku*) since it was a site where the enshrined spirits resided permanently, not temporarily like at a *shōkon-jō*. The Home Ministry denied this request on the grounds that a *shōkon-sha* is still not a shrine. This desire for a ritualist led Tōkyō Shōkon-sha to convert into Yasukuni Jinja. However, the issue established a difference between *shōkon-sha* and *shōkon-jō*. Confer Takenaka (2015, 47–50).
26 The chief ritualist of Kamikawa Jinja was appointed to look after the shrine, and several ritualists located beneath him to serve the shrine.
27 This shrine was founded in 1644, but shrine tradition traces its origins back to 1216. According to legend, an old woman named Oriyi, sometimes said to be an ancestor of the Ainu, venerated three kami who were able to bring large catches of herring to the village. After Oriyi mysteriously disappeared, the villagers continued to venerate the three kami as well as Oriyi's spirit. Confer Sutō (1971, 34–5).
28 Kajiura, along with the Commander of the Seventh, Lt. Gen. Satō Konosuke, and Adjutant General Lt. Col. Sukegawa Seiji hatched the plan in 1933 to renovate the neglected site into a splendid shrine, to be financed by a donation of the price of one cigarette from every Hokkaido resident (Shimemura 1981, 574). He served first as Assistant Adjutant General, and then Adjutant General until he was sent to Manchuria in 1935.
29 This included Nishikawa Ni'noshin, the chief ritualist of Furano Jinja discussed below.
30 Future renovation plans were dashed by the end of the war.
31 These are not the only examples of plans to establish a 'northern' version of the centre in Hokkaido. For example, a 'northern imperial villa', modelled after the

already established eastern, southern and western imperial villas, was planned to be built at the site of Kamikawa Jinja. Hokkaido was often imagined as a holographic northern version of the Japanese centre.

32 *Hokuchin*, lit. 'North (Spirit-)Pacification' can be interpreted on several registers. Since the museum held memorial items of the war dead, the spirits being pacified may be seen as those from the north (Hokkaido and Karafuto) who died on the battlefield. But *hokuchin* can also be an abbreviation for *hokuchinjufu*, lit. 'North Protection Office'. The *chinjufu* were offices charged with protecting the homeland in ancient Japan. The term *chinju* 'protector' is also used to refer to the area each shrine is charged with looking after.

33 These guns were originally planned for an assault on the Ryōjun Fort at Port Arthur, but were never used. Kajiura bought them off the Hakodate base using money donated by all the soldiers of the Seventh.

34 Onko is a term unique to Hokkaido.

35 The background to this decision includes the Chinese Rites Controversy, during which the Church allowed Catholics to take part in Confucian ritual. Confer Breen (2010).

36 After the Occupation, the name reverted to Hokkaidō Gokoku Jinja (cf. Shimemura 1981, 655–6).

37 The Furano Basin lacked significant Ainu settlements in the late nineteenth century (Segawa 2015, 28), but photographs from Furano's early history show that at least some semi-Japanized Ainu lived in Furano around the time it was being settled by migrants from the Home Islands (Furano-shi Kaiki 90 Shūnen Kinen-shi Henshū Iinkai 1994, 7).

38 Ashihara Isao, the ritualist of Chikabumi Jinja in Asahikawa, was charged with looking after his own shrine, in addition to Furano Jinja.

39 The Nishikawa family continues to serve as hereditary ritualists at Furano Jinja today.

40 A certain enmity over this is still felt today between the two communities. Confer Hokkaidō Jinjachō (2019).

41 Many smaller shrines, including Torinuma Jinja, in the lower Furano area, never sought government recognition. If requested by the shrine's local community, the ritualist of Furano Jinja might visit on major festivals, but the shrines were not formally under his care.

42 After the war, in fear the war memorial would be torn down by the Occupation, the physical remains were removed and returned to their relatives. Furthermore, the inscription was chiselled out and replaced with the name 'Tower of Peace' in an effort to preserve it. Today, Furano holds the Peace Festival on 15 June, which includes a memorial service for the war dead at the tower as well as a marching band parade by students from the local schools.

43 See Yamada and Maeda (2012, 616–759) for maps of shrines in Karafuto.
44 With forty one of the 124 shrines with known kami in Karafuto dedicated to her, Amaterasu was the most commonly enshrined kami (Yamada and Maeda 2012, 43).
45 There were also at least another 150 unregistered Shinto sites, although little is known about them. See Yamada and Maeda (2012) for a comprehensive collection of materials about shrines in Karafuto.
46 Hokkaido was briefly divided into three prefectures before its sparse population led to it being treated as a single prefecture under the Hokkaido government.
47 Poultney Bigelow, quoted in Sugiyama (1922, front matter).

Chapter 4

1 Based upon the hagiographic account by Taiwan Jinja Shamusho Hensan (1935, 9–40).
2 For example, Mason, philosopher and author of *The Meaning of Shinto*, wrote that 'One of the first actions of the Japanese, accompanying territorial expansion, is to erect Shinto Shrines' (Mason 1935, 14).
3 For an example in relation to Taiwan, see Lo (2002, 111).
4 English terminology is varying and confusing for this demographic group. They have been called 'Taiwanese', 'Chinese' or even 'natives', depending on if they are being contrasted with post-war Chinese immigrants, the indigenous Taiwanese tribes or the Japanese, respectively. I follow contemporary Japanese terminology here, using Takasago to refer to Taiwan's indigenous Austronesian peoples, Islanders (*hontō-jin, tōmin*) to refer to the Southern Chinese migrants and their descendants, and Home Islanders (*naichi-jin*) to refer to migrants from the Japanese Home Islands.
5 The treaty also ceded to Japan the Liaodong Peninsula, but the Triple Intervention of 23 April 1895 by Russia, France and Germany forced Japan to return the peninsula to the Qing. This bred severe resentment on the Japanese side and was a factor leading to the Russo-Japanese War.
6 Although many scholars both pre- and post-war treat Taiwan as Japan's first colony (Nitobe 1912, 347; Peattie 1984b, 80–1; Sugiyama 1922, front matter; Takekoshi 1907, 2), other scholars argue that Hokkaido preceded Taiwan as a Japanese colony (Mason 2012, 17; Siddle 1996, 51; Walker 2001, 13). Confer Seaton (2016a) for an overview of this argument.
7 In contrast to the 'mature barbarians'.
8 Four of them were located within Home Islander enclaves, and another two were dedicated to Kotohira. As discussed in Chapter 7, Kotohira was also a popular shrine among Japanese migrants in Hawai'i.

9 The national Japanese government had established a separate office for shrines in 1900, but regional governments like that in Hokkaido continued to maintain a single office for shrines and religious organizations.
10 *Shinshi*, the term used for pre-shrines in Korea, was also a generic term used across the Japanese empire for any small unofficial Shinto site. It was used in Korea because the legal category of pre-shrine was originally intended as a holding category for such sites. Although the legal category of pre-shrine was adopted by the Taiwan Governor-General, the term *sha* was used instead of *shinshi*. This was likely because the category was adopted in Taiwan in order to allow for the building of new Shinto sites and the term *sha* overlaps with both the second Chinese character of *jinja* (shrine) and the term used for village (Jp. *sha*, Ch. *shè*) in Taiwan.
11 Later in 1935, Tansui Middle School and Girls' School, operated by the Canadian Presbyterian church, resisted the government's requirement for shrine visits and *yōhai*, but quickly came to a compromise over the issue. See Komagome (2005, 21–3) and Ion (1999, 104–5).
12 The *jingū* appellation is only used by shrines dedicated to an imperial ancestor, such as Amaterasu Ōmikami, Emperor Jinmu or Emperor Meiji. Prince Yoshihisa, while a member of the imperial family, was not a direct ancestor of an emperor, and thus not qualified to receive the term *jingū*.
13 To compare, the government also financially contributed to Hokkaido's Sapporo Jinja, but Taiwan Jingū received far more preferential treatment. For example in 1925, Sapporo Jinja received 3,283 yen while Taiwan Jinja received 25,000 yen (Sai 1994, 24).
14 This was Taihoku's first park, established in 1896 by Taihoku's governor Hashiguchi Bunzō (Allen 2012, 95). It is perhaps not surprising that Hashiguchi, who planned Taiwan's public park system, had previous served as an attaché in the Hokkaido government and as headmaster of Sapporo Agricultural College (Hokkaido University).
15 The former site of the shrine still continues to carry associations with Maruyama Park. For instance, the Grand Hotel Taipei, which now occupies the site, is called Yuan Shan (Jp. Maruyama) Hotel.
16 Today many lanterns remain, but the names are largely effaced. I was told by one informant, who was a boy during the Second World War, that the donators often effaced their own names in fear of repercussions from the post-war Chinese government. While the amount of attachment Taiwanese Islanders had to shrines is debatable, the great number of shrine lanterns, statues and other furnishings that were preserved suggests many were at least attached to shrine furnishings.
17 For example, Shiodome Jinja, Shinchiku Jinja and Byōritsu Jinja. Confer Kaneko (2015, 32, 61, 56).
18 For an example among the Takasago, see Barclay (2018, 115).

19 For example, see Sugiyama (1916, 501) and Kanagawa Daigaku Himoji Shiryō Kenkyū Sentā (2019).
20 These visits can be included in what Hara called 'Spatial Domination' or, put another way, 'rule by space' (cf. Hara 2011).
21 Other popular trees were *Calocedrus formosana* (a Taiwanese tree), *Ficus microcarpa* (a tropical tree), *Cleyera japonica* (Sakaki), *Cinnamomum camphora* (a tropical tree) and *Michelia formosana* (a Taiwanese tree). Cf. Taiwan Jinja Shamusho Hensan (1935, 113).
22 For example, *takushoku*, or 'colonization/development', is literally 'breaking ground-planting', *kaitaku*, or 'pioneer/development' is literally 'opening-breaking ground', and *shokuminchi*, or 'colony', is literally 'planting-people-land'.
23 Cf. Chapter 2 on the 'four seasons'.
24 Ordinance 167, on 27 December 1895, defined Western Standard Time as an hour earlier than Central Standard Time.
25 Western Standard Time was abolished with Ordinance 529, with the entire empire using Central Standard Time.
26 This is an important contrast from the modern Western colonial anthropology which typically held that even the existence of local deities was a superstition. Cf. Asad (1993, 171–99).
27 Allen suggests that Taiwan Islander elites' cultural superiority in classical Chinese culture may have challenged the assumed superiority of the Home Islanders (2012, 102).
28 These *komainu* still sit at the site of Taiwan Jingū, but now guarding the Grand Hotel Taipei, instead of a shrine.
29 Yamaguchi also evoked the Chinese idea of *seisaku* (Ch. *zhèngshuò*) – renewing the calendar upon the enthronement of a new emperor – to explain the necessity for Taiwan residents to follow the new calendar and be obedient citizens (Sai 1994, 192–3).
30 Probably Percival Lowell (1895) and Arthur May Knapp (1896).
31 *Inshi jakyō* is an older term more commonly translated as 'lewd rites and evil teachings' which was connected to the more modern idea of *meishin*, or 'superstitions'. Shintoists, at least overseas, continued to utilize the older term when discussing which kami should be legitimate objects of veneration. Also cf. Josephson (2012, 175–7) on the development of *meishin*, and Odaira (2009, 187–209) on the discourse around *inshi* and restoration of the Jingikan in the Meiji period.
32 For example, the greater imperial shrine Kashii-gū was historically known as Kashii-byō.
33 As seen in Chapter 3, Hokkaidō Gokoku Jinja also began as a site after a custom of temporary *shōkon* developed. But Hokkaidō Gokoku Jinja became a *shōkon-sha* first.

34 Indian architectural elements were also often included in Japanese Buddhist temples during this period in an effort to express a pan-Asian Buddhism. Cf. Tanabe and Tanabe (2013, 20–2).
35 The Charter Oath was a foundational document of the Meiji State. The fifth clause of the Charter Oath reads: 'Knowledge shall be sought throughout the world so as to strengthen the foundation of imperial rule.'
36 Ide was fond of the Imperial Crown Style, and it was common in government buildings across Taiwan. Kenkō Jinja also includes many elements of the Imperial Crown Style.
37 This increased as the war progressed, but I have been unable to locate statistics after 1942.
38 Yasukuni Jinja lists 27,864 Taiwanese as enshrined there today, which would have made them also eligible for enshrinement at Taiwan Gokoku Jinja. However, the war situation may have meant they were not able to be enshrined in Taiwan Gokoku Jinja before it was abolished.
39 Taiwan Islanders could join in non-combat positions from 1938.
40 This last criterion allowed the enshrinement of those who had died on the Taiwan Expedition in 1874.
41 For example, Tokachi Gokoku Jinja was built next to Obihiro Jinja in Hokkaido.
42 He helped the government under Gotō Shinpei formulate the brutal 'scorched earth' policy of dealing with the Takasago.
43 For example, the *ilisin* harvest festival of the Amis tribe of the Takasago came to include elements of Japanese moon-viewing customs and often overlapped with the (pre-)shrine's annual festival (Kaneko 2018, 293). The *ilisin* festival as celebrated today still includes elements adopted from Shinto shrines (Naiseibu 2020).

Chapter 5

1 This would have been the 14th day of the 12th month of 200 AD on the lunisolar calendar.
2 Based on the accounts in the Kojiki, Nihongi, and on Tsukioka Yoshitoshi's popular woodcut of this event (1879).
3 Especially at Sumiyoshi shrines, dedicated to the kami who aided her crossing to Korea, and Hachiman shrines, dedicated to her son Emperor Ōjin.
4 Although the term Samhan originally referred to the Proto-Three Kingdoms era rather than the later three kingdoms of Koguryŏ, Silla and Paekche, by the seventh century, it was also being used to reference the latter three kingdoms.
5 *Daigongen* is a Buddhist title for kami common during this period when Buddhism and Shinto were amalgamated. Sumiyoshi-no-Ōkami were the three

kami who aided Jingū in the classics and were, like Kotohira, often venerated for maritime safety.

6   For the role Japanese settlers had in Korea's colonization, see Uchida (2011).
7   For more on the Same Ancestor theory, see Oguma (2002, 64–92).
8   Chōsen Government-General Order 82 'Shrine and Temple Regulations', 1915.
9   Chōsen Government-General Order 21 'Matter Regarding Pre-shrines', 1917.
10 Despite this, subsequent Chōsen Governors-General remained affiliated with the military. This is in contrast with Taiwan, which had several civilian governors-general.
11 There were dissenters to this theory. For example, Takekoshi Yosaburō, the historian and politician who rejected the idea that the Takasago shared racial ancestry with Home Islanders and advocated for the genocidal policy the Taiwan Governor-General sometimes took towards the Takasago, argued that Koreans were of a different race (Caprio 2009, 33–4).
12 Amaterasu's title is customarily read Ōmikami ('great honourable kami'), regardless of whether it is written with or without the character for honourable.
13 Takamatsu later went on to become Kashihara Jingū's chief ritualist in 1931 and then Sapporo Jinja's chief ritualist in 1934.
14 Takamatsu Shirō (1925–31), Achiwa Yasuhiko (1931–40) and Nukaga Ōnao (1940–5). Cf. Hiura (2013, 271) for short biographies of Chōsen Jingū's ritualists.
15 See Henry (2014, 35) for a 1919 map of Chōsen Jingū within the larger area of Kejiō.
16 Specifically, 48,410 *taima* were distributed in 1934, while 1,263,648 *taima* were in 1940 (Hiura 2013, 209).
17 Police statistics, however, give the more optimistic statistic of 20 per cent of Korean households having Jingū *taima* in 1939.
18 This resembles the origins of Hokkaidō Gokoku Jinja, which aimed to 'educate wordlessly' military recruits into a modern lifestyle. See Chapter 3.
19 Shinshū Buddhism was particularly evangelical for a Japanese Buddhist sect while Tenrikyō was a religious Sect Shinto group originating from the teachings of its founder, Nakayama Miki (1798–1887).
20 When using this phrase to call for the promulgation of Shinto across Greater East Asia, Kondō credits his inspiration to Karl Ernst Haushofer, the German geographer who helped link Japan to the Axis nations.
21 Shrine documents of Kankō Jinja, however, described Kunitama as the 'ancestral kami of developing the land', reflecting a combination of the older ancestor and pioneering interpretations of Ōkunitama (Aono 2015, 178).
22 Heijō Jinja and Taikyū Jinja were ranked as lesser national shrines in 1937, followed by Kōgen Jinja and Kōshū Jinja in 1941 and Zenshū Jinja and Kankō Jinja in 1944.

23 Keijō Jinja was not alone in this. Taikyū Jinja, another lesser national ranked shrine, also conducted funerals (Hiura 2013, 153).
24 Of course, Japanese Christians were not the only ones contesting where the line lay between the religious and secular spheres. When Kume Kunitake, a teacher at Tokyo Imperial University, questioned the Shinto-based legitimacy of the imperial house by disparaging Shinto as an 'old superstition' in the Kume Incident of 1892, he – like Uchimura and Okumura – was forced to resign (Hiura 2013, 3).
25 While rural schools often had no nearby shrine to visit, they were not free from this pressure. Schools which did not have access to a shrine or pre-shrine would build a small shrine-like structure for keeping and venerating the Jingū *taima*. Cf. Hiura (2013, 204–40).
26 See Nakajima et al. (2015, 177, 179) for maps of Heijō and Heijō Jinja.
27 To give just two examples of this, Cumings links assimilation to shrines by writing that Koreans 'were for the first time required to speak Japanese or to take Japanese names. The colonizers even forced Koreans to worship at Shinto shrines' (Cumings 2005, 182), while Young writes that 'the *kōminka* (imperialization) policy … attempted to force racial assimilation through coercive diffusion of Japanese language, Japanese names, and shrine Shinto' (Young 1998, 365). Although Shrine Shinto played a key part in Japanese colonialism, this was not necessarily the same thing as Japanese assimilation.
28 A similar suppression of itinerant ritualists had occurred in the Home Islands in the mid-nineteenth century. Confer Odaira (2009).
29 Compare this to Miyazaki Naokatsu's statement in the previous chapter about how Taiwanese kami became Japanese kami, much like how Taiwan residents became Japanese citizens, when Japan started governing Taiwan.
30 Although today Shinto is often described as a type of 'nature worship', as previous chapters have shown, Shintoists during this period saw Shinto as historical rather than mythological.
31 He previously served as the head of the Culture and Education Bureau in Taiwan.
32 While vocabulary clearly differentiated shrines (*jinja*) from pre-shrines (*shinshi*) and other Shinto sites in Japanese, for Koreans writing in Hangul the words were spelled the same (*sinsa*). Korean students understandably conflated shrines, pre-shrines and Shinto sites at schools such as the fireproof safes built for storing important documents like the Imperial Rescript on Education (Hiura 2013, 168).
33 Tenji and Saimei are usually accepted as historical figures today. The historical existence of Ōjin and Jingū are more contested. Cf. Allen (2003) for further discussion on especially Jingū's contested historicity.
34 Known as Empress Kōgyoku during this rule.
35 In contrast to only 327 households under the Empire of Korea (Sohn 2004, 308).

Chapter 6

1 Based off the accounts of Nichiman Chūō Kyōkai (1941, 86–9) and Hashimoto (1941, 112–14).
2 For example, the pamphlet *Manshūkoku no Shūkyō* (*Religions of Manchukuo*), published by the Manchukuo government in Japanese, gives a detailed overview of the major and minor religions, as well as religious-like organizations. 'Shintō' is listed as a heading under the minor religions category, but is only given a single line of text pointing out that some Japanese migrants follow Sect Shinto like Tenri-kyō and Konkō-kyō (Manshū Jijō Annai-jo 1939, 46).
3 Contemporary English-language postcard captions use this phrase, but it seems likely that 'royal' is a misprint for 'loyal'.
4 Photographic examples of all the previously mentioned war memorials can be seen in Zushi (2003, 99–120).
5 This may have been done because the town had been the site of the Battle of Liaoyang (Jp. Ryōyō) in the Russo-Japanese war.
6 See Tsuda et al. for maps of Kenkoku Chūreibyō (2007, 287–9).
7 The Chinese character used here is the same as the one used for the tombs of Japanese emperors, such as Jinmu's tumulus next to Kashihara Jingū.
8 At this rite, 24,141 glorious spirits were enshrined, with the majority of them (19,877) being Japanese subjects (Tsuda 2008, 75).
9 See Sagai (1998, 84) for a short biography of Hashimoto.
10 See Tsuda et al. for maps of Kenkoku Shinbyō (2007, 284–5).
11 This idea contrasted with the understanding of many migrants to Manchuria, who described the *taima* they received from the Ise Jingū as a divided spirit.
12 Kobayashi Iwao, Education Official of the Institute of Ritual in the Home Islands, also lays out this idea in his book. See Kobayashi (1944, 119–28).
13 The official texts of the 1935 Instruction for the People Upon Return and the 1940 Establishing the Pillar of the State edits were widely reprinted in the 1940s. See Nichiman Chūō Kyōkai (1941, front matter) or Kobayashi (1944, 134, 136) for examples.
14 The rhetoric around this 'Manchukuo Foundational Spirit' was not limited to Manchurian citizens, but was also drilled into potential Japanese migrants during their training in Japan (Sagai 1998, 92).
15 These ordinances were revised in 1943 and 1941, respectively. See Kobayashi (1944, 120–1).
16 See Chapter 2 for a discussion of this.
17 The festival day of Kikoku-sai, which was linked to Japan's Kinen-sai, was celebrated on the 6th of the 24 solar terms of the Chinese lunisolar calendar. It marked the start of the planting season.

18 This outfit resembled the Zhongsan suit ('Mao suit') developed in the Republic of China and the 'citizen's dress' introduced in Japan in 1940.
19 See Tsuda et al. (2007) for maps of Shinkyō Jinja (242–4) and other shrines along the S. Manchurian Railway.
20 Nine other shrines in the Railway Zone were given permission this year, all of them enshrining Amaterasu either alone or in combination with Emperor Meiji and/or Ōkuninushi. Cf. Tsuda et al. (2007, 210).
21 Antō Jinja, Hōten Jinja and Bujun Jinja were grouped into this same category.
22 Some shrines like Hōten Jinja and Bujun Jinja built permanent *yōhai* sites within their gardens (Tsuda et al. 2007, 248).
23 Post-war, many Chinese residents recall being prohibited from visiting the city's shrine, even if they were expected to show respect when passing in front of it. For examples, see the ethnographic research of Tsuda et al. on Bujun Jinja, Tetsurei Jinja, Kaigen Jinja, Kōshurei Jinja and Seian Jinja (2007, 256, 262, 266, 274, 279).
24 See Aoyagi (2002) for an in-depth study on Modekngei.
25 See Tomii et al. (2004) for maps of Nan'yō Jinja and other shrines in the South Seas.

Chapter 7

1 Its easternmost island (Kure Atoll, uninhabited) lies 2,790 kilometres from Japan (Torishima) and its westernmost island lies 3,674 kilometres from the US mainland (Flumeville).
2 In Hawai'i censuses, Portuguese were often counted separately since they were brought to Hawai'i as plantation labourers, similar to non-Caucasian groups.
3 This section incorporates material from Shimizu (2019).
4 Lawai Daijingū shrine on Kaua'i was also founded on the same day as Hilo Daijingū.
5 Ōmikami and Sume Ōmikami are both used seemingly interchangeably as Amaterasu's title in sources related to Hawai'i's shrines.
6 Lord Katō was a former lord of Kumamoto, and thus also a historical kami.
7 See the discussion on Kotohira Jinsha below for more on the subsumption of prefectural identity at shrines.
8 It moved again to its current location after a tsunami wiped it out twice and the land it previously stood on was bought by the state to turn into a city municipal park.
9 Some Hawai'i shrines like Hawaii Daijingū on O'ahu directly stated their 'equivalent rank' under the shrine ranking system. See Maeda (1999, 133).

10 Previous research has already noted how amulets 'help sustain the normative principles involved in kinship organization' (Swanger and Takayama 1981, 249–50). In a similar manner, this *taima* distribution process also affirmed the Confucian kinship model of the state central to the Imperial Rescript on Education.
11 See Shimizu (2019, 14) for a chart comparing Hilo Daijingū's festivals with national holidays in Japan.
12 These necklaces may have been based off ancient necklaces preserved as shrine treasures. Cf. Uchigawa (2019).
13 Other Shinto ritualists in Hawai'i also dressed like this. Cf. Goldman (2003, 83).
14 In 1940, the name was changed to Shintō Taikyō.
15 The first definition of 'temple' in the 1930 edition of *Webster's New International Dictionary* connects it to the paganism of ancient Greece and Rome by stating that it was 'anciently usually regarded as a residing place of the deity, whose presence was symbolized by a statue', and then refers the reader to columniation (Harris and Allen 1930, 2124, 443).
16 However, foreign superstitions might be acknowledged as deserving of religious freedom by broad-minded American officials. For example, the judge who ruled in favour of shrines in Hawai'i being deserving of religious protection wrote in his decision that 'I am not even prepared to find on this evidence that [the shrine] ... held beliefs which could be agreed to constitute a religion' (Kotohira *Jinsha v. McGrath*).
17 Although the shortage of men meant women were increasingly acting as ritualists during the war, women were officially allowed to become ritualists again only after the war in 1946.
18 Inari-san was venerated at officially recognized shrines such as Fushimi Inari Taisha, but Japanese officials and proper society considered the incorrect/secret veneration or ritual appeasement of foxes and fox-related kami a danger to society either as lewd rites or as superstition.
19 In 1920, 3 November was no longer a national holiday, as the Emperor Meiji had died and Emperor Taisho's birthday became the holiday. However, the Emperor Meiji continued to be popular and 3 November became a holiday again in 1927.
20 Of the 277,830 overseas Japanese living in the Americas in 1930, 103,996 of them resided in the United States and 119,740 in Brazil. In comparison, the much smaller geographic area of Hawai'i had 144,295 Japanese residents. See Young (1998, 314–15).
21 This category may also include *taima* distributed within South East Asia as well. See Zushi (2003, 260), who draws his statistics from Kondō (1943, 324).
22 Sometimes called Uetsuka Jinja.

Chapter 8: Conclusion

1. For example, Nakajima's fourfold categorization is typical in post-war Shinto studies. His first three categories of shrines are defined by their enshrined kami, while the last category lumps all overseas shrines into a single geographic category (Nakajima 2010, 22).
2. For example, the Tsu City Groundbreaking Ceremony Case, the Ehime Tamagushi Case and the Sorachibuto Shrine Case. Also see Seaton (2016b, 171–6) on the current controversy surrounding Hokkaidō Gokoku Jinja.
3. Nakajima has divided the fate of overseas shrine sites into four categories: reused, abandoned, restored as Shinto shrines or restored to their use before becoming a shrine. The last category is rare, with Nakajima giving only three examples. This is expected given that most shrines were constructed on virgin land (Nakajima 2013, 35).
4. Shrines in the Northern Territories (Kuril Islands), also occupied by the Soviets but still claimed by Japan, suffered a similar fate. See Hoppō Ryōdo Bunka Nichiro Kyōdō Gakujutsu Kōryū Jikkō Iinkai (2005).
5. In a similar manner, Occupation forces in Japan also used the garden of Meiji Jingū in the Home Islands as a site for Easter sunrise services. See Kawai (1950, 94).

Character glossary

Aburasugi	油杉
Achiwa Yasuhiko	阿知和安彦
Aida Fusae	相田房江
Aikoku Kōshinkyoku	愛国行進曲
Amaterasu Ōmikami	天照大御神・天照大神
Amaterasu Sume Ōmikami	天照皇大神
amatsukami kunitsukami	天神地祇
Amenominakanushi no Kami	天之御中主神
Amenotaneko no Mikoto	天種子命
Amenotomi no Mikoto	天富命
Antō Jinja	安東神社
Ari	阿里
Arianza Shokuminchi	アリアンサ植民地
Ashihara Isao	芦原伊佐男
Baba Nao	馬場直
Ban Yūzaburō	伴雄三郎
bekkaku kanpeisha	別格官幣社
Benten	弁天
Bogure Jinja	ボグレ神社
Bujun Jinja	撫順神社
bun'in	分院
bunrei	分霊
butsudan	仏壇
byō	廟
Byōritsu Jinja	苗栗神社
Chikabumi Jinja	近文神社
chinju	鎮守
chinjufu	鎮守府
Chinkō	鎮江
chinowa	茅の輪
chinza	鎮座
Chiya Matsue	千屋松恵
Chō Kanshō	張煥相
Chō Keikei	張景惠
Chōsen Jingū	朝鮮神宮

Chōsen Kunitama	朝鮮国魂
Chōsen Kunitama-no-kami	朝鮮国魂神
Chōsen Misogi-kai	朝鮮禊会
Chōshun	長春
chūkon-hi	忠魂碑
chūrei-tō	忠霊塔
Chūreki	中壢
Chūsei-hoku	忠清北
Chūsei-nan	忠清南
daigongen	大権現
daijingū	大神宮
Daijōsai	大嘗祭
Dai-Nana Shidan Kan Shōkon-sha	第七師団管招魂社
Dairen Jinja	大連神社
dōjō	道場
dōsai	洞祭
dōsoron	同祖論
Ebisu	恵比寿
eirei	英霊
Enpeigun Ō Shi	延平郡王祠
Ezochi	蝦夷地
Ezo-zakura	蝦夷桜
fugeki	巫覡
Fujieda Nagahira	藤枝修衡
Fukushū Jinja	福州神社
Fukutama Senkichi	福玉仙吉
Furano Jinja	富良野神社
Fushiko	伏古
Fuyo Jingū	扶余神宮
Ga Chishō	賀知章
gaien	外苑
Ganjōji	願乗寺
genshin	元神
Genshinsai-setsu	元神祭節
Genshi-sai	元始祭
Gojō Jinja	五常神社
gokoku	護国
Gokoku-byō	護国廟
gongen	権現
goshinsatsu	御神札
Goshōraku	五常楽
gotairei	御大礼

Gotō Shinpei	後藤新平
gyoen	御苑
Hachiman-gū	八幡宮
haibō	牌坊
Haimenbō	灰面坊
hairei	拝礼
Hajime no Miyako	はじめの都
Hajime no Tennō	はじめの天皇
hakkō ichiu	八紘一宇・八紘為宇
Hakugyoku	白玉
Hara Kei	原敬
Hasegawa Kiyoshi	長谷川清
Hasegawa Yoshimichi	長谷川好道
Hashiguchi Bunzō	橋口文蔵
Hashimoto Toranosuke	橋本虎ノ助
Hawaii Daijingū	布哇大神宮
Hawaii Dazaifu Tenmangū	ハワイ大宰府天満宮
Hawaii Izumo Taisha-kyō Hawai Bun'in	ハワイ出雲大社教ハワイ分院
Hawaii Jinmeiroku	ハワイ人名録
Hawaii Kotohira Jinsha	ハワイ金刀比羅神社
Heian-nan	平安南
Heijō Jinja	平壌神社
Higashikuze Michitome	東久世通禧
Hilo Daijingū	ヒロ大神宮
Hime-tatara-isuzu-hime no Mikoto	媛蹈鞴五十鈴媛
Himuka (Hyūga)	日向
Hirata Atsutane	平田篤胤
Hirota Hitoshi	広田斉
Hokkaidō Gokoku Jinja	北海道護国神社
Hokkaidō Jingū Tongū	北海道神宮頓宮
Hokkaidō Jingū	北海道神宮
Hokkaidō Jinja	北海道神社
Hokkaidō Shōkon-jō	北海道招魂場
Hokkaidō Shōkon-sha	北海道招魂社
Hokkyō Jinja	北京神社
hokō	保甲
hokora	祠
hokuchin	北鎮
Hondawake-no-mikoto	誉田別命
Hōnichi Senshō Kinenbi	訪日宣詔記念日
Honolulu Daijingū	ホノルル大神宮

Honolulu Shintō Renmei	ホノルル神道連盟
hontō-jin	本島人
Hōten Jinja	奉天神社
ichinomiya	一宮
Ide Kaoru	井出薫
Ikeda Kiyoshi	池田清
Imamura Yemyō	今村恵猛
Inari-san	稲荷さん
inshi jakyō	淫祀邪教
Inukai Tsuyoshi	犬養毅
Ise Jingū	伊勢神宮
Ishin Kinō-tai	維新勤王隊
Ishizuchi Jinsha	石鎚神社
Ishizuchihiko no Mikoto	石鎚毘古命
Isobe Misao	磯部節
Isogai Seizō	磯貝静蔵
ittoku isshin	一徳一心
Iwamura Michitoshi	岩村通俊
Iyasaka Jinja	弥栄神社
Izanagi no Mikoto	伊邪那岐命
Izanami no Mikoto	伊邪那美命
Izumi Jinja	泉神社
Izumo Ōyashiro-kyō	出雲大社教
Izumo Taisha	出雲大社
Izumo Taisha-kyō	出雲大社教
Jibyō Seiri	寺廟整理
jibyō	寺廟
jikan shihai	時間支配
jingi	神祇
Jingi-in	神祇院
Jingikan	神祇官
jingiryō	神祇令
Jingishō	神祇省
Jingū Hōsaikai	神宮奉斎会
Jingū Shichō	神宮司庁
jingū	神宮
Jingū	神功
Jingū-kyō	神宮教
Jinja Honchō	神社本庁
jinja	神社
Jinmu Tennō-sai	神武天皇祭
Jinmu	神武

Jinpū Kōsha	神風講社
jinsei girei	人生儀礼
Jōrin-ji	定林寺
Jōshin-sai	嘗新祭
Junten	順天
Kagahi Sōryū	曜日蒼龍
Kageyama Yoshikage	景山宜景
kagura	神楽
kai	華夷
Kaigai Jinja Mondai Kenkyū-kai	海外神社問題研究会
Kaigen Jinja	開原神社
kainei	会寧
Kairan Kunmin Shōsho	回鑾訓民詔書
Kaishū Jinja	海州神社
Kaitai Jinja	開台神社
Kaitai Seiō Byō	開臺聖王廟
kaitaku	開拓
Kaitaku Jinja	開拓神社
Kaitaku no Sanjin	開拓の三神
Kaitaku-shi	開拓使
Kaizan Jinja	開山神社
Kaizan Ō Byō	開山王廟
Kajiura Ginjirō	梶浦銀次郎
Kakei Katsuhiko	筧克彦
Kakizaki	蠣崎
Kami Furano	上富良野
kami	神
kamidana	神棚
Kamikawa Jinja	上川神社
Kamimusubi no Kami	神産巣日神
Kamiuchi Hikosaku	上内彦策
Kamui Kotan	神居古潭
Kamura Masaharu	加村政治
Kamu-yamato-ihare-hiko-hohodemi no Sumera Mikoto	神日本磐余彦火火出見天皇
Kangaku-sai	勧学祭
Kankō Jinja	咸興神社
kankoku heisha	官国幣社
kannagara no michi	惟神の道・随神の道
Kanname-sai	神嘗祭
Kansatsu-sho	管刹所
Kantō Jingū	関東神宮

Kantō-shū	関東州
Kanzaki Osamu	神崎長
Karafuto Gokoku Jinja	樺太護国神社
Karafuto Jinja	樺太神社
Kashihara Jingū	橿原神宮
Kashihara Jingū Kōsha	橿原神宮講社
Kashii-byō	香椎廟
Kashii-gū	香椎宮
Kashikodokoro	賢所
Kasuga Taisha	春日大社
Katō Genchi	加藤玄智
Katō Jinsha	加藤神社
Katō Kanji	加藤完治
Katō Kiyomasa	加藤清正
Kawasaki Kazoe	川崎嘉添
Kawasaki Ritarō (Masakuni)	川崎利太郎 (正郷)
Kawashima Atsushi	河島醇
Kawatsura Bonji	川面凡児
Keijō Jinja	京城神社
Keiki	京畿
Keirō Iankai	敬老慰安会
keishin sūso	敬神崇祖
keishuku-jitsu	慶祝日
Kenkō Jinja	建功神社
Kenkoku Chūreibyō	建国忠霊廟
Kenkoku Shinbyō	建国神廟
Kenkoku-byō	建国廟
Kigen-setsu	紀元節
Kikoku-sai	祈穀祭
Kimura Tomiji	木村富次
Kinen-sai	祈年祭
Kita Sadakichi	喜田貞吉
Kitahara Nobutsuna	北原信綱
Kitashirakawa-no-miya Nagahisa Shinnō	北白川宮長久親王
Kitashirakawa-no-miya Naruhisa Shinnō	北白川宮成久親王
Kitashirakawa-no-miya Yoshihisa Shinnō	北白川宮能久親王
Kodama Gentarō	児玉源太郎
kōdo	皇土
kōdō	皇道

Kōfūkai	興風会
Kōgakkan	皇学館
Kōgen Jinja	江原神社
Kōkai	黄海
Kōkei Jinja	江景神社
kōki	皇紀
kokka no sōshi	国家の宗祀
kōkoku	皇国
Kōkoku Takumin Kaisha	皇国拓民会社
Kokugaku	国学
kokuhei shōsha	国幣小社
Kokuhon Tenjō Shōsho	国本奠定詔書
Kokumin Shōgakkō	国民小学校
Kokutai Meichō	国体明徴
komainu	狛犬
Komeya Miyozo	米屋三代槌
kōminka	皇民化
Konkō-kyō	金光教
Konpira Daimyōjin	金毘羅大明神
Kōreiden	皇霊殿
Kōshi Jikkō (Jitsuo)	合志実行（実男）
Kōshi Kakuta	合志覚田
Kōshū Jinja	光州神社
Kōshurei Jinja	公主嶺神社
Kotan-ishi	古潭石
kōtei heika	皇帝陛下
Kotohira Daigongen	金毘羅大権現
Kotohira Jinja	金刀比羅神社
Kotohiragū	金刀比羅宮
Kotohira-sha	金刀比羅社
Kudō Isamu	工藤勇
Kumaso	熊襲
Kume Kunitake	久米邦武
Kume-mai	久米舞
kuni yuzuri	国譲り
kunitama	国魂
Kunitama-no-Kami	国魂神
Kunitama-no-Ōkami	国魂大神
Kuroda Kiyotaka	黒田清隆
Kurosaka Katsumi	黒板勝美
Kurozumi-kyō	黒住教
Kuzusō-hōnō	国栖奏奉納

kyō	教
Kyōbushō	教部省
kyōdōshoku	教導職
kyōha	教派
kyōkai	教会
kyōshi	教師
Kyūchū Sanden no Saishin	宮中三殿の祭神
kyūchū sanden	宮中三殿
Lawai Daijingū	ラワイ大神宮
magatama	勾玉
Maruyama	円山
Maruyama/Enzan Daihanten	円山大飯店
Matsumae	松前
matsurigoto	政・祭
matsuru	祭る・祀る
Matsuura Takeshirō	松浦武四郎
Matsuzaki Shinajirō	松崎品治郎
Meiji Jingū	明治神宮
Meiji-setsu	明治節
meikai	冥界
meishin	迷信
Minami Jirō	南次郎
Minatogawa Jinja	湊川神社
Minpū Sakkō Kyōgikai	民風作興協議会
misogi	禊
Mitaku Shina	三宅志奈
mitamashiro	御霊代
miya	宮
Miyanoshita	宮の下
Miyaō Katsuyoshi	宮王勝良
Miyaō Shigemaru	宮王重丸
Miyazaki Naokatsu	宮崎直勝
Mizuno Jun	水野遵
Mochiji Rokusaburō	持地六三郎
Mōkyō Jinja	蒙疆神社
Momoyama	桃山
Motoori Norinaga	本居宣長
mugan jinja	無願神社
Murasakita Naotane	紫田直胤
Murayama Chijun	村山智順
mushūkyō	無宗教
Myōgon-ji	妙厳寺

Myōhō-ji	妙法寺
myōjin	明神
Nagamasa Jinja	長政
nagare	流
naichi-jin	内地人
naien	内苑
naisen ittai	内鮮一体
Nakayama Miki	中山みき
Naminoue-gū	波之上宮
Nan'yō Jinja	南洋神社
Nankyō Gokoku Jinja	南京護国神社
Nankyō Jinja	南京神社
Nanzan	南山
Nanzan Daijingū	南山大神宮
naorai	直会
Nashimoto-no-miya Masako	梨本宮方子
Nawiliwili Daijingū	ナベリベリ大神宮
Negishi Takeka	根岸武香
nenchū gyōji	年中行事
Nichiren	日蓮
Nigihayahi no Mikoto	饒速日命
Niiname-sai	新嘗祭
Nikkō Tōshōgū	日光東照宮
Ninigi no Mikoto	瓊瓊杵尊
Ninomiya Sontoku	二宮尊徳
Nipponjin Jinmeiroku	日本人人名録
Nishikawa Gensai	西川玄斎
Nishikawa Kunihide	西川邦秀
Nishikawa Ni'noshin	西川仁之進
Nishiuchi Narisato	西内成郷
Nitobe Inazō	新渡戸稲造
nōkotsu jinja	納骨神社
Nōson Shinkō	農村振興
Nukaga Ōnao	額賀大直
nusa	幣
Obihiro Jinja	帯広神社
Ōdō rakudo	王道楽土
Ōdori Kōen	大通公園
Ogasawara Shōzō	小笠原省三
Ōgi-no-mai	扇の舞
Ōjin	応神
Okada Minoru	岡田実

Okakura Kakuzō	岡倉覚三
Ōkami	大神
Ōkawa Shūmei	大川周明
Okazaki Donkai	岡崎吞海
Okumura Teijirō	奥村禎次郎
Ōkuninushi no Mikoto	大国主命
Ōkuninushi no Ōkami	大国主大神
Ōkunitama no Kami	大國魂神
Okuno Jinshichi	奥野陣七
Ōmikami	大神・大御神
Ōmononushi no Kami	大物主神
Ōnamuchi no Kami	大那牟遅神
Onko	オンコ
Ontake-kyō	御嶽教
Ōnuki Maura	大貫真浦
Origuchi Shinobu	折口信夫
Oriyi	折居
Ōsako Naotoshi	大迫尚敏
Ōta Toyō	太田外世雄
Ōtaki Jinja	大滝神社
Oyama Fumio	小山文雄
Ozaki Hotsumi	尾崎秀実
Ozaki Otokichi	尾崎音吉
rei	霊
reisai	例祭
rerijon	レリジョン
Ritsuryō	律令
Ryōyō Jinja	遼陽神社
Ryūkyū	琉球
Ryūtōsan Jinja	龍頭山神社
Sagami Shin'ichi	佐上信一
Sai Nanzen	崔南善
sai-jitsu	祭日
Saimei	斉明
saisei itchi	祭政一致
Saitō Makoto	斎藤実
Sakaki Shigejirō	栄木鎮二郎
Sakaki-no-mai	榊の舞
sankan seibatsu	三韓征伐
Sanpai Insen	参拝院線

sanpai	参拝
Sapporo Jinja	札幌神社
Sapporo Sorei Jinja	札幌祖霊神社
Sarutahiko	猿田彦
Sasaki Tōichi	佐々木到一
Sasaki Yasugorō	佐々木安五郎
Satō Konosuke	佐藤子之助
Seian Jinja	西安神社
seichi	聖地
seichō	正庁
Seichō Kaizen	正庁改善
seinaru	聖なる
seisaku	正朔
Senge Son'yu	千家尊愛
sha	社
shakaku	社格
shi	祠
shibyō	祠廟
shidaisetsu	四大節
shidōkai	斯道会
Shima Yoshitake	島義武
Shimaji Mokurai	島地黙雷
Shimo Furano	下富良野
Shimoteine-mura	下手稲村
Shin Zuirin	沈瑞麟
Shinchiku Jinja	新竹神社
Shinden Kaihatsu	心田開発
shin'en	神苑
shingaku	神学
Shingon	真言
Shinkaden	神嘉殿
Shinkai Umemaro	新海梅磨
shinkaku	神格
shinkan	神官
shinkō	信仰
shinkoku	神国
Shinkyō Jinja	新京神社
shinmei	神明
Shinonome Shi	東雲祠
shinsei	神聖

shinshi	神祠
shinshoku	神職
Shinshū	真宗
shinto	神都
Shintō	神道
Shintō Honkyoku	神道本局
Shintō Jimukyoku	神道事務局
Shintō Taikyō	神道大教
Shinton Jinja	新屯神社
Shiodome Jinja	汐止神社
Shirasaki Hachimangū	白崎八幡宮
Shisei Kinenbi	始政記念日
shiu	祠宇
shōkon	招魂
shōkon-jō	招魂場
shōkon-sha	招魂社
Shōnan Jinja	昭南神社
shosha	諸社
Shōtoku Taishi	聖徳太子
shū	宗
shūkan	習慣
shuku-jitsu	祝日
shukusai-jitsu	祝祭日
shūkyō	宗教
shūkyō hōjin	宗教法人
sō	宗
sōchinju	総鎮守
sokui	即位
Somei-yoshino	染井吉野
Son Eiboku	孫永穆
Sorachi	空知
soreisha	祖霊社
Sōsei-gawa	創成川
sōshi	宗祀
Sōyama Seitarō	早山清太郎
Sue	須恵
Sugihara Miyotarō	杉原美代太郎
Sugimoto Teiichi	杉本禎一
sūhai	崇拝
Sukegawa Seiji	助川静二
sūkei	崇敬
sūkeisha	崇敬者

Sukunahikona no Kami	少彦名神
Sume	皇
Sumiyoshi-no-Ōkami	住吉大神
Susanoo-no-mikoto	素戔嗚命
Suwa Jinja	諏訪神社
Suwa Taisha	諏訪大社
Tagawa Matsu	田川マツ
tai	台
Tai-gū	太夷宮
Taihoku	台北
Taihoku Inari Jinja	台北稲荷神社
taikō	大孝
Taikyōin	大教院
Taikyū Jinja	大邱神社
taima	大麻
Tainan Jinja	台南神社
tairiku	大陸
taisha	大社
taishū	大州
Taiwan Jingū	台湾神宮
Taiwan Jinja	台湾神社
Taiwan Jinja-sai	台湾神社祭
Taiwan Jinja Shin'en-kai	台湾神社神苑会
Takachiho	高千穂
Takamatsu Shirō	高松四郎
Takamimusubi no Kami	高御産巣日神
Takasago	高砂
Takayama no Takagami	タカヤマのタカガミ
Takekoshi Yosaburō	竹越與三郎
Takenouchi-no-sukune	武内宿禰
Tanaka Chigaku	田中智學
Tei Fukuda	鄭福田
Tei Kōsho	鄭孝胥
Tei Seikō	鄭成功
Tei Shiryū	鄭芝龍
tenchi shindan	天地神壇
Tenchōsetsu	天長節
Tenji	天智
Tenjiku	天竺
Tenman Tenjin	天満天神
Tenri-kyō	天理教
Tensei-kai	天晴会

Tenso Jinja	蚕祖神社
tenson	天孫
tera	寺
Terauchi Masatake	寺内正毅
Tetsurei Jinja	嶺鉄神社
Tōa Minzoku Kyōkai	東亜民族協会
Tōgō Heihachirō	東郷平八郎
Tōjō Hideki	東条英機
Tokachi Gokoku Jinja	十勝護国神社
Tōkyō Daijingū	東京大神宮
Tōkyō Shokuminchi Jingū	東京植民地神宮
Tomi	鳥見
tōmin	島民
torii	鳥居
Torinuma Jinja	鳥沼神社
tōrō	灯籠
Toyohara Jinja	豊原神社
Toyokawa Inari Daimyō Jinja	豊川稲荷大明神社
Toyouke no Ōmikami	豊受大御神
tsukinami-sai	月次祭
Tsukioka Yoshitoshi	月岡芳年
Tsukushi	筑紫
Ubagami Daijingū	姥神大神宮
ubusuna no kami	産土の神
Uchimura Kanzō	内村鑑三
uchū no shinri	宇宙の真理
Uehara Yūsaku	上原勇作
Uetsuka Dai-ichi Shokuminchi	上塚第一植民地
Uetsuka Jinja	上塚神社
Uetsuka Shūhei	上塚周平
Ugaki Kazushige	宇垣一成
ujiko	氏子
ukiyoe	浮世絵
Umezu Yoshijirō	梅津 美治郎
Unebi Kashihara Kyōkai Hon'in	畝傍橿原教会本院
Unebi Kyōkai	畝傍教会
Urayasu-no-mai	浦安の舞
Uta Shigemaru	菟田茂丸
Wakabayashi Yoshimichi	若林嘉倫
Watanabe Kan'ichi	渡辺勘一
Yamada Nagamasa	山田長政
Yamada Tadashi	山田正

Character Glossary

Yamaguchi Tōru	山口透
Yamaki Masao	矢巻正雄
Yamato Ikejiri	大和池尻
Yamato Jinsha	大和神社
Yamato Kokushikan	大和国史舘
Yamato Shinbun	大和新聞
yamato-bataraki	日本体操
Yamazaki Nobuyoshi	山崎延吉
Yanagita Kunio	柳田国男
Yasukuni Jinja	靖国神社
Yasutake Tadao	安武直夫
Yatsuka Kiyotsura	八束清貫
yōhai	遙拝
Yoshida Kanetomo	吉田兼倶
Yoshida Sadaharu	吉田貞治
Yūshūkan	遊就館
za	座
Zenra-nan	全羅南
Zenshū Jinja	全州神社
zōka sanjin	造化三神
Zunashi	頭無

References

Abe, David K. and Allison Imamura. 2019. 'The Destruction of Shinto Shrines in Hawaii and the West Coast during World War II: The Lingering Effects of Pearl Harbor and Japanese-American Internment.' *Asian Anthropology* 18/4: 1–16.

Abrams, Meyer H. 1973. *Natural Supernaturalism: Tradition and Revolution in Romantic Literature*. New York: W. W. Norton & Company.

Adams, Romanzo. 1924. *The Japanese in Hawaii: A Statistical Study Bearing on the Future Number and Voting Strength and on the Economic and Social Character of the Hawaiian Japanese*. New York: The National Committee on American Japanese Relations.

Allen, Chizuko. 2003. 'Empress Jingū: A Shamaness Ruler in Early Japan.' *Japan Forum* 15/1: 81–98.

Allen, H. W. 1960. 'The Shinto Directive.' *Contemporary Religions in Japan* 1/2: 85–9.

Allen, Joseph R. 2012. *Taipei: City of Displacements*. Seattle: University of Washington.

Ama, Michihiro. 2011. *Immigrants to the Pure Land: The Modernization, Acculturation, and Globalization of Shin Buddhism, 1898–1941*. Honolulu: University of Hawai'i.

Anderson, Benedict. 1991. *Imagined Communities: Reflections on the Origin and Spread of Nationalism*. London: Verso.

Anderson, Emily. 2014. *Christianity and Imperialism in Modern Japan: Empire for God*. London: Bloomsbury Academic.

Antoni, Klaus and Yvonne Antoni. 2017. 'Inventing a State Ceremony: Ottmar von Mohl, Jinmu-tennō and the Proclamation of the Meiji Constitution on February 11th 1889.' *Beiträge des Arbeitskreises Japanische Religionen* 11: 1–30.

Aoi, Akihito. 2014. 'Transplanting State Shinto: The Reconfiguration of Existing Built and Natural Environments in Colonized Taiwan.' In *Constructing the Colonized Land: Entwined Perspectives of East Asia around WWII*, edited by Izumi Kuroishi, 97–122. London: Routledge.

Aono Masaaki. 2015. *Teikoku Shintō no Keisei: Shokuminchi Chōsen to Kokka Shintō no Ronri*. Tokyo: Iwanami.

Aoyagi Machiko. 2002. *Modekngei: A New Religion in Belau, Micronesia*. Tokyo: Shinsensha.

Asad, Talal. 1993. *Genealogies of Religion: Discipline and Reasons of Power in Christianity and Islam*. Baltimore: Johns Hopkins University.

Asad, Talal. 2003. *Formations of the Secular: Christianity, Islam, Modernity*. Stanford: Stanford University.

Asato, Noriko. 2003. 'Mandating Americanization: Japanese Language Schools and the Federal Survey of Education in Hawaii, 1916–1920.' *History of Education Quarterly* 43/1: 10–38.

Asato, Noriko. 2006. *Teaching Mikadoism: The Attack on Japanese Language Schools in Hawaii, California, and Washington, 1919-1927*. Honolulu: University of Hawai'i.
Barclay, Paul D. 2018. *Outcasts of Empire: Japan's Rule on Taiwan's 'Savage Border', 1874-1945*. Oakland: University of California.
Bell, Roger. 1984. *Last Among Equals: Hawaiian Statehood and American Politics*. Honolulu: University of Hawai'i.
Bellah, Robert N. 1991. *Beyond Belief: Essays on Religion in a Post-Traditional World*. Berkeley: University of California.
Blaxell, Vivian. 2009. 'Designs of Power: "Japanization" of Urban and Rural Space in Colonial Hokkaidō.' *The Asia-Pacific Journal* 35/2/9: 1-17. http://apjjf.org/-Vivian-Blaxell/3211/article.html
Boyle, Edward. 2020. 'Mapping of the Maritime Boundaries at Japan's Northern Edge in the 19th Century.' *Oxford Research Encyclopedia of Asian History*. 30 June 2020; Accessed 13 July 2020. https://oxfordre.com/asianhistory/view/10.1093/acrefore/9780190277727.001.0001/acrefore-9780190277727-e-412
Breen, John. 2009. 'Ideologues, Bureaucrats and Priests: On "Shinto" and "Buddhism" in Early Meiji Japan.' In *Shinto in History*, edited by John Breen and Mark Teeuwen, 230-51. Abingdon: Routledge.
Breen, John. 2010. 'Popes, Bishops and War Criminals: Reflections on Catholics and Yasukuni in Post-war Japan.' *The Asia-Pacific Journal* 8/9/3: 1-16. https://apjjf.org/-John-Breen/3312/article.html
Breen, John and Mark Teeuwen. 2010. *A New History of Shinto*. Chichester, West Sussex: Wiley-Blackwell.
Buntilov, Georgy. 2016. 'Common Narratives in Discourses on National Identity in Russia and Japan.' *Asian Philosophy* 26/1: 1-19.
Burchardt, Marian, Monika Wohlrab-Sahr and Matthias Middell, eds. 2015. *Multiple Secularities beyond the West: Religion and Modernity in the Global Age*. Boston: Walter de Gruyter.
Caprio, Mark E. 2009. *Japanese Assimilation Policies in Colonial Korea 1910-1945*. Seattle: University of Washington.
Chamberlain, Basil Hall, trans. 1982. *The Kojiki: Records of Ancient Matters*. Tokyo: Tuttle Publishing.
Chen, Edward I-te. 1984. 'The Attempt to Integrate the Empire: Legal Perspectives.' In *The Japanese Colonial Empire, 1895-1945*, edited by Ramon H. Myers and Mark R. Peattie, 240-74. Princeton: Princeton University.
Chōsen Sōtokufu. 1927. *Chōsen Jingū Zōei-shi*. Keijō: Sōtokufu.
Chōsen Sōtokufu. 1942 (1972). *Chōsen no Ryōdo Saishi: Buraku-sai*. Tokyo: Kokusho Kankōkai.
Christy, Alan S. 1997. 'The Making of Imperial Subjects in Okinawa.' In *Formations of Colonial Modernity in East Asia*, edited by Tani E. Barlow, 141-70. Durham: Duke University.
Cumings, Bruce. 2005. *Korea's Place in the Sun: A Modern History*. New York: W. W. Norton & Company.

Enomoto Yōsuke. 2011. *Shima Yoshitake*. Saga: Saga Kenritsu Sagajō Honmaru Rekishikan.
Fluhman, J. Spencer. 2012. *'A Peculiar People': Anti-Mormonism and the Making of Religion in the Nineteenth-Century America*. Chapel Hill: University of North Carolina.
Fujikane, Candace and Jonathon Y. Okamura. 2008. *Asian Settler Colonialism: From Local Governance to the Habits of Everyday Life in Hawai'i*. Honolulu: University of Hawai'i.
Fukuyama, Francis. 2006. *The End of History and the Last Man*. New York: Simon and Schuster.
Furano Jinja (Furano Jinja Gosōshi Hyakunenshūnen Kinen Jigyō Hōsankai Jinja-shi Henshū Iinkai), ed. 2004. *Furano Jinja-shi*. Furano, Hokkaido: Furano Jinja Gosōshi Hyakunenshūnen Kinen Jigyō Hōsankai Jinja-shi Henshū Iinkai.
Furano-shi Jinbutsu Jiten Henshū Iinkai. 2004. *Furano-shi Jinbutsu Jiten*. Furano, Hokkaido: Furano-shi Ryōdo Kenkyūkai.
Furano-shi Kaiki 90 Shūnen Kinen-shi Henshū Iinkai, ed. 1994. *Kaiki 90-nen shūnen Kinen Furano-shi Rekishi Shashin-shū*. Furano, Hokkaido: Furano-shi Kaiki 90 Shūnen Kinen-shi Kankō Iinkai.
Goldman, Rita. 2003. *Every Grain of Rice: Portraits of Maui's Japanese Community*. Virginia Beach: The Donning Company.
Grayson, James H. 2002. 'Susa-no-o: A Cultural Hero from Korea.' *Japan Forum* 14/3: 465–87.
Hachijō Tadamoto. 1999. *Igyō no Shōzoku: Meijiki no Gi Shōzoku*. Kiyō Court Dress Research Institute. Accessed 19 June 2017. http://www.kariginu.jp/kikata/igyousyouzoku.htm
Hansen, Wilburn. 2010. 'Examining Prewar Tōgō Worship in Hawaii: Toward Rethinking Hawaiian Shinto as a New Religion in America.' *Nova Religio: The Journal of Alternative and Emergent Religions* 14/1: 67–92.
Hara Takeshi. 2011. *Kashika Sareta Teikoku: Kindai Nippon no Gyōkōkei*. Tokyo: Misuzu Shobō.
Hardacre, Helen. 1989. *Shintō and the State, 1868–1988*. Princeton: Princeton University.
Hardacre, Helen. 2017. *Shinto: A History*. New York: Oxford University.
Harris, W. T. and F. Sturges Allen, eds. 1930. *Webster's New International Dictionary of the English Language Based on the International Dictionary of 1890 and 1900 Now Completely Revised in All Departments Including Also a Department of New Words a Dictionary of Geography and Biography, Being the Latest Authentic Quarto Edition of the Merriam Series*. Springfield, MA: G. & C. Merriam Company.
Hashimoto Toranosuke. 1941. 'Kenkoku Shinbyō Gosōken to Kokuhon Tenjō no Shisho.' In *Manshū Teikoku Kōtei Heika Gohōnichi to Kenkoku Shinbyō Gosōken*, edited by Nichiman Chūō Kyōkai, 106–17. Tokyo: Nichiman Chūō Kyōkai.
Hazama, Dorothy O. and Jane O. Komeiji. 2008. *The Japanese in Hawai'i: Okage Sama De*. Honolulu: Bess Press.

Henry, Todd A. 2014. *Assimilating Seoul: Japanese Rule and the Politics of Public Space in Colonial Korea, 1910–1945*. Berkeley: University of California.

Hilo Daijingū. 1928. *Kinen Enkakushi: Hilo Daijingū Sanjūnen-sai*. Hilo: No publisher listed.

Hiura Satoko. 2013. *Jinja, Gakkō, Shokuminchi: Gyaku Kinō suru Chōsen Shihai*. Kyoto: Kyoto University.

Hokkaidō Jingū. 1989. *Shashin Hyakunijū Nenshi Hokkaidō Jingū*. Sapporo: Hokkaidō Jingū.

Hokkaidō Jingū-shi Hensan Iinkai. 1991. *Hokkaidō Jingū-shi Jōkan*. Sapporo: Hokkaidō Jingū.

Hokkaidō Jingū-shi Hensan Iinkai. 1995. *Hokkaidō Jingū-shi Gekan*. Sapporo: Hokkaidō Jingū.

Hokkaidō Jinjachō. 2019. 'Hokkaidō no Jinja: Kami Furano Jinja.' *Hokkaidō Jinjachō Kōshiki Hōmupēji*. Accessed 8 October. https://hokkaidojinjacho.jp/上富良野神社

Honda, Gail, ed. 2012. *Family Torn Apart: The Internment Story of the Otokichi Muin Ozaki Family*. Honolulu: Japanese Cultural Center of Hawai'i.

Hoppō Ryōdo Bunka Nichiro Kyōdō Gakujutsu Kōryū Jikkō Iinkai. 2005. *Hoppō Ryōdo no Jinja: Chishima/Hoppō Ryōdo Shaji Kyōkai Nichiro Kyōdō Chōsa Hōkokusho*. Sapporo: Hokkaidō Jinjachō.

Howell, David L. 2005. *Geographies of Identity in Nineteenth-Century Japan*. Berkeley: University of California.

Imaizumi Yoshiko. 2013. *Sacred Space in the Modern City: The Fractured Pasts of Meiji Shrine, 1912–1958*. Leiden: Brill.

Inamiya Yasuto. 2020. 'Fuyo Jingū Zōei no Tenmatsu.' *Inamiya Yasuto*. Blog. Posted 6 June. Accessed 23 September 2021. https://note.com/inamiya/n/n8ab423ae73ef

Inamiya Yasuto and Nakajima Michio. 2019. *Shinkoku no Zan'ei: Kaigai Jinja Atochi Shashin Kiroku*. Tokyo: Kokusho.

Inoue Nobutaka. 2003. 'The Modern Age: Shinto Confronts Modernity.' In *Shinto – A Short History*, edited by Inoue Nobutaka, translated by Mark Teeuwen and John Breen, 159–197. London: Routledge Curzon.

Inoue Nobutaka. 2019. 'Gokoku Jinja.' *Encyclopedia of Shinto*. Accessed 9 October. http://k-amc.kokugakuin.ac.jp/DM/dbTop.do?class_name=col_eos

Ion, A. Hamish. 1999. *The Cross in the Dark Valley: The Canadian Protestant Missionary Movement in the Japanese Empire, 1931–1945*. Waterloo, ON: Wilfrid Laurier University.

Isomae, Jun'ichi. 2012. 'The Conceptual Formation of the Category "Religion" in Modern Japan: Religion, State, Shintō.' *Journal of Religion in Japan* 1/3: 226–45.

Itō Keitarō. 2002. 'Jinmu Tennōryō kō: Toku ni tōgaito haiji to kokugenji o chūshin ni.' In *Bunkazai to Kindai Nihon*, edited by Suzuki Ryō and Takagi Hiroshi, 57–82. Tokyo: Yamakawa Shuppansha.

Jansen, Marius B. 2000. *The Making of Modern Japan*. Cambridge: Belknap Press of Harvard University.

Josephson, Jason Ā. 2012. *The Invention of Religion in Japan*. Chicago: University of Chicago.
Josephson-Storm, Jason Ā. 2017. *The Myth of Disenchantment: Magic, Modernity, and the Birth of the Human Sciences*. Chicago: University of Chicago.
Kanagawa Daigaku Himoji Shiryō Kenkyū Sentā. 2019. 'Taiwan Jinja.' *Kaigaki Jinja (Atochi) ni Kan suru Dētabēsu*. Accessed 9 October.
Kaneko Nobuya. 2015. *Taiwan Kyū-Jinja Kochi e no Tabi Annai: Taiwan o Mamotta Kamigami*. Tokyo: Jinja Shinpōsha.
Kaneko Nobuya. 2018. *Taiwan ni Watatta Nippon no Kamigami: Fīrudowāku Nippon Tōji Jidai no Taiwan no Jinja*. Tokyo: Ushio Shobō Kōjin Shinsha.
Kang, Wi Jo. 1997. *Christ and Caesar in Modern Korea: A History of Christianity and Politics*. Albany: State University of New York.
Kanpei Taisha Nanyō Jinja Hōsankai. 1941. *Kanpei Taisha Nanyō Jinja Gochinza-sai Kinen Shashin-chō*. Palau: Kanpei Taisha Nanyō Jinja Hōsankai.
Kanzaki, Kiichi. 1921. 'Is the Japanese Menace in America a Reality?' *The Annals of the American Academy of Political and Social Science* 93: 88–97.
Kanzaki Osamu. 1941. 'Manshū Kenkoku no Seishin.' In *Manshū Teikoku Kōtei Heika Gohōnichi to Kenkoku Shinbyō Gosōken*, edited by Nichiman Chūō Kyōkai, 128–40. Tokyo: Nichiman Chūō Kyōkai.
Kashihara Jingū-chō. 1989. *Kashihara Jingū*. Kashihara, Nara: Kashihara Jingū-chō.
Kasulis, Thomas P. 2004. *Shinto: The Way Home*. Honolulu: University of Hawai'i.
Kawai, Michi. 1950. *Sliding Doors*. Tokyo: Keisen-jo Gaku-en.
Kenkō Jinja Shamusho. 1940. *Kenkō Jinja-shi*. Taipei: Kenkō Jinja Shamusho.
Kihara Takayoshi, ed. 1935. *Hawai Nipponjin Shi*. Tokyo: Bunsei-sha.
Kim, John Namjun. 2007. 'The Temporality of Empire: The Imperial Cosmopolitanism of Miki Kiyoshi and Tanabe Hajime.' In *Pan-Asianism in Modern Japanese History: Colonialism, Regionalism, and Borders*, edited by Sven Saaler and J. Victor Koschmann, 151–167. New York: Routledge.
Kleine, Christoph. 2013. 'Religion and the Secular in Premodern Japan from the Viewpoint of Systems Theory.' *Journal of Religion in Japan* 2/1: 1–34.
Knapp, Arthur May. 1896. *Feudal and Modern Japan*. Boston: Colonial Press.
Kobayashi, Gloria R. and Richard I. Nakamura. 2008. *The Yashijima Story: The History of Waiakea Town*. Hilo, HI: Pacific Tsunami Museum.
Kobayashi Iwao. 1944. *Shukusaijitsu no Hongi*. Tokyo: Meiseidō.
Komagome Takeshi. 2005. '1930 Nendai Taiwan/Chōsen/Naichi ni okeru Jinja Sanpai Mondai: Kirisuto-kyōkei Gakkō no Henshitsu/Kaitai wo Meguru Rensa Kōzō.' *Rikkyō Gakuin-shi Kenkyū* 3: 4–39.
Kondō Yoshihiro. 1943. *Kaigai Jinja no Shiteki Kenkyū*. Tokyo: Meiseidō.
Koschmann, J. Victor. 2007. 'Constructing Destiny: Rōyama Masamichi and Asian Regionalism in Wartime Japan.' In *Pan-Asianism in Modern Japanese History: Colonialism, Regionalism, and Borders*, edited by Sven Saaler and J. Victor Koschmann, 185–99. New York: Routledge.

Kotani, Roland. 1985. *The Japanese in Hawaii: A Century of Struggle*. Honolulu: The Hawaii Hochi.
Kotohira Jinsha v. McGrath, 90 F. Supp. 892 (1950).
Krämer, Hans Martin. 2011. 'Beyond the Dark Valley: Reinterpreting Christian Reactions to the 1939 Religious Organizations Law.' In *Japanese Journal of Religious Studies* 38/1: 181–211.
Krämer, Hans Martin. 2013. 'How Religion Came to Be Translated as Shūkyō: Shimaji Mokurai and the Appropriation of Religion in Early Meiji Japan.' *Japan Review* 25: 89–111.
Kuroda Toshio. 1981. 'Shinto in the History of Japanese Religion', *Journal of Japanese Studies* 7/1: 1–21.
Lewis, Martin W. and Kären E. Wigen. 1997. *The Myth of Continents: A Critique of Metageography*. Berkeley: University of California.
Li Baihao and Matsumoto Yasutaka. 2016. 'Nihon no Haisen-go ni okeru Kyū Nankyō Jinja no Ayumi: Naze Nankyō de Shaden ga Kowasarenakatta no ka.' *Himoji Shiryō Kenkyū* 13, 63–80.
Lo, Ming-Chen M. 2002. *Doctors Within Borders: Profession, Ethnicity, and Modernity in Colonial Taiwan*. Berkeley: University of California.
Louth, Andrew and Helmut Thielicke. 2014. 'Theology.' In *The Encyclopaedia Britannica*. Accessed 4 January 2020. https://www.britannica.com/topic/theology
Lowell, Percival. 1895. *Occult Japan or the Way of the Gods: An Esoteric Study of Japanese Personality and Possession*. Cambridge: The Riverside Press.
Maeda Takakazu. 1999. *Hawai no Jinja Shi*. Tokyo: Daimeidō.
Maeyama Takashi. 1997. *Ihō ni 'Nihon' wo Matsuru: Burajiru Nikkeijin no Shūkyō to Esunishitī*. Tokyo: Ochanomizu Shobō.
Manshū Jijō Annai-jo. 1939. *Manshūkoku no Shūkyō*. Shinkyō: Manshū Jijō Annai-jo.
Mason, Joseph W. T. (1935) 2002. *The Meaning of Shinto: The Primaeval Foundation of Creative Spirit in Modern Japan*. Reprint, Trafford Publishing. Citations refer to the reprinted edition.
Mason, Michele. 2012. *Dominant Narratives of Colonial Hokkaido and Imperial Japan: Envisioning the Periphery and the Modern Nation-State*. New York: Palgrave Macmillan.
Masuzawa, Tomoko. 2005. *The Invention of World Religions: Or, How European Universalism Was Preserved in the Language of Pluralism*. Chicago: University of Chicago.
Matsunaga, Diane. 1978. 'Inu-gami: The Spirit of the Dog.' In *Kodomo no Tame ni for the Sake of the Children: The Japanese American Experience in Hawaii*, edited by Dennis M. Ogawa, 73–75. Honolulu: University of Hawai'i.
Maxey, Trent E. 2014. *The 'Greatest Problem': Religion and State Formation in Meiji Japan*. Cambridge, MA: Harvard University Asia Center.
Mita, Maki. 2009. *Palauan Children under Japanese Rule: Their Oral Histories*. Suita, Osaka: National Museum of Ethnology.

Miyamoto Takashi. 2014. 'Sapporo Jinja kara Hokkaidō Jingū e: Meiji Tennō Gozōshi no Ikisatsu.' In *Hokkaidō Jingū Kenkyū Ronsō*, edited by Hokkaidō Jingū and Kokugakuin Daigaku Kenkyū Kaihatsu Suishin Sentā, 53–102. Tokyo: Kōbundō.

Miyawaki Hiroyuki. 2017. 'Manshū no Kyōiku.' *Miyagi Gakuin Joshi Jinbun Shakai Kagaku Ronsō* 26: 13–18.

Monbushō. 1874. *Chiri Shoho*. Myōdō Prefecture: Monbushō.

Monbushō. 1897. *Hokkaidō Yō Jinjō Shōgaku Tokuhon Maki no Go*. Tokyo: Monbushō.

Naiseibu. 2020. 'Karen Makotaay (Minatoguchi) Shūraku Ami-zoku Ilisin Hōnen Matsuri.' *Shūkyō Hyakkei*. Accessed 4 June. https://www.taiwangods.com/html/landscape_jp/1_0011.aspx?i=94

Nakajima Michio. 2007. 'Kyū Manshūkoku ni Okeru Jinja no Setsuritsu ni Tsuite.' In *Nichichū Ryōkoku no Shiten kara Kataru Shokuminchiki Manshū no Shūkyō*, edited by Kiba Akeshi and Tei Jōi, 139–70. Tokyo: Kashiwa Shobō.

Nakajima Michio. 2010. 'Shinto Deities That Crossed the Sea: Japan's "Overseas Shrines", 1868–1945.' *Japanese Journal of Religious Studies* 37/1: 21–46.

Nakajima Michio. 2013. *Kaigai Jinja Atochi no Keikan Henyō: Samazama na Ima*. Tokyo: Ochanomizu Shobō.

Nakajima Michio, Maeda Takakazu, Tsuda Yoshiki, Sakai Hisayoshi, Suga Koji, and Inamiya Yasuto. 2015. 'Kyū Chōsen Kitabu (Chōsen Minshu Shugi Jinmin Kyōwakoku) no Jinja Atochi wo Tazunete.' *Nenpō Himoji Shiryō Kenkyū* 11: 169–204.

Nichiman Chūō Kyōkai. 1941. *Manshū Teikoku Kōtei Heika Gohōnichi to Kenkoku Shinbyō Gosōken*. Tokyo: Nichiman Chūō Kyōkai.

Nippon Nyūsu Eigasha. 1940. *Nippon Nyūsu Dai 2 Gō*. Newsreel. June 18. http://www2.nhk.or.jp/shogenarchives/jpnews/list.cgi

Nitobe, Inazo. 1905 (2008). *Bushido: The Soul of Japan*. New York: G.P Putman's Sons. Bilingual Reprint, IBC Publishing. Citations refer to the reprinted edition.

Nitobe, Inazo. 1912. 'Japan as a Colonizer.' *The Journal of Race Development* 2/4: 347–61. https://www.jstor.org/stable/29737924

Nitta, Hitoshi. 2009. 'Shintō as a "Non-Religion": The Origin and Development of an Idea.' In *Shintō in History: Ways of the Kami*, edited by John Breen and Mark Teeuwen, 252–71. London: Routledge.

Nitta Mitsuko. 1997. *Dairen Jinja-shi: Aru Kaigai Jinja no Shakai-shi*. Tokyo: Ōfū.

Nongbri, Brent. 2013. *Before Religion: A History of a Modern Concept*. New Haven: Yale University.

Noto Kunio. 1994. 'Sapporo Matsuri no Ashiato: Meiji Jidai.' In *Sapporo Matsuri*, edited by Sapporo-shi Kyōiku Iinkai, 66–75. Sapporo: Sapporo-shi Kyōiku Iinkai.

Odaira Mika. 2009. *Jōsei Shinshoku no Kindai: Jingi Girei/Kōsei ni okeru Saishisha no Kenkyū*. Tokyo: Perikan-sha.

Oguma Eiji. 2002. *A Genealogy of 'Japanese' Self-Images*, translated by David Askew. Melbourne: Trans Pacific Press.

Okabe Minoru. 1984. 'Junan no Chūreitō.' In *Tsuzuki Furano Kobore Hanashi*, edited by Saitō Bunshō et al., 219-225. Furano, Hokkaido: Furano Shi Ryōdo Kenkyūkai.

Ōkawa Shūmei. 1940. *Nippon Nisen-Roppyaku Nenshi*. Tokyo: Daiichi Shobō.

Ōmi Toshiro. 2017. 'Kindai Bukkyō to Shintō.' *Gendai Shisō* 45/2: 282-9.

Ono, Sokyo. 1962. *Shinto: The Kami Way*. Tokyo: Tuttle Publishing.

Oshiro, George M. 2007. 'Nitobe Inazō and the Sapporo Band: Reflections of the Dawn of Protestant Christianity in Early Meiji Japan.' *The Japanese Journal of Religious Studies* 34/1: 99-126.

Peattie, Mark R. 1984a. 'Introduction.' In *The Japanese Colonial Empire, 1895-1045*, edited by Ramon H. Myers and Mark R. Peattie, 3-52. Princeton: Princeton University.

Peattie, Mark R. 1984b. 'Japanese Attitudes toward Colonialism, 1895-1945.' In *The Japanese Colonial Empire, 1895-1945*, edited by Ramon H. Myers and Mark R. Peattie, 80-127. Princeton: Princeton University.

Peattie, Mark R. 1992. *Nan'yō: The Rise and Fall of the Japanese in Micronesia, 1885-1945*. Honolulu: University of Hawai'i.

Perez, Rob. 2001. 'Raising Cane: Japanese Gift Ruffles Feathers in Honolulu.' *The Honolulu Star-Bulletin* October 28. Accessed 2019 December 30. http://archives.starbulletin.com/2001/10/28/news/perez.html

Reader, Ian and George J. Tanabe, Jr. 1998. *Practically Religious: Worldly Benefits and the Common Religion of Japan*. Honolulu: University of Hawai'i.

Ruoff, Kenneth J. 2010. *Imperial Japan at Its Zenith: The Wartime Celebration of the Empire's 2600th Anniversary*. Ithaca: Cornell University.

Saaler, Sven. 2016. 'Nationalism and History in Contemporary Japan.' *The Asia-Pacific Journal* 14/29/7: 1-17. https://apjjf.org/2016/20/Saaler.html

Sagai Tatsuru. 1998. *Manshū no Jinja Kōbō Shi*. Tokyo: Fuyō Shobō.

Sai Kindō (Tsai Chin Tong). 1994. *Nippon Teikoku-ka Taiwan no Shūkyō Seisaku*. Tokyo: Dōseisha.

Sasaki Kaoru. 2009. *Hokkaidō no Shūkyō to Shinkō*. Tokyo: Yamakawa Shuppansha.

Sasaki Kaoru. 2013. *Michinoku to Hokkaidō no Shūkyō Sekai*. Sapporo: Hokkaidō Shuppan Kikaku Sentā.

Scott, James C. 2009. *The Art of Not Being Governed: An Anarchist History of Upland Southeast Asia*. New Haven: Yale University.

Seager, Richard H. 2009. *The World's Parliament of Religions: The East/West Encounter, Chicago, 1893*. Bloomington, IN: Indiana University.

Seaton, Philip A. 2016a. 'Grand Narratives of Empire and Development.' In *Local History and War Memories in Hokkaido*, edited by Philip A. Seaton, 26-59. Abingdon, Oxon: Routledge.

Seaton, Philip A. 2016b. 'Commemorating the War Dead at Hokkaido Gokoku Shrine.' In *Local History and War Memories in Hokkaido*, edited by Philip A. Seaton, 161-78. Abingdon, Oxon: Routledge.

Segawa Takurō. 2015. *Ainu Gaku Nyūmon*. Tokyo: Kōdansha.
Shimemura Sadao. 1981. *Hokkaidō Gokoku Jinja Shi*. Asahikawa, Hokkaido: Hokkaidō Gokoku Jinja.
Shimizu, Karli. 2017. 'Shintō Shrines and Secularism in Modern Japan, 1890–1945: A Case Study on Kashihara Jingū.' *Journal of Religion in Japan* 6/2: 128–56.
Shimizu, Karli. 2019. 'Religion and Secularism in Overseas Shinto Shrines: A Case Study on Hilo Daijingū, 1898–1941.' *Japanese Journal of Religious Studies* 46/1: 1–29.
Shirano Jin. 1994a. 'Sapporo Matsuri no Ashiato: Tanoshiikana Sapporo Matsuri.' In *Sapporo Matsuri*, edited by Sapporo-shi Kyōiku Iinkai, 91–104. Sapporo: Sapporo-shi Kyōiku Iinkai.
Shirano Jin. 1994b. 'Sapporo Matsuri no Ashiato: Yōgo Mame Jiten.' In *Sapporo Matsuri*, edited by Sapporo-shi Kyōiku Iinkai, 105–13. Sapporo: Sapporo-shi Kyōiku Iinkai.
Shoji, Rafael. 2008. 'The Failed Prophecy of Shinto Nationalism and the Rise of Japanese Brazilian Catholicism.' *Japanese Journal of Religious Studies* 35/1: 13–38.
Siddle, Richard. 1996. *Race, Resistance, and the Ainu of Japan*. Abingdon: Routledge.
Smith, Graeme. 2008. *A Short History of Secularism*. London: I.B. Tauris.
Sohn Jung Mok. 2004. *Nihon Tōjika Chōsen Toshi Keikaku Shi Kenkyū*, translated by Nishigaki Yasuhiko, Ichioka Miyuki, and Lee Jong Hee. Tokyo: Kashiwa Shobō.
Stegewerns, Dick. 2006. 'The Dilemma of Nationalism and Internationalism in Modern Japan: National Interest, Asian Brotherhood, International Cooperation or World Citizenship?' In *Nationalism and Internationalism in Imperial Japan: Autonomy, Asian Brotherhood, or World Citizenship?*, edited by Dick Stegewerns, 3–16. Abingdon: RoutledgeCurzon.
Stephan, John J. 1984. *Hawaii under the Rising Sun: Japan's Plans for Conquest after Pearl Harbor*. Honolulu: University of Hawai'i.
Suga Kōji. 2010. 'A Concept of "Overseas Shinto Shrines": A Pantheistic Attempt by Ogasawara Shōzō and Its Limitations.' *Japanese Journal of Religious Studies* 37/1: 47–74.
Suga Kōji. 2014. 'Kaigai Jinja no Keifu ni Miru Hokkaidō Jingū: Sōchinju Saishin to Meiji Tennō Gochinza.' In *Hokkaidō Jingū Kenkyū Ronsō*, edited by Hokkaidō Jingū and Kokugakuin Daigaku Kenkyū Kaihatsu Suishin Sentā, 131–62. Tokyo: Kōbundō.
Sugiyama Yasunori, ed. 1916. *Taiwan Meisho Kyūseki Shi*. Tokyo: Taiwan Sōtokufu.
Sugiyama Yasunori. 1922. *Taiwan Rekidai Sōtoku no Chiseki Okuzuke*. Tokyo: Teikoku Chihō Gyōsei Gakkai.
Sutō Takanori. 1971. *Hokkaidō no Densetsu*. Toyoura, Hokkaido: San'on Bungaku-kai.
Swanger, Eugene R. and K. Peter Takayama. 1981. 'A Preliminary Examination of the "Omamori" Phenomenon.' *Asian Folklore Studies* 40/2: 237–52.
Taiwan Jinja Shamusho Hensan. 1935. *Taiwan Jinja Shi*. Taipei: Matsuzaki Sadakichi.
Taiwan Sōtokufu. 1928. *Kenkō Jinja-shi*. Taipei: Taiwan Sōtokufu.
Taiwan Sōtokufu Kōtsū-kyoku Tetsudō-bu. 1935. *Taiwan Tetsudō Ryokō Annai*. Taipei: Taiwan Sōtokufu Kōtsū-kyoku Tetsudō-bu.

Takagi Hiroshi. 1997. *Kindai Tennōsei no Bunka Shiteki Kenkyū: Tennō Shūnin Girei, Nenchū Gyōji, Bunkazai*. Tokyo: Azekura Shobō.

Takagi Hiroshi. 2006. *Kindai Tennōsei to Koto*. Tokyo: Iwanami Shoten.

Takamatsu Taketsugu. 1984 'Chūreitō to Sorachi-bashi Rakka Jiken.' In *Tsuzuki Furano Kobore Hanashi*, edited by Saitō Bunshō et al., 210–18. Furano, Hokkaido: Furano Shi Ryōdo Kenkyūkai.

Takekoshi, Yosaburo. 1907. *Japanese Rule in Formosa*, translated by George Braithwaite. London: Longmans, Green and Co.

Takenaka, Akiko. 2015. *Yasukuni Shrine: History, Memory, and Japan's Unending Postwar*. Honolulu: University of Hawai'i.

Tamura, Eileen H. 1994. *Americanization, Acculturation, and Ethnic Identity: The Nisei Generation in Hawaii*. Urbana: University of Illinois.

Tanabe, George J. and Willa J. Tanabe. 2013. *Japanese Buddhist Temples in Hawai'i: An Illustrated Guide*. Honolulu: University of Hawai'i.

Tani Kenji. 2017. 'Konjaku Mappu Kyūhan Chikeizu Tairu Gazō Haishin/Etsuran' no Kaihatsu. GIS-Rison to Ōyō GIS 25/1: 1–10. http://ktgis.net/kjmapw/index.html

Taylor, Charles. 2004. *Modern Social Imaginaries*. Durham: Duke University.

Teeuwen, Mark and John Breen. 2018. *A Social History of the Ise Shrines: Divine Capital*. London: Bloomsbury Academic.

Tetsudō-shō. 1943. *Shinkoku Nippon: Kami Mōde*. Tokyo: Tōa Ryokō-sha.

Thal, Sarah. 2005. *Rearranging the Landscape of the Gods: The Politics of a Pilgrimage Site in Japan, 1573–1912*. Chicago: University of Chicago.

Thomas, Jolyon B. 2019. *Faking Liberties: Religious Freedom in American-Occupied Japan*. Chicago: University of Chicago.

Tomii Masanori, Nakajima Michio, Otsubo Junko, and Simon John. 2004. 'Kyū Nanyō Guntō no Jinja Atochi Chōsa Hōkoku.' *Jinrui Bunka Kenkyū no tame no Himoji Shiryō no Taikeika* 2: 239–322.

Tomita Shoji. 2005. *Ehagaki de Miru Nihon Kindai*. Tokyo: Seikyūsha.

Ts'ai, Hui-yu Caroline. 2009. *Taiwan in Japan's Empire Building: An Institutional Approach to Colonial Engineering*. Abingdon: Routledge.

Tsuchiya S., ed. 1927. *Hawai Zairyū Dōhō Go-taisō Kinenchō*. Honolulu: Shōgyō Jihōsha.

Tsuda Yoshiki. 2008. '"Manshūkoku" Kenkoku Chūreibyō to Kenkoku Shinbyō no Kenchiku ni tsuite: Ryōbyō no Zōei Kettei kara Shunkō ni itaru Keika to Sono Yōsō.' *Himoji Shiryō kara Jinrui Bunka he Kenkyū Sankakusha Ronbunshū*, 71–87.

Tsuda Yoshiki, Nakajima Michio, Kim Hwaja, and Kawamura Takeshi. 2006. 'Kyū Chōsen no Jinja Atochi Chōsa to sono Kentō: Zenra-nandō, Wajun-gun wo chūshin ni.' *Jinrui Bunka Kenkyū no tame no Himoji Shiryō no Taikeika* 3, 285–382.

Tsuda Yoshiki, Nakajima Michio, Horiuchi Hiroaki, and Shang Feng. 2007. 'Kyū Manshūkoku no "Mantetsu Fuzokuchi Jinja" Atochi Chōsa kara Mita Jinja no Yōsō.' *Jinrui Bunka Kenkyū no tame no Himoji Shiryō no Taikeika* 4: 203–89.

Uchida, Jun. 2011. *Brokers of Empire: Japanese Settler Colonialism in Korea, 1876–1945*. Cambridge: Harvard University Asia Center.
Uchigawa Takashi. 2019. 'Matsuura Takeshirō no Ōkubi-kazari.' *Eureka* 51/14: 90–5.
University of South Carolina. 2019. 'Formosan New Years Procession/ Parade – Outtakes.' *Moving Image Research Collections*. Accessed 9 October. https://mirc.sc.edu/islandora/object/usc%3A2099
Uta Shigemaru. 1921. *Hajime no Tennō*. Tokyo: Kengyō Shoin.
Uta Shigemaru. 1922. *Hajime no Miyako*. Kashihara, Nara: Kanpei Taisha Kashihara Jingū-chō.
Uta Shigemaru. 1940. *Kashihara no Tohotsu Mioya*. Tokyo: Heibonsha.
Uta Toshihiko. 1981a. *Kashihara Jingū Shi Kan Ichi*. Kashihara, Nara: Kashihara Jingū-chō.
Uta Toshihiko. 1981b. *Kashihara Jingū Shi Kan Ni*. Kashihara, Nara: Kashihara Jingū-chō.
Uta Toshihiko. 1982. *Kashihara Jingū Shi Bekkan*. Kashihara, Nara: Kashihara Jingū-chō.
Van Goethem, Ellen. 2018. 'Heian Jingū: Monument or Shintō Shrine?' *Journal of Religion in Japan* 7: 1–26.
Victoria, Brian D. 2006. *Zen at War*. Lanham, MD: Rowman & Littlefield Publishers.
Walker, Brett L. 2001. *The Conquest of Ainu Lands: Ecology and Culture in Japanese Expansion, 1590–1800*. Berkeley: University of California.
Watanabe Daizo, ed. 2000. *The Centennial Celebration of the Hilo Daijingu*. Hilo, Hawai'i: Robert Okuda.
Watanabe Masako. 2008. 'The Development of Japanese New Religions in Brazil and Their Propagation in a Foreign Culture.' *Japanese Journal of Religious Studies* 35/1: 115–44.
Watanabe Natsuko. 2016. 'Fukushū Jinja Atochi Tsuika Hōkoku: Sōken Tōji ni kansuru Kikitori Chōsa ni tsuite.' *Himoji Shiryō Kenkyū* 13: 97–102.
Watanabe Shichirō. 1930. *Hawai Rekishi*. Tokyo: Ōtani Kyōzai Kenkyūsho.
Watanabe Shichirō. 1938. 'Furoku (Ni): Nipponjin Jinmeiroku.' In *Hawai Rekishi*, edited by Watanabe Shichirō, 1–217. Tokyo: Kōgakukai Kyōiku-bu.
Yamada Kazutaka and Maeda Takakazu, eds. 2012. *Karafuto no Jinja*. Sapporo: Hokkaidō Jinja-chō.
Yamada Kōshi, ed. 1915. *Kensha Kaizan Jinja Enkaku-shi Fu Son Seikō-den*. Tainan: Kensha Kaizan Jinja Shamusho. http://www.himoji.jp/database/db04/syoseki/013.html
Yamaguchi, Teruomi. 2005. *Meiji Jingū no Shutsugen*. Tokyo: Yoshikawa Kōbunkan.
Yamazaki Kin'ichiro, ed. 1939. *Taiwan no Fūkō*. No publisher listed. Accessed 23 September 2021. http://digital.lafayette.edu/collections/eastasia/cpw-nofuko/nf0044
Yang, Mayfair Mei-Hui, ed. 2008. *Chinese Religiosities: Afflictions of Modernity and State Formation*. Berkeley: University of California.

Yatsuka Kiyotsura. 1941. 'Kannagara no Michi Koko ni Tettei.' In *Manshū Teikoku Kōtei Heika Gohōnichi to Kenkoku Shinbyō Gosōken*, edited by Nichiman Chūō Kyōkai, 118–27. Tokyo: Nichiman Chūō Kyōkai.

Young, Louise. 1998. *Japan's Total Empire: Manchuria and the Culture of Wartime Imperialism*. Berkeley: University of California.

Zhang, Yijiang. 2016. *The Origin of Modern Shinto in Japan: The Vanquished Gods of Izumo*. London: Bloomsbury Academic.

Zushi Minoru. 2003. *Shinryaku Jinja: Yasukuni Shisō wo Kangaeru Tame ni*. Tokyo: Shinkansha.

Index

Ainu 57, 66–7
ancestors 39, 49, 77, 106, 209, 210. *See also* imperial ancestors, Same Ancestor theory
assimilation 16
  American 199, 211
  Home Islands 90, 105, 114, 123
  rhetoric of 127, 145–6, 151

Bogure Jinja 209, 227

Chōshun Jinja 170
civil religion 9

daijingū shrines 132–3, 140, 161, 186, 201, 207
Dairen Jinja 174

evolution 17–19, 103

filial piety 49, 104, 137
  Great Filial Rite 34, 153, 166
  and loyalty 77, 115, 118, 156, 162–3
Fukushū Jinja 174
funerals 27, 67, 69–70, 205
  prohibition of 106, 134, 140, 193, 214, 218

glorious spirits (*eirei*) 90, 113, 158, 160, 161–2, 172
Gojō Jinja 168
Gokoku-byō 158. *See also* Kenkoku-byō
Greater East Asia 13, 17, 86, 138, 139

Heian Jingū 63
Hokkaidō Jingū 60, 222, 223
Hokkyō Jinja 174

identity
  American 182, 190
  local 75, 114, 118, 152, 202, 217
  national 78, 132, 139, 156, 186
  patriotic 67, 159

imperial ancestors 26, 40–1, 48, 94, 96, 100
  Manchuria 165
Imperial Palace Sanctuaries 50, 54, 160–1, 165, 192. *See also* recycling
Imperial Rescript on Education 13, 48, 141, 162, 191, 216, 220
Ise Jingū 38, 47, 74, 134, 158, 160–1.
  See also Jingū-kyō, sacred torch
  Amaterasu 132, 162
  garden 36, 54
  recycling 60, 63, 171
  yōhai 54, 87
Iyasaka Jinja 172–3
Izumo Taisha 47, 61, 132, 203, 205, 226
Izumo Taisha-kyō 47, 200, 201, 203–6, 227

Jingū Calendar 54, 64, 65, 101–2, 190, 216
Jingū Hōsaikai 68–9, 101, 186–7, 197–8, 203. *See also* Jingū-kyō
Jingū *taima* 26, 105
  distribution of 68–9, 134–5, 174, 186–7, 189, 198, 208
  and Jingū calendar 102, 186, 216
  in the periphery 189, 215
  as shrines 130, 162, 173
Jingū-kyō 68–7, 104, 134, 194, 203
Jinja Honchō 219, 221, 222

Kaishū Jinja 148
Kaitaku Jinja 63
Kakei Katsuhiko 137, 172–3
Kami Furano Jinja 82–3
Kamikawa Jinja 75, 83, 84
Kantō Jingū 100, 175, 226
Karafuto Gokoku Jinja 59, 87, 222
Karafuto Jinja 59, 86–7, 100, 129, 222–3
Kashikodokoro. *See* Imperial Palace Sanctuaries
Katō Jinsha 198, 200, 206
Kenkoku-byō 158–60, 161
Kingly Way 153, 155, 162, 164–5, 217

Kōgen Jinja 148
Kokugaku 19, 23, 31, 33
komainu statues 103, 201, 223
Konkō-kyō 203, 206
Kotohiragū 24, 42, 47, 200, 201
Kurozumi-kyō 87, 203

leisure 48-9, 87, 100, 123, 134
　cherry blossom viewing 62, 65, 82
　lewd rites and evil teachings (*inshi jakyō*) 109, 138, 198

maps 11, 13, 34
Meiji Jingū 32, 36, 49, 53, 221
　yōhai 43, 47, 54
Minatogawa Jinja 23
Miyazaki Jingū 54
Mōkyō Jinja 175, 226

Nagamasa Jinja 175, 226
Nankyō Gokoku Jinja 225
Nankyō Jinja 175, 225
Nan'yō Jinja 100, 136, 176-7, 226
Nanzan Daijingū 128, 133, 139
national topography 63, 74, 98, 100, 150, 215
Nawiliwili Daijingū 201
Nikkō Tōshōgū 69

Ogasawara Shōzō 132, 209
Okakura Kakuzō 16, 190
Okinawa 15, 102, 176, 219, 190
one shrine per village movements 23, 94, 106, 119, 130, 147
Ontake-kyō 197, 203
Ōtaki Jinja 201-2

pan-Asianism 16-17, 42, 183, 195
public parks 32, 53, 64, 150, 171
　and leisure 36, 82, 97
　postwar 221, 224, 226
　purification basin 111, 119, 158, 201
　localization 76, 167, 171-2

recycling 31, 43, 51, 63, 83, 171
respect for the kami and veneration of the ancestors (*keishin sūsō*) 94, 143, 147, 130, 137
Ryōyō Jinja 157
Ryūtōsan Jinja 128, 139, 140

sacred torch 102, 136
Same Ancestor theory 128-9, 129, 131-2, 133, 138, 151
Sect Shinto. *See* Izumo Taisha-kyō, Jingū-kyō, Konkō-kyō, Kurozumi-kyō, Ontake-kyō, Shintō Honkyoku, Shinto Secretariat, Tenri-kyō
Shimaji Mokurai 25-6
Shinonome Shi 70, 79, 87, 206
Shinto Directive 219
Shintō Honkyoku 69, 192, 194, 197, 203
Shinto Secretariat 68-9, 104, 192, 194
Shintoization 20, 111, 217
　war dead 158, 175, 178, 218
Shinton Jinja 168
Shirasaki Hachimangū 201-2
Shōnan Jinja 175
shrine crest 87, 135, 117, 163, 169
Shrine Reorganization Movement. *See* one shrine per village movements
state religion 20, 21, 27, 140, 219
　American 6
　Great Promulgation Campaign as 4, 9
　State Shinto 26, 27, 137, 140, 220
Suwa Jinja 209

Tai-gū 168
Tainan Jinja 108, 110, 112, 136, 188, 214
Taiwan Gokoku Jinja 90-1, 96, 116-18, 223
Tenri-kyō 78, 137, 203
Tenso Jinja 210, 227
terra nullius 98, 131-2
textbooks 13-14, 65, 137, 199
　Jinmu 13, 34, 48
　shrine distribution 136-7, 143
time zones 47, 102
Tōkyō Shokuminchi Jingū 208-9, 210, 227
Torinuma Jinja 83
Toyohara Jinja 87, 222
Toyokawa Inari Daimyō Jinja 174
tree planting 32, 53, 62, 76, 81-2, 214
　indigenous 86, 97, 101, 190, 217
　volunteer 49, 62
triumphal arches 63, 134

Ubagami Daijingū 73

virgin land 63, 98, 108, 171, 214

volunteers 37, 62, 66, 78, 97, 102
   as citizenship training 49, 104, 151, 216
   labour brigades 49, 53, 158

world under one roof (*hakkō ichiu*) 17, 42, 44, 164, 221

Yasukuni Jinja 22, 72–8, 79, 156–60
   and *gokoku* shrines 70, 87, 117–18
   lese majesté 142–3
   shrine ranking system 23, 113
   yōhai 43, 54, 221

www.ingramcontent.com/pod-product-compliance
Lightning Source LLC
Chambersburg PA
CBHW052215300426
44115CB00011B/1701